The Complete Reference to
the pfSense Internet Gateway and Firewall

pfSense Essentials

By Jeremy C. Reed
Published by Reed Media Services

pfSense Essentials
The Complete Reference to the pfSense Internet Gateway and Firewall
By Jeremy C. Reed
July 2019

ISBN: 978-1-937516-04-8

Publisher: Reed Media Services

This book was written using nvi on NetBSD and generated with Dblatex version 0.3.10 and pdfTeX 3.14159265-2.6-1.40.19 (Web2C 2018) installed with pkgsrc. It uses Nimbus typefaces from the URW++ foundry.

Contents in Brief

Contents

List of Figures

List of Tables

Preface

This *pfSense Essentials* book covers many of the commonly-used features in pfSense. It corresponds to the latest supported pfSense release version at the time of this book's printing: version 2.4.4-p3. It also covers many details related to older versions. This book is a completely new rewrite done by the same book publisher of the Definitive Guide to pfSense. pfSense has changed a lot in the ten years since that long-out-of-date book was written. This book also covers installation and basic configuration through advanced networking and firewalling — using the new interface and, in many cases, new configurations and different software. For details about *pfSense Essentials: The Complete Reference to the pfSense Internet Gateway and Firewall*, please see the website at http://www.reedmedia.net/books/pfsense/.

Author

This book's author, Jeremy C. Reed, is a long-time BSD Unix enthusiast and professional. Reed has been managing BSD systems for over two decades. He has been a member of The NetBSD Foundation since 2003 and served on their corporate board for a decade. He co-founded and served on the BSD Certification Group, Inc. board. As a trainer, he has taught over a dozen professional BSD training courses and over 85 lectures covering various open source or Unix administration topics (including at BSD conferences). As an open source developer, he has contributed to many projects including Pkgsrc, X.org Windowing System, DragonFly BSD, and ISC BIND9. As a software packager, he has created and maintained hundreds of packages. As a professional administrator, Reed has worked with various versions of BSD/OS, FreeBSD, NetBSD and OpenBSD. He has implemented and professionally maintained various *BSD servers providing services for thousands of DNS zones and websites and tens of thousands of email accounts.

Reed is also a co-author of Wiley's Beginning Unix and the BIND DNS Administration Reference books. He was also the founder and editor of the BSD Today online news site. He has been researching and conducting interviews related to BSD, Unix, and Internet history for over 10 years toward a book about the history of Berkeley Unix. For the past ten years, Reed has been professionally working as a software quality assurance engineer and release manager with a focus on DNS server technologies and Internet security.

Book Development

This book was written using Docbook using NetBSD and vi. The print-ready book was generated with Dblatex version 0.3.10 with a custom stylesheet, pdfTeX 3.14159265-2.6-1.40.19 (Web2C 2018), and the TeX document production system installed via Tex Live and Pkgsrc. Several scripts and templates were created to help have a consistent document.

The book was managed using the Subversion version control software. The basic writing process included adding over 350 special comment tags in the docbook source files that identified topics to cover and for every pfSense web interface PHP script (highlighting if they were main webpages from the pfSense menu). As content was written, these special comments were updated with their current status. A periodic script checked the docbook files and the generated book and reported on writing progress and current needs. The publisher's older book was not consulted during this writing.

During this writing, nearly every interface was tested. In addition, code and configurations were often temporarily customized to simulate various pfSense behaviors and system situations. Most of the pfSense interface source code was read, which helped with identifying pfSense configurations and features that didn't display in standard setups and all of its options. The software was upgraded several times and installed and ran in multiple VMs and hardware environments with many wireless and network cards, including with IPv6. In addition, third-party documentation and even source code was researched to help explain pfSense configurations and behaviors. As part of this effort, the author documented 352 bugs or code suggestions.

The first subversion commit for this book was in July 2014. It had commits in 39 different months with 656 commits total. The book's docbook source had 3789 non-printed comments and 56,193 non-blank lines of text. The generated book has over 180,000 words.

Acknowledgements

Acknowledgement and thanks are due to the book reviewers, including Bijan Nowroozi, Walter Parker, Craig A. Fincher, and Eric J Knauer. (One of the reviewers oversaw a deployment of over 200 pfSense installations.) A special thanks goes out to the cast of hundreds of open source developers who donated time and skills toward the software that powers pfSense. This includes FreeBSD; OpenBSD and its PF packet filter, relayd, and OpenSSH; NGINX; Unbound; MPD; PHP; OpenVPN; m0n0wall (the predecessor of pfSense); bsnmpd; curl; KAME dhcp6; ISC DHCP and dhclient; dnsmasq; hostapd; ldns; minicron; miniupnd; ntpd; openldap; perl; pftop; php-fpm; python; radvd; rrdtool; scponly; sqlite3; sshguard; StrongSwan; tcpdump; tcsh; Vixie cron; wpa_supplicant; and many others. Also thank you to Benoit Guillon and the Dblatex community for their assistance. And thank you to the pfSense project — it was the firewall and router for the network where the book writing was done (with well over 50 devices and many frequent users).

1 Introduction

pfSense is a free operating system for standard computers used for deploying a network firewall and router. It is a do-it-yourself network utility appliance commonly used in small offices and homes, but is also used in many large organizations and corporate environments. It is used by novice computer operators to experienced network engineers, especially because of its rapid deployment and proven history. It provides many features also available in commercial firewalls and is viewed as a unified threat management (UTM) solution. It may be used to establish a VPN to encrypt all traffic, a wireless access point, a perimeter firewall for a DMZ (demilitarized zone network), and as an intrusion detection and prevention system. It offers time-based packet filtering, network monitoring, network address translation, IPv6 networking, Dynamic DNS, traffic shaping, a captive portal, firewall redundancy for high availability, system backups and updates, and many other features. It provides a wide-range of services like caching DNS, DHCP, web proxying, and many more. It also offers several diagnostic interfaces to troubleshoot or understand network and system behavior, including graphs, log monitoring, and network probes and traces. Additional software packages are also available for furthering its functionality.

pfSense is managed via an intuitive web interface. While pfSense is not as simple and easy to understand as some other free firewall distributions, it is considered the most feature-rich. It is known for its stability, solid performance, and its fast startup and operations.

pfSense is based on free, open source software and includes over 900 individual tools and programs for troubleshooting, diagnostics, system management, scripting, and network and system services. Its core operating system is FreeBSD, a popular Unix-type system with proven experience dating back to the 1970's but continually improved and extended for modern hardware and technologies. pfSense includes OpenSSH for remote encrypted terminal access, the NGINX HTTP server and PHP for the web-based management interface, Unbound for recursive and caching DNS service, ISC DHCP for managing IP address leases, ntpd for synchronizing clocks using the Network Time Protocol, OpenBSD's relay daemon and PF packet filtering, and much more. Using the Unix shell and direct access to the tools and servers is not required as pfSense provides a user interface for configurations, control, and analysis.

2 Installation

This chapter covers the installation, the first boot up of pfSense, and initial network interface assignments done via a text-based console. The installation is done in three parts: disk setup and copying the pfSense environment to the new disk; booting from the new disk and doing a basic network configuration; and then logging into the web-based user interface (in the following chapter) to continue with the initial installation, including basic configurations like choosing nameservers and time servers.

The free community edition of pfSense may be downloaded from the `https://www.pfsense.org/download/` webpage. There you may select the download file to use. It may also have links to source code and daily development snapshots, but this book focuses on the standard image installation.

2.1 Installation Prerequisites

The memory needs depend on the desired use of pfSense and how many clients it has connected simultaneously, etc. A lightweight use of pfSense with less than ten clients in a home setting may only need around 170 to 240 MB of RAM. 512 MB of memory should be adequate for most small office uses of pfSense. Heavy uses of Snort and Squid add-on packages could use 4 GB or more of memory.

The installer requires a hard disk larger than a gigabyte. An initial install takes around 790 MB, and other space is needed to also hold additional packages, software updates, and historical logging and statistics. It is recommended to use a disk of at least two gigabytes so you can have room for logs, monitoring data, configuration backups, and for upgrades.

The pfSense installation will also attempt to create a disk partition for swap (aka virtual memory) which should be large enough to hold the contents of the memory for troubleshooting potential crashes.

pfSense only requires one network interface, but its basic setup and common usage is with two network interfaces.

2.2 Getting pfSense

At the pfSense download page select the desired version to download in a drop-down menu. Normally the preferred or common choices are pre-defined. Depending on the selections, you may have additional menus to choose options from too — or some options may not be available.

Select the architecture for your hardware to install on in the following drop-down menu: AMD64 (64-bit) for common x86_64 systems or Netgate ADI (RCC-VE). (Note that the 32-bit i386 support is not offered in pfSense 2.4 and newer versions.)

The download webpage changes periodically. You may have an option here to then select the installer (or installation platform): USB Memstick Installer or CD Image (ISO) Installer.

Then, if available (such as selecting the *memstick* installer), select the console: serial if doing an installation (such as remotely) without a physical keyboard and monitor or VGA if doing a local installation with a monitor display and keyboard.

It may show a SHA256 hash which may be used as a download checksum verification. (Or you may click on a SHA256 Checksums link to access files containing the corresponding hashes.)

It will provide a list of download mirror locations (like Singapore or New York City). Select a reasonable closest choice in the drop-down menu and click the **Download** button.

Note if you download directly via browsing at a mirror, it may list older release versions also; so be sure to download the latest version number that you desire to use.

The downloads are gzip (LZ77) compressed and are around 95 MB to 305 MB in size. When uncompressed, the USB Memstick image is around 315 MB to 625 MB (depending on the version). On Windows, you can use *WinZip*. You can decompress it using the `gzip` tool on OS X, Linux, or BSD systems; for example:

```
$ gunzip pfSense-CE-2.4.3-RELEASE-amd64.iso.gz
```

(It won't have any output to the terminal, but the file will be replaced with the real file and the old .gz file will be gone.)

To use a CD ISO image, use your system's CD disk writing software. Do not simply drag and drop the file to the CD, but you need to burn or write using its *image* feature which will make the CD bootable and usable with the many files in the image.

For a *memstick* image, copy it to your USB flash disk to boot and install from. On a Unix type system (including OS X), use the `dd` command to copy the uncompressed USB image file to a USB disk device. Be sure to write to the correct device name. You may be able to get the device name by running the `dmesg` command immediately after inserting the USB disk. For example, with `/dev/sdb` as the target device:

```
$ gunzip pfSense-memstick-2.2.6-RELEASE-amd64.img.gz
$ sudo dd if=pfSense-memstick-2.2.6-RELEASE-amd64.img of=/dev/ ↵
    sdb
638832+0 records in
638832+0 records out
327081984 bytes (327 MB) copied, 141.6 s, 2.3 MB/s
```

This may take a few minutes.

On a Windows operating system, you can use the *rawrite2* Disk Image Tool to copy the uncompressed image to the disk. The tool is available via https://www.netbsd.org/~martin/ rawrite32/. Note that some USB flash disks won't boot, so try another, maybe newer or larger, flash disk.

2.3 Booting

Boot your system with the prepared USB flash disk or CD disk (or from a disk with pfSense already installed). Note that all of the booting, installation, and administration at the computer's console will be in all text. There won't be any windows nor graphical images. The actual pfSense user interface will available after the first part of the installation via a web browser on a different system.

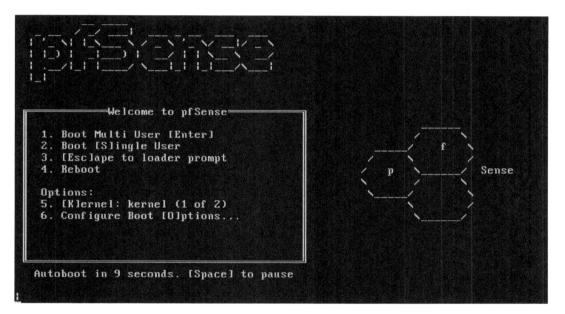

Figure 2.1: Boot Menu

The "Welcome to pfSense" boot menu for the system (as shown in Figure 2.1) will be available on the console for a few seconds — and then it will continue to boot. (Note when booting the installer, the delay is 9 seconds, but on an already-installed system, the boot menu is only available for 2 seconds.) Press the spacebar to pause the boot or press one of the numbered choices for your selection. The purpose of the boot menu is to be able to select the system you want to boot or to workaround or select different supported hardware.

The normal or main choice is to press Enter (or "**1**") to Boot Multi User — which continues on with booting the FreeBSD kernel and the pfSense console menu with installer.

The Boot Single User option ("**2**" or "**s**") is for system recovery. After booting the operating system kernel and mounting the main root file system as read-only, it will prompt you to enter the full pathname for the shell or press Enter to use the default Unix */bin/sh* shell. The system has hundreds of tools available, but note that the networking and pfSense services are not started up in this mode. Entering "**exit**" at the single-user shell will continue to boot into normal multi-user mode (which was option "**1**").

The Loader prompt (option "**3**" or Escape key) provides low-level access to the boot loader to provide system diagnostics and various options to detect hardware or other features to manipulate the boot loader. Type "**?**" to see a list of options there or type "**help** " followed by a loader command to see details, like "**help reboot**". Type "**menu**" at the boot loader prompt to get back to the main boot menu. Normal installation will not need the use of the loader prompt.

Option 5 (or press "**k**") will toggle the desired kernel between the default and the kernel.old version. For example, if using the boot loader on a preinstalled system that was upgraded, you could boot the old kernel by selecting this.

Option 6 (or "**O**") for Configure Boot Options will provide a new menu to toggle ACPI support, Safe Mode, Single User mode, or Verbose boot. Press "**d**" to reset to the defaults, or press the backspace (or "**1**") to go back to the main menu.

When booting, the operating system kernel is loaded and its system messages will be printed to the console, scrolling many lines, as it detects its hardware. Then it will do some system configurations, including setting up temporary RAM-disks.

(If you booted an old NanoBSD image, it will start up the ready-to-use, pre-configured pfSense. You won't need to continue this part of the installation, so you may skip to the following chapter.)

2.4 Installer Menus

After the operating system has booted, a copyright, trademark, and distribution notice will be displayed. Press Enter to accept it to continue.

Then the installation menus will appear. It will prompt you (as shown in Figure 2.2) to either install, launch a Unix shell, or to recover a previous pfSense configuration.

These style menus may be used with the up or down arrows to highlight menu selections. For long lists, you may use the Page Up or Page Down arrows to jump to the top or bottom of items or the contents. The Home and End keys may be used to jump to the first or last menu item or to the top or bottom of displayed content. Some of the menus have individual characters highlighted, such as the first letter of a selection. You may type that letter to make that selection. (If there are multiple selections with the same highlighted letter, it will rotate through that set.) Some of selected items may have additional information — a tool tip — displayed at the bottom of the screen. Use the Tab key or left or right arrows to switch between the buttons. If you have multiple buttons and one is highlighted, you may use the spacebar to rotate through them. Then, when the menu item and desired button are selected, press the Enter key to continue.

(Selecting **Cancel** will drop you to the FreeBSD `login:` prompt. This is unusable because no password is set at this point.)

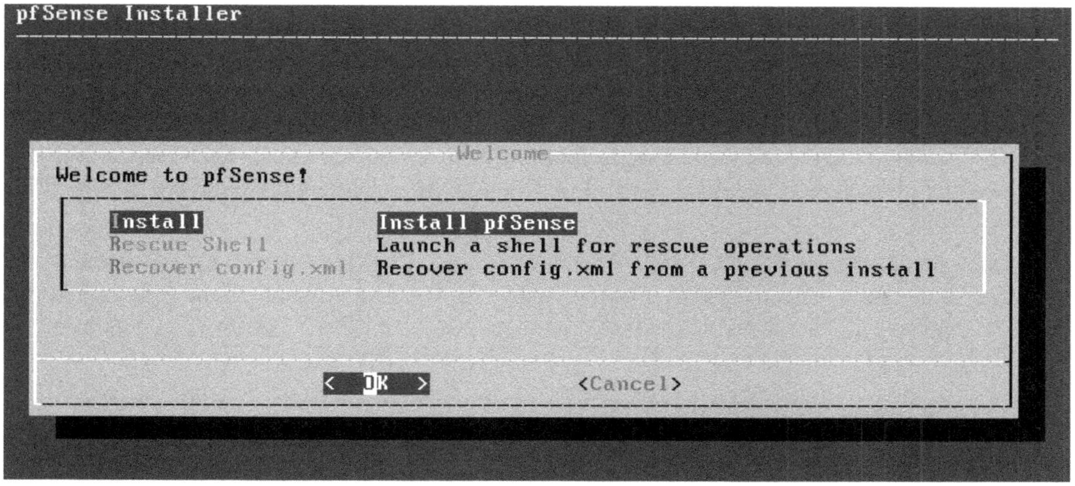

Figure 2.2: Welcome Installer Menu

2.5 Rescue Shell

The rescue shell is used by Unix administrators who are comfortable or experienced at a */bin/sh* command interpreter. The operating system below pfSense is FreeBSD which provides over 700 tools and utilities in its base system. Unix shell commands and FreeBSD and some pfSense tools may be used to diagnose or configure the system.

To use it, select the **Rescue Shell** menu item and press Enter when the **OK** button is highlighted. There are a few other ways to access the shell or use Unix commands later during the installation and with pfSense after it is installed. (See Section 7.1 and Section 37.9.)

But note that the system does not come with the associated manual pages or documentation. Actually using the shell is outside the focus of this pfSense book. To get back to the installer, terminate the shell by typing "**exit**" (and press Enter).

2.6   Recover config.xml

The `config.xml` file is pfSense's master configuration file. It contains all the settings from pf-Sense's many user interface menus, options, and selections. It also retains some history of configuration changes. The underlying firewall and server settings are generated from this single file.

Select this recovering feature and press Enter if you have a previous configuration you need to restore with. This will bring up another menu to select the disk partition that contains the file. (It does not mount each partition nor look on them in advance for you.) The selections use FreeBSD device or UUID naming (such as `ada0s1d` or `diskid/DISK-QM00002s1d`). Each choice will also indicate what file system it has (like "freebsd-ufs") and its size. Highlight the desired disk partition and press Enter for OK.

If it cannot find the file or there is some error, the messages will display too fast to read and will take you back to the main welcome menu. Obviously the file won't be available in the first installation. But you may have the file on an old hard disk that previously ran pfSense which you could have had previously plugged in to your system. Then this could be used to quickly get the new system running.

After it is installed, there are multiple other ways to recover to a previous `config.xml` configuration, if available. This is covered in Chapter 8 for the web interface and Section 37.16 for the text console interface.

2.7   Install

To install, simply select that and press OK in the menu. This will take you to a menu to choose your keyboard type and then a menu for partitioning the target disk — and ultimately creating the file system there and copying all of pfSense to it.

Note that if you cancel some submenu or have an error in some installation step, it may prompt you to exit to a shell or to restart the entire installation process. (Even if it says to exit the installer, it will take you back to the first installer menus.)

2.8   Keyboard Mapping

When installing, first it will display a menu (as seen in Figure 2.3) to select your keyboard type. The console will default to the standard US keyboard. The menu has a long list of keymapping options from Armenian phonetic layout to righthand dvorak.

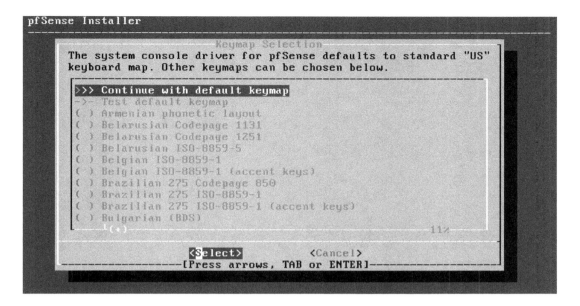

Figure 2.3: Installer: Keymap Selection

After selecting a keyboard mapping and pressing Enter for **Select**, you may test it by then selecting the **Test ... keymap** option. That will pop-up a small text line where you can type different keys to see if they match up. Press Enter to get back to the keymap selection. When ready, select the **Continue with ...** menu item.

2.9 Disk Partitioning and Installation

The next installer display (as seen in Figure 2.4) will list some choices for setting up your disk to install pfSense on. While this menu is called *Disk Partitioning* they all lead to file system creation, transferring the pfSense system to the new disk, and its initial configurations so it can boot up pfSense. Some of the steps are automated proceeding without confirmation while some require advanced configurations. The menu choices include the automated UFS setup (the default), manual setup using menus, using the command-line shell, and the semi-automated ZFS setup.

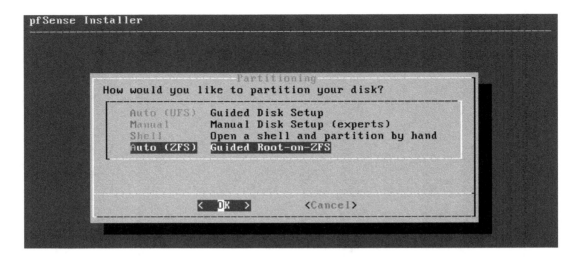

Figure 2.4: Installer: Disk Partitioning

At the end of each of these steps, after the disk(s) are prepared, it will automatically begin extracting the distribution files to the new file system. As it does this, it will display a progress bar and indicate how many files have been transferred and the files per second rate.

When this installation is complete, it will prompt if you want to use the Unix command-line shell to do some extra configurations in a chroot environment of the new file system. This defaults to **No** (but if you do use the shell, type "`exit`" to exit it). Then it will prompt you again, to either reboot (the default) or to use the shell. (Even if you use the shell, when you exit there, the installer will reboot.) Choose to reboot to continue with your pfSense setup.

Note
Be sure to quickly remove your installation USB flash disk or CD-ROM — or make sure you boot from the newly installed hard disk — before the new pfSense system starts up.

2.9.1   Auto UFS

When the pfSense installer only detects a single hard disk to install on, the **Auto (UFS)** selection does not ask nor prompt before reformatting the file system. Several displays will quickly appear (like seen in Figure 2.5) and disappear as the installer detects your available disk, partitions, formats it using the FreeBSD standard UFS aka *Fast* File System, and then extracts the distribution files.

2.9.2 Auto (UFS) Guided Install

But if you do have multiple possible hard disks, the **Auto (UFS)** feature will have multiple prompts and menus. It will list your disks. Select your choice to install to. Then it will ask if you want to use the entire disk or a specific partition. If you choose to use the entire disk (the default choice), it will ask you to confirm you want to erase that disk.

Then it will display a menu to choose how you want it partitioned. Choose one of the choices from: Apple Partition Map, BSD labels without a MBR, GPT (GUID Partition Table) which is the common default, MBR (DOS-style partitions), NEC PC-9801 partition table (PC98), and Sun VTOC8 partition table (like used on a SPARC-based Solaris system).

Next it will bring up a partition editor (which is discussed in the following section). Note that it will require a partition of at least one gigabyte in size. (If you don't have a valid partition to use, it will ask you to choose another disk or go to the partition editor.)

When completed in the partition editor, select **Finish**. Then it will ask you to confirm again to erase the disk. Select **Commit** to overwrite the disk. Then it will partition and format the selected disk and automatically install pfSense.

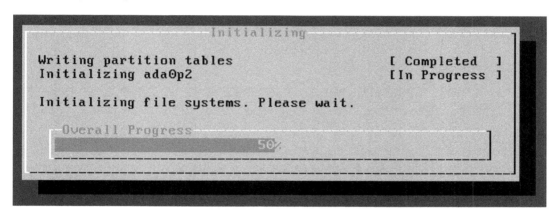

Figure 2.5: Installer: Initializing file systems

2.9.3 Partition Editor

To use menus to manually select your installation target disk and to custom partition it, select the **Manual** menu item. (You may also end up at this editor via other menus too.) As shown in Figure 2.6, it will show your disks and existing partitions (such as MBR partitions also known as *slices* in FreeBSD) and BSD label partitions (which are effectively partitions within partitions). The disks and partitions are identified using FreeBSD device names, such as `ada` (for ATA disks), and numbering (starting with 0). These will also be described with their size, the disk partitioning method, like GPT, and the file system type (like *freebsd-ufs*) or use of the partition (like *freebsd-swap* or *freebsd-boot*). You may use the up and down arrows to select the disk or partition.

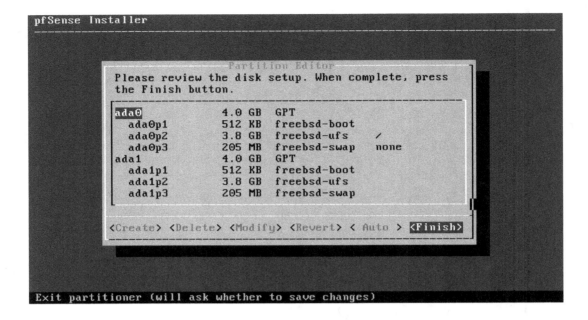

Figure 2.6: Partition Editor

There are six menu functions which may be selected using the left or right arrows or the Tab key. These features are:

Create

Create is used to either define the disk (if not defined yet) or to add another partition to the selected disk. If the disk is described as "(none)", it will bring up a menu to choose how the disk will be managed. These partition schemes include: Apple Partition Map, BSD labels without a MBR (but may be dangerous as non-BSD systems may not recognize it if needed for recovery), GPT (GUID Partition Table), MBR (DOS-style partitions), NEC PC-9801 partition table (PC98), and Sun VTOC8 partition table (like used on a SPARC-based Solaris system). On modern systems, GPT is the common choice. After defining this partition scheme, you will need to choose **Create** again to partition it.

When the disk's partition scheme is already defined, each time (up to a max allowed for the scheme) you choose **Create** a partition may be added. The input box will have fields to enter the type, size, mountpoint directory, and label for the single partition. It will also have an **Options** selection for file systems that can have further configurations. Type directly into these fields. Use the up or down arrow keys to change the field you are on. Don't use the Enter key except to activate the selected button below. You may need to use the Tab key to change focus.

The **Type** field doesn't have a menu of partition types to choose from, so manually type in the choices: *freebsd-ufs* is the standard (or default) type for where the files will be stored; *freebsd-swap* is for the swap disk; and *freebsd-boot* for a few files for booting the system. **Size** is used to define how large this partition will be. You may use suffix mnemonics like "MB" to define the size units. The size of the partition may be prepopulated with the rest of the disk space. For the actual file system(s), the **Mountpoint** needs to be set it to a directory name that exists in the pfSense installation. At the minimum one partition is required for the / (top of file system) mountpoint. Normally a separate partition is not needed for pfSense data, but you could choose to create it and select a mountpoint location. Note that using multiple partitions may or may not work as expected. The **Label** field is an optional descriptive name to identify your partition.

For "freebsd-ufs" file system types, the options menu will have checkboxes for: UFS version 1 (instead of default version 2), Soft updates (on by default for faster metadata changes including file creation and deletion), Soft updates journaling (the default to record some file system metadata changes twice so even if crashed, the file system startup may be faster), and TRIM to enable hardware-supported block delete support (common for SSD disks).

Delete

Delete will remove the highlighted partition or disk entry from the menu. If the disk is highlighted, then all its partitions are removed too. (You may use the following **Revert** action to restore a deletion to this setup.)

Modify

Modify is used to select the partition scheme for the disk or file system details for a specific partition.

Revert

Revert will restore a previously modified and deleted disk or partition file system settings. This doesn't actually restore the disk, but just for this settings menu. Nothing is actually changed on the disk until the **Finish** action is followed.

Auto

Auto will automatically figure out partitioning on its own. It will ask if you want to use the entire disk (which it identifies with its FreeBSD device name and number). That is the default choice. Or you may choose the **Partition** choice by pressing the right arrow or Tab key. Even if you select the *auto* method, it will still prompt you for more options, like for the partition scheme (as discussed with the **Create** option). It may show your current disk's partitioning. It may be good enough or you may choose to start from scratch by selecting the top disk entry and choosing **Delete**.

Finish

When ready, use **Finish** to prepare the disk and partitions per these manual settings. This prompts you to select **Commit** to confirm you want to overwrite your disk with pfSense.

2.9.4 Partitioning By Hand

Like discussed earlier about the rescue shell, if you want to use FreeBSD tools at the Unix command line to diagnose or to setup your disk partitioning manually, select the **Shell** menu item. You will be placed at the Unix command interpreter. To get back, enter "`exit`" and press Enter.

This book does not cover these manual steps such as using *fdisk*, *geom*, *bsdlabel*, *newfs*, *boot0 cfg*, *tunefs*, *zfs*, or other tools. You can run the "`bsdinstall partedit`" command to get to the menus for the partition editor which is the *manual* disk setup as covered in the previous section.

After partitioning and creating the file system, mount the new file system at /mnt and place your Unix *fstab* file at /tmp/bsdinstall_etc/fstab under that mount point.

2.9.5   ZFS

Selecting **Auto (ZFS)** will bring up a menu for configuring the ZFS file system to install and run
pfSense on. ZFS is an advanced file system technology that optionally offers multiple disk mirroring
redundancy and encryption. It requires at least one 4 GB disk. Note you will need to have at least
two 4 GB disks to use ZFS mirroring or RAID.

This menu has several options which lead to further menus or toggle or rotate through the option's
value. To get back to a parent menu, you may be able to select the **Back** or **Cancel** button. The ZFS
menu options include:

Install

When ready with the following ZFS configuration settings, highlight and select the **Install** item
to proceed. If you didn't select any or enough disks for your ZFS pool, it will prompt for that.
If you are using encryption, it will also prompt for a passphrase to use (and then confirms it).

Pool Type/Disks

This brings up an additional menu to define the ZFS Virtual Device type. By default, it is set to
Stripe which offers no redundancy and only needs one disk. You can also choose from **Mirror**
which requires two disks, **RAID 1+0** (at least four even number of disks), **RAID-Z1** (three disks
minimum), **RAID-Z2** (four disks minimum), or **RAID-Z3** (five disks minimum). (Note while
scrolling through the choices, a tool tip will display at the bottom of the screen with more
details.) When selecting this, it will also prompt you to select one or more disks to use for the
ZFS pool.

Rescan Devices

If you are using hot-swappable drives, you can select **Rescan Devices** to probe the devices to
detect when disks are changed out or to update the list of available disks.

Disk Info

Use **Disk Info** to help identify or view various details about a disk. You will be prompted
to select the disk to see the information for. (Note it will list some memory disks or maybe
other disks that you won't be enabling ZFS nor installing pfSense on.) The output may include
partition sizes, partition starting blocks, the type and make of the device, the number of heads
and cylinders, firmware revision, serial number, transfer rate, what features are enabled (like
SMART or power management), or other details. To scroll through the output, use the Page
Up, Page Down, End, and Home keys. Select **OK** and then **Back** when finished to return to the
ZFS options menu.

Pool Name

Use this to define the name for the new ZFS storage pool. It defaults to "zroot" and a name is
required. Your choice must begin with a letter and may contain periods, dashes, underscores,
and alphanumeric characters. But it may not start with the reserved "c0" through "c9" nor may
you use the reserved names "log", "mirror", "raidz", nor "spare".

Force 4K Sectors?

By default, it will use a sector size of 4 KB for best performance even in the case that the hard
disk misrepresents its sector size. If you need to have ZFS calculate based on what the drive
actually reports (like a 512 byte sector size), select the **Force 4K Sectors?** field to toggle it to
NO.

Encrypt Disk?

> By default, the ZFS pool of disks will not be encrypted. Select this to toggle to **YES** if you want it to be encrypted. After you choose **Install**, you will be prompted for the passphrase for the encrypted file system.

Partition Scheme

> This defaults to GPT (BIOS). Select it to rotate through its other values: GPT (UEFI), GPT (BIOS+UEFI), MBR (BIOS), GPT + Active (BIOS), and GPT + Lenovo Fix (BIOS). (Using a GPT is recommended,)

Swap Size

> This defaults to "2g" for a two gigabyte swap size. When selected, you can enter the size of disk space to use for virtual memory swapping and paging. Use a suffix like "m" for megabytes or "g" for gigabytes. It is recommended to use "1g" or "2g", but note that with modern systems with plentiful memory, you shouldn't be swapping. The minimum allowed is "100m" or you may enter "0" (zero) for no swap.

Mirror Swap?

> By default, the swap partition will not be mirrored. If you want it to be mirrored over the pool's drives, select this to toggle to **YES**. You should not need to mirror swap and using this may break kernel crash dumps.

Encrypt Swap?

> By default, the swap space is not encrypted. This space is used as a memory store and may contain sensitive information. If you are concerned that someone could recover system memory from your hard disk, toggle this to **YES**. This will use a temporary key so the swap cannot be recovered.

After selecting **Install**, you will be prompted to confirm to overwrite the listed disks. Select **YES** to proceed with the ZFS creation and then it will continue with the automated initial pfSense installation (as described earlier).

2.10 First Boot After Installation

After the initial installation, boot the system without the installer CD or installer USB flash disk. Depending how your boot loader is defined, you may get a brief prompt to optionally select FreeBSD (which is the base system pfSense is running on). It will automatically continue to the boot loader menu. By default, it will automatically boot the normal startup using the Boot Multi User option in two seconds. Also, as introduced in Section 2.3, you can pause the boot or select the Single User mode for recovery, select a different kernel, configure different boot options, or use the loader prompt for advanced boot needs or troubleshooting.

When booting, the console will display various details such as detected hardware and other kernel messages, mounting disks, starting up pfSense, and loading configurations. These details may be hundreds of lines of text which scroll by. (On later boots after the completed installation, it will show the IP addresses for the network interfaces too.)

2.11   Basic Networking Setup

To run pfSense, it will need to know your network interface assignments so you can login to its web-based management interface and so it can configure a default network gateway and potentially a firewall with network address translation. Note that this section covers this configuration using the text console dialog. Later network interface configurations may be also done via the web-based interface as described in Section 13.2.

If a network interface sees DHCP or IPv6 router advertisements, it may autoconfigure for your WAN network for its Internet access. In this case, you will not be prompted to assign or configure your interfaces and it will display their IP addresses and show a text menu (which is covered in the final chapter). But you may choose to manually configure (or reconfigure) your interfaces there by typing "**1**" and pressing Enter. (This section describes the same steps as if you entered the **1) Assign Interfaces** text console menu option after pfSense is installed.)

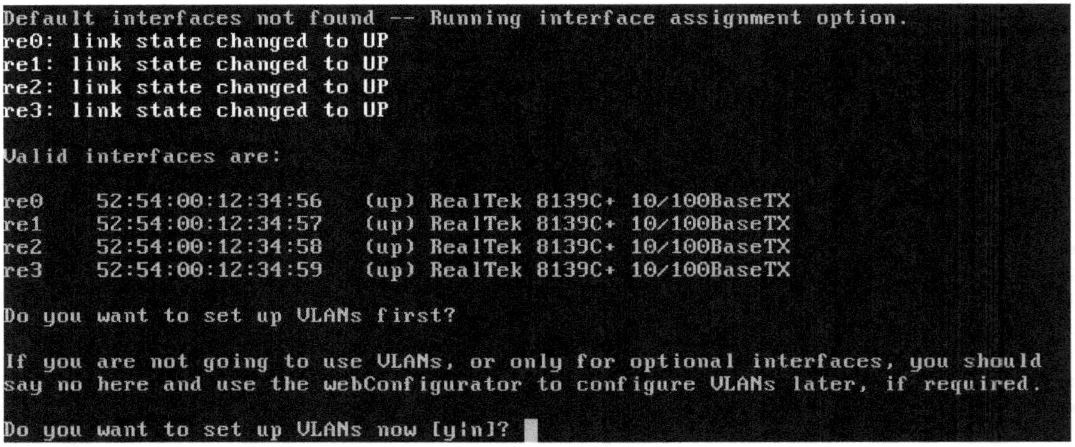

```
Default interfaces not found -- Running interface assignment option.
re0: link state changed to UP
re1: link state changed to UP
re2: link state changed to UP
re3: link state changed to UP

Valid interfaces are:

re0     52:54:00:12:34:56    (up) RealTek 8139C+ 10/100BaseTX
re1     52:54:00:12:34:57    (up) RealTek 8139C+ 10/100BaseTX
re2     52:54:00:12:34:58    (up) RealTek 8139C+ 10/100BaseTX
re3     52:54:00:12:34:59    (up) RealTek 8139C+ 10/100BaseTX

Do you want to set up VLANs first?

If you are not going to use VLANs, or only for optional interfaces, you should
say no here and use the webConfigurator to configure VLANs later, if required.

Do you want to set up VLANs now [y|n]?
```

Figure 2.7: Interface assignment option

Or the dialog (as seen in Figure 2.7) may indicate that the default interfaces were not found. It may also have kernel messages indicating that the detected network devices' link states have been changed to up — meaning that the interface is enabled and the hardware may have been re-initialized. If this was a later boot and previously-configured interfaces no longer match the hardware, it may require you to assign the new interfaces.

It will also list the interfaces it considers valid. Each listed interface is identified with the FreeBSD device driver name and number (like "em2", "re1", or "ath0"), its MAC hardware address (like "00:00:5E:00:53:FF"), whether it is "up" (or "down"), and some vendor, model and/or physical description (such as "Intel(R) PRO/1000 Network Connection 7.2.3" or "RealTek 8168/8111 B/C/CP/D/D-P/E/F PCIe Gigabit Ethernet"). It should list one or more network interfaces.

2.12 VLANs Setup

When you don't have an interface autoconfigured, it will first prompt if you want to set up VLANs. A VLAN is a *virtual* local network which may be used to group hosts and networks together even if they are not on the same physical connections. Switches and devices with network interfaces that are VLAN capable can route, send, or receive packets with an ID number to identify what VLAN they are on.

While it may be recommended to utilize VLANs, it is not required. The prompt suggests if you are not using VLANs for your standard network that you should enter "**n**" for no, and later use the webConfigurator (as seen in Section 13.6) to configure VLANs as desired.

If you have VLANs on your network and plan to use them now, enter "**y**" to set it up. It will list the interfaces that can accept or pass through VLAN-tagged packets. At the prompt, enter the parent interface name (from the list) for the new VLAN. Then provide the VLAN ID number that identifies it (choices are from 1 to 4094).

It will then list the capable interfaces again and prompt again for the new VLAN. (Note that it doesn't indicate if you already assigned one to a VLAN.) When finished with adding VLANs, press Enter without any interface name. It will list your VLAN interfaces, identified with the device name and number followed by an underscore, then the word "vlan" immediately followed by the tag ID, such as re0_vlan99.

2.13 Network Interface Assignments

pfSense will not startup without the WAN (aka wide area network) interface configured. This is the network interface which connects your pfSense system to the Internet. As seen in Figure 2.8, it will provide a list of choices — the network interface identifiers, optionally (if defined previously) the VLAN interfaces, and "a" for auto-detection.

The auto-detection may be useful if you don't know the names of your interfaces. For the auto-detection, you will disconnect all interfaces first, so you will need to have some access to the cables or physical devices. If you select "**a**" to auto-detect an interface instead of entering its name, it will pause for you to make sure that specific network link is re-connected. So basically you will connect only a single network interface and then press Enter to detect it. If it doesn't auto-detect the interface, it will say that no link-up was detected and it will allow you enter the interface name instead.

If you don't use the auto-detection, then just type in the interface name (as listed at the prompt), such as "re0".

```
If the names of the interfaces are not known, auto-detection can
be used instead. To use auto-detection, please disconnect all
interfaces before pressing 'a' to begin the process.

Enter the WAN interface name or 'a' for auto-detection
(re0 em0 or a): em0

Enter the LAN interface name or 'a' for auto-detection
NOTE: this enables full Firewalling/NAT mode.
(re0 a or nothing if finished): re0

The interfaces will be assigned as follows:

WAN   -> em0
LAN   -> re0

Do you want to proceed [y|n]? ▊
```

Figure 2.8: Installer: Assign WAN and LAN Interfaces

After defining the WAN interface, it will prompt for a LAN interface name. This is the device for the local area network. While pfSense may be used with only a single interface (the WAN), its common usage is also with a second device (the LAN). Enter the network device for your LAN selection or choose to do the auto-detection.

Beyond the WAN and LAN, if it detects additional interfaces it may ask to assign an Optional 1, Optional 2, Optional 3, and additional network interfaces. Enter the device name or you can do this auto-detection separately for each network interface.

To complete the initial network interfaces assignments, press Enter without any value. Then it will display the list of interfaces as you just selected to be assigned for the WAN, LAN, and other optional interfaces, and prompt you to enter "**y**" for yes to proceed. If you don't want those settings (and you don't enter "y"), it will restart this interface assignment setup dialog again, listing its detected interfaces, prompting about VLAN, et cetera.

pfSense will attempt to auto-configure the WAN interface using DHCP (for IPv4) or IPv6 router advertisements for Internet access for your pfSense system. pfSense will automatically assign the LAN interface to an address within the 192.168 address space. It will start a DHCP server by default for the LAN network with an auto-set range and enable network address translation (NAT) so devices on the local network can get internally-assigned addresses and have Internet access through your pfSense system. In addition, pfSense will enable some packet filtering (aka firewall) rules and a few networking services as covered in the following chapters. Figure 2.9 is an example of some of these startup messages.

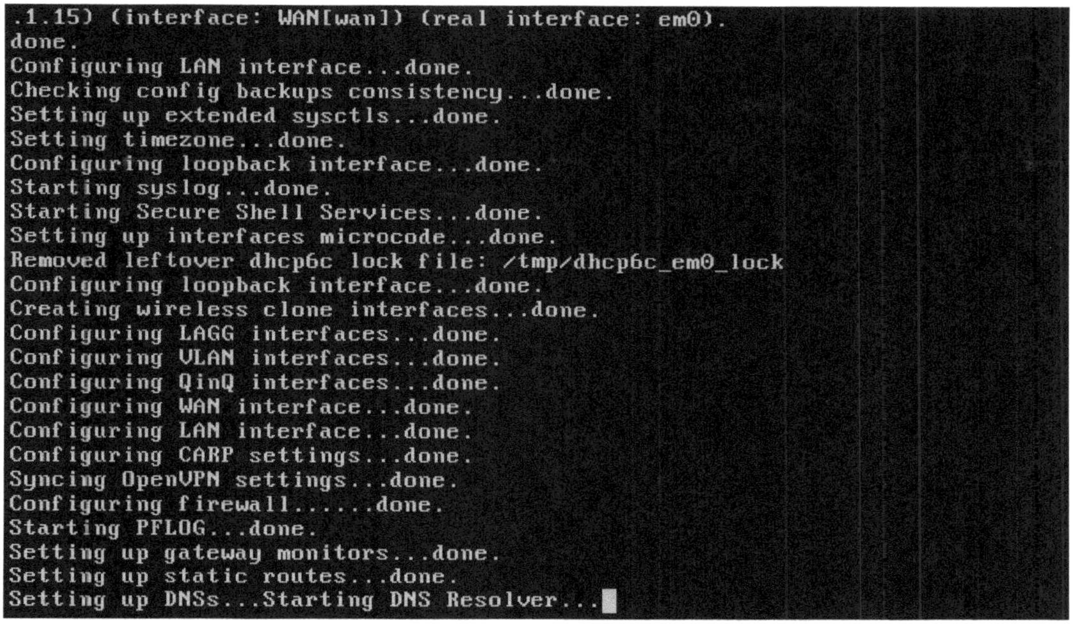

```
.1.15) (interface: WAN[wan]) (real interface: em0).
done.
Configuring LAN interface...done.
Checking config backups consistency...done.
Setting up extended sysctls...done.
Setting timezone...done.
Configuring loopback interface...done.
Starting syslog...done.
Starting Secure Shell Services...done.
Setting up interfaces microcode...done.
Removed leftover dhcp6c lock file: /tmp/dhcp6c_em0_lock
Configuring loopback interface...done.
Creating wireless clone interfaces...done.
Configuring LAGG interfaces...done.
Configuring VLAN interfaces...done.
Configuring QinQ interfaces...done.
Configuring WAN interface...done.
Configuring LAN interface...done.
Configuring CARP settings...done.
Syncing OpenVPN settings...done.
Configuring firewall......done.
Starting PFLOG...done.
Setting up gateway monitors...done.
Setting up static routes...done.
Setting up DNSs...Starting DNS Resolver...█
```

Figure 2.9: Starting Messages

If the DHCP-configured WAN IP address is wrong, or you don't use DHCP for the WAN, or you need to use a different range for your LAN, these can be changed using a web browser via the Setup Wizard as covered in the next chapter. But if you really need to change it now in the text console, because you cannot get to the web interface, see the number 2 option in the displayed text menu as described in Section 37.3.

2.14 Text Console Menus

After the network devices are initially setup and pfSense finishes its startup, a simple text-based menu will be displayed at the console with several numbered choices. This menu provides access to the Unix command-line shell, some basic settings, recovery or restoration capabilities, or simple diagnostics for pfSense. It doesn't provide easy-to-use configurations for further setting up pfSense as the normal use of pfSense is via its web-based interface.

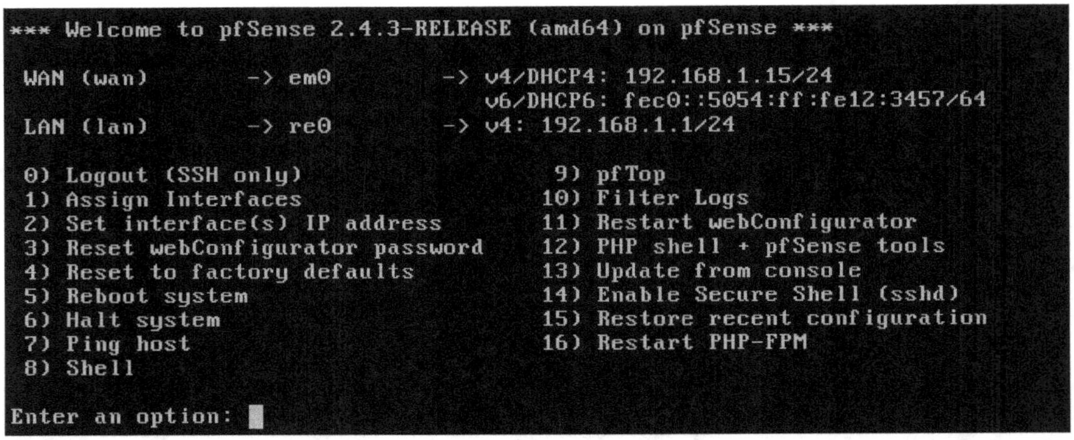

```
*** Welcome to pfSense 2.4.3-RELEASE (amd64) on pfSense ***

WAN (wan)        -> em0        -> v4/DHCP4: 192.168.1.15/24
                                  v6/DHCP6: fec0::5054:ff:fe12:3457/64
LAN (lan)        -> re0        -> v4: 192.168.1.1/24

0) Logout (SSH only)                  9) pfTop
1) Assign Interfaces                 10) Filter Logs
2) Set interface(s) IP address       11) Restart webConfigurator
3) Reset webConfigurator password    12) PHP shell + pfSense tools
4) Reset to factory defaults         13) Update from console
5) Reboot system                     14) Enable Secure Shell (sshd)
6) Halt system                       15) Restore recent configuration
7) Ping host                         16) Restart PHP-FPM
8) Shell

Enter an option: █
```

Figure 2.10: Text Console Menu

Make a note of the LAN IP address, or if you don't have that, the WAN IP address (such as seen in Figure 2.10). This will be used to access the web-based setup wizard and the pfSense user interface as covered in the following chapters.

This display will always be available when pfSense is running. No login prompt nor password is needed at the local terminal to access it. You shouldn't need to use this text-based menu at this time (and you may turn off that monitor if not needed). The final chapter, Chapter 37, covers this text console menu in detail.

3 Web Interface Setup

While pfSense does provide a text-based menu and Unix console access, its primary and most common usage is via the web-based interface known as the *webConfigurator*. The administrator uses a web browser to access over a hundred dynamic webpages (covered through the rest of this book) to configure, monitor, and manage the many pfSense networking and administration features.

This chapter covers the web login and key installation steps done via the web interface using its Setup Wizard. This includes steps for setting the hostname, configuring the DNS server to use, setting the timezone, optionally further configuring the WAN and LAN interfaces, and setting the pfSense administration password. These common settings may also be configured via alternate forms as discussed in later chapters. The next chapter continues with common web interface usage tips, the main dashboard, and the web menu panel found on all webpages.

3.1 Accessing the pfSense Web Interface

Since the webConfigurator is started by default, you can access the pfSense configuration via a web browser on the local network. The text console will show the IP address for the LAN interface. If you only have a WAN interface, you can connect to the webConfigurator using it instead. (But if you do have a LAN, the firewall will prevent access to this web-panel administration interface via the WAN.)

Use a cookies-enabled web browser to connect to that address. It will redirect to HTTPS. On its first access, your web browser should complain that the connection is not secure due to an untrusted, self-signed security certificate. You need to tell your web browser to accept the provided pfSense certificate, identified as "pfSense webConfigurator Self-Signed Certificate."

Then you will receive the Username/Password login display. By default, the username is *admin* and the password is *pfsense*.

3.2   Setup Wizard

The first time you login after a new installation, the pfSense Setup wizard will be activated. Note that most configurations in pfSense do not use multi-webpage wizards where you continue page to page, but just single webpage forms.

At the top of the webpage display will be a panel of links. Ignore that menu at this time if you want to use the setup wizard. That panel's features will be covered in detail throughout the rest of this book.

If for some reason you don't complete this setup wizard, but you do want to use it later, click the **System** menu link at the top panel and then click **Setup Wizard** in its drop-down menu to restart it from the beginning.

This setup wizard is not required. If you prefer to just configure things separately (as covered in this book), just click the pfSense logo to access the *dashboard* as described in the following chapter. The upcoming sections provide cross-references to find the similar configurations outside of using the setup wizard.

To start using this setup wizard, click the **Next** button. It may show an advertisement for some paid services or support. Click **Next** again to get to the first configurations.

3.3   General Information (Setup Wizard)

The first form of the pfSense Setup Wizard (as seen in Figure 3.1) provides a few common configurations for the general setup of pfSense.

First enter the hostname part of the name of your new system in the **Hostname** field. It defaults to "pfSense". Then enter the rest of the fully-qualified domain name in the **Domain** field. (It defaults to "localdomain".) For example, if your desired name is *pfsense.office.example.net*, then enter just "`office.example.net`" in the **Domain** field. (These two fields may also be defined via the **System** → **General Setup** webpage as covered in Section 5.1.1.)

By default, pfSense runs a local caching DNS resolver. Also if your WAN was configured via DHCP (or PPP) which provided a DNS server to use, that external DNS server will also be used as a fallback. To supplement the backup DNS servers to use for the local system's resolution, enter their IP addresses in the **Primary DNS Server** and **Secondary DNS Server** fields.

Uncheck the **Override DNS** checkbox to not use the DNS server definition provided via DHCP (or PPP) for the resolver configuration.

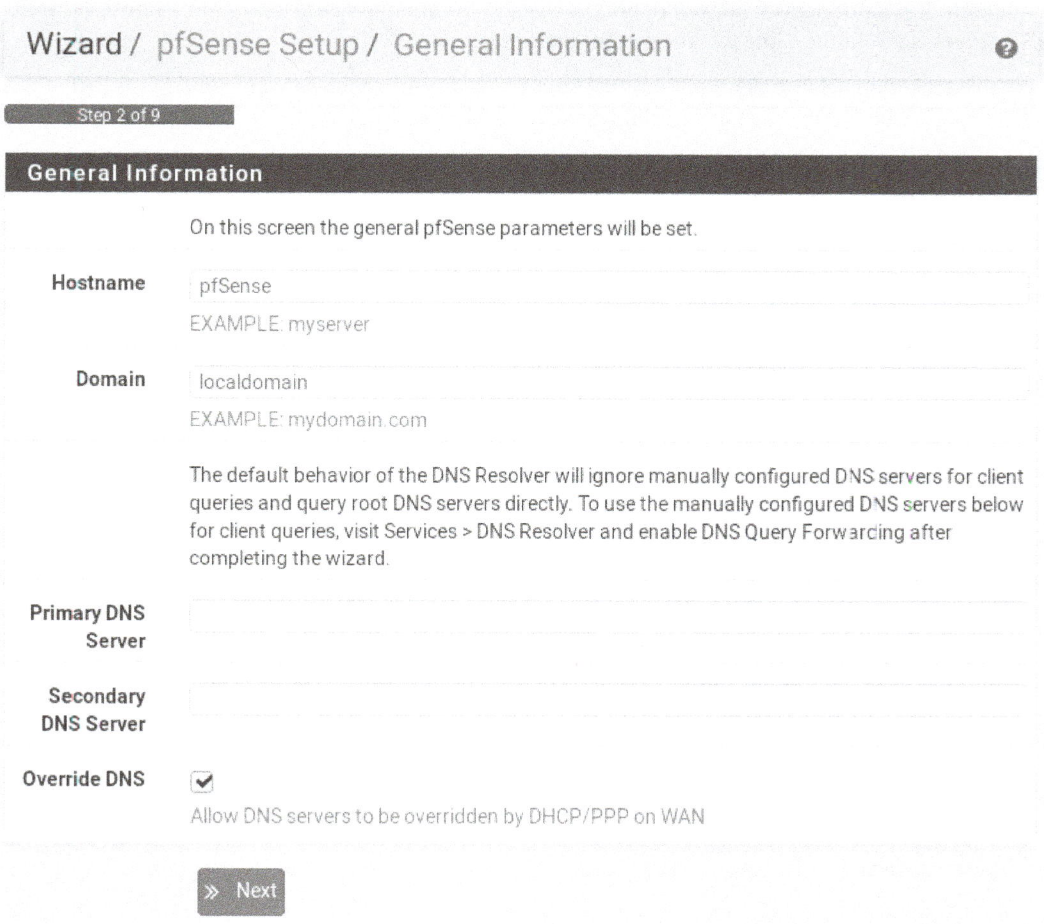

Figure 3.1: **Setup Wizard** : General Information

(These DNS settings are also found on the **System** → **General Setup** webpage in the DNS Server Settings section as further described in Section 5.1.2.)

Then click the **Next** button to continue to the next form in the wizard.

3.4 Time Server Information (Setup Wizard)

pfSense uses the Network Time Protocol to maintain its clock. It can also provide this service to other systems. This is discussed in detail in Chapter 18.

By default, it synchronizes with the pool of *0.pfsense.pool.ntp.org* upstream servers. To use a different NTP server, set it in the **Time server hostname** field.

Unix systems like pfSense generally use the standard UTC timezone for scheduling and logging. To change this, select a timezone in the **Timezone** drop-down menu.

(These time information settings may also be set at the **System** → **General Setup** webpage in the Localization section as further covered in Section 5.1.3.)

Use the **Next** button to continue in the wizard.

3.5   Configure WAN Interface (Setup Wizard)

The WAN interface was likely already configured at the text console earlier in the installation (or probably you wouldn't even have networking access to get to the webConfigurator — even though it could be via the LAN). This wizard allows you to define different ways for the WAN interface to be configured. Depending on this first selection in the **SelectedType** drop-down menu, the other configurations may be available or unavailable (greyed out). The choices are *Static*, *DHCP* (the default), *PPPoE* (PPP-over-Ethernet), and *PPTP* (Point-to-Point Tunneling Protocol).

To spoof the MAC address of the WAN interface, set it in the **MAC Address** field.

To override the default MTU or MSS, set it in the **MTU** and **MSS** fields. By default, they are 1500 bytes, except for PPPoE which uses 1492.

If you chose the *Static* type, you will need to enter the IP address and subnet mask in the corresponding fields. You will also need a default gateway for accessing the Internet; enter its IP address in the **Upstream Gateway** field. (This would be accessible on the same network.)

If you want to use IPv6 instead, see the details in Chapter 14.

When using DHCP to configure your WAN settings, you may set your DHCP client identifier in the **DHCP Hostname** field.

If you are using PPPoE to setup your WAN interface, you may need some of the following attributes defined. Enter the username and password into the corresponding fields. These details are usually provided by the ISP providing the PPPoE service. Some require a **PPPoE Service name** to select the correct profile, but normally this is blank.

Check the **PPPoE Dial on demand** checkbox to have the system establish the connection when a packet is to be sent over the link. If you have no packets transmitted, then this connection is closed after a timeout. This is disabled by default (or by setting it to 0). It may be defined in the **PPPoE Idle timeout** field using seconds, but if you aren't using the *on-demand* checkbox, then the tunnel is removed when idle.

(These PPPoE client settings and other advanced configurations are explained in more detail in Section 24.2 and they may be defined via the **PPPs** subpage linked from the **Interfaces** → **Assignments** menu.)

While the PPTP is not considered secure, you may require it for your WAN setup. Enter the PPTP username and password provided by the ISP in the required fields. Then enter your pfSense system's IP address and its subnet to be used for the PPTP tunnel in the **PPTP Local IP Address** field and drop-down menu. Then enter your ISP's IP address (also known as the *peer*) in the **PPTP Remote IP Address** field.

You can also have a virtual full-time connection by using the **PPTP Dial on demand** checkbox. The connection starts up when outgoing traffic to the PPTP peer is detected. When the **PPTP Idle timeout** is set (in seconds), your PPTP tunnel will be stopped when it hasn't had any traffic either way for that amount of time. Setting it to 0 (zero) disables this timeout. Note if you have a timeout and are not using the *on-demand* your connection will not be restarted.

(Further details and additional PPTP configurations are covered in Section 24.2 for the **Interfaces** → **Assignments** → **PPPs** subpage.)

By default, incoming traffic from reserved private IP space is firewalled from the WAN network. To allow this traffic, uncheck the **Block RFC1918 Private Networks** checkbox, Normally this is a bad idea if your WAN is direct to the Internet.

In addition, by default, pfSense will block incoming traffic over the WAN with a source address that should never appear in Internet routing tables because they are not allocated, not officially assigned, or are reserved. These are called *bogons*. If you need to allow traffic from a large periodically-updated bogons list, uncheck the **Block bogon networks** checkbox. But it may be better, to just allow the specific IP space instead with specific firewall rules.

(These reserved network blocking settings may be done via the **Interfaces** → **WAN** webpage as covered in Section 13.2.7. Also more information about the bogons is in Section 16.17.)

Then click the **Next** button at the bottom to continue in the setup wizard.

(These WAN settings and more are also accessible via the **Interfaces** → **WAN** webpage and further described in Chapter 13.)

3.6 Configure LAN Interface (Setup Wizard)

If you have a second network interface used for the LAN, you can define your local network's address range which is used for the DHCP assignments and other systems' interfaces. The defaults set with the text-based installer are 192.168.1.1 and /24 with the DHCP range as 192.168.1.100 through 192.168.1.199.

Enter your pfSense system's local address in the **LAN IP Address** field and its subnetting mask in the **Subnet Mask** drop-down menu. The subnet mask should be lower than 31. The IP address can not be the same as the subnet's network address nor broadcast address.

This setup wizard will define a reasonable address range for the DHCP service based on your settings if the existing range doesn't exist or is outside of the newly defined network. If your LAN address is in the first half of the subnet, the DHCP range will allocate addresses in the second half — or vice versa. For example, an address ending with a .1 in a /24 subnet may result in a DHCP range of addresses ending with .10 through .245.

Warning
This is the IP address used to connect to the pfSense webConfigurator where you are
making these changes. If you change this, you will need to access pfSense with the new
address.

Click **Next** again to continue in the wizard.

(These two LAN configurations and several others can also be defined at the **Interfaces** → **LAN**
webpage as covered in Chapter 13. The DHCP service configurations are explained in Chapter 19.)

3.7   Set Admin WebGUI Password (Setup Wizard)

Be sure to set a new password for the administrator's access to the pfSense webConfigurator. By
default, it is a commonly-known password and others within your same network if you are using a
LAN or others in the world if using only a WAN on the Internet may be able to login using it.

This same password is also used for access to the text console menus (and Unix shell), if you have
SSH enabled. (Enabling SSH is covered in Section 5.3.2 and Section 37.15.)

Enter your desired password twice in the **Admin Password** fields and then press the **Next** button.

(This password may also be changed via the **System** → **User Manager** webpage. On the **Users** tab
and in the Users table, click the **Edit user** pencil icon action for the *admin* user. For more details, see
Section 6.2.)

This is the end of the setup wizard. To use these new settings, click the **Reload** button. A reload-in-
process window may pop up for a few seconds.

Click the logo at the top-left of the display after the page has reloaded and you will be taken to the
main pfSense dashboard, introduced in the next chapter.

4 The pfSense webConfigurator

This chapter covers the basic usage of the *webConfigurator* web interface, its main dashboard, and introduces the web panel menu found on all of its 200-plus webpages. This menu introduced in this chapter links to around eighty main pages for many pfSense features.

As covered previously in Section 3.1, the pfSense interface is accessed using a web browser and you will need to accept its security certificate. If you are using a LAN, its default address is **https://192.168.1.1/** or use the IP address as seen above the text console menu. If you don't have a LAN setup, then you will connect to it via the WAN address.

4.1 Change Admin Password

pfSense has a default administrator username and password of *admin* and *pfsense*. If this is not changed yet, you should immediately change it as your first step. Even before you learn about the dashboard and the many menus, click the **System** menu link in the top panel. This will expand a submenu. Then click the **User Manager** menu entry. This will take you to a new page showing the pfSense user accounts. There will be a table with at least one row for the System Administrator. On the right is an **Edit user** pencil icon in the action column. Click it to go to the webpage form to change the User Properties for the *admin* account. A few fields down, set your new desired password (and confirm it by entering it again), and click the **Save** button at the bottom of the page. (This is also covered in Chapter 6.) When finished, click the logo in the top left to get back to the dashboard.

4.2 The Menu Panel

The web interface pages have a panel with links at the top (as shown in Figure 4.1). The categories are: System, Interfaces, Firewall, Services, VPN, Status, Diagnostics, and Help. (Some systems also have Gold.) Each of these is a drop-down menu with various choices (in alphabetical order) that open new displays or webpages. Those webpages provide system details, troubleshooting assistance, and allow setting configurations and starting and stopping various features. Each webpage should have this same menu panel.

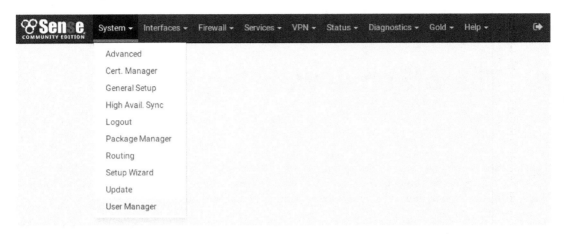

Figure 4.1: Panel (with **System** → **User Manager** highlighted)

If the browser window is narrow, the menu links panel will not be displayed at the top, but instead a standard three-line menu icon will be displayed to access the navigation menus. Click on it to expand the pfSense menu instead.

Note that some of the links take you to the remote pfSense website, such as for various help documentation. The old **Gold** option links to details about a purchased annual membership subscription which provides online backups and video conferencing. The paid Gold Membership may not provide commercial support. The **Help** menu has links to the documentation on the official website for the current page you are on, a Bug Database for reporting issues, the Developers Wiki, the FreeBSD Handbook, and the web-based community forum. (If you find any details lacking in this book or you have documentation suggestions, please send your feedback.)

4.2.1   General Web Interface Usage

The various webpages may display outputs and specific details or provide input forms to enter information and submit configurations. For multiple selection forms (including drop-down menus), use your web browser's feature, such as pressing the Control, Shift, or Command keys, to select multiple entries if desired.

Some actions or button selections may pop-up a small dialog box or prompt to verify that you really want to perform that action. This usually provides an **OK** button to proceed and a **Cancel** button to not continue. While many of the pfSense menus have this verification step, it is important to note that some critical changes may not have this second opportunity to approve the action.

Depending on the feature, making configuration changes may not be activated after clicking the **Save** button. It may prompt you to next click **Apply changes** to complete them. Also some settings may say that they were changed, but still have a submit button to close the acknowledgement about it.

If a configuration change ever causes you to get locked out of the web interface, you should be able to revert the change using the text-based console menu. If you cannot get to it via SSH over the network, you may need to have physical access to the keyboard and display or serial access via a remote KVM. The console menu has a feature to switch back the configuration database to a prior revision as covered in Section 37.16.

Many of the pages offer shortcut links for supplementary pages in the top right of the topic header. These shortcuts may include related settings, related status, and related logs (represented with icons like sliders, bar chart, and a bullet list, respectively). Users with limited privileges (as introduced in Section 6.1) may not have all the shortcuts. These may be followed by a question-circle icon to link to external documentation at the pfSense website for help or information for that page (if available there).

A lot of configurations and outputs are displayed in tables. If the browser width is too narrow, you may miss some information, but there may be a scroll bar at the bottom of the table or you may be able to use the right arrow key (after clicking in the table) to see further fields. Many tables may be sorted by clicking the column headers. Clicking them again may reverse the sorting. Some rows also have an *actions* column or other columns with buttons or clickable icons to perform tasks related to that row or entry. Hovering over various entries or icons may provide explanations or further details.

The following sections briefly introduce the menu selections as available in the default installation; as appropriate, further details within this book are cross-referenced. Note that the pfSense menus may have fewer items based on privileges. Users (and groups) may be setup to limit features as discussed in Section 6.1.

4.2.2 System menu

System → Advanced
> This allows advanced configurations for the web server and other access methods to pfSense, firewall, NAT, state timeouts, IPv6 options, network interface options, proxy support, miscellaneous hardware features, FreeBSD system tunables, and notifications from pfSense. These submenus are covered in various sections in this book, including Section 5.3.1, Section 16.8, Section 13.7, Section 5.4, Section 15.2.2, Section 16.9, Section 10.4, Section 10.5, Section 5.5, and Section 5.6.

System → Cert. Manager
> This menu allows importing existing Certificate Authorities and creating internal or intermediate CAs, importing or creating certificates and Certificate Signing Requests, exporting X.509 and PKCS#12 certificates and keys, and managing Certificate Revocation Lists (CRL). These features are covered in Chapter 12.

System → General Setup

Section 5.1.1 covers this menu. It provides configurations for the hostname, local DNS, localization (like the timezone), changing the theme, and adding other user features for the web interface.

System → High Avail. Sync

pfSense can share many of its configurations and current firewall states with another pfSense system to help run a redundant firewall. This high availability (HA) synchronization is covered in Chapter 36.

System → Logout

This menu choice will simply log you out of the pfSense webConfigurator interface. It will take you to the opening login page. Be sure to logout if using a public computer to access the pfSense web interface.

System → Package Manager

In addition to the many software programs preinstalled with pfSense, additional software suites — or packages — can be installed and enabled in pfSense. This package management is covered in Chapter 35.

System → Routing

Chapter 15 covers pointing your pfSense system to Internet gateways and configuring static network routes.

System → Setup Wizard

This menu item will take you back to the simple configuration wizard covered in the previous chapter. Normally, other menu features will be used instead for reconfigurations or further settings.

System → Update

Chapter 9 is about upgrading pfSense to a newer version using the web interface. (On old pfSense versions, you may use the **System → Firmware** feature to update the system.)

System → User Manager

pfSense can have multiple users and groups with different credentials which may be used to access the webConfigurator interface or pfSense-provided network services. pfSense can also use an external RADIUS or LDAP service for authentication. This is covered in Chapter 6. If this menu item takes you to a password reset page only, that means you don't have enough administration privilege to manage other users.

4.2.3   Interfaces menu

The **Interfaces** menu lists the already-created network interfaces such as LAN, OPT1, and WAN. (The following choices may vary based on the network interface naming you use.) The general configuration and interface-specific settings are accessible via these menu options. For details, see Chapter 13.

Interfaces → Assignments

This option is used to enable and configure a new network interface, including for wireless, bridging, tunneling, and more. This is covered in Section 13.1. (Older versions of pfSense prior to 2.4 list this as **(assign)**.)

Interfaces → WAN

This is used to configure how your pfSense system gets Internet access. This is covered in Section 13.2.

Interfaces → LAN

Section 13.2 also covers this option for configuring an interface for the internal network.

4.2.4 Firewall menu

Firewall → Aliases

You can have convenient pseudonyms for URLs, port numbers, IP addresses, and even hostnames so you may use names in various configurations. See Section 16.5 for details.

Firewall → NAT

Chapter 17 covers port forwarding, bidirectional address translation, and Network Prefix translation (NPt).

Firewall → Rules

pfSense's name is based on *PF*, the OpenBSD Packet Filter. Setting up block and pass rules for different interfaces is covered in Section 16.1.

Firewall → Schedules

Packet filter rules can be enabled for only specific dates and times. This calendaring and scheduling is explained in Section 16.9.

Firewall → Traffic Shaper

pfSense provides a bandwidth control system by queueing or dropping outbound packets. This is covered in Chapter 25. It can also instrument packet loss and artificial delays as covered in Chapter 26.

Firewall → Virtual IPs

Section 16.10 is about different types of virtual IP addresses for using additional IP addresses on single interfaces or for sharing the same IP address over multiple pfSense systems.

4.2.5 Services menu

Services → Auto Config Backup

This provides use of an offsite backup service for encrypted pfSense configurations. To use it, see Section 8.4. (This feature was added to the open source pfSense version 2.4.4.)

Services → Captive Portal

Chapter 29 is about allowing customers to gain temporary Internet access after authenticating, such as with a webpage login.

Services → DHCP Relay

You can have pfSense listen to DHCP requests and relay them on to another DHCP server. This is covered in Section 19.7.

Services → DHCP Server

Chapter 19 is about using pfSense to run a DHCP service for IPv4.

Services → DHCPv6 Relay

For relaying DHCP for IPv6 to another server, see Section 20.5.

Services → DHCPv6 Server & RA

To run your own IPv6 Router Advertisement (RA) service or DHCP for IPv6 service, see Section 20.1 and Section 20.2.

Services → DNS Forwarder

pfSense offers a simple DNS forwarding server called `dnsmasq` as covered in Section 21.3.

Services → DNS Resolver

pfSense also runs the `unbound` full-featured DNS resolver and validator introduced in Section 21.2.

Services → Dynamic DNS

pfSense can share its local IP address with an outside authoritative DNS service so your system can be found via its DNS name. See Chapter 22 for details.

Services → IGMP proxy

pfSense can forward multicast traffic to other systems using the Internet Group Management Protocol (IGMP). This is introduced in Section 13.10.

Services → Load Balancer

Chapter 34 covers setting up pfSense to forward incoming traffic to other servers to distribute the load.

Services → NTP

pfSense can provide a network time service. This is covered in Chapter 18.

Services → PPPoE Server

Chapter 31 is about setting pfSense to provide Internet access to customers using the Point-to-Point Protocol over Ethernet.

Services → SNMP

Section 27.6 is about setting up your pfSense system to send system details and stats using the Simple Network Management Protocol.

Services → UPnP & NAT-PMP

pfSense can setup port mappings for Internet access behind upstream NAT gateways by using the Universal Plug and Play Internet Gateway Device Protocol and NAT Port Mapping Protocol. This is covered in Section 17.8. This menu item is only available when your pfSense system has multiple interfaces.

Services → Wake-on-LAN

Section 13.9 covers using pfSense to send the magic WoL packet to turn on remote systems.

4.2.6   VPN menu

A VPN, or virtual private network, is used to provide secure, private communication over a public or shared network. The VPN connection is a tunnel between two endpoints. It must be authenticated to be established, using a password, digital certificate, or other method. Commonly the traffic is encrypted for confidentiality.

pfSense provides support as a VPN client (or peer) for establishing a tunnel with a remote provider or as a server so remote clients may have VPN tunnels back to the pfSense system. While there are many VPN protocols, pfSense supports IPsec (using IKEv2), L2TP, and OpenVPN technologies as a network access server. These features are available via this top **VPN** menu.

(pfSense also provides VPN-like tunneling using the Point-to-Point Protocol over Ethernet support as covered in Chapter 31.)

VPN → IPsec

pfSense can manage IPsec-based private networks. This is covered in Chapter 30.

VPN → L2TP

pfSense can provide a non-encrypted Layer 2 Tunneling Protocol (L2TP) service. This is covered in Chapter 32. (It can also be configured as an L2TP client as covered in Section 24.2.)

VPN → OpenVPN

The OpenVPN configurations as a client and server are covered in Chapter 33.

VPN → PPTP

Note that the **VPN → PPTP** menu item for implementing a Point-to-Point Tunneling Protocol server with pfSense is no longer available because that protocol is insecure.

Old versions of pfSense provided PPTP for implementing a VPN server. It has many known vulnerabilities and is considered obsolete. While PPTP client support is commonly available on many devices and operating systems, both Microsoft[1] and Apple[2] recommend using other tunneling technologies.

pfSense can still be a PPTP client, such as connecting the WAN to an ISP using PPTP as a non-secure, non-private transport. For details, see the interface configuration in Section 24.2.

---

[1]*Microsoft Security Advisory 2743314: Unencapsulated MS-CHAP v2 Authentication Could Allow Information Disclosure.* August 20, 2012. `https://technet.microsoft.com/library/security/2743314`.

[2]*Prepare for removal of PPTP VPN before you upgrade to iOS 10 and macOS Sierra.* Jul 12, 2016. `https://support.apple.com/en-us/HT206844`.

4.2.7   Status menu

The **Status** menu provides links to several pages to provide details on the current state of many of the services and various features in pfSense. Some of these pages also provide toggles or other options to disable or reconfigure the features.

Status → Captive Portal

Viewing the currently logged-in captive portal users is covered in Section 29.9.

Status → CARP (failover)

Features for managing the Common Address Redundancy Protocol (CARP) and high availability synchronization are explained in Section 16.10.2.

Status → Dashboard

This simply takes you back to the main pfSense display which you can also do by clicking on the logo (Section 4.3).

Status → DHCP Leases

Section 19.6 is about the DHCP leases that are currently assigned and the pool ranges available.

Status → DHCPv6 Leases

Read Section 20.4 about the active and static leases for DHCPv6 and IPv6 prefix delegations.

Status → DNS Resolver

The `unbound` DNS resolver infrastructure cache stats are introduced in Section 21.2.5. (This status page was added in pfSense 2.4.4.)

Status → Filter Reload

This page provides a button to reload already-configured packet filter (firewall) rules (Section 16.11).

Status → Gateways

pfSense does various monitoring, including for its known gateways. See Section 15.1.3 about the current network gateway status.

Status → Interfaces

This displays many details about the network interfaces (Section 13.3).

Status → IPsec

Section 30.2 discusses the IPsec VPN status and leases information.

Status → Load Balancer

The current state of pfSense-configured load balancers and virtual servers are covered in Section 34.5 and Section 34.6.

Status → Monitoring

An interactive graph and summary report about system utilization, networking, DHCP, and other features is covered in Section 28.2. (Note this menu item was at **Status → RRD Graphs** in versions prior to pfSense 2.3.)

Status → NTP

Details about the configured Network Time Protocol sources are displayed (Section 18.1).

Status → OpenVPN

Section 33.5 covers the list of any OpenVPN clients and OpenVPN statistics.

Status → Package Logs

If you have add-on packages installed that have their own logging (outside of **Status → System Logs**), this output may be accessed via this link (Section 35.4).

Status → Queues

Details about ALTQ-based traffic shaping are covered in Section 25.7.

Status → Services

A quick view of the running daemons (such as the monitoring service and the network time server) with shortcut actions to disable, re-configure, or view their stats and logs is available via this link. This is discussed in Section 7.7.

Status → System Logs

This link takes you to the general logs view which is explained in Section 11.4. This has subpages to view around 18 different log categories which are covered in their related chapters in this book.

Status → Traffic Graph

This links to a real-time graph showing bandwidth for a network interface. (Section 28.1).

Status → UPnP & NAT-PMP

This menu item is only available in multiple interface environments. It is used to view and reset the packet filter rules for the Universal Plug and Play and NAT Port Mapping Protocol features (Section 17.8.3).

Status → Wireless

Section 23.7 covers the local wireless access points and ad-hoc peers. This menu item will only be listed if a wireless interface is enabled.

4.2.8 Diagnostics menu

Diagnostics → ARP Table

This may be used to view or remove ARP cache entries (Section 13.8).

Diagnostics → Authentication

Section 6.8 covers verifying that a user account's password works, including for remote LDAP or RADIUS server authentication.

Diagnostics → Backup & Restore

This menu item is used to make copies and revert pfSense configurations; it is covered in Section 8.1.

Diagnostics → Command Prompt
> This feature provides ways to run PHP code and shell commands and upload and download files (Section 7.1).

Diagnostics → DNS Lookup
> This menu item allows you to do simple DNS queries (Section 21.1).

Diagnostics → Edit File
> Section 7.2 is about accessing the file system via a web interface.

Diagnostics → Factory Defaults
> This may be used to reset the pfSense system to its initial configurations and state. See Section 7.10 for details.

Diagnostics → GEOM Mirrors
> This may be used to manage a GEOM-based RAID file system as discussed in Section 10.1. This menu item is only available if pfSense was installed using a RAID1 mirror using FreeBSD GEOM.

Diagnostics → Halt System
> This is used to shutdown or poweroff the system (Section 7.3).

Diagnostics → Limiter Info
> This menu item is used to view the traffic shaping bandwidth limiters (Section 26.6).

Diagnostics → NDP Table
> Section 14.8 is about viewing the IPv6 Neighbor Discovery Protocol (NDP) table and deleting entries.

Diagnostics → Packet Capture
> Section 27.1 is about displaying or saving details about matching packets on a network interface.

Diagnostics → pfInfo
> This may be used to view the PF packet filter limits and statistics (Section 16.13).

Diagnostics → pfTop
> Real-time rule stats and active states may be displayed using the pfTop tool (Section 37.10).

Diagnostics → Ping
> A common network *ping* may be performed using this feature. See Section 27.2 for details.

Diagnostics → Reboot
> This is used to restart the pfSense system, including the hardware. See Section 7.4 for details.

Diagnostics → Routes
> Viewing the IPv4 and IPv6 network routing tables is covered in Section 15.4.

Diagnostics → S.M.A.R.T. Status
> Section 10.3 covers viewing disk diagnostics and running drive reliability tests.

Diagnostics → Sockets

This page shows listening network services and, optionally, existing two-way communication links for IPv4 and IPv6 (Section 27.3).

Diagnostics → States

Section 16.15 discussed the recent and current partial or established network connections seen through the firewall, including a way to remove a specific state.

Diagnostics → States Summary

This view gives summary counts for firewall connections, including by destination and source IP addresses. See Section 16.16 for details.

Diagnostics → System Activity

A frequently-updated view about the top CPU processes and memory usage is discussed at Section 7.5.

Diagnostics → Tables

This page may be used to view the previously-loaded IP address entries as stored as tables in the firewall (Section 16.17).

Diagnostics → Test Port

Section 27.4 discusses checking if a remote or local network service can accept TCP connections.

Diagnostics → Traceroute

This menu item may be used to perform a network *traceroute* (Section 27.5).

While there are around eighty main pages linked from this top menu, over a hundred additional feature subpages are also available as linked from these corresponding pages (and introduced throughout this book).

4.3   Dashboard

The dashboard is the main or front display webpage of the pfSense interface and by default it displays various system information and a few minor details about the configured network interfaces. To get to the dashboard at almost any time, click on the pfSense logo on the top left of the browser's display.

The dashboard contains some widgets that may be added and moved around for your desired system view and needs. A displayed widget has a titlebar with a - dash button to minimize and a **X** button to close the widget. A **+** (plus) button on the dashboard may be used to add (or re-add) a widget. Moving a widget is done by simply grabbing its titlebar with your mouse pointer and dragging it. The **Save Dashboard Layout** button may be used to save your dashboard view for the next visit.

The dashboard defaults to two columns. To change the number of columns, see the **System →
General Setup → webConfigurator** menu for the **Dashboard Columns** setting as covered in Section 5.1.1.

The default dashboard widgets are the *System Information* and *Interfaces* views as seen in Figure 4.2. (You may also have an advertising widget that you may choose to close by clicking its **X** button.)

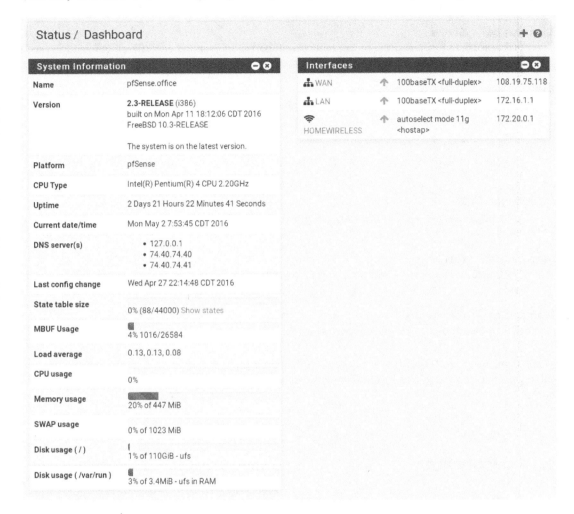

Figure 4.2: Dashboard

The System Information may vary based on what details the system detects. This may include:

- System hostname

- pfSense-derived unique identifier (Section 5.4.5)

- BIOS vendor, version, and release date

- The running pfSense version, architecture, and release date (and it may indicate if you are running the current version or out of date as covered in Section 9.2)

- FreeBSD version (that pfSense is running on)

- CPU type and features

- Kernel PTI (Section 5.4.4)

- Hardware crypto accelerator (Section 5.4.3)

- System uptime in hours, minutes, and seconds

- Current date and time

- DNS servers it uses

- Date and time for this system's last configuration change

- Firewall state table size and a link to see the states (see Section 16.15)

- MBUF (networking memory) usage

- System temperature (Section 5.4.3)

- System load averages, CPU usage percentage, memory use, and swap (virtual memory) use (which can be seen in some more detail in the **Diagnostics** → **System Activity** display as described in Section 7.5)

- Disk usage for all the mount points

Some of this system information is displayed using simple bar graphs.

The Interfaces widget shows your network interfaces on the dashboard. Each will show the selected type (like DHCP) in parentheses, if up or down (like a green up arrow), the media type (like 10baseT or 100baseTX), media settings (like full-duplex), and the configured IP address. Clicking on an interface name will take you to its specific configuration (as covered in Chapter 13).

4.3.1 Adding a Widget

Widgets may be added by clicking the **Available widgets** plus icon at the right top of the dashboard. Then on the dashboard you will have a widget that displays the list of widgets. If you have the **Available Widgets** checkbox on the **System** → **General Setup** page selected, you will have this list shown by default. (See Section 5.1.4 for details.)

The available dashboard widgets may include the following:

- Captive Portal Status

- CARP Status

- Dynamic DNS Status

- Firewall Logs

- Gateways

- GEOM Mirror Status

- Installed Packages

- Interface Statistics

- Interfaces (enabled by default)

- IPsec

- Load Balancer Status

- NTP Status

- OpenVPN

- Picture (to display an image)

- RSS (news feed reader)

- Services Status

- S.M.A.R.T. Status

- System Information (enabled by default)

- Thermal Sensors (see Section 5.4.3)

- Traffic Graphs

- Wake-on-Lan

Add a new widget to your dashboard by clicking its corresponding plus icon. It may appear immediately, but you may need to scroll down to access it.

4.3.2 Widget Configurations

Various widgets may be configured to provide different information on the dashboard. The titlebars may have a wrench icon to expand or open up a configuration section. After clicking it, see below the normal widget content.

The widgets may have various configurations or options, such as selecting an image to view or how often to update. It really varies based on the widget. For example, there may be a table listing some of the attributes for the widget each with a corresponding **Show** checkbox. Unselect a checkbox to filter out viewing of the corresponding information. To check all the checkboxes, press the **All** button.

Click the **Save** button to redisplay the widget using this new configuration.

Note that some widget's configurations may be honored by other widgets; for example, the Fahrenheit temperature scale enabled for the Thermal Sensors widget will also be used by the System Information widget.

4.4 Wizards

pfSense provides a few web-based wizards, like seen in the first installation in the previous chapter, to help simplify and automate the configuration of complex tasks. The admin is prompted step-by-step to complete different settings. Usually each page has only one or a few items to configure. To continue to the next form in the wizard, click its **Next** button. Generally you need to submit all the pages in the wizard for it to complete the configuration changes.

Note that wizards do not need to be used, but they are alternatives to configuring these same features elsewhere in pfSense. In some cases, a wizard takes more time and is less helpful than using the normal interfaces. But others may complete and activate settings for multiple features via a single interface. If you don't want to complete a wizard, just leave it by clicking the logo to go to the dashboard or go to a different menu page.

Examples in this book for wizards are:

- **OpenVPN Remote Access Server Setup Wizard** — via the **VPN** → **OpenVPN** → **Wizards** page (Section 33.1.2)

- **pfSense Setup** — via the **System** → **Setup Wizard** (Chapter 3)

- **Multiple Lan/Wan Traffic Shaper Wizard** — via the **Firewall** → **Traffic Shaper** → **Wizards** (Section 25.5)

- **Dedicated Links Traffic Shaper Wizard** — via the **Firewall** → **Traffic Shaper** → **Wizards** (Section 25.6)

4.5 Notices and Alerts

The webConfigurator may indicate notices in the right top of the panel with a red bell symbol and a corresponding number for the count of notices. Clicking on the bell (or number) will display a pop-up window with further details, such as the pfSense feature where a problem was detected, some output from a debug log, and maybe a timestamp. Example notices may be about starting to create SSH keys or when key generations are completed, when a service is started, invalid DHCP pool errors, filter reload problems, and many others.

You can click the **Close** button to close the pop-up window without acknowledging it. Or press the **Mark All as Read** button to indicate you are finished with the notices — and the notices bell on the panel will disappear. (Note that pfSense 2.2 version's panel may flash in yellow with a red arrow; its notices can be acknowledged individually or you can click the **Acknowledge All Notices** link.)

Some of the notices provide tips or instructions on how to remedy a problem. If you don't pay attention to frequent issues, this could build up to thousands of notices to scroll through.

Notices can also be relayed on via email or by using the Growl protocol when configured via the **System** → **Advanced** → **Notifications** subpage. See Section 5.6 for details.

4.6   Crash Reporter

If pfSense detects some pfSense PHP programming bug or a FreeBSD kernel crash, it will show
a dialog at the top of the dashboard to link to a view of the problem. Following the link to the
Crash Reporter page will show briefly about your FreeBSD system and these crash details. FreeBSD
kernel crash dumps may be due to hardware failures not handled well by the system or an internal
consistency check. The outputs may be very large and may require a FreeBSD kernel developer to
understand them.

If you have FreeBSD crash files or programming bugs logged, there will be buttons to download
them for further analysis and to share with others for troubleshooting. (Older versions of pfSense
allowed submitting the crash report to pfSense developers for inspection directly via this interface.)
It attempts to anonymize these details, but you may want to check it first to make sure you don't
send any confidential details. The PHP errors in pfSense's code can be discussed with the pfSense
developers.

If you'd like to ignore the crash report or handle it differently, you can remove the details by clicking
the **Delete the crash report data** button. Then it will take you back to the dashboard.

5 System Settings

This chapter covers the general settings for the pfSense system, such as the hostname, simple DNS server settings, localization, webConfigurator themes, administrator access, and external notifications, plus various advanced options like `sysctl` tunables. Some of the specific options are also discussed in further detail in later chapters related to the feature.

5.1 General Setup

The **System** → **General Setup** menu covers many of the same basic configurations as setup during the initial installation wizard.

Be sure to click the **Save** button at the bottom to apply the changes.

5.1.1 System

The **Hostname** field is the name of the local system without the domain name. The **Domain** input is for the domain name. (It is suggested that you do not use "local" as it may conflict with Bonjour or a mDNS service. It is recommended that you use your own valid subdomain or domain and not an invented top-level domain (TLD). The hostname and the domain together make the fully-qualified domain name (FQDN).

5.1.2 DNS Server Settings

IP addresses for up to four DNS servers that will provide resolver services (such as Google's 8.8.8.8, OpenDNS's 208.67.222.222, or your upstream ISP's resolver) may be listed in the DNS Server Settings. If you have a multi-WAN setup, you may use the drop-down for the **Gateway** for each to select the WAN network interface to use to access that DNS server.

If you configure to use DNS over TLS via the **Services** → **DNS Resolver** page (Section 21.2), it may need a valid hostname for TLS certificate verification. Enter the corresponding hostname (for the IP address) in the **DNS Hostname** field. The DNS over TLS feature was added in pfSense version 2.4.4 and this option was added in pfSense version 2.4.4-p3.

These defined DNS servers may also be shared with PPTP VPN clients, DHCP clients, used for DNS forwarding, and shared to clients via various features in pfSense.

By default, the **DNS Server Override** option is checked, which means the system will use the DNS servers as assigned by DHCP (or PPP) on the WAN. Note that those DNS servers will not be shared with the pfSense system's DHCP or PPTP VPN clients.

Note that pfSense also runs the *unbound* DNS resolver and recursive server and you don't need to setup these settings unless you have a particular need to use a defined server. If you check the checkbox for **Disable DNS Forwarder**, the local system won't use this local DNS service (but the local DNS server *unbound* will still run).

(If you happen to uncheck the **DNS Server Override** and check the **Disable DNS Forwarder** and also don't have any DNS servers listed, lookups will still work as the FreeBSD system will fallback to sending its queries to the local interface which will get to *unbound*. If you happen to also stop that DNS service, then you will be out of luck.)

This menu may not show the DNS server(s) in use, but they can be seen from the default dashboard's System Information.

5.1.3 Localization

The timezone used for the system clock is set via drop-down list which contains many locations from Africa/Abidjan to Pacific/Wallis and abbreviations like Etc/GMT-8, CST6CDT, UTC, and many others. The CMOS clock should be set to the time in the UTC timezone. Then for convenience, set this **Timezone** field to your local timezone.

The default NTP timeserver is "0.pfsense.pool.ntp.org". You may list different or additional servers in the **Timeservers** field. Use a space between the servers. You may use IP addresses or hostnames, but be sure to have working DNS if a hostname is used.

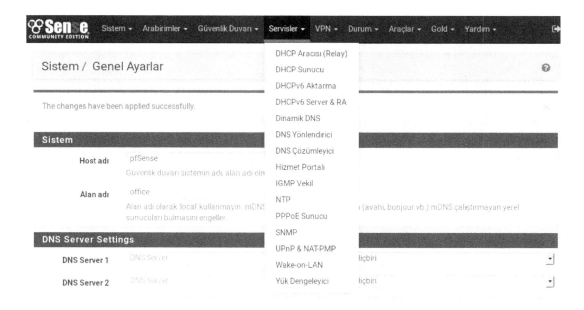

Figure 5.1: **System** → **General Setup** (in Turkish)

The pfSense webConfigurator interface has been partially translated to Türkçe (as seen in Figure 5.1), Português (brasil), and, in newer versions, to several other languages. You may choose one of these languages for the webConfigurator in the **Language** drop-down box.

This may change the characters and content used in the displays, menu titles, explanations, and much more. Note that even if you choose a non-English language, English will still be used for some settings, menu options, and descriptions.

5.1.4 webConfigurator (General Setup)

Various web interface customizations are available for the look and some basic usage of the pfSense web interfaces. Note that pfSense can have different settings for these features per interface user too. See the following section on how to enable this.

Use the **Theme** drop-down menu to select the Cascading Style Sheet (CSS) file for how the webpages will be displayed. This is for the presentation, such as fonts and colors, of the pfSense web interface. The choice labeled *pfSense* is the default. (Custom CSS files may be stored on the pfSense server in the /usr/local/www/css/ directory and then selected here.) Note that the web browser may need a hard refresh on the page to reload its cached style sheet to see the changes.

On some displays, the top navigation bar may scroll with the page. To turn this off, the user may choose to have the top menu always be displayed at the top of the web browser display even when scrolling. To select this, set the *Top Navigation* drop-down menu to *Fixed (Remains visible at top of page)*. (This is normally for large displays.) The default is the *Scrolls with page* option.

To see the pfSense server's hostname in the top navigation menu use the **Hostname in Menu** drop-down menu. By default, the top menu doesn't show the hostname, but selecting an alternative will replace the **Help** menu header with the hostname. You may select *Hostname only* to show the short name (trims off any of the domain information) and *Fully Qualified Domain Name* to display the short name with the DNS domain name (aka FQDN). Note this doesn't cause the help to keep the links local. Also note that after saving this change, the current General Setup page may not reflect the new setting yet.

By default, the front page dashboard (see Section 4.3) is split into two columns for the layout of the displayed widgets. You may choose for 1, 2, 3, or 4 columns in the **Dashboard Columns** selection.

Select the **Interfaces Sort** checkbox to sort the interfaces links in the **Interfaces** menu. Normally it shows the WAN first, then the LAN and the OPT interfaces.

The **Associated Panels Show/Hide** checkboxes are for displaying additional features on some of the web interface pages. By default the following four features are hidden. An icon is available on those pages regardless to access them. Enable the **Available Widgets** checkbox to display the Available Widgets panel on the dashboard. This is for adding more widgets easily to the dashboard as introduced in Section 4.3.1. To see the Log Filter panel by default on the **Status** → **System Logs** page as discussed in Section 11.1, check the **Log Filter** checkbox. Use the **Manage Log** checkbox to also show the Manage Log panel there (Section 11.3). Use the **Monitor Settings** checkbox to show the Settings panel by default at the **Status** → **Monitoring** page Section 28.2. (These associated panels customizations were introduced in pfSense 2.3.)

The **Require State Filter** customization is only provided for admins (and is not available in the per-user settings). It is used by the **Diagnostics** → **States** → **States** page as covered in Section 16.15 so it won't potentially display a very large state table. Activate the checkbox to not display the state table without a filter. (Note that even with this checked, by using the filter on that diagnostics page, the admin can still see a large state table.)

When the **Left Column Labels** checkbox is enabled, clicking a label in the left column in various configuration webpages will toggle or select the first item in its group of settings. This is not enabled by default.

The firewall and NAT tables allow using the mouse to move rules up and down to change their ordering. To disable this, click the **Disable dragging of firewall/nat rules** checkbox.

The pfSense login webpage is blue. If you want to have it be in a different color, select it in the **Login page color** drop-down menu. This may be useful if you have multiple pfSense systems and want to quickly identify which one by the color. This feature is only available for admins.

The **Login hostname** setting is not available per user. When the checkbox is activated by the admin, the hostname of the pfSense system will be displayed at the pfSense login screen. This is not enabled by default.

By default, the webpage title as shown at the top of the web browser or in the web browser tab will first show the pfSense server hostname followed by the specific pfSense interface page displayed. To change this order to display the current page first, followed by the hostname, check the **Display page name first in browser tab** checkbox. (Note this customization is on the user's own settings, but is not in the admin's system wide settings on this same page; see the **System** → **Advanced** → **Admin Access** page in Section 5.3.1 for the same setting.)

The admin view of the customizations also includes the **Dashboard update period** setting. This number entry form is for setting the refresh or reload timeout for frequent or infrequent updates for various widgets output, such as active VPNs, NTP status, IPsec tunnels status, interface stats, gateway stats, and the various stats and meters in the System Information widget. This update defaults to 10 seconds. (Note that NTP status timeout is six times longer than this setting, so defaults to once a minute.) The minimum allowed setting is 5 seconds and the longest update period is 600 seconds (five minutes). Note that a frequent update period will put more load on the pfSense web server. (Non-admin users cannot set this.)

Use the **Save** button to save these webConfigurator settings.

5.2 User Settings

When allowed, individual users can have customizations for the look and use of the webConfigurator interface, including many of the system-wide settings discussed in the previous section. To enable this for individual use, go to the **System** → **User Manager** → **Users** page and click the specific user's **Edit user** pencil action icon to get to the user properties. (See Section 6.2 for details.) Check the **Custom Settings** checkbox and then save that change. Then that user will have access to a new menu item: **System** → **User Settings**. (Note that selecting that checkbox will also expand the same new custom settings on the user properties page. The administrator can also make the following user-specific selections there instead.)

The first custom setting on the **System** → **User Settings** page is for the alternate CSS file. This Cascading Style Sheet defines how the webpage's HTML is displayed, including colors and fonts used. Select the choice in the **Theme** drop-down menu.

Use the **Top Navigation** drop-down menu to select *Fixed* if you want the top menu links to remain visible at the top of the pfSense webpages when you scroll down.

To see the pfSense system's short hostname or fully-qualified domain name in the top menu (to quickly help identify what system you are on), select a choice in the **Hostname in Menu** drop-down menu.

The **Dashboard Columns** selection may be used to have one through six columns of widgets on the main pfSense webpage. It defaults to two columns.

Additional panels are available on the dashboard, **Status** → **System Logs**, and **Status** → **Monitoring** pages. To enable these by default, click the corresponding **Associated Panels Show/Hide** checkboxes.

The **Left Column Labels** checkbox enables the use of column labels to also be used as a toggle for the first setting in a configuration group. (For example, when this is in use, clicking the **Left Column Labels** text will toggle the corresponding **Active** checkbox.

The **Browser tab text** checkbox is used to show the current pfSense webpage title (like "System: User Settings") first before the hostname in the web browser's identification of the website as seen in window titlebar text or web browser tabs.

Again, for more details about the above settings, also see them (amongst others) in the previous section. Click the **Save** button to store the selections. Note that some display options may not be immediately seen, but if the specific user goes to another page or reloads the page, the settings should be in effect.

5.3 Admin Access Options

Many options related to remote access into the pfSystem can be configured under the **System** → **Advanced** → **Admin Access** menu, The menu also has links along the top to access advanced settings for the firewall and NAT, networking, system tunables (also known as sysctls), notifications, and other miscellaneous settings; these are covered in later sections.

5.3.1 webConfigurator

By default, the webConfigurator is available using the HTTPS protocol and an existing TLS/SSL certificate can be selected. (See Section 12.2 about the certificates.) If the radio button for the protocol is changed to HTTP, then the **SSL Certificate** selection disappears. The TCP port field may be kept blank to use the default (port 443 for HTTPs or port 80 for HTTP), or you may enter a custom port number. (Note with HTTP, traffic to and from the webConfigurator, including the password, is sent in plain text and could be sniffed by others between you.)

The **Max Processes** selection is mostly unnecessary. By default, the `nginx` web server is configured to allow at least 1024 simultaneous connections. The number of web servers it runs initially depends on the amount of memory and if captive portals are enabled.

By default, the HTTPS web server is configured to also listen on standard port 80 and redirects the web browser client to use HTTPS instead. This is used to change from plain text to encrypted tunnel usage. The **WebGUI redirect** option may be checked to disable this HTTP redirection response configuration.

The pfSense web server uses HTTP Strict Transport Security (HSTS) which tells the browser to only use HTTPS even for plain HTTP links for the webConfigurator website. To turn this default off, click the **Disable HTTP Strict Transport Security** checkbox.

The pfSense interface web server can also use a TLS extension to use the Online Certificate Status Protocol (OCSP). To turn this on and to enable verification of OCSP responses, click the **Force OCSP Stapling in nginx** checkbox. (This feature was introduced in pfSense version 2.4.4.)

Some web browsers will allow the login credentials to be saved in the browser for quicker later logins. You may disable this by unchecking the **WebGUI Login Autocomplete** checkbox.

Successful logins to the web interface are logged, such as "/index.php: Successful login for user 'admin' from: 172.16.1.4". This specific logging can be turned off by checking the **WebGUI login messages** checkbox. These system logs can be seen in **Status** → **System Logs** → **System** → **General** page; see Figure 11.1 for details.

Behind the scenes, there is a daemon running called `sshguard` to help protect the system from brute force attacks. (Previous to pfSense version 2.4.4, it used the `sshlockout_pf` daemon.) This watches authentication logging messages for various problem logins (including for the webConfigurator) and when it reaches some failed attempts it will temporarily add the host to a packet filter table to block it via the WAN. Periodically, old block entries are removed. (Also see more details and the **Whitelist** option in the upcoming Login Protections Section 5.3.3.) To disable this automated lockout, check the **Anti-lockout** checkbox.

Warning
By default, logins are always accessible via the LAN. But when this **Anti-lockout** is checked, that automatic LAN rule is not in place. Be sure to setup a firewall rule to allow access as needed so you don't get locked out.

Also note that when using the text console menu to set an interface's IP address, this setting will be reset.

DNS rebinding is an attack techique where web browsers are used to access private network machines and then return the results to the attacker. By default, pfSense attempts to protect against this by not allowing private network addresses to be returned for public Internet names. These addresses are 10.0.0.0/8, 172.16.0.0/12, 169.254.0.0/16, 192.168.0.0/16, fd00::/8, and fe80::/10, since they should not be visible on the Internet. If this causes problems in your environment's DNS or your web interface access, you may choose to check the **DNS Rebind Check** checkbox to disable it.

Or if the DNS rebinding protection is preventing access to pfSense, you may list alternate hostnames that may be used to access the web interface. Use the **Alternate Hostnames** field; use spaces to separate multiple hostnames. Note this is for the pfSense webConfigurator access only; to add alternate hostnames for the DNS Resolver or the DNS Forwarder, see Section 21.2.4 and Section 21.5, respectively.

The web interface is also protected against HTTP_REFERER redirection. It checks to make sure that the referring webpage that submitted a form is the same pfSense system. If this causes problems with access to the web interface, such as with scripts, you can check the checkbox to disable this under **Browser HTTP_REFERER enforcement**. But note this may make you vulnerable to a man-in-the-middle attack (if someone impersonates the form submission they may have a different referer). If you cannot access the web interface due to this, see the text console menu's **shell + pfSense tools** feature for the *disablerefererchek* command (Section 37.13).

The web browser titlebar or tab text starts with the hostname followed by the current pfSense webpage. To reverse this, check the **Browser tab text**. checkbox to display the page name first.

5.3.2 Secure Shell

A few SSH server options may be configured in the **System** → **Advanced** → **Admin Access** menu. The **Secure Shell Server** option may be checked to enable secure remote access to the text console menu and Unix shell via an SSH login. Or if already enabled, the checkbox may be unchecked to turn it off. Enabling and disabling the SSH server can also be toggled via the console menu; see Section 37.15 for details. (Of course you can't SSH into it to enable it, but you could use the physical console keyboard and display or via serial access, if enabled, to access the text console menu.)

By default, this SSH access is password protected. For further security, an RSA or DSA authorized keys file (as covered in Section 6.2.3) may be used for authentication. To restrict SSH logins to use precreated authorized keys only, check the checkbox for **Authentication Method** (on pfSense versions before 2.4.4) to disable password logins. If your SSH client doesn't send a key file that matches up, it will immediately close the connection with permission denied.

Since pfSense version 2.4.4, the checkbox is replaced with a **SSHd Key Only** drop-down menu which also introduces the *both* option. Again the default is to use a SSH public key or a password. You may also select to login via a key only. Or you can configure two-factor authentication for the SSH access by selecting the *Require Both Password and Public Key* option.

Note that *root* user logins are allowed (based on the password or public key settings).

The **Allow Agent Forwarding** checkbox is used to allow `ssh-agent` private keys authentication agent forwarding via SSH sessions. (This option was introduced in pfSense version 2.4.4-p1.)

SSH service runs on TCP port 22; if you'd like to have it listen on a custom port instead, enter the number in the **SSH port** field. (By the way, if you need to access your system via SSH from the outside world, incoming firewall rules for the WAN will be needed.)

Be sure to click the **Save** button at the bottom of the webpage to activate your changes. All current SSH logins will be terminated.

5.3.3 Login Protection

The brute force detector watches for failed incoming login attempts for SSH and the web interface and probes for common web services. Certain patterns are given an attack score which is normally 10. When hitting an attack threshold within a defined time, an attacker is temporarily blocked by adding its IP address to a packet filter address collection table used for blocking incoming connections for both the SSH and webConfigurator ports. Its configurations can be tuned via these login protection settings on the **System** → **Advanced** → **Admin Access** page. (These were introduced in pfSense version 2.4.4-p1.)

With three failed login attempts — or when the accumulated attack score reaches 30 — for a single source IP address within a detection period, it will be blocked by the firewall. This attack scoring can be adjusted with the **Threshold** number field. To block on the first failure, set it to 10.

It will block the attackers for around two minutes the first time. The brute force detector will keep track of attackers and later blocks will increase this delay by 1.5 times. The initial delay in seconds can be set in the **Blocktime** number field. The actual unblocking happens randomly around that time (times the later delay factor). Note that a frequent job also runs to clear out any entries older than an hour.

Potential attackers are remembered for 30 minutes (1800 seconds). To keep track for a different time, enter it in seconds in the **Detection time** number field.

In addition to the previous **Anti-lockout** checkbox, you can also specifically whitelist single addresses or networks to make sure they are never blocked by the `sshguard` process. For the **Whitelist** setting, enter in the IP addresses or networks where admins will legitimately come from in the address and subnet mask fields. To add multiple whitelisted addresses, click the **Add address** button as needed. (Or remove a whitelist entry with the **Delete** button.)

See the **Diagnostics** → **Tables** page (Section 16.17) to view the currently-blocked IP addresses in the *sshguard* packet filter table. (Older versions of pfSense instead used the *sshlockout* and *webConfiguratorlockout* tables.)

5.3.4 Serial Communications and Console Options

With a normal install, using the serial port for console is disabled. It can be enabled by checking the box for **Serial Terminal**. The keyboard and internal video card will still be available for the console menu too.

The default serial console port speed 115200 bps, 8 data bits, no parity bits, and 1 stop bit. The speed may be modified using **Serial Speed** drop-down menu.

All consoles will display the console menu, operating system boot messages, and other console messages. The **Primary Console** selection is for where the pfSense boot script output will be displayed; its choices are *Serial Console* and *VGA console*.

The console menu via serial or the local keyboard may be password protected by enabling the **Console menu** checkbox. By default, it will automatically run the text-based menu as the *root* superuser without any login needed.

(See Chapter 37 for details about the text console.)

5.4 Advanced Miscellaneous Settings

The **System** → **Advanced** → **Miscellaneous** page is used for various types of settings, such as proxy support, power savings, cryptographic and thermal hardware, and pfSense installation feedback. See other chapters in this book for its other miscellaneous settings: load balancing (covered in Section 15.2.2), schedules (Section 16.9), gateway monitoring (Section 15.2.2), RAM disks setup (Section 10.4), and hard disk standby (Section 10.5),

5.4.1 Proxy Support

If you need to use an HTTP proxy to do remote web downloads, set your proxy server settings in the Proxy Support section. This is used for downloading firewall alias lists, updating bogon lists, downloading third-party packages, and more.

Enter the IP address or the fully-qualified domain name of the HTTP proxy server in the **Proxy URL** field. Do not include the scheme and slash characters (like "http://").

By default, some uses of the proxy will be on port 3128. You can enter your HTTP proxy port number or valid service name in the **Proxy Port** text field.

If your HTTP proxy requires user/password authentication, enter them in the **Proxy Username** and **Proxy Password** fields. The username can only contain letters, digits, periods, dashes, underscores, and at-signs. Enter the password twice to confirm it is typed correctly.

After saving these settings, various configurations will be updated to use the proxy, but it won't trigger downloads at this time. You may need to check the downloads or logs later to confirm it worked.

5.4.2 Power Savings

The power savings control daemon, `powerd`, can monitor the system's CPU's load and adjust the CPU frequency (aka clock speed) to be faster or slower, which results in using more or less electrical power, respectively. The hardware reports what frequencies it has available based on milliwatt usage which the utility will select from. This feature can be turned on by using the **Enable PowerD** checkbox.

The power saving mode choices are:

- **Hiadaptive** — This increases frequency to improve performance for interactivity when the system load rises and when the system is idle it lowers the frequency (degrading performance) to use less power. When the system load is less than 25%, it will attempt to reduce the frequency by around 3%. When the system load is greater than 37.5%, it will attempt to scale up the frequency based on the load. If the load is greater than 75%, it will try to quadruple the clock speed (up to the detected limits). For example, when the load is at 51% at a current frequency of 1203 MHz, it may change it to 2003 MHz so it can be faster (but use more power). Or when the load is low at 3% at a current frequency of 3003 MHz, it may change the clock speed down to 2403 MHz to save power.

- **Adaptive** — Like *Hiadaptive*, but tuned for less power consumption with some performance loss. When the system load is less than 50%, it will attempt to reduce the frequency by around 12%. When the system load is greater than 75%, it may scale the clock speed up based on the load. And if the system load is greater than 95%, it will attempt to double the current clock speed (within its detected limits). Commonly this is used for battery-powered systems.

- **Minimum** — Set to the lowest frequency as detected. This doesn't adapt based on the system load. This will use the least power, but may degrade the performance the most.

- **Maximum** — Set to the highest frequency as detected. This also doesn't adapt based on the system load. This will use the most power and provide the best performance.

The modes default to *Hiadaptive* for when plugged in on AC power, running from a battery, or if the AC line state is unknown. Change these as needed in the following **AC Power**, **Battery Power**, and **Unknown Power** drop-down lists. Note some systems cannot detect the power source, so use the **Unknown Power** choice as a fallback.

The current clock speed can be displayed by running "**sysctl dev.cpu.0.freq**" by using the **Diagnostics → Command Prompt** (Section 7.1) feature or at the command-line shell, for example:

```
[2.4.4-RELEASE][admin@pfSense.localdomain]/root: sysctl dev.cpu.0.freq
dev.cpu.0.freq: 3003
```

When the **Enable PowerD** option is unchecked, the CPU will run again at its default clock speed.

5.4.3 Cryptographic and Thermal Hardware

When your hardware has AES-NI cryptographic acceleration that is detected by your system, this will be noted in the System Information widget on the dashboard. This is a hardware implementation of some Advanced Encryption Standard (AES) features. To enable it, use the **Cryptographic Hardware** drop-down list. You may also select to enable the *BSD Crypto Device (cryptodev)* which allows some software (like OpenSSL, IPsec, and OpenVPN) to have access to hardware-accelerators for cryptography. Or you may choose the option to use both of these device drivers. After saving, you need to reboot the system to recognize the crypto hardware settings. No extra crypto accelerator feature is enabled by default.

By default, thermal sensor or temperature reading support is attempted using ACPI (if the hardware supports it). If needed, you can enable an on-die digital thermal sensor device driver for Intel Core or various AMD processors in the **Thermal Sensors** drop-down menu. After saving, the system will need to be rebooted to recognize this thermal hardware setting.

When the system can read its temperature, it can be seen using the Thermal Sensor widget on the dashboard. See Section 4.3.1 about enabling widgets.

5.4.4 Kernel Page Table Isolation

Some FreeBSD systems support Page Table Isolation (PTI) for the Meltdown hardware security vulnerability on Intel CPUs. This causes a significant performance regression. To turn off the meltdown mitigation, click the **Forcefully disable the kernel PTI** checkbox. (Since pfSense 2.4.4-p1, this will show your current boot loader setting for this.)

After saving this, you will need to reboot for it to take effect (Section 7.4). The System Information widget on the dashboard will also indicate if PTI is enabled or not.

5.4.5 Installation Feedback

When the dashboard's System Information widget does a pfSense version check, when doing a system update, installing packages, downloading bogons, downloading URL aliases, reporting crashes, and possibly other web-based downloads, your pfSense system is identified to pfSense — and potentially other download sites — via the HTTP User-Agent request header. A unique ID, like facade5c74e3a359dd9c, is generated using a proprietary executable and can be seen on the main dashboard in the System Information widget as the Netgate Device ID. This may be based on your system's hardware and may indicate hardware changes.

To not send this generated ID, select the **Do NOT send Netgate Device ID with user agent** checkbox. (Even when this is selected, it is still provided to Netgate when using their Auto Config Backup service as covered in Section 8.4.)

Warning
Even when the generated ID is not provided, the HTTP user agent will still disclose what version of pfSense you are running to pfSense and third-party download sites (like for alias URL downloads).

Click the **Save** button to store the changes. Note that some of the features require a system reboot (as noted) to actually use the new settings.

5.5   System Tunables

Additional advanced system options are available via the **System** → **Advanced** → **System Tunables** page. These are FreeBSD `sysctl` settings for kernel behaviors, such as for Internet networking and routing, random process IDs and random number generation, keyboard reboot, file systems, socket buffers, IPsec, CARP, socket sizing, and kernel corefiles. pfSense has other features for setting system tunables which are introduced in other sections, such as Power Savings (Section 5.4.2) and some wireless interface configurations (Section 23.4.1).

The table lists many of the standard tunables as selected by pfSense, brief descriptions, and their current values. The defaults are shown below.[1]

hw.syscons.kbd_reboot
    Enable keyboard reboot. (0)

kern.corefile
    Process corefile name format string. (/root/%N.core)

kern.ipc.maxsockbuf
    Maximum socket buffer size. (4262144)

kern.random.harvest.mask
    Entropy harvesting mask. (351)

kern.randompid
    Random PID modulus. (347)

net.enc.in.ipsec_bpf_mask
    IPsec input BPF mask. (0x0002)

net.enc.in.ipsec_filter_mask
    IPsec input firewall filter mask. (0x0002)

net.enc.out.ipsec_bpf_mask
    IPsec output BPF mask. (0x0001)

net.enc.out.ipsec_filter_mask
    IPsec output firewall filter mask. (0x0001)

net.inet.carp.senderr_demotion_factor
    Send error demotion factor adjustment. (0)

---

[1]Most of these sysctl descriptions are from the FreeBSD kernel. This book doesn't cover these advanced tunables in detail. Consult the FreeBSD documentation if curious.

net.inet.icmp.icmplim
Maximum number of ICMP responses per second. (0)

net.inet.icmp.reply_from_interface
ICMP reply from incoming interface for non-local packets. (1)

net.inet.ip.intr_queue_maxlen
Maximum size of the IP input queue. (1000)

net.inet.ip.portrange.first
Used by some programs for the beginning of available port range. (1024)

net.inet.ip.process_options
Enable IP options processing ([LS]SRR, RR, TS). (0)

net.inet.ip.random_id
Assign random ip_id values. (1)

net.inet.ip.redirect
Enable sending IP redirects. (1)

net.inet.raw.maxdgram
Maximum outgoing raw IP datagram size. (131072)

net.inet.raw.recvspace
Maximum space for incoming raw IP datagrams. (131072)

net.inet.tcp.blackhole
Do not send RST on segments to closed ports. (2)

net.inet.tcp.delayed_ack
Delay ACK to try and piggyback it onto a data packet. (0)

net.inet.tcp.drop_synfin
Drop TCP packets with SYN+FIN set. (1)

net.inet.tcp.log_debug
Log errors caused by incoming TCP segments. (0)

net.inet.tcp.recvspace
Initial receive socket buffer size. (65228)

net.inet.tcp.sendspace
Initial send socket buffer size. (65228)

net.inet.tcp.syncookies
Use TCP SYN cookies if the syncache overflows. (1)

net.inet.tcp.tso
Enable TCP Segmentation Offload. (1)

net.inet.udp.blackhole
Do not send port unreachables for refused connects. (1)

net.inet.udp.checksum
    Compute UDP checksum. (1)

net.inet.udp.maxdgram
    Maximum outgoing UDP datagram size. (57344)

net.inet6.ip6.prefer_tempaddr
    Prefer RFC 3041 temporary addresses in source address selection. (0)

net.inet6.ip6.redirect
    Send ICMPv6 redirects for unforwardable IPv6 packets. (1)

net.inet6.ip6.rfc6204w3
    Accept the default router list from ICMPv6 RA messages even when packet forwarding is
    enabled. (1)

net.inet6.ip6.use_tempaddr
    Create RFC 3041 temporary addresses for autoconfigured addresses. (0)

net.key.preferred_oldsa
    IPsec always use a new SA when the initiator reboots. (0)

net.link.bridge.pfil_bridge
    Packet filter on the bridge interface. (0)

net.link.bridge.pfil_member
    Packet filter on the member interface. (1)

net.link.bridge.pfil_onlyip
    Only pass IP packets when pfil is enabled. (0)

net.link.tap.user_open
    Allow user to open /dev/tap (based on node permissions). (1)

net.link.vlan.mtag_pcp
    Retain VLAN PCP information as packets are passed up the stack. (1)

net.pfsync.carp_demotion_factor
    pfsync's CARP demotion factor adjustment. (0)

net.raw.recvspace
    Default raw socket receive space. (65536)

net.raw.sendspace
    Default raw socket send space. (65536)

net.route.netisr_maxqlen
    Maximum routing socket dispatch queue length. (1024)

vfs.read_max
    Cluster read-ahead max block count. (32)

Each entry also has an **Edit tunable** action icon for updating the value, tunable name, or description. A FreeBSD system has many other sysctls and you can click the **New** button at the top of the table to add a new entry with a value. (If you save an existing entry with a new tunable name, a new tunable will be created.) Note that it will accept misspelled or non-existent names or invalid values without warning. After saving a new (or changed) entry, you will need to click the **Apply Changes** button for the new sysctl setting to take effect.

New tunable entries or modified settings also offer a **Delete/Reset tunable** action icon in the table. For a new tunable, it is used to delete it, and for a pfSense known tunable, it is used to reset it to its default value (and description). This will pop-up a prompt to verify to remove or reset it.

5.6 System Notifications

pfSense can send notifications to Growl, a third-party customizable notification system for OS X, Windows, Linux, Android, and other platforms. On your desktop or phone, Growl can display pop-up windows for real-time events and a rollup window for notifications you may have missed.

pfSense can also send notifications via email (aka SMTP). Note that some packages require the SMTP notifications to be configured to function properly.

These notifications may be for events such as dynamic DNS updates, SSH key creation and SSH startup, errors with synchronizing configurations, high availability clusters resuming state, load balancer gateway problems, upgrade warnings, DHCP misconfigurations, package reinstall issues, firewall filter rule loading problems, restoring backups problems, and more.

These remote notifications can be enabled and configured via the **System** → **Advanced** → **Notifications** page. After making the changes, click the **Save** button.

5.6.1 SMTP (Notification) Settings

To use the email-based notifications, uncheck the **Disable SMTP Notifications** checkbox. The **E-Mail server** and the **Notification E-Mail address** fields are also required.

Enter the IP address or the fully-qualified hostname of the SMTP mail server to relay notifications through in the **E-Mail server** text field.

If this mail server is running on an alternate port (like 587 or 465), set that port number in the **SMTP Port of E-Mail server** field. (If unset, it uses the standard TCP port 25.)

It will wait for 20 seconds for the mail server connection. To change this timeout, enter the seconds in the **Connection timeout to E-Mail server** number field.

For securing the SMTP communications, use the **Enable SSL/TLS** checkbox. It will do STARTTLS automatically if the mail server supports it. By default, the SMTP certificate is validated. If you don't want to check the certificate, because it is known to fail, but still do encrypted mail, uncheck the **Validate SSL/TLS** checkbox. (This option was introduced in pfSense version 2.4.4-p1.)

The default sender email address will be username *pfsense* at your defined hostname and domain name. To change this, put the sending email address in the **From e-mail address** field.

Enter the email address that will receive the notifications in the required **Notification E-Mail address** field.

If you need an SMTP authentication username (or identity) and its password for the remote server, enter them in the **Notification E-Mail auth username (optional)** and **Notification E-Mail auth password** fields. Leave these empty to not to use an authentication method.

The **Notification E-Mail auth mechanism** drop-down menu defaults to the ESMTP *PLAIN* authentication method. You may also change it to the *LOGIN* type. Some mail servers do not support both methods. Only change this if it is known that your mail server (such as Office365 or Exchange) doesn't work with PLAIN for authentication. This is only used if the username and password are set.

To see if the email-based notification works, save your new settings and then when back to this page use the **Test SMTP Settings** button. Then check the incoming email as defined earlier to see the notification message. The top of the pfSense webpage will also display a status line about this email test.

If a notification message can't be mailed from pfSense, an error will be logged. See the main **Status → System Logs** view and search for "`Could not send the message`" (Section 11.1).

5.6.2   Sounds

The beeps at the physical hardware when pfSense starts up and shuts down can be disabled (or enabled) at the bottom of the **Notifications** page. It is enabled by default. Check the **Disable the startup/shutdown beep** checkbox to turn of this sound.

5.6.3   Growl Settings

Uncheck the **Disable Growl Notifications** checkbox to enable sending notifications using the Growl notification system. Note that it is also disabled if the following **IP Address** is not set.

You may customize the class of the Growl notification in the **Registration Name** text field (which defaults to "PHP-Growl").

The **Notification Name** text field defaults to "pfSense growl alert."

Enter the IP address for the Growl service in the **IP Address** field. Note it will use the GNTP protocol using TCP port 23053.

Then enter the **Password** for that remote growl notification system (or device).

Verify it works by clicking the **Test Growl Settings** button to send a test Growl notification to your defined IP address. Check the receiving Growl app and also look at the top of the pfSense webpage for any status message about the test attempt.

If a Growl message can't be sent, an error will be logged. See the main **Status** → **System Logs** view and filter for "`Growl`" (Section 11.1).

6 Users and Groups

This chapter is about user and group management for users allowed to access the pfSense administration interfaces. The user accounts may be used by other features too, like the Captive Portal, IPsec, and OpenVPN. pfSense can also use an external RADIUS or LDAP service to authenticate against.

The user and group management can be accessed via the **System → User Manager** menu. Its default **Users** display will list the currently configured users with their username, full name, if disabled or not, and what groups they are part of. Action icons to edit individual user's settings or to delete the user are available.

The system always includes the default System Administrator (admin) user account which has full privileges at the pfSense web interface. In Unix terms, this is the superuser and has full *root* power at the shell too. This *admin* user cannot be removed using this interface.

6.1 Privileges

For access and use of the system, pfSense provides around 245 fine-grained capabilities to limit or extend privileges, such as Unix shell account access, web interface dashboard access and its widgets, viewing various diagnostics or logs, and access to configuration pages. By not enabling (or by removing) privileges, it can be used to disallow modifying system configurations or firewall rules, for example. This is one of the powerful features of pfSense. The following is a short example of just some of the many privileges.

- **WebCfg - All pages** — Allows access to all pfSense webpages and SSH shell access.
- **WebCfg - Crash reporter** — Allows access to a page to view and submit crash reports to pfSense.
- **WebCfg - Firewall: Alias: Edit** — Allows adding or editing aliases for IPs, networks, and ports.
- **WebCfg - Firewall: NAT: Port Forward: Edit** — Allows adding or editing port forwarding using network address translation.
- **WebCfg - Firewall: Rules** — Allows access to view, disable, or delete existing firewall rules.

- **WebCfg - Status: Logs: Settings** — Allows setting general logging options and remote syslogging.

- **WebCfg - Status: Services** — Allows viewing, restarting, and temporarily stopping various system and network services.

- **WebCfg - System: General Setup** — Allows access to changing web interface and dashboard view settings, the system hostname, DNS servers to use, and localization.

- **WebCfg - System: User Manager** — Allows access to view, add, edit, or remove users. If not allowed, then non-admin users can change their own password.

- **WebCfg - System: User Settings** — Allows changing web interface and dashboard view settings.

Users may be given capabilities directly or inherit them as being part of a group which has been assigned privileges. Most of the privileges are related to accessing or using the web interface. Note that if a user doesn't have access to a specific webpage, he or she will be redirected to a different page. The web interface menus should only display the links for the pages the user has access to. Note that some pages or widgets may have been given access, but have links to pages that the user doesn't have access for.

Warning
It is important to note that some pages offer other features and some privileges provide capabilities that may effectively give the user more privileges than expected. For example, a privilege may allow editing files or running commands on the system which would bypass other restrictions.

Enabling use of these privileges for users and groups is covered in the upcoming Section 6.2.4 and Section 6.4.1.

6.2   Add or Edit a User Account

To add a new user account, from the **System → User Manager** page, click the green **Add** button (at the bottom of the Users list). This will take you to the **Edit** page for setting User Properties and Keys. The user's scope is predefined as either SYSTEM for built-in or USER for an add-on user. Only the username and password fields are required to add a new user account — but note at this minimal addition, the account will be locked (due to no privileges) and won't be usable for logins.

Editing an existing user will offer these same entry fields, plus allow setting up the effective privileges and user certificates for the user. To edit an existing user, from the front **System → User Manager** page, click the user's corresponding edit action pencil icon.

Use the **Save** button at the bottom to complete the addition or editing of a user. This will take you back to the list of all users.

Note

By default, privileges aren't extended to new users. When logging in via the web interface, a popup will indicate that no page is assigned for the user.

The account can be set so the user cannot login by checking the **Disabled** checkbox. This will prevent access for both the web interface and text console (via SSH).

The **Username** is used for the local Unix /etc/passwd account. The username may not contain a space and the valid characters are upper and lowercase alphabet, digits, period (.), dash (-), and underscore (_). The length is limited to 16 characters.

Set the user's password by entering it twice (the second to confirm it as it cannot be seen). The password is required. (Users can later change or set their own password via the same **System** → **User Manager** menu entry as explained in Section 6.7.)

The **Full name** field is used to describe the account.

If you'd like the account to expire after a specific calendar day, enter it at the **Expiration date** field. Use the format *MM/DD/YYYY*. It may also provide a calendar popup widget to select the date. Note that the expiration kicks in after that date (at the end of the day). A background job checks this expiration configuration every few hours and will also mark the account disabled if expired. It will block logins when it reaches the expiration date.

The user can have tailored webpage formatting and some basic usage changes with the pfSense interface. To access these customizations, check the **Custom Settings** checkbox and several new input fields will appear. These several customizations are covered in Section 5.1.4 (for site-wide defaults) and Section 5.2 (for the user). Also by enabling this checkbox, the user may also be able to customize these same settings via a new **System** → **User Settings** menu item. But that is only available if that page is allowed for the user (with the "WebCfg - System: User Settings" privilege).

The **Group membership** selections are for assigning the user to one or more groups. It provides two selection lists: the left list is for the available groups this specific user is not a member of; and the right list lists the groups the user is a member of. By default, the only entry is *admins* in the left (not a member) list because that is the only group by default.

See the **System** → **User Manager** → **Groups** subpage as described in Section 6.4 to add a group. Note that multiple users at a time can be configured per group when editing on that other page.

To join a group (on the user's page), highlight the group name in the left column and click the corresponding blue **Move to the "Member of"** button. (Then the group name will disappear from the left list and be added to the right list.) To remove a group membership, select the group in the right (member) column, and click the **Move to "Not member of" list** button. (Use your web browser's feature, such as pressing the Control, Shift, or Command keys, to select multiple group names if desired.)

6.2.1 Create Certificate for User

Users may have certificates directly associated to their user account. For more details about certificates for the system, see Chapter 12 about the **System** → **Cert. Manager** features.

If you already have a private Certificate Authority (CA) configured in pfSense, a checkbox will be displayed to create a user certificate when adding a new user. If you don't have this checkbox, first create a private CA. Your CA details may be viewed or a new one added via the **System** → **Certificate Manager** → **CAs** pages as discussed in Section 12.1.

Clicking the checkbox will expand the new user addition form. It will display a few fields for creating a certificate. To create a certificate at this time, you are required to enter a name in the **Descriptive name** field. It is recommended to use the same new username as entered previously for this new user.

Then select the CA used for creating the new certificate in the **Certificate authority** drop-down menu.

The **Key length** drop-down defaults to 2048 bits which is a standard recommended minimum key size for the private key. You may choose a different size from the drop-down as needed.

The certificate will expire by default in approximately 10 years (3650 days). You may change this by entering the number of days in the **Lifetime** input field.

If you don't have a CA or don't choose to create the certificate at this time, you may choose to save this new user first and then later edit it to import an external certificate or create a certificate for the user. This is covered in the following.

6.2.2   User Certificates

Note the User Certificates section's fields are not offered when initially adding a user. After adding the user (and saving it), you can later edit the account to access this form.

If you are editing a previously-created user and you have existing certificates, the User Certificates section lists the certificates by name and the CA used for each. It also provides a remove action (trash can icon) to remove the user's association with that certificate. It will prompt to confirm it is okay to remove that user's use of that certificate by pressing the **OK** button. Note that it will not remove the certificate itself, which can be removed via the **System** → **Certificate Manager** → **Certificates** page as covered in Section 12.2.

Use the **Add** button to associate a certificate with the user. This will take you away from editing the user to the **System** → **Certificate Manager** → **Certificates** → **Edit** page to add a certificate associated for the user.

On the new page, when adding a new certificate, a descriptive name is assigned and by default it will be set to the username. Then select in the **Method** drop-down menu if you want to import an existing certificate, create an internal certificate, create a Certificate Signing Request (CSR), or choose a certificate already known to pfSense. The default is to import a certificate which is used to upload a X.509 PEM certificate and private key as generated elsewhere. For more information, see Section 12.2.1.

Selecting to create an internal certificate in the **Method** drop-down menu will bring up a new Internal Certificate form with several options. For more information, see Section 12.2.1. A new form for an External Signing Request with many options will appear when choosing to create a Certificate Signing Request. For more information, see Section 12.2.1.

You may also use a previously imported or generated certificate, by selecting **Choose an existing certificate**. Then a new form appears with a drop-down menu to select an existing certificate. The certificates will be identified with their descriptive name and reference ID. It may also indicate if it is a CA (Certificate Authority), is revoked, or in use (meaning the system already has the same certificate configured for another use).

Click the **Save** button to complete adding the certificate for the user. This will take you back to the user list — so to see the certificate for the user, click the edit action (pencil icon) for that user to see its User Certificates list.

6.2.3 Keys

The Keys section is used to enter the authorized SSH public keys that are permitted for logging in to the console and an IPsec Pre-Shared Key.

For SSH, enter one public key entry per line in the **Authorized SSH Keys** textbox. The public SSH key is provided from a SSH key generation utility (like `PuTTYgen` on Windows or `ssh-keygen` on Mac OS X). It contains optional options, the protocol keytype (like ssh-rsa), the public Base64-encoded key, and a comment (or identifier). (Behind the scenes, pfSense stores the SSH public keys in the user's `~/.ssh/authorized_keys` file on the pfSense server.)

The **IPsec Pre-Shared Key** field is used to set a pre-shared secret (PSK). It is used by pfSense's VPN daemons to authenticate other hosts.

 Warning
While the SSH public key is designed for sharing and does not need to be confidential, the IPsec secret should be protected.

These IPsec pre-shared keys may be viewed and managed via the **VPN → IPsec → Pre-Shared Keys** subpage as described in Section 30.5.

6.2.4 Effective Privileges

The Effective Privileges section is only displayed after the user is already created — so after adding a new user (and saving it), click the **Edit user** pencil icon from the Users list for the specific user to access this. The Effective Privileges section will show a table listing the privileges available for the user indicating the group it is inherited from (if applicable), its name and description, and an action. The table is empty by default.

To remove a single privilege, click the corresponding **Delete Privilege** trash can icon. This will pop-up a prompt. Click **OK** to remove it (or press **Cancel** to keep it). This may immediately deactivate some monitoring page for that user, for example.

Click the green **Add** button to assign privileges for the specific user. This will take you to the **System → User Manager → Users → Edit → Add Privileges** page. The **Assigned privileges** menu lists the 200-plus available capabilities (other than those already assigned but not inherited via group privileges).

To reduce the displayed list, you may use the **Filter** field. Just enter a partial keyword or phrase, like "**dhcp**" or "**virtual server**" and press Enter (or click the **Filter** button) — and the **Assigned privileges** list will show only the matching choices. Use the **Clear** button to reset this filter (and display all possibilities again).

A brief one-line description for a single selected item is displayed at the bottom of the page (below the buttons).

Select the desired privilege or multiple privileges and click the **Save** button. Then it will take you to the top-level **System** → **User Manager** → **Users** page. Click again the **Edit user** (pencil) icon for the previous user to see its new effective privileges.

6.3   Removing Users

Users may be removed by clicking the **Delete user** trash can icon in the Users table on the **System** → **User Manager** page. It will prompt to ask if you are sure you want to delete the user; click the **OK** button to proceed (or you may click **Cancel** to not remove the user).

A checkbox is also available to select and remove multiple users at one time. After selecting the users, use the red **Delete** button at the bottom of the table. It will also provide a pop-up prompt to confirm you want to remove the selected users.

If you want to temporarily deactivate an account (instead of removing), the user can be marked as disabled. See Section 6.2 for details.

6.4   Groups

A *group* is used to enable privileges for multiple user accounts. Individual users inherit the capabilities from the groups they are a member of. When you have a lot of users that should have similar characteristics, using groups eases their management. The available groups are managed via the **System** → **User Manager** → **Groups** menu. This lists the existing groups by name with a description and count of members per group. The actions allow editing the group and, optionally, remove the group.

By default, there are two *system* groups: *all* which has no privileges and *admins* allows access to all pages and to the Unix shell.

A group can be removed from the groups list page by clicking its corresponding **Delete group** action trash can icon. It will prompt to confirm if you want to remove a group. Click **OK** to proceed (or you may cancel this action). Note that removing a group does not delete its members, but those users will no longer inherit any privileges related to that previous group.

To edit a group setup, click its corresponding pencil icon for the **Edit group** action.

To setup a new group, click the green **Add** button. This will bring up the Group Properties form (which is also available when editing an existing group).

Enter a unique group identifier in the **Group name**. The valid characters are the upper and lowercase alphabet, digits, a period (.), dash (-), and underscore (_). The maximum length is 16 characters.

The **Scope** drop-down menu is for selecting if the group is *Local* or *Remote*. (A third scope which can not be selected is *system* which is for the built-in predefined groups.) The *Local* scope is used to setup a Unix /etc/group entry for sharing Unix group privileges (such as used via the Unix shell). (If the scope is set to *Remote*, the group name may also contain space characters.)

You may optionally enter a brief explanation about the group in the **Description** field.

The **Group membership** selection lists are for assigning a user to one or more groups. The left list is for the available users this specific group does not include, and the right lists the users in the group. By default (with a new group), the left column will list the *admin* and all the pfSense users that have been previously created.

To assign a user to the group, highlight the username in the left column and click the corresponding blue **Move to "Members"** button. (Then the username will disappear from the left list and be added to the right list.) Multiple users may be selected or you may assign one at a time. To remove a user from the group's membership, select the username in the right column, and click the **Move to "Not members" list** button (and then the user will appear in the left column).

Note that per-user setup for multiple groups can be configured via the **System → User Manager → Users → Edit** page as described in Section 6.2.

Click the **Save** button to save the new group settings. It will take you back to the previous page listing all the groups.

6.4.1   Group Privileges

When editing an existing group, you will also have an Assigned Privileges section. This will list the privileges with descriptions associated with this group. To remove a single capability, click its corresponding **Delete Privilege** action trash can icon and to confirm this action click **OK**. By default (with a new group), the lists of privileges will be empty.

Click the **Add** button to add a privilege to the group being edited. This will take you to the **System → User Manager → Groups → Edit → Add Privileges** page.

The webpage interface for assigning privileges for a group is similar to the assigning privileges to a user as covered in Section 6.2.4. Select one or more privilege identifiers in the **Assigned privileges** options menu. The list will not include the group's currently-assigned privileges. For convenience, enter a partial keyword in the **Filter** text field and press the **Filter** button for the list of available privileges to only show matching items. (Click the **Clear** button to reset the filter so all privileges are listed.)

Click the **Save** button to add those privileges to that group. You will be taken back to the **System → User Manager → Groups → Edit** page. Note that this doesn't replace the previous assignments, so to make changes use the **Delete Privilege** trash can icon to remove privileges (one at a time).

6.5   Settings

The **System** → **User Manager** → **Settings** page is used to set the system-wide pfSense web interface idle timeout and the user authentication server.

Logins to the pfSense web interface will timeout at four hours of no use. The webpage may still display the current page, but if you click on any menu link or submit button, you will be logged out and taken to the login page. To change this default for all users, use the **Session timeout** dialog to choose the time in minutes.

 Warning
If the session timeout is configured as 0, then this idle timeout will be disabled for all users. This means a user will be logged in indefinitely, so someone else using that web browser could go to a pfSense page and have instant access.

The **Authentication Server** drop-down menu is used to select how users to the pfSense web interface are authenticated, such as LDAP or RADIUS. By default, the web users just use the standard Unix local user password database, which is defined as the *Local Database* option. In a default installation, this will be the only option. To configure the other authentication server methods, first go to the **System** → **User Manager** → **Authentication Servers** page which is covered in the following section.

To save your settings, click the **Save** button. You may test an LDAP authentication backend by clicking the **Save & Test** button.

6.6   Authentication Servers

Users may login to pfSense by authenticating against a local Unix password database (the default), a RADIUS server, or a remote LDAP service. This authentication is for accessing the pfSense web interface, and for captive portal logins (and accounting), IPsec Mobile Clients support, and Open-VPN connections. The **System** → **User Manager** → **Authentication Servers** page lists the current authentication server types and allows you to add a configuration to access a LDAP or RADIUS authentication server.

No RADIUS or LDAP authentication servers are configured by default. Click the **Add** button to setup this alternative authentication method. This will bring up a new page with a Server Settings form.

Or to edit existing settings for connecting to a RADIUS or LDAP server, click the **Edit server** action (pencil icon) that corresponds to the entry in the list. This will take you to the same form (covered in the following) that was used to add the entry, but you won't be able to change the descriptive name nor type.

To remove a server from the list, click the **Delete server** action (trash can icon) for the server. It will prompt in a pop-up to confirm if you want to remove that authentication server; click the **OK** button to proceed.

Note

You won't be able to edit nor delete the Local Database authentication server as this is the built-in method.

On the new page for adding an authentication server, enter a unique name in the **Descriptive Name** text input box. This field is required. (This field cannot be changed when editing existing settings.) It is recommended to use a name that includes the following type as part of the name ("ldap" or "radius") so it can be easily recognized in other parts of pfSense offering use of this defined authentication server.

The **Type** drop-down form is used to choose between LDAP and RADIUS. The following form reflects the server settings for that type choice. (This type also cannot be changed for an existing setup.)

Note

The `freeradius` package may be installed to run your own RADIUS service. See the **System** → **Package Manager** feature as covered in Chapter 35 to install it. pfSense doesn't provide a pre-packaged LDAP server daemon solution.

6.6.1 LDAP Server Settings

Enter the remote LDAP server's hostname or IP address in the **Hostname or IP address** text input field. This field is required. When using SSL or STARTTLS TLS (as defined in the following **Transport** drop-down menu), the CN (common name) contained within the certificate presented by the LDAP server must match the resolved LDAP server address.

The **Port value** may be used to connect with an LDAP server on a custom port. The default is defined by the following **Transport** selection. *TCP - Standard* or *STARTTLS* use port 389 and the *SSL* choice uses port 636. This field is required.

The **Transport** drop-down menu is used to select the type of LDAP to use. The default choice is *TCP - Standard*. The secure options are *TCP - STARTTLS* and *SSL - Encrypted* (also known as *LDAPS*) which are the LDAP protocols over TLS/SSL for encrypted communication. Note that selecting the transport will reset any custom port setting above.

When using STARTTLS or LDAPS, a Certificate Authority (CA) may be used. If your pfSense system has already been configured to know about one or more CAs, they will be listed in the **Peer Certificate Authority** drop-down menu. Note when using an Active Directory (AD), its CA must match.

If no CAs have been defined, it will link you to the **System** → **Certificate Manager** → **CAs** page where you can add a certificate. This is covered in Section 12.1.1.

The **Protocol version** drop-down is for selecting the LDAP protocol to be used when connecting to the LDAP server. It defaults to 3 and the other choice is 2. Note that some LDAP 3 servers may choose not to talk using protocol 2 if needing LDAP 3 protocol features.

To specify the number of seconds to wait for LDAP search results and for network timeouts, use the **Server Timeout** number input field. It defaults to 25 seconds.

For **Search scope**, the **Level** drop-down menu defaults to *One Level* which is for returning information only below the following **BaseDN** (such as a single directory results). The other option is *Entire Subtree* which is equivalent to searching an entire directory. (The *One Level* scope may be much faster.) The Distinguished Name is used to reference LDAP objects with a sequence of attributes (separated by commas). Enter it in the **BaseDN** text field.

The **Authentication containers** text field is for entering semicolon-separated relative distinguished names (which may be multiple with commas) to prepend to the BaseDN. This is used to do the LDAP searches using different attributes. If this includes a "DC=" Domain Component, the LDAP search will not use the BaseDN as part of the search. This field is required. Here are two examples:

```
CN=Users;DC=example,DC=com
```

or

```
OU=Staff;OU=Freelancers
```

To the right of that field is the **Select a container** button. Clicking this will use the various settings to connect to the server to search for all organizational unit entries or users. If successful, it will bring up a new form for selecting LDAP containers for authentication. Use the checkboxes to select the desired entries and click the corresponding **Save** button.

Note if there is a problem and it cannot connect to the LDAP server, a note may be displayed at the bottom of the webpage. You may need to check your settings and try again.

To add additional attributes to the LDAP query, click the **Enable extended query** checkbox. This will bring up the **Query** text input field to enter a filter addition. An example is:

```
&(objectClass=inetOrgPerson)(mail=*@example.com)
```

LDAP has minimal authentication. By default, pfSense will do a simple authentication between itself and the LDAP server without a DN (Distinguished Name) and password. To actually use a DN and password, click the **Use anonymous binds to resolve distinguished names** checkbox to *uncheck* it. When this anonymous bind feature is not enabled, two new **Bind credentials** text input fields appear for the User DN and the password to use for the authentication.

When adding a new authentication server, the form will also display an **Initial Template** drop-down menu with *OpenLDAP* (the default), *Microsoft AD*, and *Novell eDirectory* choices. Selecting one of these LDAP implementations will preset the following three required attributes. (Note that the template choices are not available when editing existing LDAP server settings, but you can still edit the individual following attributes.)

The **User naming attribute** text field is used to refer to the logon username. For OpenLDAP and Novell eDirectory the default is "**cn**" (Common Name). The Microsoft AD attribute is *samAccountName*, used with old Windows NT 4.0 and Windows 98. This field is required and is used to prefix the LDAP filter.

The **Group naming attribute** text field defaults to "**cn**" (for all three template types). This field is required.

The required **Group member attribute** text field is used to for getting group information. The default attribute name for OpenLDAP is "`member`", Microsoft AD is "`memberOf`", and Novell eDirectory is "`uniqueMember`".

By default, it will use RFC 2307bis Active Directory style group membership. To use members listed on the group object (**Group Object Class** with **Group member attribute**) rather than using groups listed on user object (the **User naming attribute**), check the **RFC 2307 Groups** checkbox. The following text field, **Group Object Class** is only used if the **LDAP Server uses RFC 2307 style group membership** is checked. The default is "`posixGroup`" (and "`group`" is another common value for the object class).

Some LDAP servers store their information in UTF-8 character encoding format (so they can support accents, extended alphabets, Chinese characters, emojis, et cetera). This may be required, but note that some LDAP servers don't support it so it is disabled by default. Use the **UTF8 Encode** checkbox to convert LDAP parameter strings before sending them to the server.

If usernames used in pfSense contain an @ (at) sign, by default, it is removed with any text following it for use with LDAP filtering. To not strip away the parts of the username, check the **Username Alterations** checkbox.

Use the **Save** button to store the LDAP Server Settings and you will be returned back to the **System → User Manager → Authentication Servers** page.

6.6.2 RADIUS Server Settings

RADIUS is an authentication and accounting service. The acronym is for Remote Authentication Dial-In User Service and was commonly used in the past for dial-up servers and routers. It is still used for centralized user management for multiple systems and networks.

To use RADIUS for authentication, add a server via the **System → User Manager → Authentication Servers** subpage. Then after entering the **Descriptive name** like described earlier, select *RADIUS* in the **Type** drop-down menu.

The **Protocol** drop-down is for selecting how it will communicate with the RADIUS server. It defaults to *MS-CHAPv2*, Microsoft's second version of the Challenge-Handshake Authentication Protocol. The other choices are *PAP* Password Authentication Protocol; *MD5-CHAP* where the CHAP response is hashed with MD5; and *MS-CHAPv1* Microsoft's first version of CHAP.

Enter the RADIUS server's hostname or address in the required **Hostname or IP address** field. Enter the shared secret for that server host in the required **Shared Secret** field. This may be any length, but the protocol uses only the first 128 characters.

The **Services offered** drop-down menu is used to select *Authentication and Accounting* (the default), *Authentication*, or *Accounting*. You will need to select an authentication service (and not only accounting) to have this configuration be available and used for user logins, such as with the captive portal (Section 29.3.6), for example. (The accounting-only mode is only used for IPsec VPN. It is used for statistical purposes such as billing, and not for validating a user login.)

The standard RADIUS Authentication port number is 1812. The standard RADIUS Accounting port number is 1813. If the server is using a custom port, enter it in the **Authentication port** and/or

Accounting port input fields as needed. Note that if you select the *Accounting* service above, then it will only use the **Accounting port** setting. If you select the *Authentication* service, then it will only use the **Authentication port** setting. Otherwise it will use both ports.

The **Authentication Timeout** number input form is used to set the time in seconds that the RADIUS server must respond by. It defaults to five seconds. A common default for RADIUS clients is three seconds, but if you are using two-factor authentications, be sure to have enough time for the user to receive and enter a token.

It will attempt to authenticate two times before giving up. This is a built-in setting and is not configurable.

The **RADIUS NAS IP Attribute** selection field lists your interfaces, like WAN and LAN, and their primary IP addresses. This is used to identify your pfSense server to the RADIUS server when requesting access. (It is not the visitor's IP address.) It may also be used for authentication and accounting by setting the *Called-Station-Id* attribute (for non-Cisco RADIUS). This normally defaults to the WAN's IP address. (This option was introduced here in pfSense version 2.4.4.)

Click the **Save** button to save the server settings. This will return you to the list of authentication servers.

6.7   User Password

For pfSense systems that have been setup with users that haven't been given the "WebCfg - System: User Manager" privilege to manage other users, the menu link for **System** → **User Manager** takes them instead to a **System** → **User Password** page. This allows a user to change their own local password. They enter their new choice twice (to avoid typing errors) and click the **Save** button to reset it.

Administrators can change passwords for themselves or other users via the different **System** → **User Manager** page via the **Edit user** pencil icon for the specific user (as covered in Section 6.2).

6.8   Testing Authentication

The **Diagnostics** → **Authentication** menu may be used to verify if a user account exists and that the password works. By default, there is only a single **Authentication Server** choice to test with — pfSense's *Local Database*. Additional authentication backends of LDAP and RADIUS may be added via the **System** → **User Manager** → **Authentication Servers** menu (which can be also accessed via the **Related settings** icon on the header bar) as explained in the previous Section 6.6.

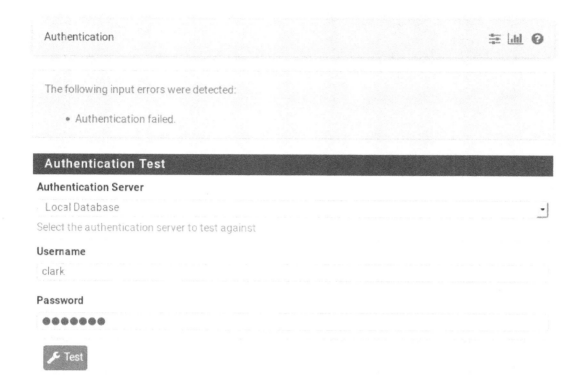

Figure 6.1: **Diagnostics** → **Authentication** failure

Select the **Authentication Server**, enter the username and password, and click the **Test** button. It will report if it could authenticate successfully and will list the group names the user is a member of. If the user doesn't exist or the password is wrong, it will report an "Authentication failed" error (as shown in Figure 6.1).

7 System Management

This chapter is about additional pfSense operating system management that is unrelated to its main use as a router, firewall, or network server. It includes details on running commands, transferring files, editing files, rebooting or shutting down the system, viewing system memory and load details, starting and stopping various services (temporarily) via a single interface, resetting to the initial pfSense defaults, and about a hidden pfSense feature to view lots of system information in a single report.

7.1 Command Prompt and File Transfers

The **Diagnostics** → **Command Prompt** feature provides ways to run shell commands, run PHP code, download files, and upload files via the pfSense web interface.

Warning
The Command Prompt features are for advanced users and the interface warns that they can be dangerous. It provides superuser privilege for the base system.

Unix shell commands, including arguments and special characters, can be entered in the field under Execute Shell Command. Click the **Execute** button to run it. The shell output will be displayed at the top of the webpage (as seen in Figure 7.1). Use the double left arrow («) icon to use the previous sent command and the right double angle quotes (») icon to go forward in the shell history. The current command line can be reset by pressing the **Clear** button.

For normal shell access, see Section 37.9 about the console (or SSH) shell.

Figure 7.1: **Diagnostics** → **Command Prompt** shell example

To download a file from the pfSense server, enter the complete path name (such as /etc/ascii-art/ pfsense-logo-small.txt) and click the **Download** button.

To upload a file, click the web browser's **Browse...** button and use the web browser's widget to select a local file. Then click the **Upload** button. The file will be saved under the pfSense server's /tmp directory.

As an alternative for uploading or retrieving files and even browsing the pfSense directories, see the **Diagnostics** → **Edit File** page as described in the following Section 7.2.

Multiple PHP commands, even a PHP script, can be entered into the Execute PHP Commands text input box. It will also silently prepend your code to include pfSense PHP utility functions so you can access the pfSense environment configurations. Press the **Execute** button there to run your PHP code on the server and the PHP Response output will be displayed.

If there is a PHP error, you should receive response output about it and it may indicate where the problem is. (Note that pfSense may detect the programming mistake as a bug in its own system and its crash detection may prompt you to report it to the pfSense project — if you see this, just delete it. See Section 4.6 for more details.)

7.2   Directory Browser and File Editor

The **Diagnostics** → **Edit File** feature allows browsing around the FreeBSD file system, displaying and editing text files, and saving files to the system. At the top is a blank text input box; this may be used to enter a filename to load or save or a directory name to browse. For example, to view the user database, enter /etc/passwd and click the **Load** icon; it will then display that file in the larger text input box below the icons. (Do not edit and save this file with the same filename.) A good use of this feature is as a file viewer.

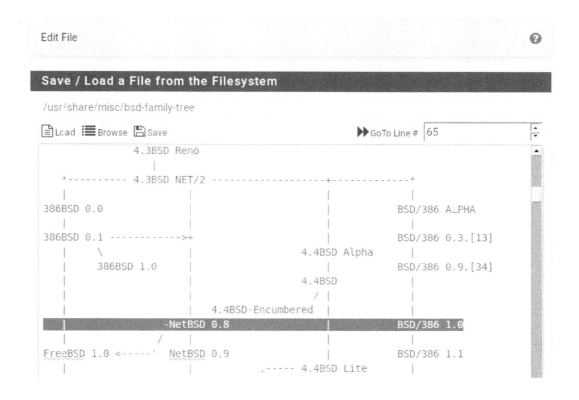

Figure 7.2: **Diagnostics** → **Edit File** — **Load** example

If the input text box contains a valid directory starting with a slash (/) and you click the **Browse** button, it will generate a list of directories and files to browse as seen in Figure 7.3. If the input text box is empty, it starts at the top (root) of the file system. If you click on a folder, the browser display will take you to that directory. If you click on the "**. .**" (dot dot) folder, it will browse up one level.

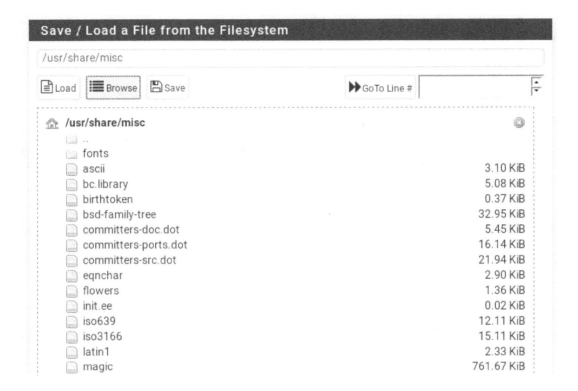

Figure 7.3: **Diagnostics** → **Edit File** — **Browse** example

If you click on a file (or click **Load** with a filename in the input field), regardless of the file type, it will load it into the text area edit box. So a binary file, like an ELF executable or a JPEG image, will be displayed as unreadable text or Unicode placeholders.

Once a file is loaded, you can press the **Browse** button again to get back the folder view, but note that this will lose your edits in the simple editor.

The input field on the right top side is to jump to a line number within the text area. To use it, enter a number (or use the up or down arrows to select a number), and click the corresponding **GoTo Line#** button — and it will highlight that line in the displayed file. (See Figure 7.2 for an example.)

Warning
The **Edit File** feature is dangerous; it can overwrite or corrupt important files.

If you want to make changes, type in the simple text edit box and click the **Save** icon. You may change the filename in the path name input box to save it in a different location or with a different name. Note that it will not create a directory, so will fail to write a file that contains a non-existent path.

To download or upload a file, also see the **Diagnostics** → **Command Prompt** feature as covered in the previous section.

7.3 Halt System

The **Diagnostics** → **Halt System** menu option may be used to shutdown the pfSense system. It will stop any captive portal services and add-on programs, and following a clean shutdown of the system, it will power off the hardware.

Click the **Halt** button to proceed. It will prompt you to confirm first. It may take around a minute for the system to turn off. Note that the webpage doesn't indicate when actually shutdown though.

To keep the system running, just click **Cancel** to return to the dashboard.

You may also use the text console menu option 6, as discussed in Section 37.7, to halt the system.

If you want to restart the system instead of powering it off, use the **Diagnostics** → **Reboot** page as covered in the following.

7.4 Reboot

The pfSense system's hardware can be rebooted using the **Diagnostics** → **Reboot** menu item. If you don't want to reboot, just click the top left pfSense logo or press **Cancel** to go back to the dashboard. To reboot, click the **Reboot** button. It will shutdown captive portal accounting, stop running add-on software, and runs the system's shutdown scripts, before temporarily shutting down and booting back up. The webpage will indicate it is rebooting and the page will reload periodically and see if the system is back online. It may take 90 seconds or longer for the pfSense system to come back up.

To power off the system instead, see the previous section about the **Diagnostics** → **Halt System** option.

The text console menu, as described in Section 37.6, may also be used to restart pfSense without a hardware reset, reboot to the console single user mode, or to force a file system check when rebooting.

7.5 System Activity

The report at **Diagnostics** → **System Activity** provides a quick snapshot about the operating system as shown in Figure 7.4. It shows the system load averages, how long the system has been up (a number before a plus + sign is for the days), how many processes (programs) the system is running, the memory and swap (virtual memory) usage, and then a table of the top 18 processes sorted by the CPU use percentage. This display is automatically refreshed every 2.5 seconds; exit to another page like the dashboard to stop this continual job.

The load averages are the average number of jobs in the run queue for the last 1, 5, and 15 minute periods. The load average may not be useful for comparing between systems, but you may want to make a mental note of these numbers as a baseline for later same-system comparisons. Generally, a low load average would be less than one and near 0.00. This load average is also shown on the System Information widget on the dashboard (Section 4.3).

The physical and virtual memory allocations show current use:

Active

> The memory used by processes.

Inact

> The inactive memory that is still cached but is freed.

Wired

> This is memory used by the kernel and cannot be swapped out to disk. This includes the networking stack, such as seen in the MBUF Usage on the dashboard's System Information view.

Cache

> This is used to cache data and can be freed immediately if needed.

Buf

> This is the disk cache buffers. It is used to improve disk read performance by reading already cached disk sections from memory instead. This memory can be freed quickly as needed.

Free

> The ready-to-use memory. (The inactive, cache, and buffers can become free too.)

The swap is the memory that has been transferred to a swap device as *virtual* memory, like a disk swap partition. If the free swap is frequently less than 95% of the total swap, maybe you need more physical RAM. The dashboard's System Information widget also summarizes this as percentages and visually with its Memory usage and SWAP usage graphs.

Diagnostics / System Activity

CPU Activity

```
last pid: 50236;  load averages:  0.16,  0.16,  0.15  up 9+22:22:14    15:06:01
118 processes: 2 running, 97 sleeping, 19 waiting

Mem: 41M Active, 278M Inact, 98M Wired, 1184K Cache, 110M Buf, 21M Free
Swap: 1024M Total, 4884K Used, 1019M Free


   PID USERNAME    PRI NICE   SIZE     RES STATE    TIME    WCPU COMMAND
    11 root        155 ki31    0K      8K RUN     232.1H  98.19% [idle]
 63413 root         28    0 63908K 26244K piperd   0:41    2.49% php-fpm: pool nginx (php-fpm)
    12 root        -92    -    0K    152K WAIT    78:04    0.00% [intr{irq18: r10 fwohc}]
    12 root        -92    -    0K    152K WAIT    44:16    0.00% [intr{irq17: r11}]
     0 root        -92    -    0K    120K -       32:04    0.00% [kernel{dummynet}]
     7 root        -16    -    0K      8K pftm    11:11    0.00% [pf purge]
    12 root        -92    -    0K    152K WAIT     9:23    0.00% [intr{irq19: ath0}]
    12 root        -60    -    0K    152K WAIT     7:40    0.00% [intr{swi4: clock}]
   337 unbound      20    0 45928K 34320K kqread   5:26    0.00% /usr/local/sbin/unbound -c /va
  5748 root         52   20 10456K  2020K wait     2:57    0.00% /bin/sh /var/db/rrd/updaterrd.
    15 root        -16    -    0K      8K -        2:14    0.00% [rand_harvestq]
    22 root         16    -    0K      8K syncer   1:57    0.00% [syncer]
 97990 root         20    0 10628K  1816K nanslp   1:30    0.00% [dpinger{dpinger}]
 48108 root         20    0 13008K 13040K select   1:26    0.00% /usr/local/sbin/ntpd -g -c /va
  4815 dhcpd        20    0 16332K  8160K select   1:26    0.00% /usr/local/sbin/dhcpd -user dh
 43195 root         20    0 24716K  5308K kqread   1:16    0.00% nginx: worker process (nginx)
     4 root        -16    -    0K     16K -        0:48    0.00% [cam{doneq0}]
 14566 root         20    0 10232K  1872K bpf      0:34    0.00% /usr/local/sbin/filterlog -i p
```

Figure 7.4: **Diagnostics → System Activity**

The *top* processes table shows the process with the highest CPU usage percentage first. For each process, it displays the following:

PID

The process ID. While the PID is unique, it may display multiple rows for the same PID for different threads.

USERNAME

The user that's running the process.

PRI

The current priority level pertaining to the process' or thread's scheduling. The lower the number (even negative numbers) the higher its priority. The range of numbers varies from system; for example on some systems the base number may be 20 and on others it may be 44. Note that the priority of processes may change frequently.

NICE

The scheduling priority. For normal processes, this is between -20 and 20. The lower the number the more CPU time it gets. The *nice* level adjusts the priority level as discussed previously. Interrupt threads or timesharing processes may be listed with a "-" dash. Kernel threads may be prefixed with a "k" and idle kernel threads are prefixed with "ki".

SIZE

The total size of the program's machine instructions (text), variables data, and temporary storage (stack) displayed in kilobytes.

RES

This is the kilobytes of real RAM used by the process (also known as resident memory).

STATE

The current state of the process, such as LOCK (waiting to acquire a lock), RUN or CPU*n* (runnable process), WAIT (short-term uninterruptible disk wait), ZOMBIE (a dead process), accept (listening for connections), kqread (blocked on kqueue), nanslp (thread is sleeping), select (blocked on synchronous I/O), and several others.

C

This is an optional column for only SMP systems which shows the processor number the process is running on.

TIME

The amount of system and user CPU seconds used.

WCPU

The weighted CPU percentage. It is based on more than one sample interval and after awhile should reflect a better average. Often many of the processes will show only 0.00%.

COMMAND

The name of the running command or this may be status information from the command if displayed in brackets. (Note that all this output is cropped by pfSense to fit within 105 characters width.)

Again, this view doesn't show all processes; on a general install of pfSense you may have between 70 and 120 processes commonly running at any given time, but this only shows the top CPU users.

A historical view of some of these and additional details can be graphed via the **Status → Monitoring** page as explained in Section 28.2.

7.6   CPU Utilization

A graph of the non-idle CPU time percentage may be watched at the **Status → CPU Load Graph** page. This is a hidden page that isn't linked within pfSense. It can be accessed at your pfSense URL with `/status_graph_cpu.php` (such as `https://172.16.33.1/status_graph_cpu.php`).

It starts without any value and will work its way up to showing the graph for the last two minutes as seen in Figure 7.5. Note that the graph uses SVG which is built-in to most modern web browsers, but if not, you may need to install a SVG viewer.

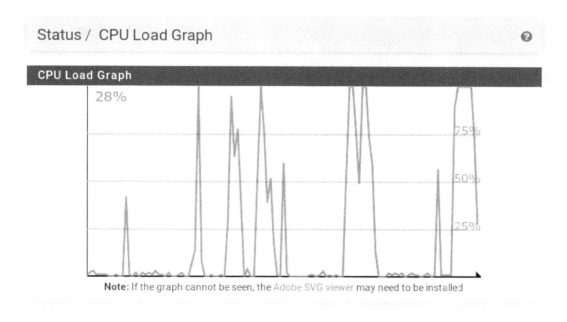

Figure 7.5: CPU Load Graph

The number in the top left corner of the graph is the current CPU usage. Note that this number is different than the load averages as seen at **Diagnostics** → **System Activity** which also shows system activity per software process. See Section 7.5 for more information.

7.7 Service Status and Control

The **Status** → **Services** feature quickly provides a view of most of your enabled and running network services on a single page. It lists the service name and its brief description along with a status indicator showing if it is running, stopped, or disabled.

The entry may also have one or more actions. If it is running, you can click on the **Restart Service** circle arrow icon or the **Stop service** pause button icon to reload configurations or halt the feature, respectively. Note when the service is stopped here, the configurations don't record that, so a later reboot or other watchdog process may restart it. If the service is already stopped, you can attempt to start it with the **Start Service** play button icon. When these actions are clicked, a new icon may indicate the progress and there may be a short delay.

You may also have icons that link to the **Related settings** to make configuration changes, **Related status** to view its feature specific details, and **Related log entries** for its debugging outputs.

On a new or bare install, you will only have a few entries. The list will include your installed packages (see Section 35.3) and the following network services if enabled:

- *bsnmpd* — SNMP Service (Section 27.6)

- *captiveportal* — Captive Portal for each zone (Chapter 29)

- *dhcpd* — DHCP Service (Chapter 19)

- *dhcrelay* — DHCP Relay (Section 19.7)

- *dhcrelay6* — DHCPv6 Relay (Section 20.5)

- *dnsmasq* — DNS Forwarder (Section 21.3)

- *dpinger* — Gateway Monitoring Daemon (Section 15.1.2)

- *igmpproxy* — IGMP proxy (Section 13.10)

- *ipsec* — IPsec VPN (Chapter 30)

- *miniupnpd* — UPnP Service (Section 17.8)

- *ntpd* — NTP clock sync (Chapter 18)

- *openvpn* — OpenVPN for each server and client (Chapter 33)

- *radvd* — Router Advertisement Daemon (Section 20.1)

- *relayd* — Server load balancing Daemon (Chapter 34)

- *sshd* — Secure Shell Daemon (Section 5.3.2)

- *unbound* — DNS Resolver (Section 21.2)

Note that a few network services may be omitted from the list even when they are enabled. To start and stop or perform other actions see the following. For DHCPv6 service, see the **Services → DHCPv6 Server & RA** page as covered in Chapter 20. For the PPPoE VPN service, go to **Services → PPPoE Server** as described in Section 31.1. And for the L2TP VPN, see the **VPN → L2TP** page as covered in Section 32.1.

7.8   Hidden Detailed Status Page

Another secret page that isn't linked from the pfSense menus or other pages is at the filename /status.php (such as https://172.16.33.1/status.php). It provides a snapshot about the system on a single webpage, including its version, date the pfSense software was built, and over 80 linked sections (on the same webpage) providing status of the many following features.

- DHCP Configuration
- DNS Resolution Configuration
- Listing of /conf/ directory
- Disk Free Space
- Mounted Filesystems
- ZFS Pool List
- ZFS Properties
- Firewall Ruleset Limiters
- IPFW Firewall Limiter Info
- IPFW Firewall Rules for Captive Portal
- pf Firewall Info
- pf Firewall OSFP
- pf Firewall Show All
- pf Firewall Tables
- pftop Firewall Long
- pftop Firewall Rules
- pftop Firewall Speed
- USB Hardware Devices
- IPsec SAD
- IPsec Status
- Load Balancer Redirects
- Load Balancer Summary
- DHCP Log
- Filter Log
- IPsec Log
- NTP Log
- PHP Errors Log
- PPPoE Server Log
- System Log
- relayd Log
- Network Listen Queues
- Gateway Status
- Interfaces
- Network-Switch Configuration
- Network Protocol Statistics
- Network Sockets
- Local Boot Loader Configuration
- Package Manager Configuration
- Virtual Memory Stats
- Kernel Boot Message Buffer
- Uptime
- Netgate Crypto ID / Public Key
- Process List

- DHCPv6 Configuration
- filterdns Daemon Configuration
- Listing of /var/run/ directory
- Disk GEOM Mirror Status
- ZFS List
- ZFS Pool Status
- Firewall Ruleset
- Firewall Ruleset Limits
- IPFW Firewall Queue Info
- pf Firewall Firewall Rules
- pf Firewall NAT Rules
- pf Firewall Queues
- pf Firewall State Table Contents
- pftop Firewall Default
- pftop Firewall Queue
- pftop Firewall Size
- PCI Hardware Devices
- IPsec Configuration
- IPsec SPD
- IPsec strongSwan Configuration
- Load Balancer Relays
- Captive Portal Authentication Log
- DNS Log
- Gateways Log
- L2TP Log
- OpenVPN Log
- PPP Log
- Routing Log
- Wireless Log
- ARP Table
- Network Buffer and Timer Statistics
- Interface Statistics
- Network Mbuf Usage
- NDP Table
- Routing Tables
- Boot Loader Configuration
- Installed Packages
- Kernel Environment
- Kernel Boot Messages
- Upgrade Log
- Sysctl Values
- pfSense Main config.xml
- Process Top Usage

Some details may not be provided based on your system setup. This is mostly output from diagnostic tools, system configuration files, and the most recent log entries. The page can easily be tens of thousands of lines long from the generated outputs.

These many details can be hidden from regular web interface users using the privileges system as covered in Chapter 6. The privilege name is "WebCfg - Hidden: Detailed Status" to allow or deny access.

 Warning
Be careful sharing this **Detailed Status** data as it contains sensitive information. It can contain passwords, shared secret keys, private keys, and lots of other possibly-confidential details.

Click the **Download** button to get a tarball snapshot of all this data as many individual files. For example, the `status_output.tgz` may be around 225 KB in size.

7.9   Hidden Upload Configuration Page

The hidden **Upload Configuration** page is not covered in this book. It provides a way to replace the system configuration database by uploading *config.xml* file data, installing it as the main configuration, and rebooting.

Consider not allowing pfSense users access to this feature via the "WebCfg - Hidden: Upload Configuration" privilege (Section 6.2.4).

You can also replace the pfSense configuration using previous backups. See the following chapter about a few different ways.

7.10   Factory Defaults

The **Diagnostics → Factory Defaults** is used to remove all of your custom configurations. This will also have the WAN interface get its address via DHCP, and set the LAN to be configured as an internal DHCP server with address of 192.168.1.1. The username and password will be set to the defaults of "admin" and "pfsense".

To return to the dashboard without the reset, click the **Keep Configuration** button.

To lose your existing settings, click the **Factory Reset** button. It will popup a prompt to confirm this factory reset; click **OK** and it will install the default settings and it will immediately reboot.

The reset to factory defaults is also available via option 4 in the text console menu, as covered in Section 37.5.

8 Backups

pfSense provides some easy ways to backup all or selected configurations. pfSense also automatically saves the previous configuration file when it has updates and writes out a new configuration. In addition, an add-on package may be used to select directories to backup. This chapter covers these backups and how to restore from older configurations. An alternative method for synchronizing the configurations to another pfSense system for providing high availability is described in Chapter 36.

As for additional system backup methods, pfSense comes with Unix standard `dump` and `restore` file system backup commands; `cpio`, `pax`, and `tar` file archive tools; `cpdup` directory mirroring tool; and the SSH `scp` remote file copy program. These may be ran via the command-line terminal. While this book doesn't cover using these Unix tools, note that if you use `scp` (or SSH for scripted backups) to connect to pfSense to use the *root* user account instead of the *admin* user (with the same password), because it has a needed working login shell (even when not logging in).

8.1 Backup and Restore of Configurations

pfSense offers a backup solution to download all configurations or specific configurations as XML — or the reverse: upload a previous configuration XML file and restore the configuration using it. The menu is available under **Diagnostics** → **Backup & Restore**. The configuration choices include:

- All
- Captive Portal
- DNS Forwarder
- DHCP Server
- Firewall Rules
- IPSEC
- OpenVPN
- RRD Data
- Syslog
- Static routes
- SNMP Server
- VLANS

- Aliases
- Captive Portal Vouchers
- DNS Resolver
- DHCPv6 Server
- Interfaces
- NAT
- Package Manager
- Scheduled Tasks
- System
- System tunables
- Traffic Shaper
- Wake-on-LAN

The backup configuration menu options include selecting the backup area, and if you want to backup package information and RRD data. You may also choose to encrypt the configuration file with a password (using a 256-bit AES in CBC mode cipher). For the backup areas, only the features available in the configuration are listed in the drop-down box (so your choices may be different than this list). Only one feature area may be selected per backup download (or you may select *All*).

Click the **Download configuration as XML** button and a file will be generated named after the system's hostname and a datestamp (down to the second), e.g., config-pfSense.office-20160514083617.xml. If a specific backup area is selected, then the filename is prefixed with that feature name. Your web browser should prompt you to save the file.

By default, the backup will include configurations for your installed packages (if any). To skip package configurations, check the **Do not backup package information** checkbox.

A simple configuration without RRD data may only be around 20 KB. The RRD data — such as IPsec and WAN traffic counters and memory and processor usage stats — is skipped by default. If the checkbox for it is unchecked, the download backup file may increase by three or more megabytes (depending on how much RRD data your pfSense system has).

8.1.1 Restore Configuration

To restore a system to a previously saved XML configuration, use the same menu, **Diagnostics →** **Backup & Restore**, and under **Restore Backup**, click the **Browse** button to select the file to upload. If it is an encrypted file, click the checkbox and enter its password. Optionally select the **Backup area** (which defaults to *All*) for the only desired feature configuration to restore. Click the **Restore Configuration** button and then a pop-up browser window may appear to confirm if you want to restore the configuration; okay it to proceed.

After restoring a full configuration, the system will reboot automatically. If there was only a specific area restored, it may warn you that the system may need to be rebooted; you may use **Diagnostics →** **Reboot** manually if desired. Depending on the configuration, you may only need to restart a specific service instead (see Section 7.7 about the **Status → Services** feature).

8.2 Configuration History

On the **Config History** subpage via the **Diagnostics → Backup & Restore** page, the most recent configurations may be compared, downloaded, deleted, or used. These were automatically saved on manual or automated configuration updates. (Note this is different than the retrieved backups described in the previous sections.)

The page displays a series of radio buttons for each backed-up configuration with the date stamp, configuration file version, the file size, and a brief description of the change, which may include the username, the IP address of the administrator, and the tool used to make the configuration change (like seen in Figure 8.1). The versions don't match the pfSense release version, but are for internal configuration versioning, such as "12.0" for pfSense 2.2.6 and "15.0" for pfSense 2.3.

Each old entry also has icons for actions to revert, download, or delete the specific old configuration.

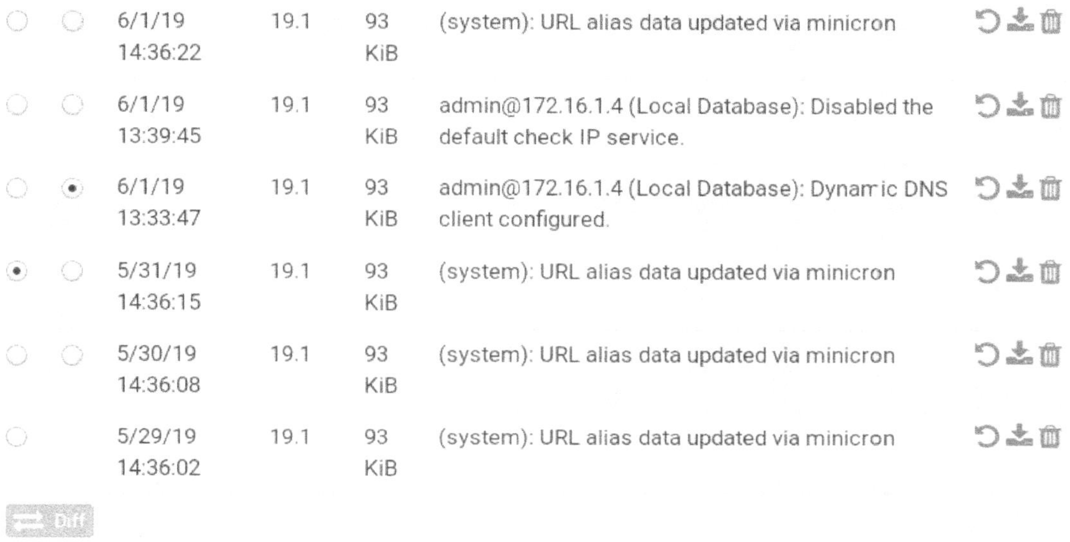

○	○	6/1/19 14:36:22	19.1	93 KiB	(system): URL alias data updated via minicron	↺ ⬇ 🗑
○	○	6/1/19 13:39:45	19.1	93 KiB	admin@172.16.1.4 (Local Database): Disabled the default check IP service.	↺ ⬇ 🗑
○	◉	6/1/19 13:33:47	19.1	93 KiB	admin@172.16.1.4 (Local Database): Dynamic DNS client configured.	↺ ⬇ 🗑
◉	○	5/31/19 14:36:15	19.1	93 KiB	(system): URL alias data updated via minicron	↺ ⬇ 🗑
○	○	5/30/19 14:36:08	19.1	93 KiB	(system): URL alias data updated via minicron	↺ ⬇ 🗑
○		5/29/19 14:36:02	19.1	93 KiB	(system): URL alias data updated via minicron	↺ ⬇ 🗑

⇄ Diff

Figure 8.1: **Diagnostics** → **Backup & Restore** → **Config History**

To compare a configuration with a previous configuration, check a right radio button for the newer entry and a left radio button for an older entry and then click the **Diff** button. It will display the XML changes using a colored unified diff format. Lines prefixed with a "-" minus sign and in pink are the lines in the old (or selected with the left radio button) file that aren't in the new file (or selected with the right radio button). Lines prefixed with a "+" plus sign and in a green color are the newer lines (that aren't in the old file).

To replace the current configuration with one of these old versions, click the circle-arrow **Revert config** icon on the corresponding entry. A pop-up window will appear to confirm this decision; click **OK** to proceed.

The text console menu also has an alternative method for reverting to an old configuration version; see Section 37.16 for details.

8.2.1   Configuration Backup Cache Settings

By default, pfSense will save a maximum of 30 backups of configurations in XML format under the /conf/backups/ directory. (Each filename will be prefixed with "config-" and a timestamp using Unix epoch seconds format.) Clicking the **+** plus icon at the end of the "Configuration Backup

Cache Settings" header (or "Saved Configurations" on older versions) will expand the menu to allow updating the backup count and to display the current diskspace used by the backups. To change the count of maximum backups to keep, enter a number and click the **Save** button.

This expanded view will also show the total disk usage of the configuration backup directory. (For example, 30 revisions may be around two megabytes.)

8.3   Backup Package

The add-on *Backup* package may be installed to provide the **Diagnostics** → **Backup Files/Dir** menu item. Package installations are covered in Chapter 35.

It uses the `tar` command to create and compress selected directories to (default) `/root/backup/pfsense.bak.tgz`. This generated tarball is also provided via the web browser as a file download.

Later that file can be used or uploaded and extracted replacing the desired file system locations.

Some recommended directories to backup include `/cf/conf` for the pfSense configuration database and its automated backups and `/var/db/rrd` for the graphing data files (as discussed in Chapter 28).

8.4   Auto Config Backup

The **Services** → **Auto Config Backup** feature is used to upload the main pfSense `config.xml` configuration for offsite backups to Netgate. The pfSense configuration is encrypted using 256-bit AES in CBC mode and uploaded in base64 format using HTTPS. This is a free service and Netgate will store up to one hundred most recent backups per pfSense system. (This configuration backup feature was added in pfSense version 2.4.4. Previously it was available as an add-on package. The old package way is known as the *legacy* option.)

At the top of the page are links for the settings and to backup now (for a manual upload) as introduced in the following sections.

When you have backups, they will be listed in a table by the date and configuration description with action icons to **Restore this revision**, **Show info**, and **Delete config**. At the bottom, it will display a count of the total offsite backups. (But by default, there are no offline backups.)

When choosing to restore a revision, you will be prompted to confirm it first. Then after it downloads it and reverts to the configuration, it will have a popup message suggesting to reboot to activate any changes.

The show information action also downloads a previous configuration file and displays details about it, including its SHA256 hash checksum, the encrypted base64-encoded data, and the decrypted configuration. You can click on the **Install this revision** button to use that pfSense configuration.

Deleting a single configuration with the trash can icon will remove it from the remote storage. First it will prompt you to confirm the removal. Then it won't be listed for a later download. (The delete action won't be available for backups using a different device key.)

If your pfSense system is different from the system your configuration was uploaded from, you can enter the other identification in the **Device key** text field. Then click the **Submit** button to refetch the list of available backups, but based on this other key instead. Or use the **Reset** button to use this pfSense system's generated device key again.

If you have the legacy service, configure it on the settings page as described in the following. Then use it here by clicking the **Use legacy "Gold" repository** button and this page's table will show the backups from that instead. The legacy service identifies the backups based on hostnames.

8.4.1 Auto Config Backup Settings

The **Services** → **Auto Config Backup** → **Settings** subpage is used to configure the automated configuration backups. To use this service automatically, check the **Enable ACB** checkbox.

The automated uploads to Netgate only happen when your main pfSense configuration is changed. For the **Backup Frequency** radio buttons, select as desired to backup immediately whenever a configuration change is saved or on a regular schedule (also only uploading if the configuration changed since the previous backup). (Note it does not backup frequent Captive Portal voucher database synchronization configuration changes.)

When backing up on a schedule, you will have fields to enter its timing for the following **Hour** (0-23), **Day of month** (1-31), **Month** (1-12), and **Day of week** (0-6) fields. (For the week day, zero is Sunday.) You may also use some *crontab* style configurations for these fields. For example:

- all using asterisk ("*")

- range using hyphen (like "7-11")

- range step using slash (like "*/2" or "0-9/3")

- list using commas (like "1,4,7" or "5-10,25-30")

You can not use names for fields. The timing is at the top of the hour (as the minute of zero is not configurable). Either the day of the week or the day of the month must match for backing up on a schedule. The default is configured to check for configuration changes daily for a daily backup, with the hour set to 0 (for midnight) and the other fields with asterisks.

Enter in a password to be used for encrypting the configuration files in the required **Encryption Password** field (and confirm it). Note it needs to be at least eight characters. This password will also be used to later decrypt a configuration if restoring it.

Each backup is identified using a 64-character key which is generated in two parts: a SSH Ed25519 authentication identity and then a SHA256 hash of that. This is automatically used for the automated offsite backups. (Your Netgate Device ID and pfSense version is also provided.) The **Identifier** text field may be used to enter some details to help identify the encrypted backups. Note that this string is provided without being encrypted.

If you have the old *Legacy Gold* backup service, click the **Legacy "Gold" settings** button. Then you can enter the username, password, and encryption password used for the legacy backup account.

Click the **Save** button to store these Auto Config Backup settings which may include enabling the backup schedule.

8.4.2   Auto Config Backup Manual Backup

The **Services** → **Auto Config Backup** → **Backup now** subpage may be used to do a manual backup. This requires that the feature is enabled and the encryption password is set per the settings subpage previously discussed.

To explain why the manual configuration backup is to be done, enter an explanation in the **Revision Reason** text field. (If this is unset, it may use the last configuration description.) Then submit this to trigger the manual backup.

You should keep track of the special identification key listed in the **Device key** text field or you won't be able to access your backed-up configurations if you are using a different system or if your SSH identity key file changed.

After the backup is done, it will display a message about it completing successfully.

Each time a backup to Netgate happens it will be logged in the **Status** → **System Logs** → **System** → **General** log view (Section 11.4). See the "`configuration backup`" message entries using the log filter.

9 Upgrading pfSense

This chapter is about upgrading the pfSense operating system to a newer version using the web interface. Behind the scenes, it will download the new software, copy it into place, migrate some configurations as needed, and reboot the system so it will start using the updated software.

Both the dashboard's System Information widget and the **System** → **Update** page will display if a new version of pfSense is available for an upgrade. The dashboard will display a cloud icon when there is a new version and it may be clicked to get to the same update page. On older versions you may have a **System** → **Firmware** menu selection instead.

Updating to a newer version of pfSense can also be done via the text console menu (as introduced in Section 37.14).

Consider doing a backup of your pfSense system before doing a system upgrade. See Chapter 8 for backup details. When upgrading, you may want to have physical access to the system's keyboard and display or via serial with a remote KVM, but most pfSense upgrades never need remote hands support. While most upgrades can be completed in a few minutes, plan for 30 minutes or more of downtime.

9.1 System Update

The **System** → **Update** page will show you the version for your currently-in-use system and the version for the available download version. It will indicate that the system is "Up to date" when the versions are the same. If a newer version (Latest Base System) is available (such as in Figure 9.1) confirmation will be required to update the system and a **Confirm** button will be available.

You may have a **Branch** drop-down menu which lists the main branch version numbering for the stable version of pfSense. (For example, if you are running a 2.4.1 version, it will show "2.4.x".)

You may choose to use the bleeding-edge code from pfSense by selecting the *Latest development snapshots* option (in the **Branch** menu). Note that this includes experimental software which is still in testing and may have more bugs or changes than you may be prepared for. Nevertheless, using the development version on a staging or second system may be useful to get familiar with its interface changes. When the experimental version is selected, it will report its latest base system version with a date-stamped string like "2.5.0.a.20190419.1725". (As it says, use the development branch at your own risk!)

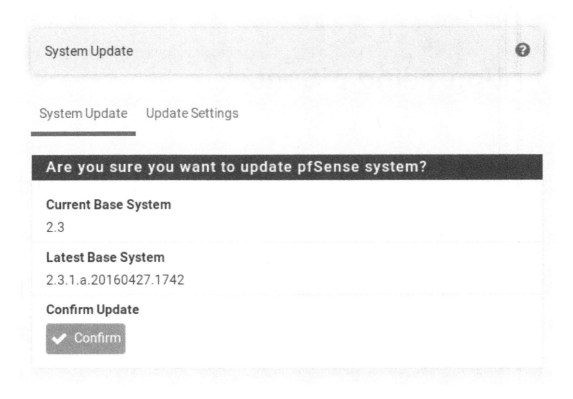

Figure 9.1: System Update - Confirm

Upgrading the system will require plenty of disk space to download and extract new software and to backup some old settings. While upgrade output may indicate you need around 55 MB to download (as an example), a minor upgrade may use an additional 123 MB of disk. Running out of disk space may not be noticed during an upgrade and it may even indicate it was successful, but stay at the old version. It is recommended to have at least a few hundred free megabytes of disk space to do an upgrade.

If you are sure you want to update the pfSense system, click the **Confirm** button (in the System Update screen). The entire upgrade and reboot process may take a few minutes to run.

Warning

The system update will make your system unavailable for over a minute at the minimum. This means that firewall rules, routing, and other network services used via your pfSense system will be down. Existing SSH and other connections may be dropped. In addition, it is possible that some services or various configurations may not start back up as expected. (For example, the SSH host key may be changed.) You may want to plan in advance for the downtime.

The system update will show the software downloads and the automated installation steps in a scrolling "Updating System" window (as seen in Section 9.3). The message "System update successfully completed" will be displayed near the top of the same display when this update is finished. Then it will indicate the system is rebooting and the page will show a countdown timer too when it will reload the page. If a slow system isn't booted yet, it may also say the system is "Not yet ready" and it will retry again after 20 seconds. (This may delay multiple times.)

Sometimes if the update fails, repeating it will work. Also sometimes it may indicate it failed by outputting error messages or your browser may lose access to the webConfigurator (times out) — but your console may still show the upgrade running and may reboot when completed.

After the system comes back up, you will be back at the login webpage. Reload the webpage if needed.

9.2 Update Settings

An additional menu **Update Settings** (under **System** → **Update**) is used to select some settings applicable to when doing a later upgrade (such as via the other webpage). You may use the **Branch** dropdown menu here to select the default branch for the update — between the default stable firmware branch or a development branch to update to. Again note that the development branch is for testing new features and bleeding-edge code and may not be as well tested and may be unstable.

The dashboard's System Information widget (see Section 4.3) displays the currently running version of pfSense and indicates if the system is running the latest available version or will report what new version is available. This check is done at most every two hours when the dashboard page is reloaded or immediately when a refresh icon is clicked. It updates the available packages list and installs any latest pfSense metadata package(s) that indicate what pfSense versions are now available. It does not auto-upgrade the system. (Also see Section 5.4.5 about disclosing details about your pfSense system.)

This remote version check can be turned off by checking the **Disable the automatic dashboard auto-update check** checkbox and clicking the **Save** button.

9.2.1 GitSync

If you have the GIT tool installed, it will display a GitSync section which may be used to update
parts of pfSense using GIT during the upgrade. GIT is a source code revision control system used
by developers to collaborate their work. This feature is used to supplement a system upgrade by
retrieving some files outside of the normal upgrade which may be used to customize your pfSense
setup. Basically this is very advanced feature as it can overwrite or replace almost any part of the
pfSense system based on what it checks out. For safety it will limit it from overwriting some crucial
files:

- /etc/crontab — Scheduled commands configuration

- /etc/fstab — File system mount points table

- /etc/group — Unix group permissions fole

- /etc/master.passwd — Unix system password file

- /etc/passwd — Standard abbreviated version of Unix system password file

- /etc/platform — File that indicates this is pfSense

- /etc/syslog.conf — System logging configuration

- /etc/ttys — Console terminals initialization configuration

- /boot/device.hints — Hardware device resource hints used by boot loader

- /boot/loader.conf — System boot loader configurations

- /boot/loader.rc — System boot loader script

- /root/.shrc — Unix shell configuration or shell login startup script

- /root/.tcshrc — Unix CSH shell configuration or shell login startup script

- /conf — Symlink and /conf* directories for pfSense configurations

- /cf — Directory for pfSense main configurations

- /tmp — Makes sure the permissions of the temporary files directory are still open

The GIT tool can be added via the **System** → **Package Manager** → **Available Packages** page (see
Chapter 35). (This tool may also be installed using the gitsync feature via the text console **PHP
shell + pfSense tools** menu as introduced in Section 37.13.)

To enable this, check the **Auto sync on update** checkbox. Then enter or update the **Repository URL**
and **Branch name** fields. They will contain the location of the GIT rep and which GIT branch to
checkout from.

The **Sync options** checkboxes are used to change the behavior of the upgrade using the GIT-based
synchronization. The **Minimal** feature will attempt to copy into place files that have been updated
instead of all files in the GIT repo. The **Diff** feature is used to only copy in place files that don't exist

or are different from your main pfSense system. The **Show Files** feature will output a list of all the files that will be copied when using the minimal or diff features. Use **Show Command** checkbox to show the Unix tar commands that will be ran. The **Dry Run** checkbox, when enabled, means it will do the checkout steps but doesn't actually overwrite or install the files to your main pfSense system.

Click the **Save** button to record any new settings.

9.3 Updating System (output)

The following is example output as displayed during the system update. Your output may also indicate about new packages being installed, for example.

```
>>> Updating repositories metadata...
Updating pfSense-core repository catalogue...
pfSense-core repository is up-to-date.
Updating pfSense repository catalogue...
pfSense repository is up-to-date.
All repositories are up-to-date.
>>> Upgrading pfSense-repo... done.
>>> Unlocking package pfSense-kernel-pfSense... done.
>>> Downloading upgrade packages...
Updating pfSense-core repository catalogue...
pfSense-core repository is up-to-date.
Updating pfSense repository catalogue...
pfSense repository is up-to-date.
All repositories are up-to-date.
Checking for upgrades (42 candidates): .......... done
Processing candidates (42 candidates): .......... done
The following 42 package(s) will be affected (of 0 checked):

Installed packages to be UPGRADED:
  php56-zlib: 5.6.23 -> 5.6.26 [pfSense]
  php56-xmlwriter: 5.6.23 -> 5.6.26 [pfSense]
  php56-xmlreader: 5.6.23 -> 5.6.26 [pfSense]
  php56-xml: 5.6.23 -> 5.6.26 [pfSense]
  php56-tokenizer: 5.6.23 -> 5.6.26 [pfSense]
  php56-sysvshm: 5.6.23 -> 5.6.26 [pfSense]
  php56-sysvsem: 5.6.23 -> 5.6.26 [pfSense]
  php56-sysvmsg: 5.6.23 -> 5.6.26 [pfSense]
  php56-sqlite3: 5.6.23 -> 5.6.26 [pfSense]
  php56-sockets: 5.6.23 -> 5.6.26 [pfSense]
  php56-simplexml: 5.6.23 -> 5.6.26 [pfSense]
  php56-shmop: 5.6.23 -> 5.6.26 [pfSense]
  php56-session: 5.6.23 -> 5.6.26 [pfSense]
  php56-readline: 5.6.23 -> 5.6.26 [pfSense]
  php56-posix: 5.6.23 -> 5.6.26 [pfSense]
  php56-pdo_sqlite: 5.6.23 -> 5.6.26 [pfSense]
```

```
php56-pdo: 5.6.23 -> 5.6.26 [pfSense]
php56-pcntl: 5.6.23 -> 5.6.26 [pfSense]
php56-openssl: 5.6.23 -> 5.6.26 [pfSense]
php56-opcache: 5.6.23_1 -> 5.6.26_1 [pfSense]
php56-mcrypt: 5.6.23 -> 5.6.26 [pfSense]
php56-mbstring: 5.6.23 -> 5.6.26 [pfSense]
php56-ldap: 5.6.23 -> 5.6.26 [pfSense]
php56-json: 5.6.23 -> 5.6.26 [pfSense]
php56-hash: 5.6.23 -> 5.6.26 [pfSense]
php56-gettext: 5.6.23 -> 5.6.26 [pfSense]
php56-filter: 5.6.23 -> 5.6.26 [pfSense]
php56-dom: 5.6.23 -> 5.6.26 [pfSense]
php56-curl: 5.6.23 -> 5.6.26 [pfSense]
php56-ctype: 5.6.23 -> 5.6.26 [pfSense]
php56-bz2: 5.6.23 -> 5.6.26 [pfSense]
php56-bcmath: 5.6.23 -> 5.6.26 [pfSense]
php56: 5.6.23 -> 5.6.26 [pfSense]
pfSense-rc: 2.3.2 -> 2.3.2_1 [pfSense-core]
pfSense-kernel-pfSense: 2.3.2 -> 2.3.2_1 [pfSense-core]
pfSense-default-config: 2.3.2 -> 2.3.2_1 [pfSense-core]
pfSense-base: 2.3.2 -> 2.3.2_1 [pfSense-core]
pfSense: 2.3.2 -> 2.3.2_1 [pfSense]
perl5: 5.20.3_13 -> 5.20.3_15 [pfSense]
libxml2: 2.9.3 -> 2.9.4 [pfSense]
libidn: 1.31 -> 1.33_1 [pfSense]
curl: 7.49.1 -> 7.50.3 [pfSense]

Number of packages to be upgraded: 42

56 MiB to be downloaded.
Fetching php56-zlib-5.6.26.txz: .. done
Fetching php56-xmlwriter-5.6.26.txz: .. done
Fetching php56-xmlreader-5.6.26.txz: .. done
Fetching php56-xml-5.6.26.txz: .. done
Fetching php56-tokenizer-5.6.26.txz: . done
Fetching php56-sysvshm-5.6.26.txz: . done
Fetching php56-sysvsem-5.6.26.txz: . done
Fetching php56-sysvmsg-5.6.26.txz: . done
Fetching php56-sqlite3-5.6.26.txz: .. done
Fetching php56-sockets-5.6.26.txz: .... done
Fetching php56-simplexml-5.6.26.txz: ... done
Fetching php56-shmop-5.6.26.txz: . done
Fetching php56-session-5.6.26.txz: ... done
Fetching php56-readline-5.6.26.txz: .. done
Fetching php56-posix-5.6.26.txz: . done
Fetching php56-pdo_sqlite-5.6.26.txz: .. done
Fetching php56-pdo-5.6.26.txz: ..... done
Fetching php56-pcntl-5.6.26.txz: .. done
Fetching php56-openssl-5.6.26.txz: ..... done
Fetching php56-opcache-5.6.26_1.txz: ...... done
Fetching php56-mcrypt-5.6.26.txz: .. done
```

```
Fetching php56-mbstring-5.6.26.txz: .......... done
Fetching php56-ldap-5.6.26.txz: .. done
Fetching php56-json-5.6.26.txz: .. done
Fetching php56-hash-5.6.26.txz: .......... done
Fetching php56-gettext-5.6.26.txz: . done
Fetching php56-filter-5.6.26.txz: .. done
Fetching php56-dom-5.6.26.txz: ...... done
Fetching php56-curl-5.6.26.txz: ... done
Fetching php56-ctype-5.6.26.txz: . done
Fetching php56-bz2-5.6.26.txz: .. done
Fetching php56-bcmath-5.6.26.txz: .. done
Fetching php56-5.6.26.txz: .......... done
Fetching pfSense-rc-2.3.2_1.txz: . done
Fetching pfSense-kernel-pfSense-2.3.2_1.txz: .......... done
Fetching pfSense-default-config-2.3.2_1.txz: . done
Fetching pfSense-base-2.3.2_1.txz: .......... done
Fetching pfSense-2.3.2_1.txz: . done
Fetching perl5-5.20.3_15.txz: .......... done
Fetching libxml2-2.9.4.txz: .......... done
Fetching libidn-1.33_1.txz: .......... done
Fetching curl-7.50.3.txz: .......... done
Checking integrity... done (0 conflicting)
>>> Upgrading pfSense kernel...
Updating pfSense-core repository catalogue...
pfSense-core repository is up-to-date.
Updating pfSense repository catalogue...
pfSense repository is up-to-date.
All repositories are up-to-date.
Checking integrity... done (0 conflicting)
The following 2 package(s) will be affected (of 0 checked):

Installed packages to be UPGRADED:
    pfSense-kernel-pfSense: 2.3.2 -> 2.3.2_1 [pfSense-core]
    pfSense-rc: 2.3.2 -> 2.3.2_1 [pfSense-core]

Number of packages to be upgraded: 2
[1/2] Upgrading pfSense-rc from 2.3.2 to 2.3.2_1...
[1/2] Extracting pfSense-rc-2.3.2_1: .... done
[2/2] Upgrading pfSense-kernel-pfSense from 2.3.2 to 2.3.2_1...
[2/2] Extracting pfSense-kernel-pfSense-2.3.2_1: .......... done
===> Keeping a copy of current kernel in /boot/kernel.old
Upgrade is complete.  Rebooting in 10 seconds.
>>> Locking package pfSense-kernel-pfSense... done.
Success
```

9.4   Security Vulnerabilities

While you may choose to delay upgrades, you should periodically consult third-party vulnerability lists to understand if your pfSense system should be updated or if features should be disabled due to security exploits. A thorough, frequently-updated database is the U.S. government-sponsored MITRE Common Vulnerabilities and Exposures (CVE) list which contains publicly-disclosed cybersecurity vulnerabilities and exposures: `https://cve.mitre.org/cgi-bin/cvekey.cgi?keyword=pfsense`

That feeds the U.S. government's National Vulnerability Database (NVD) which provides further details, such as specific versions, severity scoring, and the impact of the flaws: `https://nvd.nist.gov/vuln/search/results?query=pfsense`

Both reports may contain links to further information for specific vulnerabilities. In addition to just searching for "pfsense" known security issues, you may want to search for key software running on your system. While pfSense has hundreds of programs that run, the main software includes:

• bsnmpd	• curl
• dhclient	• dhcp6 (KAME)
• dhcp (ISC)	• dnsmasq
• freebsd	• hostapd
• ldns	• minicron
• miniupnd	• mpd
• nginx	• ntpd
• openldap	• openvpn
• openssh	• perl
• php	• php-fpm
• python	• radvd
• relayd	• rrdtool
• scponly	• sqlite3
• sshguard	• strongswan
• tcpdump	• tcsh
• unbound	• wpa_supplicant

This list is certainly not exhaustive. In addition, review your currently-installed add-on packages at the **System** → **Package Manager** page (Chapter 35) and consider checking them against the vulnerability databases.

10 Disk Management

This chapter introduces software RAID, embedded pfSense, S.M.A.R.T. disk status, memory disks for temporary or non-critical files, and putting a hard disk into standby mode.

If you installed pfSense using a ZFS filesystem (Section 2.9.5), you may see ZFS details in the very long hidden status report as introduced in Section 7.8.

10.1 GEOM Mirrors

GEOM Mirror (also known as *gmirror*) is a software RAID implementation for FreeBSD used for automatically synchronizing identical copies of data on more than one disk drive. The **Diagnostics** → **GEOM Mirrors** page is for managing an existing disk mirror. The menu item may not be available if your system doesn't have it in use. The page is not for creating new mirrors. A mirror would have been setup at installation time or via booting an old version's recovery disk using the optional Setup GEOM Mirror feature.

If you have a mirror, the GEOM Mirror Information will show the name, size, status, and component details. If a disk is degraded, you may use the **Forget Disconnected Disks** icon to forget all disks that aren't connected. This is useful if a disk has failed; a failed mirror could be repaired by using **Forget** on the mirror and then inserting a new disk.

The **Rebuild** button is used to force a rebuild of the mirror (versus autosynchronization). The **Deactivate** button button will mark the component as is inactive meaning it will not (automatically) connect to the mirror. The **Remove** button removes the component and its metadata from the mirror.

The Consumer Information section displays the available physical disks by the FreeBSD disk device name (such as ada1s1) and the disk size in bytes. In GEOM terminology, a disk is known as a *consumer*. The **Reactivate on** button is used to make the components automatically connect to the mirror. The **Clear Metadata** button is used to remove old mirror metadata from a disk no longer running as a mirror.

The **+** (plus) icon may be used to insert an additional disk to the mirror. Physical disks can only be added to the RAID mirror if they are larger than the mirror size. The previous contents will be overwritten with data from the other mirror disk(s).

10.2 NanoBSD

The menu option **Diagnostics** → **NanoBSD** is only available for older embedded installed versions of pfSense. Known as *NanoBSD*, this was a ready-to-use system image used for running pfSense on a compact flash (CF) card or similar storage disk. It has been deprecated by pfSense since version 2.4.

If you have this page on an older NanoBSD install, it shows the current embedded image size and allows some advanced options for NanoBSD pfSense administration.

If you have multiple installs of pfSense (also known as partitions), you can use the **Switch Slice** button to select the default boot slice.

NanoBSD platforms previously ran on flash disks using read-only mode. Prior to configuration changes or other updates needing the disk, pfSense would temporarily change the disk's mount status to read-write. Old versions of pfSense allow changing the status to and from Read/Write and Read-Only (it would show the current status and provide a button to toggle this). New versions of pfSense using NanoBSD are always Read/Write. (Old versions also provided a **Keep media mounted read-/write at all times** checkbox which could be used if you neeeded to make manual changes to the file system, because the Read/Write toggle was usually a temporary change due to other features resetting it periodically.)

The **Duplicate** button (which will indicate the slices to duplicate from and to) is used to do a block-by-block copy of the working boot partition to an alternate partition. Note that pfSense won't automatically boot from the new partition, so you could use the **Switch Slice** button mentioned previously.

The **View log** button will output to the bottom of the webpage about the previous NanoBSD upgrade, including about package updates, files upgraded, firmware updates, and disk partitioning.

10.3 S.M.A.R.T. Status

S.M.A.R.T (Self-Monitoring, Analysis and Reporting Technology) is meant to give sufficient warning about wear-and-tear or damage and to predict failures in storage devices. The **Diagnostics** → **S.M.A.R.T. Status** menu item may be used to retrieve information from a capable disk and to perform tests.

Each of the options on the page includes a **Device: /dev/** drop-down menu which lists one or more disks by their FreeBSD device names. Select your desired disk device to analyze that disk's S.M.A.R.T. details. Normally this would be for FreeBSD-known disk devices: ad legacy IDE hard drives, ada ATA Direct Access and SATA devices, da SCSI Direct Access devices, and the nvme NVM Express controller.

Note that the outputs displayed from the various features here don't indicate this FreeBSD device name, so be sure to remember which device was selected when viewing the outputs.

10.3.1 S.M.A.R.T. Information

The Information view can print diagnostic information about a disk. The **Info type** selection is used to select the type of output. Click the **View** button to output the report. A new page will display with the output from the `smartctl` utility. Click the **Back** button at the end of the report to return to the main S.M.A.R.T. options page.

The output may use green color for *PASSED*, red for *FAILED*, and yellow for *Warning*. If S.M.A.R.T. is not available or disabled, the output will tell you.

Note

The S.M.A.R.T. feature may not be enabled or available for your disk. If it's supported, but it is not enabled, use the Unix shell command prompt as covered in Section 7.1 or Section 37.9 to run:

> `smartctl -s on /dev/device_name`

Replace *device_name* with the desired FreeBSD device name for the disk as listed in this page's **Device: /dev/** drop-down (such as `da0`).

The *Info* selection is used to print information about your disk, including its model name, serial number, firmware version, and disk size. It will also indicate if S.M.A.R.T. capability is supported and if it is currently enabled.

The default view is *Health* which provides a brief (one line) summary of the overall-health self-assessment. If the result is *FAILED*, you should get your data backed up someplace safe as soon as possible. (See Section 8.1 about the **Diagnostics → Backup & Restore** feature.)

The *S.M.A.R.T. Capabilities* selection will print generic capabilities (such as if self-test is supported), values, and internal recommendations. It can also report on current self-test progress, how long tests commonly take, and if the device supports various features.

The *Attributes* selection is used to view the vendor-specific S.M.A.R.T. attributes and thresholds. Normally this may be around 25 to 30 entries listed by ID numbers and attribute identifiers. For example, the "Raw Value" for #12 Power_Cycle_Count shows how many times the disk has been powered up.

Choosing the *All* radio item will provide all the previous information, plus most recent device error logs and results from self-testing (as started in the next section). You may need to carefully read the long output to recognize or understand any warnings or errors.

10.3.2 Perform Self-Tests

The **Test type** choices include a few ways to start self-tests of the device. These tests may take several seconds to hours to complete. Clicking the **Test** button will trigger the testing but won't display the results. It may report how long the test may take and when it should complete by. Use the **Back** button to return to the main **Diagnostics → S.M.A.R.T. Status** page.

Note you cannot start a new self-test run when a current self-test in progress. The **Abort Test** button may be used to cancel a self-test. You can also use the **Abort** button at the bottom of the **Diagnostics** → **S.M.A.R.T. Status** page to abort an in-progress self-test on the selected device. This may prompt to confirm that you want to stop the self-tests.

To see if a self-test is currently in progress, use the *S.M.A.R.T. Capabilities* view as introduced earlier. It may report output such as the following:

```
Self-test execution status:      ( 244) Self-test routine in   ↩
    progress...
            40% of test remaining.
```

Some types of errors may be reported in the S.M.A.R.T. error log as described in the following section. The Self-test log (also in the following section) will also show results, as seen in Figure 10.1.

The *Offline* self-test is used to immediately trigger a one-time run of the short offline test. (Some disks offer this as a feature to scan the drive every few hours.) Its error results will appear in the error log or by updating the Attribute values (seen in the Information view). On some systems, this selection will just result in doing the following short run.

The default test type is *Short*. It is used to run a self test that is usually quicker than ten minutes to hopefully rapidly detect a defective drive. It may test the mechanical, electrical, and small read performance of the disk.

The *Long* selection is for running the extended and thorough self-test which may take tens of minutes or even hours. In addition to the short tests, this will do a read and verify test of the entire disk.

The *Conveyance* self-test is used for ATA disks only to identify if damage occurred during transportation, such as checking the disk the first time. Note that some disks don't support running this self-test; the *S.M.A.R.T. Capabilities* information view may list if it is supported or not.

10.3.3   View Logs (S.M.A.R.T.)

The View Logs view is for listing the recent S.M.A.R.T. Error Log entries or the recent self-test results. (These can also be seen using the *All* option in Information view discussed earlier.)

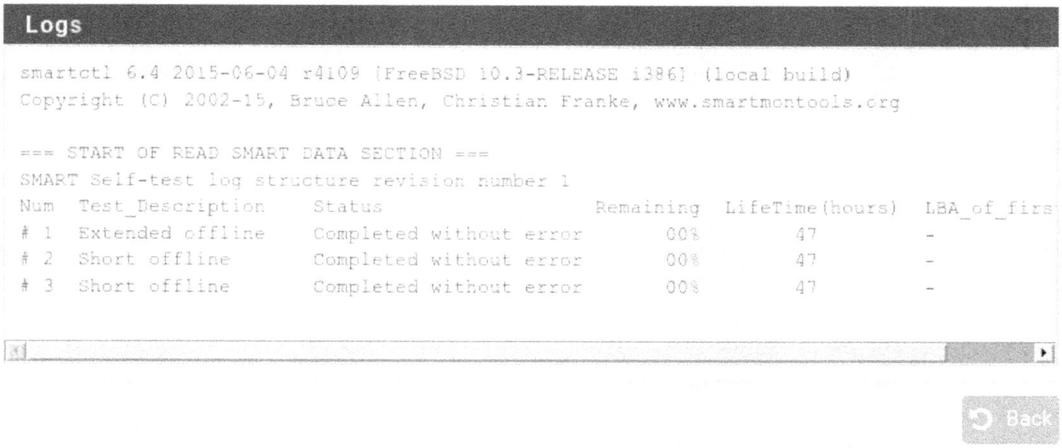

Figure 10.1: **Diagnostics** → **S.M.A.R.T. Status** Self-test logs

Use the **Log type** selection to select *Error* (the default) or *Self-test*, highlight your desired disk device, and click **View** to see these details.

Note that some self-tests can be monitored by periodically watching the log — or you may need to wait for the test to complete to see any results.

10.4   RAM Disk Settings

By default, pfSense uses a small 4 MB memory disk to store /var/run system information files which are generated on system startup (or when enabling new services). For performance of frequently updated or writing transient files, you can choose to use two larger memory systems instead for the /var and /tmp directories for multi-purpose and temporary files. This can be enabled via the **System** → **Advanced** → **Miscellaneous** subpage for the RAM Disk Settings by checking the **Use RAM Disks** checkbox.

The temporary file scratch space size can be set in the **/tmp RAM Disk Size** field in megabytes. It will default to 40 MB which is the minimum allowed size. (You don't need to include a size suffix.) Of course, your hardware will need enough RAM memory available to use this feature. Generally 1 GB of RAM is enough for pfSense and this default should be plenty.

The /var directory can be quite large and varies based on how many services you have running, what logging debugging levels are enabled, the defined maximum sizes of log files, the amount of monitoring stored, and other settings. Around 90 MB is a common size, but it can easily be much larger. You can find out its current usage in megabytes by running "**du -sm /var**" at the console shell or via the **Diagnostics** → **Command Prompt** page (Section 7.1).

This default memory file system size will be set to 60 MB, so you may want to increase it in the **/var RAM Disk Size** field. (The minimum allowed is 60 MB.) (Note that not all files normally under /var will be on the new memory file system; for example, the package database and the package downloads will be moved to a real disk instead.)

When using this memory file system, the system logging, monitoring statistics, the DHCP leases database, and downloaded URL alias tables are saved at system shutdown. All other temporary, transient, or spool files under /var (and, of course, /tmp) are not preserved. If you are concerned about more frequent permanent storage of the system logging, monitoring statistics, or the DHCP leases database in the case of a system crash, you can enable backups up to once an hour. Set the **Periodic RAM Disk Data Backups** fields to how many times a day to do the backups (up to 24 times a day) for the RRD (monitoring stats), DHCP leases, and logs. Keep a field empty or set to 0 (zero) to not backup on the hour (but it will still store the files on a clean shutdown).

When you click the **Save** button, a popup will tell you that the pfSense system requires a reboot to enable (or disable) these memory file systems. You may later use the **Diagnostics** → **Reboot** page (Section 7.4) to reboot the system after saving any RAM disk settings.

10.5   Hard Disk Standby Time

By default, the hard disks are always on. A **Hard disk standby time** drop-down form on the **System** → **Advanced** → **Miscellaneous** subpage (under the Hardware Settings) may be used to spin down the drives when not in use. Select the amount of time before putting a supported hard disk into the ATA STANDBY mode. And then click the **Save** button at the bottom of the page.

Note that there may be a delay in accessing the disk after it has been put into the standby state. To deactivate this feature, set it back to the default *Always on* choice. This feature is not needed for flash disks.

11   Logging

pfSense keeps a large collection of different recorded events, system messages, and debugging outputs. Its logging service uses special circular log files. These files have a fixed size (512 KB by default) and don't grow and don't need to be rotated, so are convenient for a self-maintaining pfSense system. The logging will overwrite from the beginning whenever it hits the end of the log file. Depending on the amount of activity or level of debugging some log entries may get overwritten frequently — so the oldest entries may be months old in some log files while other log files may only contain messages just from the most recent day.

If you need to look at or search these logs from the Unix command line (see Section 37.9), use the `clog` tool to read the special circular logging format files. For example:

```
clog /var/log/system.log | grep -i "invalid user"
```

Most of this logging is available via the **Status → System Logs** menu item. Links are available for subpages for viewing different logging which are described throughout this book.

Status → System Logs → System → General	Section 11.4
Status → System Logs → System → Gateways	Section 15.1.4
Status → System Logs → System → Routing	Section 15.5
Status → System Logs → System → DNS Resolver	Section 21.6
Status → System Logs → System → Wireless	Section 23.8
Status → System Logs → Firewall → Normal View	Section 16.18
Status → System Logs → Firewall → Dynamic View	Section 16.19
Status → System Logs → Firewall → Summary View	Section 16.20
Status → System Logs → DHCP	Section 19.8
Status → System Logs → Captive Portal Auth	Section 29.10
Status → System Logs → IPsec	Section 30.3
Status → System Logs → PPP	Section 24.2.2
Status → System Logs → VPN → PPPoE Logins	Section 31.2
Status → System Logs → VPN → PPPoE Service	Section 31.3
Status → System Logs → VPN → L2TP Logins	Section 32.3
Status → System Logs → VPN → L2TP Service	Section 32.4
Status → System Logs → Load Balancer	Section 34.7
Status → System Logs → OpenVPN	Section 33.6
Status → System Logs → NTP	Section 18.2

If you have extra packages installed, you may also have corresponding logging for those features too. These are available via the **Status** → **Package Logs** menu item. For details about package logs, see Section 35.4.

Depending on the logging view, you may have a variety of shortcut links. The standard shortcuts on all views are the **Log filter** funnel icon and the **Manage log** wrench icon as covered in the upcoming sections. You may also have shortcuts for **Restart Service** (repeat icon), **Stop Service** (stop circle icon), **Start Service** (play circle icon), **Related settings** (slider icon), and **Related status** (barchart icon), as applicable.

The standard logging display shows the date and time of each entry, the process or program name and its PID number (process ID) that the logging message came from, and the logged message string. Note that the year is not recorded and precision is only down to the second (as is standard with *syslog*-style log messages). Also some logs may not have a PID recorded. Note that the firewall log entries use a different format.

You may click on the column headers — **Time**, **Process**, **PID**, or **Message** — to sort the list by that column. Click the header again to reverse the order. Note that if you do click on the column header to order the entries, it won't base its output from the entire corresponding log file, but only for the last amount already loaded and displayed. To sort more entries, use the **GUI Log Entries** configuration discussed later.

Several of the logs are empty by default and their log pages will indicate "No logs to display." Also local logging may be disabled; see the **Local Logging** checkbox in the **Status** → **System Logs** → **Settings** page as covered in Section 11.2.

11.1   Advanced Log Filter

The pages for viewing logs provide a **Log filter** funnel icon in the shortcuts to provide Advanced Log Filter settings. Or the advanced log filter options may be displayed by default by enabling the **Log Filter** checkbox on the **System** → **General Setup** page (Section 5.1.4). This provides fields to filter the log output using regular expressions format. The standard fields for most of the logs include: **Time**, **Process** (or command) name, **PID** number, and **Message** — the actual logged string. Some log viewers may have additional or different fields for searching the logs. (Note that the Filter logging has different matching as covered in Section 16.18.)

It uses the PHP implementation of the Perl-compatible Regular Expressions. Prefix a field with an exclamation mark (!) to exclude the matching lines.

The **Quantity** number field can be used to limit how many log entries to display. This maximum can also be set in the **Status** → **System Logs** → **Settings** page (as covered in Section 11.2) or via the **Manage General Log** overrides (Section 11.3). The output will show this number as the maximum. It will also show you a count of how many entries were actually matched by the filter. Note that the log file size may be limited per the settings so it may not have enough logs saved to reach the maximum even if all matched.

Press Enter or click the **Apply Filter** button to apply the regular expression filter(s) and re-display the logged output. Once you use the filter the output will change from just showing the *Last* log entries to then show the *Matched* log entries.

11.2 General Logging Options

Various logging options may be configured via the **Status → System Logs → Settings** page. Some of these options may be overridden for specific logs via the **Manage log** shortcut (wrench icon) as discussed in Section 11.3.

The log entries views show the oldest messages first (at the top). If you want to see the most recent messages first, click the **Forward/Reverse Display** checkbox to check it.

The logging pages show up to 50 messages by default. If you want to see more or fewer logs, change the count number in the **GUI Log Entries** field. It must be at least 5 and at most 2000. This is for the display and not the size of the log files. This count is also used for viewing packages via the **Status → Package Logs** page (Section 35.4).

By default, each log file holds up to around 500 KB of messages. The amount of logging depends on how long the individual log messages are; full (500 KB) log files may vary from around 2000 lines to 7300 lines for example. To increase the default per-circular log file size, enter the desired number of bytes in the **Log file size** field. Because the log files use the circular log format and are in use, a new size will not be used until a log file is cleared or deleted. To do so immediately, save this size setting and then when the settings page reloads, click the **Reset Log Files** button.

Note

If you increase the allowed log size, the total amount of disk space used will be multiplied. Your system may have around 18 or more log files which will all be resized.

There are also settings for the packet filter logging as seen via the **Status → System Logs → Firewall** pages (see Section 16.18). To disable the default block rules logging, uncheck the **Log packets matched from the default block rules in the ruleset** checkbox. Check the **Log packets matched from the default pass rules put in the ruleset** checkbox to log *pass* matches. Uncheck the respective **Log packets blocked by 'Block Bogon Networks' rules** or **Log packets blocked by 'Block Private Networks' rules** checkboxes to disable the packet filter logging for blocked Bogons and private networks. The **Where to show rule descriptions** drop-down menu is used to optionally display the rule descriptions (or labels) in the normal firewall logs output. For further details about these firewall log settings, see Section 16.18.1.

Web server errors for the Captive Portal or the webConfigurator may be seen in the default system log (**Status → System Logs → System → General**). (Filter it for "php" or "nginx" for example.) When the **Web Server Log** checkbox is enabled, errors from the *nginx* web server should be logged to the `/var/log/nginx.log` file. This file also contains access logs (hits) to the pfSense webpages. It can be viewed using the `clog` command at the Unix console. (To see other web server error logs, you may need to directly view the non-circular `/var/log/nginx/error.log` file via the Unix console or the **Diagnostics** → **Edit File** feature,)

Some of the log page views may filter, parse, or format the related log data. This could potentially lose some data that is logged on additional lines, for example. To prevent this loss, enable the **Raw Logs** checkbox. Note this *raw* view may cause the logs to be less readable. Also, when it is checked, the log pages do not show the *Process* and *PID* fields.

The IGMP forwarding service logs at the warning or higher severity levels by default. To make it more verbose to also log informational and notice messages, check the **IGMP Proxy** checkbox. (For details about this logging, see Section 13.10.)

If you don't want log messages recorded in log files on your pfSense system, check the **Disable writing log files to the local disk** checkbox. This applies to everything. If you want to use remote centralized logging only, you may want to combine this with the following remote logging configurations.

Use the **Reset Log Files** button to clear all the log files. Be sure to save other settings on this page first before clicking this so you don't lose those settings. This reset will also restart the DHCP daemon.

11.2.1 Remote Logging Options

Logging via the *syslog* service may be forwarded to a remote *syslog* server in addition to logging to local circular log files. In the Remote Logging Options section, enable the **Enable Remote Logging** checkbox. This will bring up further options.

If you need your local *syslogger* to use a specific host for connecting to the remote *syslog* server, select a choice in the **Source Address** drop-down menu. The *Default* selection means it may use any IP address for the interface it connects via. Normally this will be okay. Other choices may be for your defined interface names (like WAN and LAN) and the *Localhost*.

If the previous option isn't set to *Default* and you need to use IPv6, then select that in the **IP Protocol** drop-down.

When the remote logging is enabled, it is required to enter at least one destination. Enter the remote *syslog* server's hostname or IP address in the first **Remote log servers** field. Up to three servers may be listed. If it is not running on the standard UDP 514 port, you may enter the port number after the hostname, delimited with a colon.

No remote logging is done even when enabled and a remote server is defined. You will need to select what log message types you want forwarded in the Remote Syslog Contents section. All are unchecked by default. To forward all log messages, check the **Everything** checkbox. Or if you want to only forward specific log messages, select them instead from the other checkboxes. These include standard *System Events* through *Wireless Events*.

Note
To forward logging, the remote *syslog* server needs to allow the incoming log messages and configured to log the message types.

Click the **Save** button to use your new logging settings.

11.3 Manage Log

By default, the logging is managed and displayed per the general log settings. These may be customized for specific logs by clicking the Manage logs shortcut wrench icon on the various log display pages which will bring up the Manage Log settings at the top of the current page. The manage logs options may be displayed by default when the **Manage Log** checkbox on the **System → General Setup** page is checked (Section 5.1.4). These options may be used to override the system-wide configurations available on the **Status → System Logs → Settings** page (as covered in Section 11.2). To hide these log settings, just click the wrench icon again or the minimize (bar) icon on the Manage Log titlebar.

To show the most recent logs at the bottom of the page, select the **Forward** radio button for the **Forward/Reverse Display** setting. Or select **Reverse** to display the most recent log entries at the top.

The **GUI Log Entries** number input field is used to limit how many lines of the logs to display on the webpage. This doesn't change how many lines are in the log itself, which is limited by the **Log file size (Bytes)** setting.

The **Formatted/Raw Display** setting is used to change how each line is displayed, but both should share the same information. By default, the log entries may be organized into multiple columns. Selecting the **Raw** radio button will just list entry by the timestamp and then the originally logged message.

Some log output pages have additional options. For the firewall logs, see Section 16.18.1.

Use the **Save** button to store these settings for later (specifically for this type of logs) and to redisplay the current log output.

The **Clear log** button will re-initialize the current corresponding log file (losing all its entries). If the circular log file size is changed, it will also set it to that new size. Note that the all system-wide logging will be temporarily stopped so when clicking this button some other logs may be lost.

11.4 General System Log Entries

The default logging view for **Status → System Logs** is for the general system. These are a variety of logs that don't correspond to the other logging pages, but there also may be some overlap in this view (and in other views) where they contain some duplicate log entries.

This view may contain log messages for conditions that possibly should be reviewed and handled. The general system logs may contain:

- messages from the security subsystems

- informational messages for generic system daemons (that are not defined for other logging views)

- informational messages from the authorization system (for login attempts)

- FreeBSD kernel debugging messages

- critical mail server errors

Figure 11.1 shows an example of abusive attempts to the SSH server and the NTP server starting.

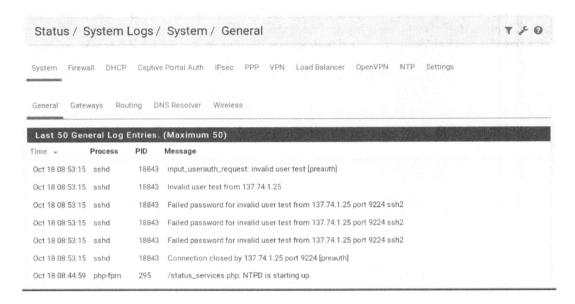

Figure 11.1: **Status → System Logs → System → General**

12 Certificates Management

X.509 certificates may be used in pfSense for the HTTPS web interface, OpenVPN server, OpenVPN client, LDAP, IPsec, Captive Portal, and for some software packages. Users may also have certificates associated to them for their use.

If you need to generate a new certificate for HTTPS webConfigurator access without using the web interface, use the text console's **PHP shell + pfSense tools** feature (Section 37.13) with its *generateguicert* script.

pfSense can be its own Certificate Authority (CA) to create or sign certificates or it may import certificates issued by third-party CAs. It can also use *intermediate* certificate authorities which are used to sign certificates in behalf of offline CAs. pfSense can also generate a Certificate Signing Request (CSR) to apply for signing by a third-party CA.

The **System → Cert. Manager** menu allows importing existing Certificate Authorities, creating internal or intermediate CAs, importing or creating certificates and Certificate Signing Requests, signing certificates, exporting X.509 and PKCS#12 certificates and keys, revoking certificates, and managing Certificate Revocation Lists.

12.1 Certificate Authorities

The main view of the **System → Cert. Manager** page is a table listing the Certificate Authorities (CAs). The table is empty by default. Once CAs have been defined for pfSense use, it will show for each its name, identify if it is internal (generated locally), its issuer (such as *self-signed* or *external*), the number of its certificates, its *Distinguished Name* which shows the subject attributes (like Country, State, Organization Unit, email address, and others) and the start date and end date for the certificate. It will also indicate if it is in use with an OpenVPN server or client, IPsec tunnel. LDAP server, or with some package.

Each certificate has corresponding actions: **Edit CA** (pencil icon) to access the certificate data or make changes as shown in the following section; **Export CA** (star icon) to download the X.509 file via your web browser; **Export key** (key icon) to download the private key (if available) as a file with the web browser; and **Delete CA and its CRLs** (trash can icon) to remove the CA reference and any Certificate Revocation Lists for the CA (if the CA is not in use)

Use the **Add** button to create a CA. This will take you to the **System** → **Certificate Manager** → **CAs** → **Edit** page.

12.1.1   Create / Edit CA

To create a new Certificate Authority, enter a required identifying name into the **Descriptive name** field. This is used within pfSense to identify it and for filenames.

In the **Method** drop-down menu, select whether you want to *Import an existing Certificate Authority*, *Create an internal Certificate Authority*, or *Create an intermediate Certificate Authority*. This choice will change the following form for using an existing or creating a new CA. Be sure to click the **Save** button to complete the changes.

Import Existing Certificate Authority

To import an existing CA, insert its X.509 PEM format certificate into the **Certificate data** field. This is required when importing an existing CA. (To recognize the correct format, its text starts with BEGIN CERTIFICATE and ends with END CERTIFICATE.)

Then optionally enter its private key in the **Certificate Private Key** field. (Its private key is needed for revocations.)

Each certificate to be issued by this CA has a unique number, called a *Serial Number*, to help identify it. When creating new certificates it will start with 1 (one). If you want to change its start number, enter a positive integer in the **Serial for next certificate** field.

Press the **Save** button to import it.

Internal Certificate Authority

When the **Method** is set to *Create an Internal Certificate Authority* a form will be available for defining many attributes for generating a CA. It has several fields with preset values. (In pfSense versions prior to 2.4.4, the state or province, city or locality, organization, and email address fields are required to be set.)

The **Key length (bits)** drop-down form allows selecting various bit sizes from 512 to 16384 bits. A key length below 2048 bits (the default) is considered weak.

The **Digest Algorithm** drop-down menu is used to select SHA1, SHA224, SHA256, SHA384, SHA512, or Whirlpool algorithm. It is not recommended to use SHA1. It defaults to SHA256.

Use the **Lifetime (days)** number entry to choose how many days the generated certificate will be valid. It defaults to 3650 days (which is approximately 10 years).

Enter the name in the **Common Name** text field. By default, it is set to "internal-ca".

Select the two-letter ISO country code for where your organization is located in the **Country Code** drop-down form. It contains 234 countries from AX (Aland Islands) to ZM (Zambia). It defaults to US (United States of America). This is used for the Country Name.

Then enter the full non-abbreviated state or province name, such as "Berkshire" or "Washington" in the **State or Province** text field.

Also enter in the **City** field the non-abbreviated locality name, such as "Newbury" or "Marysville".

The **Organization** text field is for entering the non-abbreviated legal name of the organization. (It may include suffixes like "LLC" or "Inc.") The following field is for the department or division in that organization that is handling this certificate. (Spell out ampersands "&" as "and" and avoid other special characters too.)

Enter an email address that may be used for contacting your organization in the **Email Address** field.

Click the **Save** button to generate the new private and public key pair and the new CSR (Certificate Signing Request) based on the supplied Distinguished Name information. Then it self-signs that certificate using the private key. The x509 certificate is generated using the *v3_ca* extension, using the provided bit size and algorithm for a RSA key type.

Intermediate Certificate Authority

If you select the *Create an intermediate Certificate Authority* method, an extended Internal Certificate Authority form will appear.

In addition to the fields described (and required) in the previous section, it also includes a drop-down menu for selecting a required **Signing Certificate Authority**. Select the CA there which this intermediate CA will be a subordinate of. If the drop-down is empty, you will need to import or create a CA first.

12.2 Certificate Manager

Certificates are listed and can be added or created via the **System → Certificate Manager → Certificates** subpage. Its default table (as seen in Figure 12.1) shows the previously-autogenerated webConfigurator certificate. (Notice that its *valid from* date may be from when your pfSense was installed.) You may have multiple of these certificates. The table may show lots of information.

Figure 12.1: **System** → **Certificate Manager** → **Certificates : More Information**

It will show the certificate name, whether it is a server certificate or user certificate (or maybe it has no type associated to it), and if it is a CA certificate, and if it is a certificate for TLS Web Server Authentication (identified with *Server: Yes*).

The *issuer* is the CA that issued the certificate. If the certificate is for Certificate Signing Request (CSR), this will show "external - signature pending." Or the issuer may show "self-signed" for created certificates (as it is its own owner) or "external" for imported certificates (when no local certificates are associated with it).

The *Distinguished Name* column identifies the owner or *subject* of the certificate. These attributes identify the entity it is associated with. It will also show the start and end date and time that the certificate is valid for. A **More Information** icon may be available to expand further details (as seen in the Figure 12.1). It includes the signature digest algorithm; associated names (Subject Alternate Name or SAN) such as DNS names or email addresses; and its purpose or what the certificate may be used for (Key Usage or KU and Extended Key Usage or EKU). This popup icon won't be there if these extensions aren't found.

The *In Use* column will indicate what's using the certificate, such as the webConfigurator, OpenVPN server or client, IPsec tunnel, the Captive Portal, or some package. Or it will indicate if it is a user certificate or if it has been revoked.

The table entries for the certificates also have various action icons depending on the type of certificate. These actions include:

Export Certificate (asterisk icon)
        allows you to download the X.509 certificate file via your web browser for storage or sharing.

Export Key (**key icon**)

>   allows you to download the private key file via your web browser.

Export P12 (**file cabinet or folder icon**)

>   allows you to download the personal key and certificate as a PKCS#11 format file.

Update CSR (**pencil icon**)

>   opens a new page sharing the signing request and an input box to enter the corresponding certificate from a third-party CA. This is covered in the following Section 12.2.2.

Export Request (**right arrow or sign-in icon**)

>   allows you to download a CSR which may be shared with a CA for signing.

Delete Certificate (**trash can icon**)

>   which will prompt you to confirm to remove a currently-unused certificate.

Use the **Add/Sign** button, below the table, to import or create a certificate. (On older pfSense systems, it may be a **Add** button.) This will bring up a new page as covered in the following sections.

12.2.1   Add or Sign a Certificate

When adding (or signing) a new certificate, the **Method** drop-down menu selections will bring up different forms on the page to *Import an existing Certificate*, *Create an internal Certificate*, *Create a Certificate Signing Request*, or *Sign a Certificate Signing Request*. These methods are explained in the following sections.

All require that a **Descriptive name** to be entered for the new certificate. This is used in pfSense to identify the certificate and to name it for export download filenames.

Import Existing Certificate

For importing an existing certificate, it is required to enter a descriptive name and to paste in the existing certificate and private key in the text boxes. These must be in a valid X.509 PEM format.

Create Internal Certificate

See the previous Section 12.1.1 about the several attributes to select for creating a certificate. The signer for this certificate is selected in the **Certificate authority** drop-down menu. When creating an internal certificate, the common name is required. It is not set by default. Generally this is a fully-qualified domain name — the server name when it is for a server.

It also has an optional section for adding attribute extensions to further identify the certificate. It defaults to be a user certificate (for Key Usage). To identify for server certificate use instead, select that in the **Certificate Type** drop-down menu.

You may add one or more associated names (Subject Altername Name or SAN). In the **Alternative Names** drop-down menu select a type of SAN from *FQDN or Hostname*, *IP address*, *URI*, or *email address*. Then enter its value in the corresponding field. You may enter more SANs by clicking the **Add** button. Remove a SAN entry by clicking its **Delete** button.

Create External Certificate Signing Request (CSR)

This is used to create a CSR which is shared with a third-party CA to sign.

Section 12.1.1 has more details about the various attributes for generating a signing request. Creating a CSR requires that the state or province, city, organization, email address, and the common name be entered. (Note that the CSR doesn't define the CA nor its lifetime.)

It can also have further identifying attributes (like Key Usage and SANs) as explained previously, but note that these attributes may be ignored or changed by the signing CA.

After this is saved (generated), you may use its **Export Request** action icon in the table view of certificates to download it so you may provide it to your CA. When your CA provides back the signed certificate for this CSR, use the **Update CSR** action icon to paste it in. (See the upcoming Section 12.2.2 about this.)

Sign CSR

You may also sign CSRs with pfSense by selecting the *Sign a Certificate Signing Request* method. To sign a CSR, the descriptive name is required.

The **CA to sign with** menu will list your available CAs to use for signing.

Then select the existing CSR in the **CSR to sign** menu. If you select its default *New CSR (Paste below)* option (which you may use if you don't have a CSR already imported or created), you will have two text boxes to paste in the CSR and optionally its corresponding private key.

Or in that drop-down menu, if available, you may select existing CSRs known to pfSense. Then you don't need to paste in the CSR data.

The resulting certificate will be valid for approximately 10 years (3650 days) by default. To change this, enter the number of days in the **Certificate Lifetime** number field.

It will use SHA256 as the algorithm for signing the CSR. To select a different Secure Hash Algorithm, use the **Digest Algorithm** drop-down menu. (SHA1 is not recommended.)

As described previously, identifying certificate attributes, like the Key Usage type and SANs, may be entered which will be used for the resulting (signed) certificate.

Then click the **Save** button to finish adding the certificate. This will take you back to the table listing its details with action icons to further manage it. Use other features in pfSense to then select the certificate.

12.2.2 Complete Signing Request

When a CSR has been created to be signed by a third-party, the **System** → **Certificate Manager** → **Certificates** table will indicate that with "external - signature pending" in the *Issuer* column. There are two ways to get this CSR to provide it to your external CA:

Use the **Export Request** action icon to download the certificate request as a file.

Or click the **Update CSR** (pencil icon) action icon to access a form which displays the PEM "CERTIFICATE REQUEST" data which may be copied.

Submit it to your third-party CA. When you receive the signed certificate back from the CA, use the **Update CSR** (pencil icon) action icon to open a page to upload it. Paste the new signed certificate into the **Final certificate data** text box and click the **Update** button.

12.3 Certificate Revocation

pfSense can also revoke certificates and manage lists of certificates that have been revoked. A *Certificate revocation list* or CRL contains certificates that have been invalidated or rescinded prior to expiring, because the client no longer has permission, the certificate has been superseded, its affiliation or operation has changed or ceased, or the key or CA has been compromised. Various features such as IPsec and OpenVPN can check against this revoked list to deny access, for example. The **System** → **Certificate Manager** → **Certificate Revocation** subpage is used to revoke certificates and to view and manage the CRLs.

The CRLs may be associated with an *internal* pfSense-managed CA. When using pfSense as a CA and creating self-signed certificates, you may also revoke your created certificates. CRLs may also be imported for an external *existing* CA.

The page has a table of *Additional Certificate Revocation Lists*. These are for CRLs that are mapped to CAs. When a CRL exists, the table will list it by its descriptive name and indicate if it is internal with a check icon or if not with a times (X) icon. It will show a count of certificates in the CRL (zero if none or "Unknown" if imported); and if it is in use with a check icon or, if not, with a times icon.

The entries will also have various actions. Click the **Export CRL** download icon to save it as an encoded X.509 CRL file on your computer. Click the **Edit CRL** pencil icon to modify the internal or imported CRL settings. This will take you to a new page showing your currently revoked certificates for the named CRL (as explained in Section 12.3.2).

Use the **Delete CRL** trash can icon to remove the CRL from pfSense management. Note it won't allow you to remove a CRL that is in use by an OpenVPN configuration (see Section 33.1.1).

By default, pfSense does not have any CRLs defined, but this table will list your internal or external certificates authorities with a corresponding **Add or Import CRL** button. You can add or managed the CAs via the **CAs** link near the top of the page as covered earlier in Section 12.1.

12.3.1   Create CRL

When creating a new CRL for your internal CA, you may create an internal CRL or import a CRL. Use the **Method** drop-down menu to select your choice. You won't have a selection to create a CRL when associated to an external CA — so your only option is to import it. Depending on the selected method, you will have some different fields available.

Enter a name about this CRL association in the **Descriptive name** field. This is required.

The CA it is associated with is selected in the **Certificate Authority** drop-down menu.

When creating an internal CRL, you will have fields to enter the lifetime and the serial number. Enter the number of days before the CRL expires or the next CRL is due in the **Lifetime (Days)** field. It defaults to 9999 days (over 27 years). On some platforms this will be limited to the days through the year 2038. The serial number of the issued certificate may be entered in the **Serial** field. This is optional and defaults to 0.

When importing an existing CRL, paste the X.509 CRL formatted text into the **CRL data** text box. (This text would start with "-----BEGIN X509 CRL-----" and complete with "-----END X509 CRL-----" markers.)

Press the **Save** button to store the new CRL.

12.3.2   Current Revoked Certificates

Clicking the edit action icon for a CRL will take you to the list of currently revoked certificates for that specifically. If none are revoked it will indicate that no certificates are found.

Each currently revoked certificate in a CRL is listed with is certificate name, the reason it was revoked, and the date and time when it was revoked.

A single action is available as a trash can icon to delete it from the CRL. When clicking it, you will be prompted to confirm its removal.

12.3.3   Revoking a Certificate

To revoke a certificate, click the **Edit CRL** action icon for a CRL on the main **System** → **Certificate Manager** → **Certificate Revocation** subpage. Below the currently revoked certificates list, if you have certificates that can be revoked, you will have a section to choose a certificate to revoke. (Else it will indicate there are no certificates found for the selected CA.)

In the **Certificate** drop-down menu select the certificate to revoke. Then select why in the **Reason** menu. It defaults to *No Status*. The other reason choices are: *Unspecified, Key Compromise, CA Compromise, Affiliation Changed, Superseded, Cessation of Operation, Certificate Hold*, and *Privilege Withdrawn*.

Then click the **Add** button to revoke the selected certificate and add it to the list. This will take you back to the previous **Certification Revocation** page. The count of certificates in the CRL will have increased. You can press the edit action icon for the list to see the new revoked certificate with your reason and the time it was revoked. Also on the **System** → **Certificate Manager** → **Certificates** subpage you will see "Revoked" for that certificate in the *In Use* column.

13   Networking Interfaces

This chapter covers the standard network setup options, like configuring interfaces to use pre-defined addresses, DHCP for network assigned addressing, PPP, virtual LANs (VLAN), bridging, and much more.

Most of pfSense also supports the Internet Protocol version 6 (IPv6). IPv6 settings are described in the following chapter.

The basic interface configuration was done during installation at the text console or the setup wizard (as covered in Section 2.11, Section 3.5, and Section 3.6). Or it may be done later via the text console menu (as covered in Section 37.2 and Section 37.3). But those only provide limited network interface configurations and the text console way is normally used only when there is no access available to the webConfigurator. This may happen when booting the pfSense system with changed networking hardware, which may result in an interfaces mismatch detected which would be reported and need to be fixed via the console.

When an enabled network interface is not configured, the dashboard's Interfaces widget will show it with a red "no carrier" (X) icon, the status will say "none," and the addressing will show "n/a" (not applicable). If using DHCP to configure it, the **Status** → **Interfaces** page will have a **Renew** button as seen in Figure 13.1.

13.1   Interface Assignments

To add a new network interface or to view your interface names as associated with a device (and MAC address), click **Assignments** in the **Interfaces** drop-down menu. (Old versions of pfSense have this menu entry listed as **(assign)**.)

This page will have links to subpages near the top: **Interface Assignments** (the main page), **Interface Groups** (covered in Section 16.4), **Wireless** (Section 23.1), **VLANs** (Section 13.6), **QinQs** (Section 24.1), **PPPs** (Section 24.2), **GREs** (Section 24.3), **GIFs** (Section 24.4), **Bridges** (Section 13.5), and **LAGGS** (Section 13.4),

The **Related status** barchart icon in the shortcuts (or the **Status** → **Interfaces** page) may be used to view the settings and counters for all of your assigned interfaces.

The **Interfaces** → **Interface Assignments** view shows the available network hardware listed by your existing interface names (such as WAN or LAN).

The **Network port** drop-down menu lists the pfSense-detected networking interfaces. Hardware interfaces are identified with the interface abbreviated name (as known by the FreeBSD system) followed by its detected number and the MAC hardware address in parentheses. The device may also be a software-based or virtual device, such as L2TP, POES, IPsec (Section 30.8), or OVPN (OpenVPN as introduced in Section 33.3). It will not list wireless devices (in pfSense versions 2.4 and later) until they have been predefined via the **Interfaces** → **Assignments** → **Wireless** subpage (as discussed in Section 23.1).

If you have network hardware or a virtual device that has not yet been assigned in pfSense, you can add a new assignment or change an existing interface to use a different device instead.

To add a new interface, select in the drop-down menu your desired network interface. If you only have one free network card, then it will only show one. Then click its corresponding **Add** button on the right to add this selected interface. (This button is only available when an unassigned interface is also available.) pfSense will auto-generate a proposed name and reload this page. (For example, if it is the second interface, it may be known as the "LAN" or if is the fourth interface it may be shown as "OPT2".)

Click on that new interface name to then enable and configure it. (The new interface name should also be available via the top **Interfaces** menu.) This will take you to the specific **Interfaces** page for the interface (such as the WAN, LAN, and OPT1) where you will first setup its general configuration (as seen in Section 13.2.1).

 Warning
If you add a LAN and you are using the WAN for the webConfigurator or SSH access, you may get locked out as new firewall rules will block access to pfSense administration from the WAN.

13.1.1   Change Network Port

Existing interfaces may be reassociated with a different network device via the **Network port** drop-down menu. After making your selection(s), click the **Save** button at the bottom. You may not assign two network devices to the same interface on this page.

13.1.2   Removing an Interface

To remove an interface, click its corresponding **Delete** button. This will prompt you for confirmation.

Warning
If you remove the interface you are using the pfSense web configuration or SSH text console with, you will be locked out.

13.2 Interface Configurations

The configured network interfaces may be selected for configuration by clicking on the interface name (like WAN or LAN) in the Interfaces widget on the dashboard, at the **Interfaces** menu link at the top of the web interface, or via the **Interfaces** → **Interface Assignments** page. This interface's configuration will show the current settings with fields or choices to make changes, such as defining if the interface receives some settings via DHCP or is a VPN interface.

To see the assigned network settings and counters for an interface, click on the **Related status** bar-chart icon in the shortcuts or go to the **Status** → **Interfaces** page (as covered in Section 13.3).

13.2.1 General Configuration

This general configuration has a checkbox to enable the interface; if unchecked (disabled), then the configurable options disappear.

The **Description** field is used to set the *name* for the interface, such as describing what the interface connects to. Common defaults include WAN, LAN, and OPT1. You may want to add a brief few-word description to describe its intended purpose, like "StudentLab". Note that it will remove any spaces and references for it will mostly be all capitalized. Also this name cannot match an Interface Group name.

The **IPv4 Configuration Type** is a drop-down menu with choices of *None*, *Static IPv4*, *DHCP*, *PP-PoE*, *PPTP*, and *L2TP*. Then you can enable if and how the interface is configured for IPv6 too. The **IPv6 Configuration Type** is often set to *None* for no IPv6 usage. For the IPv6 types, see the following chapter.

If you plan to use a bridged configuration, keep these as *None* (see Section 13.5).

Note that when an address type is selected, the later configuration options change accordingly as covered in the following sections. In addition when changing this type, after saving, the previous settings are removed. (If you need to recover a previous configuration, try using the **Diagnostics** → **Backup & Restore** → **Config History** feature as explained in Section 8.2.)

If you need to spoof this interface's MAC address, enter it in the **MAC address** field. The format is six hexadecimal two-digit numbers delimited with colons, for example "F7:E8:E0:87:C2:45". Usually you would just leave this blank to use the manufacturer's provided hardware address.

The maximum transmission unit or MTU is the largest packet size in bytes which may sent over the network interface. Normally, this not set and the device's default, such as 1500 bytes, will be used. To use a custom MTU, enter the integer number in the **MTU** field. Acceptable numbers are within 576 and 9000. (GIF interfaces only allow 1280 to 8192.)

The maximum segment size or MSS is a TCP option that specifies a limit for bytes received in a single packet. A pfSense system defaults to 536 bytes for the MSS. This size doesn't include the IP and TCP header sizes (40 bytes). Setting this in the **MSS** field will set up a packet filter rule for enforcing it when matching TCP packets. Note that it will be reduced by 40 bytes for the combined IP and TCP headers. The accepted values are 576 and 65535 bytes. (MSS clamping can also be defined for IPsec interfaces; for details see Section 30.6.)

Most network interfaces support media types, modes, and options such as selecting 100 Mbps (Fast Ethernet) versus 10 Mbps operation, choosing 802.11g versus 802.11b wireless mode, forcing half or full duplex operation, or hardware flow control. These vary from types of hardware. Generally the driver's or device's default or auto-selected settings (such as to auto-negotiate speeds) are fine, but if you need to force certain types, modes, or options, see the **Speed and Duplex** drop-down menu. (This option may be missing if your network interface doesn't report or allow different network interface media types or links.) It defaults to **Default (no preferences, typically autoselect)**. You may have around 15 to 34 choices as reported by your interface.

 Warning
Don't force a speed or duplex if the other end of this network connection isn't also defined the same way or your networking may fail.

13.2.2   Static IPv4 Configuration

Enter the static IPv4 address in the **IPv4 Address** field. Then select its network's subnet mask in the corresponding drop-down number menu. It defaults to /32 for a single host. If you will be providing a DHCP service on this interface, you will need to select a netmask of 30 or smaller (for a larger network).

Instead of entering the router's IP address for the gateway, pfSense can maintain a list from which one may be selected in the **IPv4 Upstream gateway** drop-down menu. Your local network interfaces (like the LAN) don't need their own gateway, so keep them set to *None* (or if you aren't using a gateway for an Internet connection).

To use a gateway, you will need to add its definition first. See the **System → Routing → Gateways** page (Section 15.1) to view gateway details or to add a gateway.

Or click the **Add a new gateway** button. This will popup a small form to enter its IP address. It will automatically give it a name (like "LANGW") or you can enter your own name to identify it. You can also enter a description. If this will be the fallback gateway for routing, check the **Default gateway** checkbox there. (See Section 15.1.1 about the alternative way to select the the default route.)

13.2.3 DHCP Client Configuration

This configuration section only appears if the **IPv4 Configuration type** is set to DHCP. In most uses, you don't need to use any of the following DHCP client configurations.

Note

If you are running a DHCP server on the same interface, you can not have it also act as a DHCP client.

If your DHCP server provider needs a DHCP client identifier or name of the client, you can enter what it would use for matching in the **Hostname** field. If this is not set, this identification is not sent.

If you want to use a permanent IP address for the same interface even when using DHCP, you may set it in the **Alias IPv4 address** field and optionally select its network subnet in the corresponding drop-down menu (which defaults to /32 for a single host). (This will be in addition to the address provided over DHCP.)

If you know of a broken or rogue DHCP server that you want to ignore, you may list its IP address (or its subnet) in the **Reject leases from** field to avoid being configured by it.

If the interface you are using for DHCP is a VLAN interface, you will have an option to assign the VLAN priority for the outgoing packets. To use this, check the **Enable dhcpclient VLAN Priority tagging** checkbox. (For details on VLANs, see Section 13.6.) Choose your 802.1p Priority Code Point (PCP) in the **VLAN Prio** drop-down menu:

- Background (BK, 0)

- Best Effort (BE, 1)

- Excellent Effort (EE, 2)

- Critical Applications (CA, 3)

- Video (VI, 4)

- Voice (VO, 5)

- Internetwork Control (IC, 6)

- Network Control (NC, 7)

The DHCP client for the interface will try to reach a DHCP server frequently starting around one second between attempts up to 15 seconds and then try again every 15 seconds. If it cannot contact the DHCP server after one minute, your client will use any valid, unexpired lease it had previously recorded. It will take the first offer it sees if there are multiple DHCP servers on the same network. These behaviors may be changed by clicking the **Advanced Configuration** checkbox option. It will bring up several additional inputs below for DHCP timing behavior and DHCP options.

The **Protocol timing** number input fields include the following. They are all set in seconds.

- **Timeout** — When the DHCP client will fall back to use a previously-recorded unexpired lease.

- **Retry** — How much time before the client tries again if it cannot reach a DHCP server.

- **Select timeout** — How many seconds should the client wait for offers from additional DHCP servers.

- **Reboot** — How much time before it tries to discover a new address instead of reacquiring the previous address.

- **Backoff cutoff** — The maximum amount of time between requests.

- **Initial interval** — The amount of time before the second attempt. This will exponentially increase with some randomness up to the **Backoff cutoff** setting.

These six timing values are all empty by default. They may be auto-defined by using the **Presets** radio selection. Choosing **FreeBSD default** or **pfSense default** enters (or resets) common timings. The default selection is **Saved Cfg** which means it will use the values previously entered in the input fields and saved. You may also select the **Clear** radio button to clear all these timing fields.

Lease Requirements and Requests

The **Lease Requirements and Requests** section is also available when the **Advanced Configuration** checkbox is selected. This provides a way to handle custom DHCP options if required by your DHCP service provider as follows. (Note that this book doesn't introduce the various DHCP options.)

To have your DHCP client send custom details to the DHCP server (so that server can recognize your client), enter them in the **Send options** text field. Normally a DHCP option is a keyword followed by a value (sometimes in quotes). Separate each of the keyword / value pairs with commas, for example:

```
dhcp-client-identifier 1:0:a0:24:ab:fb:9c , dhcp-lease-time 3600
```

When using the **Advanced Configuration**, there also some special macros which may be substituted for values from your pfSense system; these are covered in the following Section 13.2.3.

By default, the DHCP client asks for *broadcast-address*, *domain-name*, *domain-name-servers*, *hostname*, *routers*, *subnet-mask*, and *time-offset* DHCP options which the server may respond with. The **Request options** text field may be used to customize this list. These values are comma separated.

If you don't want your client to accept a DHCP offer unless certain DHCP options are provided, then enter these required options in the **Require options** text field. Again these are separated with commas.

You can also customize your DHCP client to supplement or only use DHCP options that you provide by entering them in the **Option modifiers** text field. The modifiers start with a special keyword as follows:

- **default** — use this value if no value is provided via DHCP.

- **supersede** — use this value (instead of the value from the server).

- **prepend** — also use these values at a start of a list (if supported).

- **append** — also use these values at the end of a list (if supported).

Note that each triplet of modifiers (keyword, option, and value) are delimited with commas. For example:

```
prepend domain-name-servers 127.0.0.1 , supersede domain-name    ↩
    "example.com"
```

DHCP Client Configuration Override

Some providers may require only specific DHCP options be provided. The **Configuration Override** checkbox is used to allow using an uploaded DHCP client configuration file instead of using these pfSense options. When checked, a **Configuration File Override** field will appear and the other DHCP client configurations will disappear. If using a custom DHCP configuration file, enter its full absolute filename. The configuration syntax is for the Internet Systems Consortium DHCP Client, `dhclient`, as extended by OpenBSD. It is documented in the file formats manual at `http://man.freebsd.org/dhclient.conf`.

Your custom file may contain some special macros (marked with braces) to be replaced with settings from your pfSense system. These substitutions include:

- **{interface}** — The pfSense interface's FreeBSD device interface name and number (like `re0`).

- **{hostname}** — This is the DHCP client **Hostname** settings as covered above. Note that it is hidden so toggle the **Configuration Override** checkbox to set it.

- **{mac_addr_asciiU}** — This interface's hardware address in uppercase and not delimited, such as 0022B0CEF1DC.

- **{mac_addr_asciiU }** — This interface's hardware address in uppercase and delimited with a space ( ), such as 00 22 B0 CE F1 DC.

- **{mac_addr_asciiU:}** — This interface's hardware address in uppercase and delimited with a colon (:), such as 00:22:B0:CE:F1:DC.

- **{mac_addr_asciiU-}** — This interface's hardware address in uppercase and delimited with a dash (-), such as 00-22-B0-CE-F1-DC.

- **{mac_addr_asciiU.}** — This interface's hardware address in uppercase and delimited with a period (.), such as 00.22.B0.CE.F1.DC.

- **{mac_addr_asciiL}** — This interface's hardware address in lowercase and not delimited, such as 0022b0cef1dc.

- **{mac_addr_asciiL }** — This interface's hardware address in lowercase and delimited with a space ( ), such as 00 22 b0 ce f1 dc.

- **{mac_addr_asciiL:}** — This interface's hardware address in lowercase and delimited with a colon (:), such as 00:22:b0:ce:f1:dc.

- **{mac_addr_asciiL-}** — This interface's hardware address in lowercase and delimited with a dash (-), such as 00-22-b0-ce-f1-dc.

- **{mac_addr_asciiL.}** — This interface's hardware address in lowercase and delimited with a period (.), such as 00.22.b0.ce.f1.dc.

- **{mac_addr_hexU}** — This interface's hardware address with each hexadecimal number converted first to uppercase and then that corresponding digit as an ASCII character converted to a non-delimited hexadecimal number. For example f1 becomes 4631.

- **{mac_addr_hexU }** — This interface's hardware address with each hexadecimal number converted first to uppercase and then that corresponding digit as an ASCII character converted to a hexadecimal number each delimited by a space. For example f1 becomes 46 31.

- **{mac_addr_hexU:}** — This interface's hardware address with each hexadecimal number converted first to uppercase and then that corresponding digit as an ASCII character converted to a hexadecimal number each delimited by a colon. For example f1 becomes 46:31.

- **{mac_addr_hexU-}** — This interface's hardware address with each hexadecimal number converted first to uppercase and then that corresponding digit as an ASCII character converted to a hexadecimal number each delimited by a dash. For example f1 becomes 46-31.

- **{mac_addr_hexU.}** — This interface's hardware address with each hexadecimal number converted first to uppercase and then that corresponding digit as an ASCII character converted to a hexadecimal number each delimited by a period. For example f1 becomes 46.31.

- **{mac_addr_hexL}** — This interface's hardware address with each hexadecimal number converted first to lowercase and then that corresponding digit as an ASCII character converted to a non-delimited hexadecimal number. For example F1 becomes 6631.

- **{mac_addr_hexL }** — This interface's hardware address with each hexadecimal number converted first to lowercase and then that corresponding digit as an ASCII character converted to a hexadecimal number each delimited by a space. For example F1 becomes 66 31.

- **{mac_addr_hexL:}** — This interface's hardware address with each hexadecimal number converted first to lowercase and then that corresponding digit as an ASCII character converted to a hexadecimal number each delimited by a colon. For example F1 becomes 66:31.

- **{mac_addr_hexL-}** — This interface's hardware address with each hexadecimal number converted first to lowercase and then that corresponding digit as an ASCII character converted to a hexadecimal number each delimited by a dash. For example F1 becomes 66-31.

- **{mac_addr_hexL.}** — This interface's hardware address with each hexadecimal number converted first to lowercase and then that corresponding digit as an ASCII character converted to a hexadecimal number each delimited by a period. For example F1 becomes 66.31.

Either of the MAC address substitutions may use a "U" or "L" to uppercase or lowercase the provided address. The MAC address delimiter substitutions can be a " " space, ":" colon, "-" dash, "." period, or nothing for no delimiter added.

This override file may be uploaded using SSH `scp`, with the file upload feature via **Diagnostics** → **Command Prompt** (see Section 7.1), or entered (or pasted) using the **Diagnostics** → **Edit File** page (Section 7.2).

Even if your custom or alternative configurations don't work, the pfSense interface may say that the changes have been applied successfully. The **Status** → **Interfaces** view (Section 13.3) may show a status of "no carrier" and DHCP is "down" for the interface. If the **Status** → **System Logs** → **System** → **General** log view (Section 11.4) shows an error for `php-fpm` or `/sbin/ahclient`, you may have details available in an output file. Either use the text console or the **Diagnostics** → **Edit File** feature to load the output file (see Section 7.2). The DHCP client output may be in a file named after the FreeBSD network device name, such as `/tmp/ath0_wlan0_output`. Regardless of what you find, fixing custom DHCP client configurations is beyond the focus of this book. (Have fun!) You may need to revert to use the non-advanced DHCP configurations.

To release or renew the DHCP for this interface, go to the **Status** → **Interfaces** page and click on the **Release** button (as covered in Section 13.3).

13.2.4 PPP Configuration

The PPP configuration is used to create a networking interface using a point-to-point connection via a modem (or related hardware) to an external provider or GSM carrier. This requires a dial-out serial port or modem card.

Note that pfSense has two different places to configure PPP. This is via the normal interfaces configuration when the configuration type is set to *PPP*. The other configuration is from clicking the **PPPs** link at the top of the **Interfaces** → **Interface Assignments** view. That second configuration is also accessed by clicking the **Advanced PPP** button at the bottom of PPP configurations.

pfSense provides a database of over 600 providers with near 600 with GSM and around 72 for CDMA. Selecting a country in the **Country** menu and then the **Provider** and **Plan** drop-down lists help provide preset values for the PPP connection. Choosing a plan may set a pre-defined username and password (for APN or CDMA), phone number, and the Access Point Name. It may also pre-define DNS servers to use.

Or you may enter your own PPP details in the **Username, Password** (and confirmation), and **Phone number** fields. A phone number is required. Commonly, it is #777 for CDMA networks and *99# for GSM.

If you need to enter an APN, such as for 3G connections, enter it in the **Access Point Name** field.

Selecting the device in the **Modem port** for the connection is required. Your pfSense system must have detected a FreeBSD `/dev/cua` dial-out serial device for this. If it is set to *None*, you will not be able to use this PPP feature.

The **Advanced PPP** button links to a different page to add your new PPP configuration and to edit some different PPP settings. This is covered in Section 24.2.1. Save any new changes here before clicking, as they may be lost.

For PPP logging, see the **Status** → **System Logs** → **PPP** page covered at Section 24.2.2.

13.2.5 PPPoE Configuration

A PPPoE tunnel can also be configured via the **PPPs** link from the **Interfaces** → **Interface Assignments** page. That alternate configuration may also be accessed by clicking the **Advanced and MLPPP** button below. See Section 24.2.1 for more details.

For PPP-over-Ethernet, enter the required **Username** and **Password**.

If your PPPoE service provider supplied a service name, enter it in the **Service name** field.

If using an idle timeout, the PPPoE interface is brought down if there aren't any outgoing or incoming packets transmitted for a defined time. To have a virtually full-time connection instead, check the **Dial on demand** checkbox. Then it will automatically bring the link back up when it sees local traffic. The PPPoE program, *mpd*, will re-configure the interface and adjust the routes as needed.

The idle timeout is disabled by default. If you want it to stop the PPPoE connection when it hasn't seen any traffic for awhile, set the number of seconds in the **Idle timeout** number input field. Set it to 0 (zero) to disable it again.

In addition to the idle timeout and dial-on-demand, you can reload the PPPoE interface on a schedule. This is scheduled by first selecting a choice in the **Periodic reset** drop-down menu. This is disabled by default. Selecting *Pre-set* will bring up four radio selectors. You may select one of reloading every first day of the month, every Sunday, or every day — all at midnight. Or it can be reloaded at the start of every hour.

If you need the PPPoE connection to be reloaded at a specific hour and minute or specific date, select *Custom* in the **Periodic reset** menu. This will bring up fields to enter the hour and minute; or month, day, and year (use digits delimited by slashes).

For Multilink PPPoE or other advanced settings, click the **Advanced and MLPPP** button. This will take you to a new page as covered at Section 24.2.1. Note you must save any changes here first before following that link.

13.2.6 PPTP/L2TP Configuration

A PPTP and L2TP tunnels can also be configured via the **PPPs** link from the **Interfaces** → **Interface Assignments** page. For details, see Section 24.2.1. These alternate configurations may also be accessed by clicking the **Advanced and MLPPP** button below.

 Warning
Note that PPTP is considered insecure and is not recommended.

For PPTP and L2TP, enter the required **Username** and **Password** (twice to confirm typing it correctly).

For PPTP, the local IP address is required. Enter it in the **Local IP address** field with its subnet in the corresponding drop-down field.

Then enter the IP address for the remote peer in the **Remote IP address** field. (This field is required.)

Check the **Enable Dial-On-Demand mode** checkbox to have the PPTP or L2TP interface brought up when there is outgoing traffic.

Use the **Idle timeout (seconds)** field to enter the number of seconds without traffic to stop the PPTP or L2TP connection. Setting it to 0 (zero) disables this idle-based disconnect.

To use the other PPTP or L2TP configuration instead, click the **Advanced and MLPPP** button. Note your settings here will be lost unless you saved them.

13.2.7 Reserved Networks

The **Block private networks and loopback addresses** checkbox is used to enable a firewall rule to block incoming traffic from standard internal addresses. This includes loopback networks (127/8), RFC 1918 Private Internets (192.168/16, 172.16/12, and 10/8), and RFC 4193 Unique Local IPv6 Unicast Addresses (fc00::/7). These addresses for local communication are not intended to be routed on the global Internet. This is commonly enabled for WAN to block internal addresses from coming in from the outside. In normal pfSense use, this would never be enabled for the LAN or internal interfaces.

pfSense provides a list of over 100,000 networks that should not appear on the public Internet. These are reserved addresses or addresses that aren't yet assigned. (This doesn't include the localhost, RFC 1918, nor RFC 4193 address space covered previously.) These may be use for automatic firewall rules to block this source traffic especially for the WAN since its use is normally invalid or possibly malicious. To enable this, click the **Block bogon networks** checkbox.

The bogons database is updated periodically per a setting on the **System** → **Advanced** → **Firewall & NAT** page (see Section 16.8.1). Packet filter logging for these blocks can be enabled at the **Status** → **System Logs** → **Settings** page as explained in Section 11.2.

Warning
If your Internet service provider uses addressing in the private or reserved networks, enabling these for your WAN may block your Internet access. In addition, you don't want to block these for your LAN or internal networks if you are using that address space.

If you need to use an HTTP Proxy to download the bogons, use the settings on the **System** → **Advanced** → **Miscellaneous** subpage (Section 5.4.1).

After these many changes, click the **Save** button at the bottom of the page. After the page is reloaded, you may receive an **Apply Changes** button to press to actually restart or enable the interface with these new configurations.

Note

When changing an IP address for an interface or changing it to not use a static IP address, if the DHCP server was enabled for that interface, you may also need to separately go to the **Services** → **DHCP Server** page to adjust the **Range** or disable the DHCP service for that interface (Chapter 19). You may also need to adjust any firewall rules for your new interface's network or if you have address changes. On the **Firewall** → **Rules** page, click the tab for your corresponding interface name at the top. (See Section 16.1 for details.) This may be applicable for manual Outbound NAT or other address translation rules too. Check those also as covered in Chapter 17.

13.2.8   Disable an Interface

To disable an interface, go to the **Interfaces** drop-down menu and click the interface name. Then under the **General Configuration** section (at the top), uncheck the **Enable interface** checkbox, and then click the **Save** button at the bottom of the page. A new screen will come up indicating your interface configuration changed. Click the **Apply Changes** button to complete this step.

The disabled interface will still be available via the **Interfaces** menu, but won't be listed on the Interfaces widget on the dashboard.

13.3   Interface Details and Stats

To see a quick view about the setup and usage of your network interfaces, see the **Status** → **Interfaces** page. It will have different sections for each of your interfaces covering a wide variety of details as seen in the following list. The **Status** field will indicate if the interface is *up*, *down*, or has *no carrier*, for example. Features not available or not used for the interface are not displayed.

- BSSID
- Bridge
- Cell Current Down
- Cell Current Up
- Cell Downstream
- Cell Mode
- Cell SIM State
- Cell Service
- Cell Signal (RSSI)
- Cell Upstream
- Channel
- Collisions
- DHCP
- DHCP6
- DNS servers
- Gateway IPv4
- Gateway IPv6
- IPv4 Address
- IPv6 Address
- IPv6 Link Local
- In/out errors
- In/out packets (block)
- In/out packets (pass)
- L2TP
- LAGG Ports
- LAGG Protocol
- MAC Address
- MTU
- Media
- PPP
- PPPoE
- PPTP
- RSSI
- Rate
- SSID
- Subnet mask IPv4
- Subnet mask IPv6
- Total interrupts
- Uptime

Some of the fields may have buttons or checkboxes to update the interface details, such as **Connect** or **Disconnect** buttons for L2TP, PPP, PPPoE, or PPTP network interfaces. Note if you have a dial-on-demand connection, disconnecting it here may only be temporary as a packet may tell it to reconnect.

DHCP and DHCPv6 entries will have a **Release** button to turn off the DHCP client process for that interface. If its corresponding **Relinquish Lease** checkbox is checked, it will also notify the DHCP server that you wish to release the assigned IP address. If you are using DHCP and your status is down, you will have a **Renew** button (as seen in Figure 13.1). Using this will attempt to bring that interface back up using DHCP.

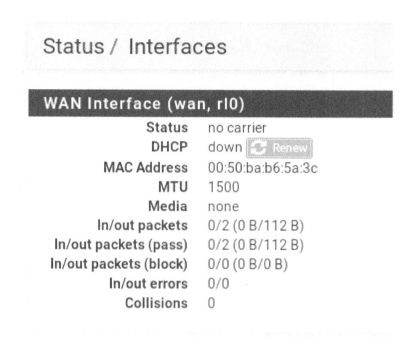

Figure 13.1: Interface no carrier status with DHCP Renew button

13.4 LAGG Interfaces

A LAGG (Link Aggregation) interface is used to combine multiple network interfaces as one virtual interface to help provide failover, load balancing, or roaming support. It has different protocols to define how it used for incoming and outgoing traffic:

- **LACP** — Traffic is balanced for the greatest total speed and fault tolerance using the Link Aggregation Control Protocol. Negotiation is done with a connected device's ports, such as a Cisco switch.

- **FAILOVER** — The first interface is the master. When unavailable, the next interface is used. Only traffic is sent or accepted through the single active interface. This can be used for setting up roaming between different networks,

- **FEC** — Cisco Fast EtherChannel is old-style load balancing support. FEC is deprecated and was removed from pfSense in version 2.4.4.

- **LOADBALANCE** — This accepts traffic from any active interface. This does not monitor the link nor negotiate aggregation.

- **ROUNDROBIN** — This accepts incoming traffic from any active interface. Outbound traffic is distributed through any active interface based on a round-robin scheduler.

- **NONE** — Disable traffic without disabling the LAGG interface.

No LAGG interfaces are setup by default. When created, the page's table shows the interface name (such as LAGG0) and the interfaces it knows about.

Use its corresponding action icons to edit the LAGG configuration or to remove it. Note you cannot delete the LAGG interface until it corresponding pfSense network interface is removed first. (See Section 13.1.2 for details.)

Use the **Add** button to add a LAGG interface.

13.4.1   LAGG Configuration

Select one or more interfaces in the required **Parent Interfaces** menu. (Use Control-click or your web browser's feature to make multiple selections.) These are identified using the FreeBSD interface naming followed by the hardware MAC address. Note that some interfaces are not capable of LAGG support even though they may be selected and saved here.

Then select the protocol to use with the LAGG interface in the **LAGG Protocol** drop-down menu as described previously. It defaults to *NONE* which passes no traffic.

Optionally enter a purpose about this LAGG interface in the **Description** text field.

After you save your configuration, the LAGG interface will be created.

To use the LAGG interface, configure it with an address. Go to the **Interface → Assignments** page and select and add it under the available network ports. It may be given a pfSense-assigned name (which can be changed) like *OPT1*. Click on the new interface name for the LAGG device to configure and enable it.

13.5   Bridging

Bridging is used to connect multiple Ethernet-like networks together, including wireless 802.11. It learns and caches the MAC addresses of the devices on its bridge interfaces and forwards traffic from one interface to another (like a switch) if the source and destination MAC addresses are on different networks. When a destination MAC address is not in its cache, then the packet will be forwarded to all the members of the bridge. Also note that the bridge uses the smallest MTU of its members.

Bridges are viewed and managed at the **Interfaces** → **Bridges** subpage found via the **Assignments** menu link. When a bridge is setup, the page will list its members by their interface names. The bridge will also have corresponding actions to edit and delete the interface bridge configuration. Note that a bridge may not be removed if it has been assigned as an interface.

To add a bridge configuration, click the **Add** button.

13.5.1 Bridge Configuration

The bridge name is automatically defined with a number, starting with *BRIDGE0*. (But some places in pfSense show this as lowercase.)

To get started at least one interface needs to be selected in the **Member Interfaces** option list. The choices include your previously setup interfaces, such as the WAN, LAN, and OPT1. You can select multiple entries by using the shift or control keys while clicking with the mouse pointer.

Note
Wireless interfaces must be in access point (hostap) mode to be a participating member in your bridge.

A description may also be entered to help explain the purpose of this bridge setup.

Clicking the **Save** button will create the bridge pseudo-device (as an interface) and configure its bridge parameters.

13.5.2 Advanced Bridging Options

Bridging has many options. To access these, click the **Display Advanced** button.

The bridge's address cache defaults to size of 2000 entries. This may be changed in the **Cache Size** field.

Enter the number of seconds before the address cache entries timeout in the **Cache expire time** field. It defaults to 1200 seconds (20 minutes). Set it to 0 (zero) to not expire the entries.

A network tap for snooping traffic by copying all frames to an additional interface can be implemented using the **Span Port** menu. Select the interfaces (which aren't a member of the bridge) to copy the frames to.

Edge ports are ports connected to servers or hosts and not switches and won't cause a loop when changing the topology. You may configure a port as an edge so it can transition to the forwarding state, by selecting the interface in the **Edge Ports** menu. Edge ports can be automatically identified. These may be selected in the **Auto Edge Ports** menu.

To define point-to-point links, select the interfaces in the **PTP Ports** menu. Or for automatic point-to-point link detection, select the interfaces in the **Auto PTP Ports** menu.

Even if an address in the cache is seen on a different interface, it can be set as static so it isn't replaced nor timesout. Select the interfaces with static addressing in the **Sticky Ports** menu.

To not forward traffic between private interfaces, select them in the **Private Ports** menu.

To use automatic link-local address configuration (stateless autoconfiguration) as part of IPv6 neighbor discovery for the bridge interface, check the **Enable IPv6 auto linklocal** checkbox. (The bridge member's will not use automatic link-local address configuration.)

13.5.3   Spanning Tree

The spanning tree protocol is used to detect and remove loops. This protocol may be activated for the bridge by checking the **Enable RSTP/STP** checkbox.

It defaults to the faster Rapid Spanning Tree Protocol (RSTP), but can downgrade ports to the legacy protocol if needed for compatibility. You may force it to use the legacy Spanning Tree Protocol (STP) in the **Protocol** menu.

Select the specific interfaces to enable the spanning tree protocol in the **STP Interfaces** menu.

The Spanning Tree Protocol configuration may be valid for 6 to 40 seconds which may be selected in the **Valid time** number field. It defaults to 20 seconds.

When the spanning tree is enabled, by default, 15 seconds must pass before the interface forwards packets. Change this delay in the **Forward time** number field within 4 seconds to 30 seconds.

The Spanning Tree Protocol broadcasts configuration messages every two seconds. For the legacy protocol (not RSTP), this may be changed from one to two seconds (with tenths of a second) in the **Hello time** field.

All the bridges are assigned a bridge priority. To have one of the bridges be the top of the spanning tree (the root bridge), set it to the lowest number in the **Priority** field. Commonly these are defined in increments of 4096 and the maximum allowed is 61440. Bridges default to 32768 which means the bridge with the lowest MAC address is the root bridge.

By default, six packets may be transmitted before being rate limited. For this maximum transmission rate limit, this may be changed in the transmit **Hold Count** field. The allowed count is within 1 to 10.

A spanning tree port priority is used to define ports that are put into forwarding state and what are blocked. By default, the ports have a priority of 128. To have a higher priority, set a lower number in the interface's corresponding **Priority** field. Or use a higher number for ports to be selected last for the forwarding state. It has increments of 16 from 0 through 240.

If a loop occurs, the spanning tree uses a path cost calculated from the media speed. To change it from the default (0), enter a number from 1 to 200000000 in the interface's **Path cost** field. The lowest number means the interface is selected first.

13.5.4 Bridge Status

The bridge members can also be seen at the **Status** → **Interfaces** page. These interfaces will be identified with a **Bridge** field and in parentheses it will list the name (and number) of the bridge it is a member of. A working bridge member should indicate it is "forwarding," while a newly configured or incomplete bridge may indicate it is "learning."

If the spanning tree protocol detects a loop in the network, the member is flagged in bold as "blocking." If you see this, then check your setup for redundant paths that may be causing the loop.

13.6 Virtual LANs (VLANs)

pfSense supports 802.1Q Virtual LAN tagging. This VLAN tagging provides a way to separate traffic on a single connection into logical networks. (A VLAN is like a LAN within a LAN.) Each VLAN is identified with a tag number (also known as a *VID*) between 0 and 4095. Traffic going through the VLAN interface will be diverted to its associated physical (parent) interface with 802.1Q VLAN encapsulation, Traffic on the physical interface with a VLAN tag will be diverted to its VLAN pseudo-interface as identified with the same VLAN tag. A single physical interface can have multiple VLANs assigned to it — each with a different tag number.

While many network devices are capable of full VLAN processing, some may not and will use a reduced MTU which may break Path MTU Discovery. Older devices may silently drop tagged packets too.

The table of VLAN interfaces shows the physical interface (by FreeBSD device name and pfSense interface name in parentheses), its VLAN tag (identification number), a priority, and the optional description. Each VLAN interface listed also has corresponding action icons to edit or remove its configuration.

No VLANs are setup by default. Click the **Add** button to set it up. (For stacked VLANs aka QinQ, see Section 24.1.)

13.6.1 VLAN Configuration

Your network devices that are VLAN capable are listed in the **Parent Interface** drop-down menu with their FreeBSD device name, MAC address, and pfSense interface name (if assigned). Select the device you want to associate the VLAN to.

Enter a number within 1 and 4094 in the required **VLAN Tag** field that will be used to identify this pseudo-interface. This same number will also be used by other devices (such as a Cisco switch) on the same network to separate the traffic.

Set the priority number in the **VLAN Priority** field. Valid integers are 0 through 7. It defaults to 0 which is the best effort.

You may optionally describe this VLAN interface in the **Description** text field.

Clicking the **Save** button will activate these changes.

To use the VLAN, you need to assign the interface. At the **Interfaces** → **Assignments** page, select the new VLAN in the **Available network ports** drop-down menu. This entry should indicate the VLAN tag number and the device and interface it is associated with. Then click its **Add** button. This will create a numbered *OPT* interface. Click on that new interface to get to its general configuration where you should enable it via a checkbox. You may also give it a new identification name in the **Description** text field (such as "VLAN_*number*"). Then you can also configure it, such as with a static IPv4 address. (Be sure to click **Save** and then, when prompted, **Apply Changes** to activate it.)

Once the pfSense interface is setup, you will be able to see it under the **Firewall** → **Rules** page where you may create rules to limit or allow its usage. You may also need to create firewall rules for the VLAN's parent interface (like the LAN) to allow packets for the VLAN. In the **Source** and the **Destination** drop-down menus you may see the new VLAN interface named for the "net".

Also in the firewall rules, you can match on VLAN priorities and assign VLAN priorities.

13.7   Advanced Network Interfaces Options

The **System** → **Advanced** → **Networking** page contains various settings applicable for supported interfaces. For the advanced IPv6 options, see Section 14.7.

Some computational tasks can be handled by the network interface hardware instead of the host CPU. This is called *offloading*. By default, it will support checksum calculations for received and transmitted data on the interface hardware. This can be disabled by checking the **Disable hardware checksum offload** checkbox.

The **Disable hardware TCP segmentation offload** checkbox is checked by default. If you want TCP4 and TCP6 Segmentation offloading done on the Ethernet interface, uncheck it.

The **Disable hardware large receive offload** checkbox is also checked by default. If you want to support the Large Receive Offload capability, uncheck it.

By default, the FreeBSD kernel will log "moved from" when a host has an ARP reply from a different Ethernet address than cached and "got reply from" when it sees physical connections on multiple interfaces. If this is too noisy or fills your logs, such as for hosts with frequent address changes, frequent cable changes, or with many mobile hosts, check the **Suppress ARP messages** checkbox.

To automatically flush all the packet filter tracking states for the WAN interface when its IP address changes, check the **Reset all states if WAN IP Address changes** checkbox.

Use the **Save** button after changing any of these checkboxes. You may need to reboot or restart a network interface configuration to activate the offloading changes.

13.8 ARP Table

ARP, or the Address Resolution Protocol, is used to map between layer 3 IPv4 addresses and layer 2 Ethernet machine addresses. This translation table, available via **Diagnostics** → **ARP Table**, displays the pfSense interface label name, the IPv4 address, the unique physical address known as the MAC (media access control), and, if available, the hostname associated with the IP address. (By default, FreeBSD will cache external ARP entries for 20 minutes.)

ARP Table				
Interface	IP address	MAC address	Hostname	Actions
LAN	172.16.1.1	00:e0:18:79:29:39	pfSense.office	🗑
LAN	172.16.1.4	00:7f:28:35:b7:ad	Wireless_Broadband_Router	🗑
HOMEWIRELESS	172.20.0.1	a4:2b:b0:f9:dc:5f		🗑
WAN	47.185.12.1	78:19:f7:3f:af:c2		🗑
WAN	47.185.12.100	00:50:ba:b6:5a:3c		🗑

Figure 13.2: **Diagnostics** → **ARP Table** failure

The ARP table, as seen in Figure 13.2, also has an Actions column. You can click on the trash can icon to delete the corresponding ARP cache entry. It will popup a prompt to confirm to delete it. Note that it may allow you to attempt to delete an ARP entry for a local interface and say it was successful, but the permanent entry is still there (as expected).

For IPv6, see Section 14.8 about viewing the Neighbor Discovery Protocol (NDP) table.

13.9 Wake-on-LAN

The **Services** → **Wake-on-LAN** page may be used to remotely turn on or awake computers that support the Wake-on-Lan (WoL) *magic* packet technology. The remote system's network card and host system must be properly configured for its support. (Note, for example, that some Apple OS X systems will only wake up when in sleep mode.) It is targetted by its MAC address so it must be local to one of the pfSense system's network interfaces.

To send a magic packet, select the network interface the target system is connected to (such as WAN or LAN) in the **Interface** drop-down menu, enter its MAC address, and click the **Send** button. The magic packet will be broadcast on the subnet for the interface. Note that the SecureON password feature is not available.

If you want pfSense to keep track of local systems for your convenience of waking up later, click the **Add** button. This will take you to a new page to enter the details. When you have target systems defined, the **Wake-on-Lan Devices** table will list each with the interface it is connected to, its MAC address, optional description, and action buttons. Click the **Edit Device** pencil icon to update its configuration. Use the **Delete Device** trash can icon to remove a corresponding WoL entry.

To send the magic packet to a specific device, click its corresponding **Wake Device** power button icon. To attempt to wake up all the pre-recorded entries, press the **Wake All Devices** button.

13.9.1   Add or Edit WoL Entry

Using the **Add** button or an individual entry's pencil icon action, you can create or modify a Wake-on-Lan entry. In the **Interface** drop-down menu select the network interface (such as WAN or LAN) that the target is connected to. Enter its hardware address (not IP address) in the **Mac address** field. You can provide a brief explanation in the optional **Description** field. Click the **Save** button to record these settings.

Note that adding or changing an entry here doesn't trigger sending the packet. To actually do so, use the main **Services** → **Wake-on-LAN** page and use the corresponding entry's power button action icon.

If you are providing DHCP service, the **Status** → **DHCP Leases** page may offer these Wake-on-LAN features. In the leases table, use the **Add WOL mapping** plus icon in the actions column. This will add that interface and MAC address to your Wake-on-LAN list. It will use the hostname for the WoL description. You can also send the magic packet to offline DHCP lease entries by clicking the **Send WOL packet** power button icon. (To see the offline leases, click the **Show all configured leases** button.)

The **Status** → **DHCPv6 Leases** page also may provide an action button to add an entry to your Wake-on-LAN list.

If you are using pfSense configuration synchronization (as covered in Chapter 36) and want your Wake-on-LAN configurations sent to your other pfSense server, be sure to check the **WoL Server settings** checkbox on the **System** → **High Availability Sync** page.

13.9.2   Wake-on-LAN Dashboard Widget

The main pfSense dashboard provides a WoL widget. To enable it, on the dashboard, click the **Available widgets** plus button and then click **Wake-on-LAN** in the list.

The new widget will show the entries from your previously-defined list with a corresponding **Wake up!** power button to send the magic packet. The table will also show a green up arrow or red down arrow to indicate that target device's current status.

If you have a lot of entries in your WoL list and don't want your dashboard to display them all, use the widget's wrench icon button to open up the widget's configuration to define which entries to display. For more details on widget configuration, see Section 4.3.2.

13.10   IGMP Proxy

Multicasting is the transmission of packets from a single source to multiple destinations using a single address. This multi-destination delivery could be used for group gaming and live content streaming, for example. The Internet Group Management Protocol (IGMP) is used for hosts to request a membership to a multicast group. pfSense provides a simple IGMP proxy daemon, known as *igmpproxy*, that acts as a multicast client and dynamically forwards multicast traffic to other clients.

Access to view its settings or to enable IGMP forwarding is available via the **Services → IGMP proxy** page. By default, no IGMP proxying is setup. When entries are configured. a table will show the following details: the interface the proxying is on; whether it is an *upstream* interface for outgoing traffic for communicating to multicast sources or a *downstream* interface for distribution and where clients can join and receive multicast data from; optional alternate remote source networks; and an optional description for an entry.

The entries will also have corresponding actions to modify or remove it. Click the **Edit IGMP entry** pencil icon to got to the page to make changes. Use the **Delete IGMP entry** trash can icon to remove it.

To add a configuration, click the **Add** button. This will take you to a new page discussed in a following section. Note that a single IGMP Proxy configuration requires multiple entries that are added separate times. You need at least one upstream interface and one or more downstream interfaces.

After editing, removing, or adding an entry, you may need to activate changes (which may start or stop the IGMP Proxy daemon) by clicking the **Apply Changes** button.

Note that the IGMP Proxy daemon is configured to quickly send upstream a *Leave IGMP* message if it receives that message from any downstream. It also doesn't do any rate limiting.

The *igmpproxy* daemon can be restarted and stopped (or started) via the **Status → Services** page. (For details on using this generic feature, see Section 7.7.) It doesn't have an option to disable it. To turn it off permanently, you need to remove all of its configurations.

13.10.1   IGMP Proxy Logging

The IGMP Proxy logging can be viewed via the **Status → System Logs** menu item for its default **System → General** log entries page. You may use the **Log filter** funnel shortcut to enter "**igmp**" in the **Process** field and press the **Apply Filter** button to see recent matching log entries. (For details about logging, see Chapter 11.)

By default, only warning or more severe messages are logged for this service. To get more verbose informational and notice messages also, check the **IGMP Proxy** checkbox on the **Status → System Logs → Settings** page (see Section 11.2). And then save the new setting. You will then need to restart the *igmpproxy* daemon via the **Status → Services** page. A verbose logging example is seen at Figure 13.3.

Mar 28 08:21:43	igmpproxy	60202	select() failure; Errno(4): Interrupted system call
Mar 28 08:21:43	igmpproxy	60202	Got a interupt signal. Exiting.
Mar 28 08:21:43	igmpproxy	60202	All routes removed. Routing table is empty.
Mar 28 08:21:43	igmpproxy	16340	adding VIF, Ix 0 Fl 0x0 IP 0x962ab92f rl0, Threshold: 1, Ratelimit: 0
Mar 28 08:21:43	igmpproxy	16340	adding VIF, Ix 1 Fl 0x0 IP 0x010110ac rl1, Threshold: 15, Ratelimit: 0
Mar 28 08:21:43	igmpproxy	16340	joinMcGroup: 224.0.0.2 on rl1
Mar 28 08:21:43	igmpproxy	16340	RECV Membership query from 172.16.1.1 to 224.0.0.1

Figure 13.3: IGMP Proxy restart verbose logging

Note that a log message for it showing "select() failure; Errno(4): Interrupted system call" may just indicate that pfSense stopped the daemon when restarting it. Generally this may be ignored if this happened from you manually restarting or stopping the service or if you applied changes to its configuration.

13.10.2 Add or Edit an IGMP Proxy

The IGMP forwarding configurations are added or edited separately in pfSense for each interface. Use the **Services** → **IGMP proxy** page and click its **Add** button or pencil icon action to edit an existing interface configuration.

Select the network interface to use in the **Interface** drop-down menu. This defaults to the WAN. If this is for the upstream, then this is the outgoing interface for communicating to multicast data sources. If this is a downstream, this is a distribution interface for joining groups and receiving multicast data on the destination networks. You should use a different interface for each configuration.

Note
Your local subnet should not be the same as the multicast source.

Enter an optional explanation for this configuration in the **Description** text field.

Select the role of this network interface configuration in the **Type** field. This defaults to the **Upstream Interface**. The other option is the **Downstream Interface**. You may have multiple downstreams but only one upstream.

By default, IP multicast packets with a Time To Live (TTL) lower than one second are ignored. You can raise this in the optional **Threshold** seconds input field. It accepts a valid integer between 1 and 255.

The IGMP Proxy will accept multicasting and IGMP data from the network for the defined interface. Alternate sources, such as a remote source for the upstream, may be defined by entering one or more network addresses. Enter the network and CIDR in the **Networks** fields. You may add more fields for more sources by clicking the **Add network**. If you don't know your ISP's multicast sources, try enabling the verbose logging as described previously and look for messages for "RECV Membership query" and "member report" for the "from" address. You can use those to help figure out the source networks.

You may remove a source by clicking its corresponding **Delete** button. (Or set the network address field to empty.)

Click the **Save** button when complete. Back at the table view of network interface configurations for the IGMP Proxy, click the **Apply Changes** to start the daemon with the new settings.

Note

The pfSense configuration for the IGMP Proxy is problematic, so consider checking the logs (see Section 13.10.1) and the **Status** → **Services** page (Section 7.7) to make sure the `igmpproxy` daemon is running.

You may also need to configure your packet filter to allow the 224.0.0.0/4 IPv4 multicast range. (Setting up rules is covered in Chapter 16.)

14 IPv6 Networking

IPv6, or Internet Protocol version 6, is not a new protocol and has been included in FreeBSD since 2000, but wasn't fully supported in pfSense until 2013 in pfSense version 2.1.

This chapter covers the general and advanced IPv6 network interface configurations. Throughout this book, you will see many features, diagnostics, status reports, and network services offer IPv6 details or support.

A network interface's configuration is accessed by clicking the interface name in the **Interfaces** menu link, via the **Interfaces** → **Interface Assignments** page, or by clicking its name within the dashboard's Interfaces widget. Most of its common settings are discussed in the previous chapter. If you need to add the interface first, see Section 13.1.

First make sure the interface is enabled using the checkbox. Then you can enable how the interface is configured for IPv6. The **IPv6 Configuration Type** drop-down menu choices in the interface's general configuration are:

- *Static IPv6* — manually assign an address;

- *DHCP6* — get an address and other parameters via DHCPv6;

- *SLAAC* — use stateless autoconfiguration to generate an address using Router Advertisements;

- *6rd Tunnel* — use IPv6 over IPv4 tunnel using an ISP's shared IPv6 prefix;

- *6to4 Tunnel* — enable a border router to tunnel IPv6 2002::/16 over an IPv4 tunnel;

- *Track Interface* — track IPv6 configurations from another network interface; and

- *None* — for no IPv6 usage.

(If using a bridged configuration, as covered in Section 13.5, keep this as *None*.)

When the IPv6 type is selected, the upcoming configurations change or appear for that selection.

When ready, use the **Save** button at the bottom and then the **Apply Changes** button to assign the interface with an IPv6 address or otherwise activate IPv6 networking parameters. (Note this will restart the IPv4 settings for the same interface too.)

Then you can visit the **Status** → **Interfaces** page to see some of the IPv6 details (Section 13.3). If you encounter problems, consult the logging via the **Status** → **System Logs** → **System** → **General** page (Section 11.4) or other logs linked from there.

Note that you may need to adjust your firewall rules as needed for IPv6 needs. The basic enabling of this is by making sure the **Allow IPv6** checkbox on the **System** → **Advanced** → **Networking** page is checked (Section 14.7).

14.1   Static IPv6

Choosing *Static IPv6* for the **IPv6 Configuration Type** will bring up a few fields to manually assign your interface with one or more IPv6 addresses. IPv6 interfaces are identified with 128-bit addresses (79 octillion times larger space than IPv4). With so many possible unique node addresses, workarounds for address shortage are not needed.

Private IPv6 address ranges — or Unique Local IPv6 Unicast Addresses — are within fd00::/8 which provides seventy-two quadrillion addresses. This unique range should not be routed outside of your organization.

Enter the address in the **IPv6 address** field. Then select its prefix length (or subnet) in the corresponding drop-down field which defaults to 128 bits for only one address. The smallest recommended subnet is /64 (which is 18 quintillion addresses). Note you may not enter an IPv6 link local address within the fe80::/10 address space. (These are automatically configured for use on a single system.) It also cannot conflict with an existing static route nor be in use by another interface.

If your IPv6 setup needs to use an IPv4 connection (like PPPoE), check the **Use IPv4 connectivity as parent interface** checkbox.

If this is for your Internet connection, select the IPv6 gateway in the **IPv6 Upstream gateway** drop-down menu. It defaults to *None* which should be used for your local networks (LANs). If needed, click the **Add a new gateway** button to add an IPv6 gateway to this list. This will pop-up a window to add it. (Or you may add it via the **System** → **Routing** → **Gateways** page as covered in Section 15.1.2.)

14.1.1   New IPv6 Gateway

If this is the main fallback router for your Internet connections, click the **Default gateway** checkbox.

You may enter an identity for this gateway's configuration in the **Gateway name** text field. It defaults to the interface name with "GWv6" appended.

Enter the router's IPv6 address in the **Gateway IPv6** field.

For the pfSense admin's records, you may explain about this gateway in the **Description** text field.

Click the **Add** button to return to the Static IPv6 Configuration form with this new gateway selected in the **IPv6 Upstream gateway** option. (Or click **Cancel** to not add it.)

The new gateway won't be added until you actually save the new static IPv6 configuration. You can later view it or edit it via the **System** → **Routing** → **Gateways** page.

14.2   DHCPv6 Client

The client configuration for Dynamic Host Configuration Protocol version 6 for IPv6 (DHCPv6) appears when the **IPv6 Configuration Type** option is set to DHCP6. In its common use, the remote DHCPv6 server provides IPv6 addressing details to the client when requested. (If you don't need this tracked as a lease, you could use stateless DHCPv6 covered in the following SLAAC section.)

The client will also request the Domain Name Server addresses and a DNS search path to use, by default. If you need your own DHCPv6 options, use the following **Advanced Configuration** or **Configuration Override** features.

Note that you cannot use this DHCPv6 client if you are also running a DHCPv6 server on the same interface. To run a local server (see Section 20.2), it must be on an interface with a static IPv6 configuration as explained in the previous section.

Clicking the **Advanced Configuration** or **Configuration Override** checkbox will bring up additional options as explained in the following sections. These two features may not be used at the same time.

The **Use IPv4 connectivity as parent interface** checkbox implies it won't accept ICMPv6 Router Advertisement messages nor use DHCPv6 for the interface. It will attempt to use the IPv4 connection to get the IPv6 prefix details.

When the **Request only an IPv6 prefix** checkbox is unchecked, it will tell the server it wants to use non-temporary address allocation for stateful address assignment. Check it to not request an IPv6 address, but to request an IPv6 prefix instead.

Use the **DHCPv6 Prefix Delegation size** form to have the client initiate prefix delegation. The choices are *None* to not use prefix delegation or 48, 52, 56, 59, 60, 61, 62, 63, and 64 for the prefix your client wants to be delegated. (It defaults to 64.) This prefix will only be requested if the **Send IPv6 prefix hint** checkbox is checked. Note that the server may choose to ignore this.

By default, the DHCPv6 client logs debugging messages. This logging is identified with "dhcp6c." For even more debugging details, click the **Debug** checkbox. See Section 20.6 for details about viewing DHCPv6 related logs.

To get configured without using Router Advertisements, use the **Do not wait for a RA** checkbox. Some network service providers may need this. (This implies that the `rtsold` router solicitation daemon is not used. Normally it will transmit one Router Solicitation packet to get a Router Advertisement.)

To stop the remote DHCPv6 server from managing a new address if the DHCPv6 client is restarted, use the **Do not allow PD/Address release** checkbox. This means it won't ask for a release when the client stops.

You can use 802.1Q VLAN queueing priority (such as *Best Effort*) in the firewall for the DHCPv6 traffic by checking the **Enable dhcp6c VLAN Priority tagging** checkbox. It defaults to the lowest priority (*Background*); this may be changed in the **VLAN Prio** drop-down menu. This is further explained in Section 16.2.2 for the firewall rules' Advanced Options.

14.2.1   DHCPv6 Client Configuration File

When the **Configuration Override** checkbox is selected, some options disappear and a field to enter the filename for your own custom DHCPv6 client configuration file appears. Enter the complete filename in the **Configuration File Override** field.

As explained in Section 13.2.3, the configuration file may use some macros to substitute values for the DHCPv6 client settings.

The file can be uploaded using the `scp` command or via the web interface with the **Diagnostics** → **Edit File** (Section 7.2) or **Diagnostics** → **Command Prompt** (Section 7.1) features.

The DHCPv6 client implementation included with pfSense is the FreeBSD version originally from the WIDE (Widely Integrated Distributed Environment) KAME project. This book doesn't cover its many configuration statements. For details, consult the `dhcp6c.conf` (section 5) manual at `http://man.freebsd.org/`.

14.2.2   Advanced DHCP6 Client Configuration

Check the **Advanced Configuration** checkbox to see the additional DHCPv6 client options.

To not receive an IPv6 address or other stateful configurations, check the **Information only** checkbox. It may still receive DNS server addresses and other information.

To send your own DHCPv6 options to the remote server, enter them in the **Send options** text field. Each option and its optional value should be separated by commas. You may also use substitution macros here as explained in Section 13.2.3.

If the client wants the server to send *top-level* options to it, list them in the **Request Options** text field. This is also comma-delimited and you may use the substitution macros.

The DHCPv6 client runs a shell script that is ran every time an address or prefix is acquired or other messages are received. This script helps change the network interfaces and local DNS resolution and other settings based on details received from the DHCPv6 server. To use your own custom script that handles messages (like INFOREQ, REQUEST, RENEW, REBIND, RELEASE, and EXIT), enter its full filename in the **Scripts** field. The script may be uploaded using the `scp` command or via the **Diagnostics** → **Command Prompt** page (Section 7.1) or **Diagnostics** → **Edit File** page (Section 7.2). This book does not cover this programming. For details, see the `dhcp6c` (section 8) manual at `http://man.freebsd.org/`.

The client and server uses unique identifiers to know what parameters to be used. This is known as *Identity Association*. The advanced options allows setting custom values for the **Non-Temporary Address Allocation** and **Prefix Delegation** by checking the corresponding checkbox and entering the values:

ID

> This is the decimal number for the Identity Association type and identifier. It is usually 0 (zero) by default.

IPv6 address or prefix

> To specify the IPv6 address the client wants to be allocated or the prefix that it wants to be delegated.

pltime

> The preferred lifetime in seconds of the address or prefix. The word "infinity" may be used to never expire.

vltime

> The valid lifetime in seconds of the address or prefix. The word "infinity" may also be used to not expire. Note that this valid lifetime cannot be shorter than the preferred lifetime. If this valid lifetime is not set, it will use the preferred lifetime's value (**pltime**).

When using prefix delegation, your client may be configured with a site-level aggregator (SLA) identifier value. This may be entered in the **Prefix Interface sla-id** field. This is combined with the prefix delegated to the client to be configured for the network interface.

The **sla-len** field is for the length of the previous ID in bits (i.e. the network mask0. Valid numbers are within 0 and 128. It defaults to 16 if not set. This is also combined with the delegated prefix.

For example, if the custom **sla-id** is set to 1 and the **sla-len** is set to 16 and the delegated prefix is 2001:db8:ffff::/48, the interface will be configured with the combined values as 2001:db8:ffff:1::/64.

Use the **Prefix Interface** form to choose the interface for this prefix delegation. Note that it may default to the WAN, even if you are configuring networking for a different interface.

The **Authentication statement** fields are used to confirm that DHCPv6 messages are not modified and that the source is identified. Most DHCPv6 server implementations do not support this feature. To use authentication, enter both a unique identification string in the **Authname** field and "delayed" (in lowercase) in the **Protocol** field,

pfSense's client only supports the DHCPv6 Delayed Authentication Protocol. It also only supports HMAC generation algorithm with the MD5 hash, so enter "HMAC-MD5" for the **Algorithm** or leave it blank. The **RDM** field is for the replay detection method. It uses a monotonically increasing counter to help with replay attacks (to prevent reuse of a previously valid message). This is the default method and "monocounter" is the only one supported.

The **Keyinfo statement** fields are used to define a secret key shared with the server for authentication. These are used to generate the message authentication code. Enter some arbitrary string in the **Keyname** field to be used in logging only. The **Realm** is the identifier for the key. It is commonly a domain name. The **KeyID** is a decimal number which is used with the realm name to identify the secret key. Then enter the base-64 encoded shared sting in the **Secret** field. These previous four fields are required to configure the *keyinfo*. Talk to your DHCPv6 server administrator to receive these key details.

The *keyinfo* **Expire** field is used to define the key's end of life (when it can no longer be used). By default, the key never expires or you may enter the word "forever" for that. To set a time enter it like *HH:MM* for 24-hour clock and minute, *mm-dd HH:MM* to also include the month and day, or *yyyy-mm-dd HH:MM* to include the year.

DHCPv6 uses a unique client identifier (DUID) for the server to recognize and remember it to reproducibly return parameters. It will generate a time-based identifier (DUID-LLT), but pfSense will not store it in its configuration. If you have the DUID to use, it is recommended to save it via the **System** → **Advanced** → **Networking** subpage (Section 14.7).

An alternative way to automatically configure the IPv6 interface is covered in the following section.

14.3   SLAAC Stateless Configuration

SLAAC, or Stateless Auto Address Configuration, is a simple way to assign an IPv6 address. It listens to ICMPv6 Router Advertisements (RA) from routers on the local link. Using the Link Prefix from the RA combined with the unique interface identifier (EUI) derived from the interface's MAC address, it creates an IPv6 address.

In addition to SLAAC, this option also uses the DHCPv6 client to request the DNS servers and default DNS domain name to use. Known as stateless DHCPv6, it does not request nor get the IPv6 addressing details from the DHCPv6 server (which doesn't keep track of a lease for this client).

Choosing *SLAAC* does not bring up a new configuration section.

Note that the ICMPv6 router solicitation daemon will only send one probe to the interface. If it doesn't see the router advertisement before it exists, it won't get configured.

You can learn more about DHCPv6 and Router Advertisements in Chapter 20.

14.4   6rd Rapid Deployment Tunnel

Some ISPs offer IPv6 support via an IPv4 tunnel using IPv6 Rapid Deployment (6RD) as defined in RFC 5569. Compared to the following 6to4 tunneling, 6RD uses the ISP's own IPv6 prefixes to improve routing.

The ISP provides an IPv6 prefix with is derived from the ISP's prefix and an assigned IPv4 address. Enter this ISP-provided 6RD-delegated prefix in the **6RD Prefix** field. This must be a valid IPv6 address with slash (/) prefix.

Outbound IPv6 traffic seen by the pfSense system which is not within the locally-configured 6RD prefix is tunneled to the ISP's Border Relay router using IPv4. Enter that router's IPv4 address (as provided by the ISP) in the **6RD Border relay** field.

6RD uses IPv6 address space to map IPv4 address space. A mask length may be entered into the **6RD IPv4 Prefix length** number input box to specify how many bits are common for this mapping. It defaults to zero which implies that all 32 bits of IPv4 address space is used.

14.5   6to4 Tunnel

6to4 (also known as *stf*) is the transitional protocol for providing IPv6 support by tunneling IPv6 traffic over IPv4. Selecting the *6to4 Tunnel* IPv6 configuration type will enable your system to be a 6to4 border router. It does not have an additional configuration section. Note that only one interface can be setup with 6to4.

This requires that a public IPv4 statically-defined address to be previously configured that is not in the private address ranges (so not in 10.0.0.0/8, 100.64.0.0/10, 172.16.0.0/12, nor 192.168.0.0/16). An IPv6 address will be generated in the 2002::/16 network (unlike 6RD) that has the static IPv4 address embedded in it.

6to4 is not very dependable and is not recommended. Talk to your ISP to get native IPv6 instead.

14.6   Track IPv6

The *Track Interface* feature will allow this interface to use IPv6 configurations from another dynamically-assigned IPv6 interface, such as with 6to4, 6RD, or DHCPv6. For example, this may be used so the LAN interface and even its LAN clients can use the same IPv6 subnet as the WAN which is configured via DHCPv6.

Select the other interface that has a dynamic IPv6 setup, in the **IPv6 Interface** menu. This may be empty if you don't have another interface with an IPv6 6to4, 6RD, or DHCPv6 client configuration.

Tracked networks each use a /64 subnet. If you have multiple interfaces using the same tracked network, you can split it up in multiple /64 subnets by entering a hexadecimal number in the **IPv6 Prefix ID** field. Normally, you'd leave this at the default 0 (zero), but if you only have one LAN, any number between 00 and FF may be used. For a second tracked LAN, enter "1" or enter the unique number (in hexadecimal) for which subnet you want to use.

Note if your ISP doesn't delegate larger than /64 for you, you may be able to request a larger network in the other interface's DHCPv6 client configuration by selecting a smaller number (like /60 or /56) in the **DHCPv6 Prefix Delegation size** field and checking its corresponding **Send IPv6 prefix hint** checkbox. (See the earlier Section 14.2 for further details.)

14.7   Advanced IPv6 Networking Options

The IPv6 options are accessed via the **System** → **Advanced** → **Networking** page.

The **Allow IPv6** checkbox is used to enable various IPv6 behaviors in pfSense:

- ICMP for IPv6 for neighbor solicitation and advertisement is allowed through the firewall.

- ICMPv6 router solicitation and advertisement, echo service requests and replies (pings), and essential ICMP for IPv6 packets are allowed for link-local, including for IPv6 multicast routing, addresses.

- TCP and UDP port 0 is blocked.

- DHCPv6 traffic is allowed in and out.

- Block IPv6 bogons with an IPv6 bogons table when blocking bogons is also enabled (see Section 13.2.7).

- Outbound IPv6 traffic is allowed.

- NTP status includes IPv6 details.

- Dynamic IPv6 gateways are also setup.

- The DNS resolver (`unbound`) when setup will answer and send DNS queries via IPv6.

When unchecked, the packet filter rules block all IPv6 traffic except on the loopback interface.

When the **Enable IPv6 over IPv4 Tunneling** checkbox is checked, address translation is setup in the firewall for all IPv6 traffic on the WAN interface is redirected to the IPv4 address defined in the **IPv4 address of Tunnel Peer** field.

Dual stack setups need to choose between IPv6 and IPv4 for initiating communication. The FreeBSD kernel uses a policy table, like a routing table, that gives IPv6 addresses a higher precedence over IPv4. Check the **Prefer IPv4 over IPv6** checkbox to change the policy table to give IPv4 addresses a higher precedence instead.

By default, `/etc/hosts` entries for the local hostname lookup database are added for the IPv6 interfaces. If you have IPv4 interfaces, you may have entries for the same hostname for both IPv4 and IPv6 addresses. To not add the entries for IPv6, click the **Do not generate local IPv6 DNS entries for LAN interfaces** checkbox.

A DHCPv6 server uses DHCP Unique Identifiers (DUID) which identify clients to select configuration parameters. It should be globally unique and persistent across system reconfigurations, upgrades, and reboots. The permanent unique identifier for a DHCPv6 client may be defined multiple ways. The **DHCP6 DUID** drop-down menu is used to select from the following types: *Raw DUID: As stored in DUID file or seen in firewall logs, DUID-LLT: Based on Link-layer Address Plus Time, DUID-EN: Assigned by Vendor based on Enterprise Number, DUID-LL: Based on Link-layer Address*, and *DUID-UUID: Based on Universally Unique Identifier* Depending on this selection, you will have other fields to input below it.

When *Raw DUID* is selected, you will have a **DHCP6 DUID** text input box to enter your own unique identifier. It must be a valid DUID format, including the two-byte DUID type and the rest of the unique data, with hexadecimal values with valid lengths. The different types have different lengths. If your system already ran the DHCPv6 client, it will already have generated a DUID (using the DUID-LLT type). This will be shown as the placeholder and you may click the **Copy DUID** button to use it. (Or it may have a different type, based on the latest usage.)

When DUID-LLT is selected, the number of seconds since midnight (UTC) January 1, 2000 is in the first **DUID-LLT** field. If needed, you could adjust this, but it should be a valid time so there won't be collisions of two identical DUIDs. Enter the **Link-layer address** in the next field. The specific interface doesn't matter as all IPv6 interfaces will use the same DUID for DHCPv6. These details plus the hardware type (Ethernet) will be used to generate the DUID.

If DUID-EN is selected, select the device vendor's IANA registered Private Enterprise Number in the **DUID-EN** number field and enter the vendor-assigned unique identifier in the **Identifier** text box. The enterprise number is a positive 32-bit integer. (At the time of this writing, the largest assigned number is 53701.) The identifier must be unique to the specific device. It is eight hexadecimal values delimited by colons.

When DUID-LL is selected, you may enter the link-layer address as colon-delimited hexadecimals in the **DUID-LL** field. This is commonly used for a permanent network interface that is unlikely to ever be used elsewhere. This is combined with the hardware type to create the DUID. It is also used for all network interfaces connected to the device. (Note the implementation of pfSense at the time of this book's writing restricts this to six hexadecimal bytes even though DUID-LL specification allows it to be variable length.)

And finally, when DUID-UUID is selected, you may enter the Universally Unique Identifier in the **DUID-UUID** field. Also known as GUIDs (Globally Unique IDentifier), it is 16 hexadecimal bytes long.

Click the **Save** button at the bottom of the page to store the IPv6 advanced options. Section 13.7 tells you about the other advanced settings for the interfaces which aren't specific to IPv6.

14.8   NDP Table

Similar to the ARP table, the NDP (IPv6 Neighbor Discovery Protocol) table displays the mapping of neighboring IPv6 addresses with their MAC addresses (also known as linklayer addresses). It also lists the network interfaces associated with the entries, and, if available, the resolved hostnames. These NDP entries are shown using the **Diagnostics → NDP Table** menu option. See Figure 14.1 for an example.

NDP Table

IPv6 address	MAC address	Hostname	Interface	Expiration	Actions
2001:470:1f15:121:232:12ff:fe56:b34d	0:23:21:56:b3:4d		OPT4	20h24m25s	🗑
2001:db8::10:3	21:12:43:34:65:56		OPT3	permanent	🗑
2001:db8::abcd:feff:fe:ba:dcfe	ba:dc:fe:ba:dc:ef		OPT3	21h32m14s	🗑
2001:db8:1f0f:2ce:3157:9b8f:c464:d676	ac:72:98:ec:3b:1e		WIFI	6h0m39s	🗑
2001:db8:1f0f:2ce::1	00:22:b0:ec:f1:dc		WIFI	permanent	🗑
2002:81c7:d236::	0:3:d6:1a:b1:9b		OPT5	permanent	🗑
2002:81c7:d236::1	(incomplete)		OPT6	permanent	🗑
2002:81c7:d236:0:203:6dff:fe1a:b19b	0:3:d6:1a:b1:9b		OPT5	permanent	🗑
2002:81c7:d236:1::	0:14:58:85:27:b3		OPT7	permanent	🗑
2002:81c7:d236:1:214:85ff:fe85:27b3	0:14:58:85:27:b3		OPT7	permanent	🗑
fe80::a7e2:89ff:feec:3b1e%ath0_wlan0	ac:72:98:ec:3b:1e		WIFI	4h8m25s	🗑
fe80::222:bf0f:fece:f1dc%ath0_wlan0	00:22:0b:ce:f1:dc		WIFI	permanent	🗑
fe80::f6f2:d6ff:fe00:b757%re1	4f:f2:6d:00:b7:57		LAN	permanent	🗑
fe80::baca:f6ff:fedf:499d%re0	8b:ac:6f:df:49:9d		WAN	permanent	🗑

Figure 14.1: **Diagnostics → NDP**

The rows have a corresponding trash can icon action which may be used to delete the NDP entry from the address mapping table.

For IPv4 addresses' Address Resolution Protocol table, use the **Diagnostics → ARP Table** page as discussed in Section 13.8.

15   Routing and Gateways

Manually setting up networking routing tables and optional gateways is done via the **System** →
Routing page. It defaults to the **Gateways** view with additional links to the **Static Routes** and
Gateway Groups pages.

A gateway is a next-hop intermediary router in which your pfSense system's outbound packets could
be routed. But in pfSense terminology, a *gateway* is a configuration to represent one of these routers
that is not necessarily ever used unless other configurations are put in place to use it. These configurations can be used as a fallback option if the default gateway is down, for configuring static routes,
and implementing policy-routing with firewall rules.

The configured entries are usually frequently checked to make sure they are usable. This monitoring
is done by one or more `dpinger` processes that continuously watch these possible network gateway
connections. It logs about latency and loss and can trigger alarms based on the network health.
These monitoring details can be seen via the **Status** → **Gateways** and **Status** → **System Logs** →
System → **Gateways** pages (both described in upcoming sections) and via **Status** → **Monitoring**
(Section 28.2).

In addition, a set of multiple gateways may be used in a *Gateway Group*. This may be used for
round-robin load balancing of specified outgoing traffic over the multiple gateways in the group. This
is a multi-WAN setup to use multiple ISP connections to possibly lower costs and bandwidth (per
gateway) and improve reliability. (This is also called *multihoming* for the external interfaces.) This is
configured using firewall packet filter rules by selecting a group in the **Gateways** drop-down menu in
a rule's **Advanced Options**. (Further details are in this chapter.)

If your gateway changes, the IP to reference your system may change. To automate some uses of
this, a group may be used with other features in pfSense. It may be used for IPsec Phase 1 local
endpoint configurations with the **Interface** drop-down menu covered in Section 30.7. It may be
used for OpenVPN server or client endpoints as configured with the **Interface** menus as explained in
Section 33.1.1 and Section 33.2. A gateway group may also be used to define the IP address to be
used for the **Services** → **Dynamic DNS** features using a web-based service (Section 22.1) or RFC
2136 DNS UPDATE (Section 22.2).

Static routes are used to configure alternate ways to reach remote hosts or networks. When your
system doesn't have any route defined to find a remote host, it falls back to use its *default* gateway
entry as the last routing option. In any normal setup, your system routing table would always have
your default gateway entry after pfSense is installed. This default is generally a router located with
your ISP. (Note if you are using pfSense as a default gateway for other system, it is still not its own
gateway.)

While you may have multiple gateways configured with pfSense, only one is actually in use by the routing table at a time. (This is separate than the multi-WAN setup using packet filter policy routing with the gateway groups.) pfSense can monitor your gateways and it can be configured so an additional gateway may be put into use as a fallback when the first gateway is down (by changing the routing table entry).

Systems prior to pfSense 2.4.4 have a **Enable default gateway switching** feature on the **System** → **Advanced** → **Miscellaneous** subpage in the load balancing section. This checkbox was used for changing the IPv4 and IPv6 routes for the default gateway if the default gateway goes down. Normally, gateway groups are recommended and this option was unnecessary. It was disabled by default.

The **Diagnostics** → **Routes** page (Section 15.4) may be used to view your system's current routing table.

15.1 Gateways

The **System** → **Routing** → **Gateways** page is used to setup or change your additional gateways as used by the various features introduced previously. It has a Gateway's table which should list at least your *default* entry.

The table columns list the name used in pfSense for referencing this gateway configuration, its default tier (priority) name, what interface it is connected to, the IP address of this next-hop router, an IP address used to monitor it, and an optional description. The beginning of the column will also indicate if the gateway is active, inactive, or disabled with an icon. Active doesn't imply that it is used by the system's routing table, but that it is able to be used in the configuration because the interface exists. (If the interface in its configuration doesn't exist, it will be marked as inactive.)

Actions for the entries are also available to modify and duplicate the setting. Click the **Edit gateway** pencil icon or **Copy gateway** clone icon to modify it or to make a new configuration based on it. If it is a custom gateway (and not your *default* router), then you will also have action icons to disable (or enable) the entry or to remove it. When clicking the trash can icon to delete the corresponding entry, it will prompt you to confirm that.

Note that the **Delete gateway** trash can icon will not be available for your default gateway as pfSense expects it has at least one smart router to handle your traffic.

If you have custom gateways, you can also re-order the gateway entries by selecting one or more gateways in the first column checkboxes and then clicking the anchor icon to move them to there. This ordering is useful for an automatic selection of the default gateway. If making changes, click the **Save** button below the table. (This feature to order entries was introduced in pfSense 2.4.4.)

To add another gateway configuration, click the **Add** button.

The shortcuts at the top are available to restart or stop the routing service (or start the service if it is down). The **Related status** shortcut will take you to the **Status** → **Gateways** page covered in Section 15.1.3. The **Related log entries** shortcut leads to the logging for the gateway monitoring, as discussed in Section 15.1.4.

15.1.1 Default Gateways

Below the list of the gateways, you can define your default gateway for IPv4 and IPv6. These may be set to *Automatic* by default which means it will use the first gateway detected as available or the first one that is unmonitored. To manually choose a gateway versus the automatic selection use the drop-down lists. The choices will include previously-created gateways or gateway groups (as covered in the following sections).

This feature was introduced in pfSense version 2.4.4. Prior to this, it could be defined via the **Default Gateway** checkbox when adding or setting up a gateway (Section 15.1.2). A default gateway can also be defined for static IPv4 or IPv6 configurations when setting up an interface as covered in Section 13.2.2 or Section 14.1.1, respectively.

15.1.2 Add or Edit a Gateway

The **Edit Gateway** form has several input fields. Only a name for the gateway is required. The form is accessed by selecting the edit (pencil icon) or copy (clone icon) action for an entry on the **System → Routing → Gateways** table. Or by clicking the **Add** button there.

To keep this configuration but to not actual use it, select the **Disable this gateway** checkbox.

In the **Interface** drop-down menu, select the interface (like the LAN) that this gateway will be used on. This defaults to the WAN.

Choose IPv4 (the default) or IPv6 in the **Address Family** drop-down menu.

Enter an identifier in the required **Name** field. This name must contain a letter, but also may include digits and underscores. The maximum length is 31 characters. (The name may be used in the PF filter rules.) This identifier can be seen in the gateways' logging, status, or setup pages.

Enter the router's IP address in the **Gateway** field. Normally this address is within the subnet for its interface (but see the upcoming **Use non-local gateway** checkbox option). If this is an automatically-assigned (dynamic) gateway, this field will be disabled.

pfSense versions prior to 2.4.4 had a **Default Gateway** checkbox to set if this gateway assignment is the default or fallback router. This implies that outbound traffic on this interface that doesn't match a different route will use this gateway. Since version 2.4.4, selecting the default gateway is done via the form on the main **System → Routing → Gateways** page (Section 15.1.1).

The gateway is periodically checked if it is up (as discussed in upcoming sections). Click the **Disable Gateway Monitoring** checkbox to not monitor it. (When this is checked, the following **Monitor IP** field is not available.)

When the monitoring detects that a gateway is lost or is available again, it will reload any dynamic DNS and OpenVPN settings for the gateway, reload any IPsec DNS settings, and regenerate and reload all the firewall rules. Check the **Disable Gateway Monitoring Action** checkbox if you don't want these settings to be restarted.

If ICMP ECHO (ping) requests and replies don't work for monitoring this gateway, then you can enter an alternate IP address to monitor instead in the **Monitor IP** field.

Firewall rules can use policy routing to route packets to specified interfaces and gateway address (instead of possibly any matching route). This is done via the Firewall's **Advanced Options** using the **Gateways** drop-down menu (Section 16.2.2). Selecting the **Mark Gateway as Down** checkbox here will disable this forced gateway routing at the packet filter level. The status monitoring will indicate it is offline, but it may still be enabled as a normal gateway with other firewall rules allowing it.

You may optionally enter an explanation for this gateway in the **Description** text field.

Advanced Gateway Settings

Click the **Display Advanced** button to bring up further gateway configuration options, including several options used for the monitoring (which uses *dpinger*).

The **Weight** number selection is to help choose how often this gateway will be used in a gateway group. The higher number implies it may be used more for outgoing connections.

By default, the packet size sent in each ICMP ECHO monitoring probe is 28 bytes. This can be changed by entering a number in the **Data Payload** number field (which adds to it). The maximum allowed entry is 65487 bytes for IPv4 and 65507 bytes for IPv6.

If the latency is more than 500 milliseconds by default, it will trigger an alert. This milliseconds threshold can be changed in the second **Latency thresholds** field. It can not be longer than the following **Loss Interval** setting. The first field is for the low or warning visual cues on the status page (Section 15.1.3) and is not used for automated action-based monitoring, (The second field must be greater than the first field.)

The monitoring will also trigger if the packet loss percentage is greater than 20 percent. This percentage can be changed in the second **Packet Loss thresholds** field. The first field is for the low warning on the status page and is not used for automated triggers. These need to be set within 1 to 100. (Again the second field must be greater than the first field.)

The monitor will do an ICMP ECHO check once every half a second (500 ms). This can be changed by entering the milliseconds in the **Probe Interval** number field. This needs to be shorter than the upcoming **Alert Interval** setting. If you increase this time, you need to also increase the upcoming **Time Period** setting. The maximum is 86400 (which is less than a minute and a half).

If the ICMP ping doesn't get a response in two seconds (2000 ms) it is considered lost. This response time can be changed by entering the number of milliseconds in the **Loss Interval** number field. This time must be greater than the high latency threshold. If this is increased, the following time period needs to be adjusted too.

The loss percentage is calculated on how many response packets were lost versus received within one minute (60000 milliseconds). To change this, enter the milliseconds in the **Time Period** field. This needs to be greater than the loss interval combined with twice the probe interval. Also this time period cannot be 65536 times greater than the **Interval** setting.

The triggers won't happen more frequently than once per second (1000 ms). To change this, enter the milliseconds in the **Alert Interval** field. This needs to be longer than the **Probe Interval** setting (as it doesn't make sense to trigger alerts more frequently than the monitoring checks).

If you need a gateway that is not within your interface's local subnet, check the **Use non-local gateway** checkbox. When this is checked, a route is added for the IP address which should be directly reachable via the interface (as defined in this configuration). Using a non-local gateway means that there is a gateway usable via that router. This is a non-standard setup.

When finished, use the **Save** button to store the new gateway settings. If prompted, press the **Apply Changes** button to possibly activate the new gateway.

Note

Your routing table generally will not be updated with the new gateway entry. In pfSense, the "gateway" is a special configuration that is used with other configurations.

15.1.3 Gateways Monitoring Status

Your gateways with details from the monitor may be viewed via the **Status → Gateways** page. It may indicate "Pending" if there is no status available via the monitor, A table displays the gateway configuraton names and if currently the *default*, its IP address, the IP address used for monitoring (usually the same IP), monitoring stats, its current status, and the configurable description. The latency of the monitoring ping times is averaged every 30 seconds; this is displayed in the round-trip time (RTT) column. The standard deviation of the latencies is in the RTTsd column (meaning most of the ping times averaged this amount). The loss column is the percentage of the packets that were lost (a response was not seen by the monitor). Historical records of these monitoring details may also be viewed in graphs via the **Status → Monitoring** using the *Quality* axis (covered at Section 28.2).

The gateway status indicates quickly if there is a problem or if all is okay with the monitored gateway. Some statuses are based on thresholds which may be customized in your advanced gateway settings as just described in the previous section.

Offline (forced)
> The gateway is manually marked as down in the gateway settings. This implies it won't be used for any firewall rules that specifically selected it for policy routing. The gateway may still be up in use.

Offline
> The gateway is down. This may be shown if packets loss percentage is greater than 20% or the average latency (RTT) is greater than a half a second (or as custom defined).

Danger, Packetloss
> The packets loss percentage is greater than 20% (by default).

Warning, Packetloss
> The packets loss percentage is greater than 10% but not greater than 20%.

Danger, Latency
> The average latency (RTT) is greater than half a second (500ms).

Warning, Latency

> The average latency (RTT) is greater than 200 milliseconds, but not greater than half a second (500ms).

Online

> The gateway IP is monitored and its latency and packet loss is within the defined thresholds (so not too low and not too high).

Online (unmonitored)

> The gateway IP is unknown so is not monitored.

The column headers may be clicked on to sort the rows by that field. Shortcuts are also available at the top to restart or stop the routing daemon service (or start if applicable), to jump to the gateway settings, or to view the logs as seen in the following section.

15.1.4 Gateway Log Entries

The *dpinger* monitoring logs are available via the **Status → System Logs → System → Gateways** subpage. Here is an example log entry:

```
send_interval 500ms loss_interval 2000ms time_period 60000ms    ←
    report_interval 0ms data_len 0 alert_interval 1000ms    ←
    latency_alarm 500ms loss_alarm 20% dest_addr 10.185.42.1    ←
    bind_addr 10.185.42.150 identifier "WAN_DHCP "
```

The common entries include the following fields:

send_interval

> Time interval in milliseconds between sending ECHO requests.

loss_interval

> Time interval in milliseconds before a sequence is treated as lost,

time_period

> Time period in milliseconds for averaging results.

report_interval

> Time interval between reports in milliseconds. This is always 0ms because the unused reporting thread is disabled.

data_len

> Length of the message to transmit to the target.

alert_interval

> Time interval in milliseconds between alert checks.

latency_alarm

> Time threshold in milliseconds for triggering alarms based on latency

loss_alarm
> Loss percentage threshold for triggering alarms.

dest_addr
> Destination address to monitor. This is the remote gateway.

bind_addr
> Local IP address for local socket binding. This is the IP address of the local interface using the remote gateway.

identifier
> Identifier text included in output. This is the name of the gateway being checked.

When there is an alert, "Alarm" is logged with the latency in microseconds, standard deviation (std-dev) in microseconds of the total packets received, and the loss percentage. The trigger logs with "Clear" when the monitor sees the gateway again.

Oct 30 15:12:20	dpinger	WAN_DHCP 47.185.79.1: Alarm latency 4654us stddev 2426us loss 21%
Oct 30 15:20:04	dpinger	WAN_DHCP 47.185.79.1: Alarm latency 4479us stddev 1601us loss 24%
Dec 17 14:27:21	dpinger	WIFIGWv6 2620:11c:f004::157: Alarm latency 0us stddev 0us loss 100%
Jan 2 20:29:23	dpinger	WAN_DHCP 47.185.79.1: Alarm latency 12168us stddev 9131us loss 25%
Feb 10 06:14:40	dpinger	WAN_DHCP 47.185.47.1: Alarm latency 3970us stddev 852us loss 0%
Feb 10 06:14:50	dpinger	WAN_DHCP 47.185.47.1: Clear latency 4201us stddev 1233us loss 0%
Apr 10 02:47:18	dpinger	OPT2GWv6 2001:470:1f07:2ce::1: Alarm latency 59us stddev 19us loss 21 %

Figure 15.1: Gateway Logs (filtered)

The logging may also show errors. Some monitoring errors you may see include:

sendto error: 50
> The networking is down (ENETDOWN).

sendto error: 55
> The pfSense system had no buffer space available, maybe due to high network load (ENOBUFS).

sendto error: 64
> The remote host is down (EHOSTDOWN).

sendto error: 65
> You have no route to a host or it is unreachable (EHOSTUNREACH).

This log output may be searched or adjusted using the **Log filter** and **Manage log** shortcuts as covered in Section 11.1 and Section 11.3. The logging filter is useful to see triggers since there are many log entries. Search for "stddev" in the message field to see the alerts (as seen in Figure 15.1) and not frequent checks. Or search for "error" to see other problems.

15.2 Gateway Groups

As explained earler in this chapter, a grouping of gateways may be used for load balancing using the packet filter and other features. This is available via the **Gateway Groups** link on the **System → Routing** page. Note the gateway configurations need to be defined first as shown in the previous sections.

When a group exists, the table shows its group name, the gateways that are part of the group, and their priority (aka tier) numbers. (Only the lowest numbered working tier is in use at a time.)

Corresponding to a group are action icons. Click on the **Edit gateway group** (pencil) icon to modify its settings. You can create and edit a new group based on the existing group with the **Copy gateway group** (clone) icon.

To remove a gateway group, click its trash can icon. You will be prompted to confirm you want to delete it. To remove a gateway member from the group, edit it and change the specific gateway's **Tier** drop-down to *Never*.

To create a grouping of gateways, click the **Add** button. But note that just because a grouping configuration exists, nothing else uses it by default. You will need to setup other features to use it as desired.

15.2.1 Add or Edit Gateway Groups

The gateway group needs an identifier or label used to reference it (and may be used in the packet filter rules). Enter this in the required **Name** field. It can only contain latters, digits and/or an underscore (_). It is limited to 31 characters maximum length and cannot be only a number. (Note if editing an existing group, you can not change its name.)

Then select the members of the group in the **Gateway Priority** section. This lists the previously created (and not disabled) *gateways* with their names and descriptions.

Each is set to a **Tier** of "Never" which implies it is not part of the group. To add the entry, select in that drop-down an option from "Tier 1" to "Tier 5." This defines the priority of the member in the group. The lower number is the higher priority. You may have multiple members with same tier number. If you are doing load balancing, you should have multiple gateways at the same tier number.

Note

Only the one tier will be used by the feature using the gateway group. If no member is available due to being disabled or monitoring indicates it is not a good candidate, then the next tier is considered.

The **Virtual IP** column drop-down will list "Interface Address" and virtual IPs (if any). These virtual IPs are for CARP, IP Aliases, or Proxy ARP like defined via the **Firewall → Virtual IPs** page as covered in Section 16.10. This is for when the group is used for Dynamic DNS or for IPsec or OpenVPN endpoints using a virtual IP. If you aren't using a virtual IP, just leave it at the default.

Of course, you will need at least one member to have a group.

When a gateway in the group is down per the monitoring, it is not used. The **Trigger Level** drop-down menu may be used to select other conditions where it won't be used either, such as if the monitoring detected packet loss or high latency. If you want your possible gateway group to more strict, choose a different selection. (The changes in a gateway group may be logged or notifications done via email or Growl as covered in Section 5.6.)

You may enter an explanation about the group in the **Description** text field.

When done, click the **Save** button. Then click **Apply Changes** when prompted to reload with the new configuration.

Note

A firewall packet filter definition is added for the gateway group, but no rules actually use it until a rule is configured to use it.

15.2.2 Multi-WAN Load Balancing with Gateway Groups

Outbound load balancing with a gateway group is enabled via the **Firewall** → **Rules** feature. In a specific rule's **Advanced Options** section, you can select a group of external gateways for your WANs in the **Gateways** drop-down menu. For details, see Section 16.2.2.

For a group of gateways, the matching rule's outgoing traffic will be load-balanced (using the round-robin technique) over the multiple gateway choices.

When the **Use sticky connections** feature is enabled, traffic from the same source will go to the same gateway. This option is found in the load balancing section under the **System** → **Advanced** → **Miscellaneous** subpage. This is used to implement a load balancing technique when your pf-Sense system has multiple gateways (aka *multi-wan*) called *source tracking*. When enabled, later connections from the same source address will result in using the same gateway.

When sticky connections is enabled, the current source tracking entries can be seen on the **Diagnostics** → **States** → **Source Tracking** display as covered in Section 16.15.1. Matching source/destination pairs may be removed via that same page. All the entries can be flushed on the corresponding **Reset States** page as covered in Section 16.15.2.

By default, when sticky connections is enabled, this source tracking will be removed once the last state expires. If you want it to persist longer for later connections, set the corresponding source tracking timeout in seconds. This field is only available if sticky connections is enabled. (See Section 16.8.2 about other firewall state timeouts.)

A packet filter policy routing rule is created for the pool of all these gateways. Gateways that are down aren't defined in this rule. To not setup a partial firewall policy routing rule (because a gateway is not available), check the **Skip rules when gateway is down** checkbox on the **System** → **Advanced** → **Miscellaneous** subpage in the Gateway Monitoring section.

By default, firewall filter states, including for the policy routing rule, and address translation states are still tracked even when a gateway is down. To automatically flush these states when monitoring detects the gateway is down, click the **Flush all states when a gateway goes down** checkbox (also on the **System** → **Advanced** → **Miscellaneous** subpage).

(For other load balancing techniques, see Chapter 34.)

15.2.3   Gateway Groups Status

The current state of your groupings is available at the **Status** → **Gateways** → **Gateway Groups** subpage. This table shows a snapshot of the gateways in the gateway groups organized by groups, tiers, and then gateways. Colors are used to quickly identify gateways that are down or offline (light red), have packet loss or latency (delay) issues (light yellow), or are online (light green). If the monitoring doesn't know yet, it indicates it is gathering information with a light blue.

15.3   Static Routes

Commonly a gateway router is used to get to the Internet and other outside (or wide-area) networks. Instead of a dynamic routing protocol to direct to other networks, a manually configured static router may be defined to access some remote host or network. This may be because the target device isn't known via normal routing or maybe dynamic routing doesn't make the best decision. The **System** → **Routing** → **Static Routes** page is used to add or list your manually added next hop routes.

Generally static routes are not used and the table will be empty. To setup a static route, click the **Add** button. This will take you to a new page.

The table will show the network (or specific host) of the destination, its manually-defined gateway, what network interface it is via, and the optional description. Actions are available to edit, copy, disable, or delete the static route. When a route is active, the first column will show a check in a circle. When a route is disabled, it will show instead a line in a circle (ban icon) and the text will be a light gray color.

The static routes may also be viewed via the **Related status** shortcut or the **Diagnostics** → **Routes** page (see Section 15.4).

15.3.1   Add or Edit Static Route

To add (or modify) a static route, enter the IPv4 or IPv6 address for the target in the **Destination network** field and the network mask in its corresponding drop-down menu. The mask will reset to /32 (for a single host) as the default when entering an IPv4 address. You may also use an alias name instead of an IP address. (See Section 16.5 about the **Firewall** → **Aliases** → **IP** feature.) You cannot have multiple static routes with the same destination network.

Then select a previously-defined router which will be used to access that network in the **Gateway** drop-down menu. These were added with the **System** → **Routing** → **Gateways** page as covered in the previous Section 15.1.2. (Or click the "add a new one first" link to add one.) This menu should contain at least your main gateway listed by name (like WAN_DHCP) and its IP address.

To setup a blackhole route to just discard packets for that destination, select **Null4 - 127.0.0.1** or **Null6 - :1** from the menu.

If you want to have a static route configuration that is not used (such as temporarily deactivating it), check the **Disabled** checkbox.

You may optionally enter an explanation about this static route in the **Description** text field.

Click the **Save** button to store the new settings. When prompted, click the **Apply Changes** button to actually add (or change) the static route. (Then you can see it on the **Diagnostics** → **Routes** page covered in the next section).

15.4 Routing Tables

The **Diagnostics** → **Routes** page displays separate IPv4 and IPv6 routing tables as actually known by the system. The columns in the tables include the destination address, the gateway address, routing flags (as shown in Table 15.1), the count of packets sent using that route (*use*), the MTU for the path, the name of the interface used for the route, and lifetime for the route (*expire*). (Often tables don't have values in the Expire column, but if the route is not responding to traffic, this may indicate how many seconds before this route is deleted.)

B	Blackhole, just discard packets (during updates)
b	The route represents a broadcast address
D	Created dynamically (by redirect)
G	Gateway, destination requires forwarding by intermediary
H	Host entry (otherwise is network)
M	Modified dynamically (by redirect)
R	Reject, host or net unreachable
S	Static, manually added
U	Up, route usable
X	External daemon resolves name to link address
1	Protocol specific routing flag #1
2	Protocol specific routing flag #2
3	Protocol specific routing flag #3

Table 15.1: Route Flags

The common routing flags indicate if the gateway is up (U) or down (no U); if it is a gateway (G), a host (H), or a network (no H); or if it was manually added (S).

The destination known as *default* is the fall-back route to access the Internet; it should be marked with flags U and G. Destination networks may be identified with a subnet using slash (/) notation; these don't have a H or G flag. Gateway addresses may be identified with *link#* and a number representing the network interface as known to the operating system. Note that a gateway address may be identified as colon-delimited MAC hardware address.

This page has provides three display options available in the form at the top of the page. Changing these will update the display even if the **Update** button is not pressed. If you check to enable the **Resolve names** checkbox, it will show hostnames (if found) instead of IP addresses. (Note this name resolution may delay the routes display.) This resolve option is a nice feature in pfSense, as the command-line `netstat` routing output will crop long names and lose subnet notation.

By default, it limits the display to 100 rows of output. This may be changed using the **Rows to display** drop-down menu to select a number choice or *all*.

The **Filter** text field is used to enter a regular expression to match any table fields; for example, it could be used to list only certain addresses, list based on parts of hostnames, or show only specific interfaces.

The route tables display is updated every five seconds. (You should see counter changes in the *Use* column.) To have it update once quickly, press the **Update** button. Click the top-left pfSense logo to go to the dashboard or go to another page to stop this continual network routes status update.

The related settings icon on the rop right will take you to the **System** → **Routing** → **Static Routes** page covered in previous section. The related log entries will take you to **Status** → **System Logs** → **System** → **Routing** page as covered in the following section.

15.5   Routing Log Entries

The logging for the dynamic routes is available via the **Status** → **System Logs** → **System** → **Routing** subpage. This may include log messages from the `radvd` IPv6 router advertisement daemon (Section 20.1), `routed` RIP and router discovery routing daemon, `oslrd` Optimized Link State Routing protocol daemon, `zebra` Quaga routing manager (for RIP, OSPF and BGP), `ospfd` OSPF routing engine for Quagga/Zebra, `bgpd` BGP routing engine for Quagga/Zebra, and `miniupnpd` UPnP Internet Gateway Device daemon. Some of these services are installed via pfSense packages.

Some of the logging may be very frequent and may fill the log file. This log output may be searched or adjusted using the **Log filter** and **Manage log** shortcuts as explained in Section 11.1 and Section 11.3.

16 Firewall

The pfSense Firewall features a stateful packet filter that can restrict or allow various types of IPv4 and IPv6 packets that pass through the pfSense network interfaces. The individual filter steps or definitions are called *rules*. This chapter covers viewing and understanding existing rules, logging of traffic that went through the packet filter device, adding and maintaining rules, and tuning the packet filter. Aliases can be setup to conveniently assign a name to one or more addresses or port numbers. Rules can be enabled based on date and time schedules. These are also covered in this chapter.

Note

Various rules and aliases may be created and maintained via other configurations within pfSense. Even without manually setting up the following packet filtering features, you may have some settings already enabled and in use.

This packet filtering technology is FreeBSD's version of the OpenBSD PF packet filter. This also powers the Network Address Translation (NAT) for redirecting and sharing addresses (or ports) and bandwidth control for prioritizing traffic and Quality of Service. Those features, found via the **Firewall** → **NAT** and **Firewall** → **Traffic Shaper** pages, are covered in Chapter 17 and Chapter 25, respectively.

16.1 Firewall Rules

Your packet filtering rules can be viewed, created, or maintained via the **Firewall** → **Rules** page. The page shows a dynamic table describing the existing rules plus has various features and actions to re-order, edit, copy, disable, delete, and add rules.

Near the top of the page several tabs (links) are used to select the packet filter rules to view and maintain. The default view is generally for the WAN interface. These selections include **Floating** for the stateful firewall to match packets on any interface, *Interface Groups* if you have any defined (see Section 16.4), various interfaces like WAN and LAN, **L2TP VPN** if you have an L2TP server enabled (see Chapter 32), **PPPoE Server** (see Section 31.1), **IPsec**, (see Chapter 30), and **OpenVPN** (see Chapter 33). Note that some of these may not have any rules already defined. You may add a new rule as described in a following section.

Warning

Some interfaces or rule categories may default to block all incoming connections. Pass rules may be needed to allow traffic. Alternatively, some interfaces may default to open — allowing incoming connections. You may want to consider adding blocking rules to limit traffic.

Text and icons in rows that are dim or lighter than others indicate that rule is disabled. The configuration exists, but it is not used.

Near the start of each row there may be status icons for each rule to represent the following: traffic is passed, traffic is blocked, traffic is rejected, or traffic is matched, For custom rules, these icons may be clicked to disable the rule. Or it if already disabled, then clicking it will enable it.

It may have other icons to represent if the entry is a *Quick* rule (to skip later rules on matches), is an advanced setting (like matching a Source OS or a DSCP value), or if the traffic is logged. Hovering over the icons may provide more details, in particular the advanced settings may show various behaviors.

Note

After reordering (moving), disabling, or making other changes to any rules, a dialog at the top of the pfSense page will provide an **Apply Changes** button so the firewall rule changes will take effect. You may make multiple changes prior to applying them.

Custom rules have a checkbox that may be used to highlight one or more rules. This can be used to move rules above or below the selection(s) or to delete multiple rules.

The rules may have additional action icons in the final column. These are used to copy, delete, disable or enable, edit, or move rules. The special **Settings** cog icon is used to go to a different configuration page to enable or disable special built-in rules.

The **Move checked rules** anchor icon is used to move the corresponding rule above a previously selected (checkbox) rule. (It does nothing if no entries are selected.) When another rule is highlighted, the anchor will display an up (or down) arrow instead to move that rule to immediately before the earliest (highest in table) checked rule. By clicking the shift key, the anchor will display a down arrow when hovering over it. Shift-clicking on that down arrow (or anchor icon) will move the corresponding rule to immediately after the latest (lowest in table) checked rule.

Rules may also be ordered by grabbing the row and dragging it up or down in the table. You should see a hand cursor; then click to drag and release the mouse click to finalize the move. (Be sure to click the **Save** button at the bottom to save this reordered ruleset.)

The **Edit** pencil icon action will take you to a different page to modify that specific firewall rule. This is covered in the following Section 16.2.

The **Copy** (clone icon) action is used to duplicate the existing rule. Clicking this will take you to the edit form page (as discussed in the following section) with all the details preset to the original rule's settings. Make your changes there and save the new rule. Note you may want to use an optional new description (in the Extra Options section). The new rule will be ordered immediately after the rule it was based on.

Click the **Disable** (ban icon) or the **Enable** (checked checkbox icon) to define whether the corresponding rule is used or not. Toggling this will change that action icon and will dim or brighten the entry.

An individual rule may be removed by clicking the **Delete this rule** trash can icon. It will prompt to confirm this action.

Below the Rules table are additional buttons for adding a new rule, deleting rules, saving the entries, and to add a separator.

To remove multiple entries at a time, check them and click the bottom **Delete** button. It will pop-up a prompt to confirm you want to delete the highlighted rules.

The **Save** button is used to save the ruleset after you moved any entries. (This button cannot be used if no reordering was done.)

Separators may be used to visually help the admin review, organize, or describe sections in a ruleset. Use the **Separator** button to add one. Clicking it will popup an entry at the bottom of the rules table where you may optionally enter some descriptive text. It defaults to blue, but you can click a color ball at the end of the row to select a different color. Click its **Save** button to create the separator. (Or use the **Cancel** button to not add this new separator.)

Then use the mouse to drag a separator row in the ruleset to help divide it up. Note that a separator is just a user interface bar and is not a real rule.

The other two **Add** buttons at the bottom are for adding a new rule at the top of the list or at the bottom of the list. Clicking either of these buttons will take you to a new page with a form to enter the new rule. Note this page says "Edit" even though all the fields are blank or have defaults. Section 16.2 tells you more about this.

In addition to the checkbox, the status icons, and the action icons, the Rules table has the following columns:

States

> Many PF rules track the connections as stateful rules. This value will show the current states used and total bytes (shown with a "B") passed through this rule (separated by a slash). The states number may be rounded to nearest thousands or millions identified with "K" and "M" units. The bytes may be rounded to "KiB" and "MiB" units. Clicking on this states value will take you to the **Diagnostics** → **States** → **States** page (Section 16.15) to view the individual states for the related rules.

> Hovering over this field will popup further information for understanding the rule's usage. See the upcoming Section 16.12 for details and an example.

Protocol

> This shows the Internet Protocol like IPv4 or IPv6. Or if both are applicable it may show IPv4+6. It may also show the protocol transport type like TCP or UDP. If it is ICMP, it may offer a hover-over popup that shows its subtypes. An asterisk (*) implies that it matches any protocol type.

Source

> The source field shows host or networks that the rule needs to match where the packet originated from. This may be an IP address or / (slash) CIDR network. If the source is an alias, you may

hover on it to see its details or click on it to go to the page to view or edit its alias configuration (as covered in Section 16.6). An asterisk (*) indicates this will match *any* source address.

Port (Source)

This will list the source port number or numbers (a range uses a dash) for matching the rule. Well known port names, like DNS, HTTPS, SSH, IMAP, and others, will also be listed by name, An asterisk (*) indicates that it is undefined and any source port will match it. If this source port is an alias, you can hover over it to get details or click on it to view or edit it (see Section 16.5).

Destination

The destination field shows host or networks for rule matching for the target of the packet. This may be an IP address or / (slash) CIDR network. If this destination is an alias, you may hover on it to see its details or click on it to go to the page to view or edit its alias configuration (as covered in Section 16.6). An asterisk (*) indicates this will match *any* destination address.

An inverted destination is prefixed with an exclamation mark (!). This represents "not" for matching any destinations that do not match this value.

Port (Destination)

This will list the destination port number or numbers (a range uses a dash) for matching the rule. It will also list well known port names. An asterisk (*) indicates that it is undefined and any destination port will match it. If this destination port is an alias, you can hover over it to get details or click on it to view or edit it (see Section 16.5).

Gateway

This is used for policy-based routing. Normally it uses the default system routing table and displays an asterisk (*). If this is defined, it will show the gateway name for this rule's outgoing traffic. These additional gateways are defined in the **Gateways** and **Gateway Groups** pages via the **System** → **Routing** menu item (Chapter 15). If the individual gateway is manually marked as down on the **System** → **Routing** → **Gateways** → **Edit** configurations page (Section 15.1.2), then it won't be used with the packet filter rule. If this is a gateway group with multiple members, this will implement load balancing (at least for that one rule). This feature is configured when adding or editing a rule in the **Gateways** drop-down menu in the upcoming **Advanced Options** Section 16.2.2.

Queue

If you have ALTQ queues defined for traffic shaping (or QoS) and this rule is using this advanced option, it will display the Acknowledgement (ACK) Queue and Default Queue names. One or both will link to their corresponding entries at the **Firewall** → **Traffic Shaper** → **By Queue** page (see Section 25.2). This is configured in the **Ackqueue / Queue** drop-down menus in the **Advanced Options** section (see Section 16.2.2) when adding or editing a rule. It will display "none" if no queue is defined with this rule.

Schedule

A firewall rule may be configured in the **Schedule** drop-down menu in the **Advanced Options** section (when adding or editing a rule as described in Section 16.2.2) to use a time-based rule. The day/time ranges are defined via the **Firewall** → **Schedules** page (see Section 16.9).

This column will show a status icon and the schedule name if a schedule is enabled for this rule. Hovering over the icon will describe its current state such as traffic matching is currently being denied, traffic matching is currently being allowed, or the rule is not active because the time period has expired. Hovering over the schedule name may show its description. Clicking the name will take you to a page to view or edit its schedule details as covered in Section 16.9.1.

Description

This helps describe the purpose or provide a reference for the rule. It is optionally entered by the administrator under the **Extra Options** section when adding or editing a firewall rule. (See Section 16.2.1.) Various built-in or autogenerated rules also provide a description.

The table's entries may start with some auto-created rules which are enabled via other pfSense administration pages, such as: "Anti-Lockout Rule" for a LAN via the **System** → **Advanced** → **Admin Access** page (covered in Section 5.3.1); and WAN rules for "Block private networks" for RFC 1918 networks source and "Block bogon networks" for reserved IP addresses not allocated for public use — both enabled via the **Interfaces** menu for the specific interfaces (as covered in Section 13.2.7).

In the default installation, pfSense has various packet filtering rules pre-configured for common firewalling techniques. Some of these aren't even listed via these rule tables.

16.2 Add or Edit Firewall Rules

Editing or adding a new firewall rule for an interface is accessed via the **Firewall** → **Rules** page. A new form has several preset values, so saving it will introduce a valid pass rule for IPv4 TCP from any source to any destination on the selected interface. Be sure to set it up correctly before enabling it.

First set the rule type in the **Action** drop-down menu. Its choices are: *Pass* (default) to allow the traffic; *Block* to silently drop the packet; and *Reject* to discard the packet and attempt to terminate the connection by returning an ICMP UNREACHABLE for UDP and other packets or a TCP Reset (RST) for TCP. Floating rules also have a *match* action. This doesn't effect the block or pass state of a packet, but may be used to set other parameters, like the upcoming options, or to assign packets to traffic shaping queues.

To keep the rule configuration but don't load nor use it in the packet filter check the **Disabled** checkbox.

Floating rules include a **Quick** checkbox. Enable it to skip the following rules if this rule matches.

Note

Corresponding packet filtering rules may be automatically setup when network address translation rules are created (see Section 17.1). If the rule you are editing here is one of these NAT *associated* rules, you won't be able to modify the interface, protocol, source, or destination to match on as described in following paragraphs.

Select where the packets this filter will match are coming in on or going out through in the **Interface** menu. The **Interface** will default to the firewall rule category you edited or added the rule from. New *floating* rules do not have a default. For floating rules you may choose to not select any or select more than one interface options (using Shift- or Control-click).

The selections include the WAN and other interfaces you setup. It may also include *Interface Groups* which may represent a set of interfaces (see Section 16.4), or L2TP VPN, PPPoE Server, IPsec, OpenVPN, and other options.

Non-floating rules are only applied to incoming packets. Floating rules also include a **Direction** drop-down menu. It defaults to *any* which means the floating rule can match on incoming or outgoing packets. Its other options are *in* and *out* to match packets in a specific direction only.

Choose either IPv4 (the default) or IPv6 in the **Address Family** drop-down. If you want rules for both, select the *IPv4+IPv6* option (and two rules will be generated from this single configuration). (Note you cannot use both *IPv4+IPv6* if using a custom **Gateway** option in the Advanced Options.)

Select the Internet protocol for the rule matching in the **Protocol** drop-down menu. The several choices include ANY (to match on all protocols), TCP (the default), UDP, both TCP and UDP, ICMP, ESP (for IPsec), AH (for IPsec), GRE, IPV6 (for matching 6to4 tunnels with IPv4), IGMP, PIM, OSPF, SCTP, CARP, and PFSYNC.

If you selected ICMP as the protocol, you will be able to select ICMP type classifications to match on in the **ICMP Subtypes** selection box. There are over 40 options for IPv4 or IPv6 such as *althost* (alternate host address) through *wrureq* (who-are-you request) as listed in Table 16.1. This defaults to *any* for matching all ICMP types.

Where the packet originates from for the matching is set in the **Source** form section. This defaults to *any* so the rule will match from all sources. The other types include: *Single host or alias*, *Network*, *PPPoE clients*, *L2TP clients*, *WAN net*, and *WAN address*. You will also have options for your other interfaces such as: *LAN net*, *LAN address*, *OPT1 net*, and *OPT1 address*. If you are using a floating rule, you will also have *This Firewall (self)* option to represent all current and future addresses assigned to all the interfaces.

When using the *Single host or alias* selection, also enter in the IP address or alias name in the corresponding field. If selecting *Network*, then enter the network address and the required netmask number (bit count). Note that most selections don't allow setting the address as they are automatically set. If setting the address, use the same address family as defined previously. If you chose both IPv4 and IPv6, then you cannot enter any IP address.

Use the **Invert match** checkbox if you want the source to match on the sources that are the opposite of (or everything but) what is defined here.

If you are matching on a TCP or UDP protocol, use the **Display Advanced** button if you need to define the source port range. This will bring up drop-down menus with corresponding optional input fields. For many services or client requests, the source port is random and generally is not the same as the destination's service port. Keep these set to *(other)* and blank to not match on any specific port. Or select *any* to match on all source ports.

To match on a single TCP or UDP source port select it by name such as DNS (53), HTTPS (443), or SSH (22), in the **From** drop-down menu. See Table 16.2 for the common choices. (Note that some of these ports may not make sense for UDP or for TCP.)

althost	Alternate host address	IPv4 only
dataconv	Datagram conversion problem	IPv4 only
echorep	Echo service reply	both IPv4 and IPv6
echoreq	Echo service request	both IPv4 and IPv6
fqdnrep	FQDN reply	IPv6 only
fqdnreq	FQDN query	IPv6 only
groupqry	Group membership query	IPv6 only
grouprep	Group membership report	IPv6 only
groupterm	Group membership termination	IPv6 only
inforep	Information reply	IPv4 only
inforeq	Information request	IPv4 only
ipv6-here	IPv6 I-am-here	IPv4 only
ipv6-where	IPv6 where-are-you	IPv4 only
listendone	Multicast listener done	IPv6 only
listenrep	Multicast listener report	IPv6 only
listqry	Multicast listener query	IPv6 only
maskrep	Address mask reply	IPv4 only
maskreq	Address mask request	IPv4 only
mobredir	Mobile host redirection	IPv4 only
mobregrep	Mobile registration reply	IPv4 only
mobregreq	Mobile registration request	IPv4 only
mtrace	mtrace messages	IPv6 only
mtraceresp	mtrace resp	IPv6 only
neighbradv	Neighbor advertisement	IPv6 only
neighbrsol	Neighbor solicitation	IPv6 only
niqry	Node information query	IPv6 only
nirep	Node information reply	IPv6 only
paramprob	Invalid IP header	both IPv4 and IPv6
photuris	Photuris	IPv4 only
redir	Shorter route exists	both IPv4 and IPv6
routeradv	Router advertisement	both IPv4 and IPv6
routersol	Router solicitation	both IPv4 and IPv6
routrrenum	Router renumbering	IPv6 only
skip	SKIP	IPv4 only
squench	Packet loss, slow down	IPv4 only
timerep	Timestamp reply	IPv4 only
timereq	Timestamp request	IPv4 only
timex	Time exceeded	both IPv4 and IPv6
toobig	Packet too big	IPv6 only
trace	Traceroute	IPv4 only
unreach	Destination unreachable	both IPv4 and IPv6
wrurep	Who-are-you reply	IPv6 only
wrureq	Who-are-you request	IPv6 only

Table 16.1: ICMP Types

CVSup	5999
DNS	53
FTP	21
HBCI	3000
HTTP	80
HTTPS	443
ICQ	5190
IDENT/AUTH	113
IMAP	143
IMAP/S	993
IPsec NAT-T	4500
ISAKMP	500
L2TP	1701
LDAP	389
MMS/TCP	1755
MMS/UDP	7000
MS DS	445
MS RDP	3389
MS WINS	1512
MSN	1863
NNTP	119
NTP	123
NetBIOS-DGM	138
NetBIOS-NS	137
NetBIOS-SSN	139
OpenVPN	1194
POP3	110
POP3/S	995
PPTP	1723
RADIUS	1812
RADIUS accounting	1813
RTP	5004
SIP	5060
SMTP	25
SMTP/S	465
SNMP	161
SNMP-Trap	162
SSH	22
STUN	3478
SUBMISSION	587
Teredo	3544
Telnet	23
TFTP	69
VNC	5900

Table 16.2: Common Port Names

To enter your own port number, keep it set to *(other)* and enter a valid number within 1 and 65535 in the corresponding field. You may also use a previously-defined port alias name there as defined via the **Firewall** → **Aliases** → **Ports** subpage (see Section 16.5). Note if you use a port alias, then it must be the same for both the *To* and *From* fields (which implies you cannot use a number with an alias at the same time).

Note

Don't read **From** and **To** as source and destination ports. It is the start and stop of the range of port numbers, like 5000 to 5999. If you set the **To** only, it will silently ignore that setting and the rule won't work as expected. If you only have a single port to match against, list it in **From** field(s).

To have the source port match against a range of ports, the beginning port number is set with the **From** field(s) and the ending port number is set in the **To** field(s).

Then configure the target for the packet to match in the **Destination** fields. This is done the same as setting up the previous **Source** fields. It defaults on matching for *any* destination. Use the drop-down menu to select other destinations, such as *WAN address* or *WAN net*. If you select *Single host or alias* or *Network*, then enter the address details in the corresponding field(s) as described previously. Note that the destination address must be in the same address family (IPv4 or IPv6) as the source.

To match the rule on a destination TCP or UDP port or port range, set it up in the **Destination Port Range** fields. Note again that the *(other)* option implies that can enter your valid port number or custom port alias name in the corresponding fields. If you leave them blank, it defaults to match on all destination ports. Remember this **From** is not the source port, but it is the destination port. You can leave the **To** field(s) unset if you only have a single destination port to allow. The **From** to **To** is for a range of ports, like if you want to match on ports from 21000 to 21999.

To match on the inverse of this configured destination, check the **Invert match** checkbox.

16.2.1 Extra Options (Firewall Rules)

Additional configurations for the packet filter may also be set in the *Extra Options* section of the form.

Use the **Log** checkbox to record a log message for the first packet that establishes the firewall state for this rule match. (This is not for debugging only as the action still occurs.) Note that on a busy firewall with many unique connections, this may generate a huge amount of logs. This logging can be seen via the **Related log entries** shortcut or via the **Status** → **System Logs** → **Firewall** subpage as covered in Section 16.18. (The log entry will be labeled with "USER_RULE.")

To include a custom label to better identify the rule in the logs, enter it in the **Description** text field. This description is also displayed in the table showing the rules. (Text longer than 52 characters may be cropped.)

Several other options are available for configuring the packet filter rules. Toggle the **Display Advanced** or **Hide Advanced** button to display or undisplay the following form. This view is displayed by default when editing an existing rule that already has some advanced option defined.

16.2.2 Advanced Options (Firewall Rules)

Click the **Display Advanced** button for Advanced Options in the Extra Options section to expand several additional settings. (Toggle the button, displaying **Hide Advanced**, to not show these options.) Note that some of these rules are only applicable for TCP and some require other pfSense features to be setup first.

A packet filter rule can attempt to match against a remote operating system that originates an IPv4 TCP connection. (It will not match on already established connections.) pfSense includes a database of SYN (synchronize) fingerprints that describe the TCP options, size of initial packet, presence of *Don't Fragment* (DF) bit, the IP Time-to-live (TTL), and the TCP window size for various operating systems, including some specific to version and patchlevel of the operating system. This is called passive OS fingerprinting and can be used to attempt to prevent traffic from old or insecure operating systems or to only allow approved systems. But note that some fingerprints may match other operating systems and attackers could craft the SYN packets to change its appearance (and behavior).

The **Source OS** drop-down menu lists over 350 operating systems from AIX to Zaurus. To attempt to match on a single source operating system select it in the list. If you select an operating system without a version or patchlevel, it will attempt to match on all versions for that OS. It defaults to *Any* meaning that it won't evaluate based on the source operating system.

The packet filter can match on the Differentiated Services Code Point (DSCP) bits. DSCP can be used to classify traffic (such as with Avaya VOIP phones) and some devices (like Cisco routers) can then prioritize it. The **Diffserv Code Point** drop-down menu lists several commonly-used DSCP values and class selector (cs) IP precedence values as shown in Table 16.3. It also provides a few common values: 0x01, 0x02, and 0x04. Keep it empty (blank) to not filter based on DSCP bits.

IPv4 IP options and IPv6 routing extension headers are blocked by default by the firewall. To allow these packets, check the **Allow IP options** checkbox.

Non-gateway rules and floating non-*match* action rules use symmetric routing enforcement in the firewall so outgoing packets will go out the same interface that the incoming connection came in on. To not force this routing, check the **Disable reply-to** checkbox.

Multiple rules may be combined using tagging to implement policy filtering. A text string entered in the **Tag** field may be used to identify a matching packet. Then a different rule will use that same string in its **Tagged** field. This match will then require that the packet was previously tagged.

The following stateful tracking options — maximum states, maximum connections, and state timeout — can only be specified for *Pass* rules (as set in the **Action** menu). These stateful tracking options may only be used with the *keep state* or *sloppy state* methods as set in the upcoming **State type** option. The *synproxy state* also works with these settings, but cannot be used to apply them.

To limit how many concurrent tracking states this single rule can create, enter a positive integer in the **Max. states** input field. This means that until existing entries time out, later packets that match this rule will be dropped. To limit the concurrent states based on all source addresses, set this in the **Max. src nodes** field. Or to limit this for a single source address, set its maximum in the **Max. src. states** field.

Limiting the simultaneous TCP connections (after its completed TCP handshake) is set in the **Max. connections** field.

af11	Lowest Priority (Low Drop)
af12	Lowest Priority (Medium Drop)
af13	Lowest Priority (High Drop)
af21	Immediate (Low Drop)
af22	Immediate (Medium Drop)
af23	Immediate (High Drop)
af31	Flash (Low Drop)
af32	Flash (Medium Drop)
af33	Flash (High Drop)
af41	Flash Override (Low Drop)
af42	Flash Override (Medium Drop)
af43	Flash Override (High Drop)
VA	Voice Admit
EF	Expedited Forwarding
cs1	Priority
cs2	Immediate
cs3	Flash
cs4	Flash Override
cs5	Critical
cs6	Internet
cs7	Network

Table 16.3: Differentiated Services Code Point (DSCP) Values

To restrict the rate of new TCP connections over a seconds time interval use the two fields: **Max. src. conn. Rate** and **Max. src. conn. Rates**. The first field is a positive integer for the number of connections allowed within your defined seconds (1 to 255) in the second field. An example of this is protecting a web server from clients making too many connections (such as over 100 connections in 10 seconds).

Note

When hitting the maximum source connection rates, the firewall will immediately flush all existing states for the abuser and silently block it for one hour — so be careful with restricting this too low. Your firewall logs will show these with the label "virusprot overload table."

The TCP state tracking for fully-established connections doesn't timeout for one full day. To change this, enter the seconds in **State timeout** field (such as 43200 for 12 hours). (Note this is different than the FreeBSD kernel's TCP/IP stack TTL value which defaults to 64 seconds.)

By default, the rules used to track the states for new TCP connections also must have their TCP SYN flag set and the ACK flag unset. To change this to have the packet filter inspect different or no flags, set it in the **TCP Flags** section of the form. There are several checkboxes for the TCP flags (as seen in Figure 16.1): FIN (Finished), SYN (Synchronize), RST (Reset), PSH (Push), ACK (Acknowledge), URG (Urgent), ECE (Explicit Congestion Notification Echo), and CWR (Congestion Window Reduced).

TCP Flags

	FIN	SYN	RST	PSH	ACK	URG	ECE	CWR
set	☐	☑	☐	☐	☐	☐	☐	☐
out of	☑	☑	☑	☐	☑	☐	☐	☐

☐ **Any flags.**

Figure 16.1: **Firewall** → **Rules** TCP Flags

First set the *out of* checkboxes for the flags to inspect and the *set* checkboxes indicate what flags must be set and must not be set. To use this feature, check at least one of the *out of* row flags (for the inspection). Flags not defined in the *set* (first) row but are checked in the *out of* (second) row must not be set in the packet's TCP flags for the rule to match. Be careful with using this, as these flags are primarily used with the creation of state entries.

For example, to set the default, you would check SYN in the first row and SYN and ACK in the second row. As another example, the screenshot shows that it will inspect four flags and the SYN must be on and the ACK, FIN, and RST flags must be off. (The pfSense firewall scrubs any SYN and RST or SYN and FIN combinations by default.)

If you don't want to have any flags checked, then click the **Any flags** checkbox.

> **Warning**
> Not checking TCP flags has the benefit of tracking or synchronizing states for existing connections, but may miss important connection details and NAT and the synproxy state connections may hang.

How the packet filter further handles its states is defined via the **State type** drop-down menu. The default is *Keep* (to track the connection state). The other choices are: *Sloppy*, *Synproxy*, and *None*. The *Sloppy* state uses the default *Keep* in situations where the firewall doesn't see all the connection's packets so it doesn't check sequence numbers. The *Synproxy* state is only valid with TCP while using the default **Gateway** setting. The packet filter proxies new TCP connections to first handle the TCP handshake before the connected packets are forwarded between the endpoints. Use *None* if the connection should not be tracked in the state table. (If this is set to *None*, then you cannot also set the various maximum states, maximum connections, or state timeout.)

pfSense can synchronize its packet filter state table with other firewall systems to provide redundant firewall consistency. This is covered in Section 36.1. To prevent this rule's state from being synchronized even when that feature is enabled, check the **No pfSync** checkbox.

If you do not want to synchronize this filter rule configuration to another pfSense CARP-based firewall, check the **No XMLRPC Sync** checkbox. (See Section 36.2 for details.)

Similar to matching on the DSCP field, the packet filter can also match on the 802.1p Priority Code Point (PCP) in a 802.1Q VLAN header. (This is used for traffic prioritization for QoS.) To only match packets which are assigned a PCP priority, select it in the **VLAN Prio** drop-down menu. The options — with 0 at the lowest priority and 7 the highest — include:

- Background (BK, 0)

- Best Effort (BE, 1)

- Excellent Effort (EE, 2)

- Critical Applications (CA, 3)

- Video (VI, 4)

- Voice (VO, 5)

- Internetwork Control (IC, 6)

- Network Control (NC, 7)

Keep it at *none* to not match on any given queueing priority.

Instead of matching on a 802.1p priority, the **VLAN Prio Set** drop-down menu is used to assign a priority to a packet. For traffic sent over a VLAN interface, this priority is assigned in the VLAN header's PCP bits (which another system will use for matching). (See Section 13.6 for information about VLANs.) In pfSense, the default *none* will act at the Critical Applications (3) priority.

The **Schedule** drop-down is for enabling this packet filter rule to only be in place based on a day or time. By default, this is set to *none* which implies the enabled rule is always loaded. No calendar and clock schedules exist in a new installation. They may be manually created via the **Firewall** → **Schedules** page. This is discussed in Section 16.9.

To use an alternate gateway for outgoing traffic for this rule, select it in the **Gateway** drop-down menu. Its default is to use the system's default gateway. The gateway options are defined with the **System** → **Routing** → **Gateways** and **Gateway Groups** features as covered in Chapter 15. Outgoing load balancing among the gateways can be implemented for this specific rule by selecting a gateway group with multiple gateways. Note you cannot use an IPv4 gateway for IPv6 rules or vice versa (as defined in the **Address Family** selection). If you are configuring a *floating* rule, then you must also choose if it is inbound or outbound in the **Direction** menu.

If the gateway is forced offline via the **Mark Gateway as Down** option in its single gateway configuration, then this policy routing will not be used. (See Section 15.1.2 for details.)

The **In / Out pipe** drop-down menus are used to use traffic shaping limiters as described in Chapter 26. Choose in the first menu the previously-defined limiter (also known as a *dummynet pipe*) for the incoming (or upload) traffic via the external network. Optionally select a different limiter in the second menu for the outgoing (or download) traffic. (If you also apply a limiter to traffic leaving the interface, it cannot be the same limiter for the incoming traffic)

This is not used by default as seen with the *none* selections. (Anyways, no limiters are defined by default with pfSense.) When using a dummynet pipe with a floating rule and the direction is set to *out*, then also select a gateway in the previous setting.

The **Ackqueue** / **Queue** drop-down menus are for selecting the Acknowledge (ACK) Queue and Default Queue, respectively, for changing the ALTQ-based priority of this rule's traffic. The available list is defined via the **Firewall** → **Traffic Shaper** page. They both default to *none* (and no queues are available in a new installation). If the ACK Queue is set, then the Default Queue must also be set and to a different queue. The Default Queue may be defined even if the ACK queue is not defined. For more information, see Chapter 25.

Existing rules have a Rule Information section below the input forms. This contains a tracking ID number that the packet filter uses to identify the rule and timestamps for when this rule was added and when it was last updated and by who.

Click the **Save** button when finished with creating or editing the rule. After saving one or more firewall rules, you need to click the **Accept** button near the top of the display to actually load the firewall rules.

Note that if you add a rule to the bottom of the ruleset, it may never get matched. For example, a previous rule may allow traffic so a blocking rule at the end may never be seen. You can check the checkbox to select rules to move and then use the anchor icon to move the selected rules above (or earlier) than that rule.

16.3   Example Firewall Rule: Incoming DNS

DNS Resolver access from third-parties generally requires two openings — one for the packet filter and the other in the local DNS Resolver configuration. The following example shows a way to allow incoming DNS queries from the outside world (the WAN) through the packet filter. To first allow access to your local pfSense DNS Resolver, also see Section 21.2.2 about the DNS Resolver Access List.

On the **Firewall** → **Rules** page, select the **WAN** view. Add a rule with a *Pass* **Action** (for the *WAN* **Interface**). For the **Address Family** use *IPv4* (or adjust as needed). DNS can use both TCP and UDP, so for the **Protocol** select both with *TCP/UDP*. And in the **Source Address** field and corresponding network put in same values as in the DNS Resolver Access List.

The **Source** drop-down menu should just be *Network* to accept traffic from anywhere. (In the advanced display, a source port range is not needed since DNS should come from various ports.) Set the **Destination** to *WAN Address*. For the **Destination port range**, leave the **From** empty (other) and set the **To** drop down to DNS (53).

Set a **Description** such as "Allow customer to use our DNS Resolver." Then click the **Save** button, followed by the **Apply Changes** button. Then you should be able to do DNS queries from an outside system using your pfSense server.

If needed, you may need to also allow in the packet filter for the outgoing DNS responses to get back to the remote DNS client.

16.4   Interface Groups

An Interface Group is a way to use a custom name to represent one or more interfaces in your firewall rules. You can use that nickname instead and be able to switch the underlying interfaces without having to reconfigure many firewall rules, for example. It allows the convenience of using a meaningful name for interfaces, such as *wlan* for multiple wireless interfaces or *egress* for the external interfaces for the default routes. In addition, because a group can contain multiple interfaces, firewall rules may be reduced by using a group name (versus having multiple rules for each interface name). An interface may also be listed in multiple groups.

When you have one or more interface groups defined, they are listed in rule links at the top of the **Firewall** → **Rules** page so you can conveniently view rules that were specifically defined for that group of interfaces. (The new group names are also listed in the **Interface** drop-down menu when editing or adding a rule.)

These are viewed or setup via the **Interfaces** → **Interface Groups** subpage (found via the **Assignments** menu entry). This displays a table listing the group name, the interfaces (members), and an optional description for each group.

The table entries will also have actions to edit (pencil icon) and remove (trash can) the group.

To add a group, click the **Add** button.

The QinQ feature (also known as VLAN stacking) offers a group named *QinQ*. Members can be added to it via the **Interfaces** → **QinQs** subpage as covered in the Section 24.1.

Note that aliases (covered in the following section) provide an alternative technique for providing a nickname to represent IP addresses (instead of specific network interfaces).

16.4.1   Interface Group Configuration

The **Group Name** is required to identify an interface group. Use letters, numbers, and underscores (_). This name cannot end with a number. (Do not use the same name as an alias name.)

If your name doesn't adequately explain its purpose, optionally enter an explanation about it in the **Group Description** field.

Then select one or more of the interfaces in the **Group Members** selection list. Note you may have multiple groups with the same interface members assigned to them. (Individual interfaces may be reused.)

Click the **Save** button to store the definition and to return to the table view of all the interface groups.

Then you use the Firewall Rules to select the new Interface Group by its group name instead of using the specific interfaces' names.

16.5   Firewall Aliases

The **Firewall** → **Aliases** menu feature may be used to list and view alternate symbolic names used for conveniently referencing IP addresses, hostnames, networks, or port numbers. An alias's values may be remotely downloaded using its convenient URL feature. For example, a third-party may have a block list of IP addresses which you may periodically update with.

Note
You will still need to setup firewall rules to actually utilize these aliases.

Aliases are different than providing a nickname for interfaces which is available with the **Interfaces** → **Interface Groups** subpage, as discussed in the previous section. Do not use the same names with aliases and interface groups.

The default view is **Firewall** → **Aliases** → **IP** and displays the defined aliases table for IPs or hosts. The other table views are for Ports, URLs, or All which lists all the alias types. These are available as tab links near the top of the page.

The tables list the aliases by their local administrative identifier (aka nickname) and what its value is (like an IP address, network, hostname, port number, or a URL). This column will only show the first few entries, even if the alias contains many entries, The description column either provides an admin-provided or a pfSense-generated explanation.

Each alias in the table will also have actions: the pencil icon to edit the alias setup and the trash can icon to remove the alias. To add an alias, click the **Add** button. The add or edit is the same for all views as described in the upcoming section.

An additional way to add (but not edit) an alias in bulk is to use the **Import** button (but it is not available for the URLs feature). This is covered in the upcoming Section 16.7.

Alias values that use hostnames are resolved periodically so their current IP addresses are available to the PF packet filter. The frequency of these lookups is defined by the **Aliases Hostnames Resolve Interval** field via the **System** → **Advanced** → **Firewall & NAT** page (see Section 16.8).

Aliases for IP addresses can also be added via the **Diagnostics** → **DNS Lookup** feature (as covered in Section 21.1). These are identified in the table with the "Created from Diagnostics-> DNS Lookup" description.

The aliases can also be reviewed (and also removed) via the **Diagnostics** → **Tables** menu item or the **Related status** icon link on the top right as covered in Section 16.17.

16.6   Add or Edit a Firewall Alias

When adding or editing an alias, the **Name** field is required. It must begin with an alphabetical letter, and can also contain digits or an underscore (_). It cannot be over 32 characters long. Use a word that helps explain its purpose, but for further details, optionally enter its explanation in the **Description** field.

When adding an alias, the type defaults to *Hosts(s)*. This can be changed in the **Type** drop-down menu. The other selections are: *Network(s)*, *Port(s)*, *URL (IPs)*, *URL (Ports)*, *URL Table (IPs)*, and *URL Table (Ports)*. Depending on the selected type, the pfSense page will provide additional form fields for what the alias represents. Each entry for the alias has an optional description field which may be used to explain its purpose or it may later get auto-filled to contain the date when the alias entry was added.

Host(s)

> The hosts may be entered as IP addresses, networks using slash notation (like 172.16.1.1/28), or ranges of IP addresses using a dash (like 172.16.1.1-172.16.1.10). Note that when using ranges or netblocks, that they are separated and represented as single hosts — you may want to use the *Network(s)* type instead. You may also use fully-qualified hostnames that will be periodically looked up and the firewall alias rules updated.
>
> If adding a hosts alias, there will be an **Add Host** button to add additional fields for entering more hosts. These will also have corresponding **Delete** buttons to remove a single host address field.

Network(s)

> Like hosts, these are defined as hostnames, IP ranges using a dash, or with / slash notation. Each entry has a drop-down menu to select the CIDR mask. Use the **Add Network** button to add additional fields for more networks assigned to the same alias.

Port(s)

> Click the **Add Port** button to assign additional numbers to the same alias. A single valid port number may be entered or you may enter a range using a colon like "5:10" for five through ten. You may also have an alias that refers to another alias by its existing name.

URL (IPs)

> Enter the URL to download a list of IP addresses to assign to an alias. It is recommended that the downloaded file have fewer than 3000 IP address entries. If you need a larger list, see the upcoming *URL Table (IPs)* type. Use the **Add URL** button to have more than one download for a single alias.

URL (Ports)

> Enter the URL to download a list of port numbers to assign to an alias. It is recommended that the downloaded file have fewer than 3000 port number entries. For a larger list, use the upcoming *URL Table (Ports)* type. Again use **Add URL** for more downloads for one alias.

URL Table (IPs)

> This *table* type only allows entering a single URL which is a downloadable file listing IP addresses or subnets. This data is stored in a PF table. Its main difference is that it offers a drop-down menu to select how often the URL is downloaded (from one day to 128 days). It defaults to once every 128 days.

URL Table (Ports)

> This *table* type only allows entering a single URL which is a downloadable file listing port

numbers or port ranges. These port numbers are stored in a PF table. The form has a drop-down menu to select how often the URL is downloaded (from one day to 128 days). It defaults to once every 128 days.

Click the **Save** button to save or update the alias. You will be taken back to the **Firewall** → **Aliases** → **IP** page. Click the **Apply Changes** button to reload the firewall with the updated details. You may need to select a different tab link, like **All**, to see the alias.

To enable certificate checking for HTTPS URLs, enable the **Check certificate of aliases URLs** checkbox on the **System** → **Advanced** → **Firewall & NAT** page (Section 16.8). If you need to use an HTTP Proxy to access the alias URLs, see the Proxy Support section on the **System** → **Advanced** → **Miscellaneous** subpage (Section 5.4.1). Also note that details about your specific pfSense system are disclosed to remote download sites as discussed in Section 5.4.5.

The URL-based aliases can be re-downloaded later by using the **Update** button on the **Diagnostics** → **Tables** page (Section 16.17).

16.7   Bulk Importing Aliases

Clicking the **Import** button on the **Firewall** → **Aliases** → **IP** or **Ports** pages will take you to the **Firewall** → **Aliases** → **Bulk Entry** page which will allow you to paste in (for bulk entry) many values into a textbox.

For the **IP** or **All** views, this will allow you to paste in a long list of IP addresses, hostnames, networks, or IP ranges into the **Aliases to import** text box. For importing ports, you can paste in single port numbers or ranges using the colon (:) notation.

Each entry optionally may have a description following the value (separated by a space).

Also enter a descriptive alias name. This is required. It must start with an alphabetical letter and can also contain digits or an underscore (_). It cannot be over 32 characters long. You may also optionally enter an explanation in the **Description** field.

Click the **Save** button to upload the aliases. Then use the **Apply Changes** button to have the firewall reload with the new alias entry. The imported alias's first few values will be shown in the table views.

Note that you cannot use an existing alias name to replace its values with this bulk import method. You will need to edit it using the pencil icon in the table view and then edit it one field at a time. You may find it easier to just create and use a new *import* alias or use the URL feature.

16.8   Advanced Firewall Configurations

Several advanced configurations related to the packet filtering and NAT firewall are available via the **System** → **Advanced** → **Firewall & NAT** page. In most uses of pfSense, these following custom settings aren't needed.

For the Network Address Translation (NAT) advanced settings, see Section 17.3.

By default, the firewall will buffer fragments before passing on the completed packet to the filter. (This is part of *scrubbing*.) It will drop fragmented packets with the "do no fragment" (DF) bit set. If you need to accept these DF packets, enable the **IP Do-Not-Fragment compatibility** checkbox. This will clear the bits instead of dropping these packets. (As an example, Linux NFS may generate these strange packets.) Note that some operating systems generate DF packets with a zero IP identification header field; it is recommended to also enable the following option for random IDs.

Some operating systems will use predictable IDs for outgoing packets. Enable the **IP Random id generation** checkbox to replace the IPv4 identification field with random values. Note that this will only apply to the outgoing packets that aren't fragmented after the packet reassembly.

The packet filter has some built-in TCP state timeouts that are optimized for different environments. Use the **Firewall Optimization Options** drop-down menu to select your environment. The default is *Normal*; its values are listed in the following State Timeouts section. The *high-latency* (also known as *satellite*) provides a minute longer timeout for the initial first connection and slightly longer other timeouts. The *aggressive* selection may reduce memory usage substantially by dropping idle connections significantly earlier. The *conservative* selection provides extremely long timeouts to help avoid dropping legitimate connections, but note that it may use more processor and memory. In addition to TCP, the UDP timeouts are also increased by several minutes in the *conservative* mode (by pfSense).

Warning
The optimization timeouts may be overridden by the **Firewall Adaptive Timeouts** scaling and the custom **State Timeouts** settings.

The packet filtering may be turned off by checking the **Disable Firewall** checkbox. pfSense will still do routing, but the filter rules including NAT will not be used.

Warning
Network Address Translation will be turned off by the **Disable Firewall** option. See the **Disable Outbound NAT rule generation** mode in the **Firewall → NAT → Outbound** menu (as covered in Section 17.4) if you only want to disable NAT (and not the firewall rules).

If you don't want the firewall to normalize packets, such as fragment reassembly, check the **Disable Firewall Scrub** checkbox. Note that this does not disable setting the MSS as optionally defined in an interface's general configuration (see Section 13.2.1).

All timeouts are reduced when the state entries exceed the Adaptive start value (first field) in **Firewall Adaptive Timeouts**. By default (when blank) it is set to 60% of the state limit (as defined in the following **Firewall Maximum States** option). The Adaptive end value is set to 120% of the state limit, but the number of states won't reach that high. These two values create a factor to scale the timeout values: (adaptive end - number of current states) / (adaptive end - adaptive start). For example, using a default limit of 44000 states, if the state table is at 30000 entries, the scaling factor is 0.86363, so the default TCP Established timeout would drop from one day to 74617 seconds (approximately 20 hours and 43 minutes). This adaptive scaling can be disabled by setting both values to 0.

By default, pfSense will allocate 10% of the system memory for the state table size. To change the maximum number of connections tracked in the state table, set it in the **Firewall Maximum States** field. (Note it will show the default state size.)

pfSense may have several tables which contain lists, such as IP addresses, which are used by packet filter rules and may be modified without reloading the filter rules. This may include aliases, bogons, bogonsv6, snort2c, sshguard, sshlockout, virusprot, webConfiguratorlockout, and other tables. If you need to support a large number of combined table entries, set the **Firewall Maximum Table Entries** option. The default is 200000 maximum combined table entries on systems with at least 100 MB of physical memory; 100000 entries maximum by default for smaller memory systems. When using IPv6 and bogons, this limit needs to be at least 400000.

The packet filter will allocate, by default, 5000 entries in a memory pool for *scrub* fragment reassembly. This may be changed using the **Firewall Maximum Fragment Entries** field.

If you have static routes defined in **System** → **Routing** → **Static Routes** (as covered in Section 15.3), you may select the **Static route filtering** checkbox to bypass your packet filter rules for traffic that enters and leaves through the same interface. This is used to pass traffic between statically-routed subnets.

By default, when VPNs are setup, packet filter rules are added for outbound and inbound ISAKMP, and if enabled, NAT-T, IPsec Authentication Headers (AH), and Encapsulating Security Payloads (ESP). By checking the **Disable Auto-added VPN rules** checkbox, these automatic VPN rules are not added.

By default, outgoing packets are routed through the same WAN interface that the incoming connection arrived on. This symmetric communication option is called *reply-to*. It may be turned off by enabling the **Disable reply-to** checkbox. With bridging, when the gateway IP of the hosts on the bridged interface is different than the WAN gateway's IP, then this feature must be disabled. (For more information, see Section 13.5.)

The firewall is automatically configured to pass related traffic to VPN networks to nullify policy routing. When the **Disable Negate rule on policy routing rules** checkbox is enabled, this rule won't be created and you will probably need to manually create rules for those networks.

The firewall allows defining *aliases* which are admin-defined variables to be used later to simplify configurations. (For details, see the previous Section 16.5 about **Firewall** → **Aliases**.) For aliases for hosts that use a hostname, the hostnames are looked up every five minutes (300 seconds) using a daemon called `filterdns` (which looks up hostnames and adds or deletes addresses from PF tables). This DNS update interval may be changed by using the **Aliases Hostnames Resolve Interval** field to set the number of seconds.

The aliases feature also allows downloading a list of aliases via a URL. When the **Check certificate of aliases URLs** checkbox is enabled, it will verify the authenticity of the certificate used for HTTPS before downloading. Note in the default configuration, this HTTPS end-point verification is disabled and the communication may be insecure.

16.8.1 Bogon Networks

Bogons are IP addresses that are reserved or shouldn't be used. On the first of each month, the list of bogons will be updated via remote downloads from the pfSense website. (This is introduced in Section 13.2.7.) Use the **Update Frequency** drop-down selection to update this weekly or daily instead.

To manually re-download the bogons list at other times you can use the **Update** button via the **Diagnostics → Tables** page as covered in Section 16.17.

(Note that some of your pfSense system details are shared with the remote webserver as discussed in Section 5.4.5.)

16.8.2 State Timeouts

The state timeouts are for setting global expirations in seconds for when stateful connections are removed from the tracking by the packet filter. By default, the state timeouts' fields are all blank, meaning these are tuned to the PF defaults. Timeouts may be lowered to remove state entries earlier. Note if the seconds are too short, it may drop valid connections still in use, but this may also improve the performance of the firewall.

While UDP and some other protocols don't have a defined start or stop of communications, PF can still can keep track of how long it has been since there has been a matching packet.

The defaults are based on the normal optimization as defined earlier in the **Firewall Optimization Option** setting. You may want to use that selection instead. In addition, the true timeouts may be scaled by **Firewall Adaptive Timeouts** settings.

TCP First
> This is the timeout in seconds after receiving the first TCP packet that initializes a connection. The default is 120 seconds.

TCP Opening
> This is for TCP states that are not fully established. Its default is 30 seconds.

TCP Established
> The timeout for fully established connections (both sides of the connection are established). The default is 86400 seconds (one day).

TCP Closing
> One side of the connection is closing by sending a FIN (finish bit) message. The default is 900 seconds.

TCP FIN Wait
> The connections have both indicated they are finished. The default is 45 seconds.

TCP Closed
> The client has acknowledged that the server is finished. The default is 90 seconds.

UDP First

This is the state after the first UDP packet. The default is 60 seconds.

UDP Single

This is the state when the destination has never sent a packet back after the source has sent multiple UDP packets (unidirectional). The default is 30 seconds.

UDP Multiple

Both sides have sent UDP packets (bidirectional). The default is 60 seconds.

ICMP First

This is the state after the first ICMP packet. The default is 20 seconds.

ICMP Error

This is the state when an ICMP error response to an ICMP packet. The default is 10 seconds.

Other First

This is the state after the first packet (other than TCP, UDP, or ICMP). The default is 60 seconds.

Other Single

This is the state when the destination has never sent a packet back after the source has sent multiple packets other than TCP, UDP, or ICMP (unidirectional). The default is 30 seconds.

Other Multiple

Both sides have sent packets other than TCP, UDP, or ICMP (bidirectional). The default is 60 seconds.

It also has other expiration timeouts which aren't configurable. It will purge at least one expired packet every second. Expired source tracking entries (Section 15.2.2) will be expired every ten seconds. Unassembled fragments will be expired after 30 seconds and then be purged every ten seconds. Also for TCP timestamping it will give 30 seconds of leeway in case a previous packet got delayed.

16.9 Firewall Schedules

Packet filter rules can be enabled for a specific month and day, day of week, or time ranges, specific up to every quarter hour (:00, :15, :30, and :45). Multiple dates, days, and/or times and ranges can be defined in the same named schedule. You may choose to have some firewall rules drop packets on certain days or times and other firewall rules allow traffic based on a schedule, for example.

The scheduling definitions (but not the packet filter rules) are found via the **Firewall → Schedules** page. If you have any defined, the table there will show its identifying name, its days and hours (with additional helpful descriptions), and optional description. These are not used unless a packet filter rule has a schedule selected. By default, no schedules exist and no packet filters are on a schedule.

If a schedule is currently active, the table will show a corresponding clock icon for the entry. This doesn't mean a firewall rule is associated with it, but just means currently it is the same day and time as represented within that schedule. To see if a firewall rule is using it, see its table entry via the

Firewall → **Rules** page in the Schedule column. It will list the schedule name it uses and have a red circle X icon indicating that it is active to currently match traffic. (Clicking the schedule name there, will take you to its edit form as describe in the following section.)

An entry in the Schedules table will also have action icons to edit or delete it. Clicking the **Edit schedule** pencil icon will take you to a form to update its configuration. (Note this will not edit the packet filter rule.) Clicking the **Delete schedule** trash can icon will allow you to remove the schedule entry. Note that it won't remove the schedule if it is in use by a packet filter rule.

To define a new schedule, click the **Add** button on the **Firewall** → **Schedules** page.

Then to use a schedule, edit (or add) a firewall rule via the **Firewall** → **Rules** page and in the expanded **Advanced Options** section (as covered in Section 16.2.2), select your pre-defined schedule in the **Schedule** drop-down menu.

Note that when a schedule's time range ends, any active connections permitted by a firewall rule using that schedule become disabled by killing their packet filter states. If you do not want those existing connections to be terminated on a schedule expiration, check (and save) the **Schedule States** checkbox on the **System** → **Advanced** → **Miscellaneous** page.

16.9.1   Add or Edit Scheduling Details

A schedule may represent multiple days or weekdays with specific start and end times. A single configured schedule may also have different time ranges for different days. You may choose to create different schedules for each event or use one schedule with several events. This will depend on your use case and how you want your firewall to use this scheduling.

In the schedule information input form, first enter a unique identifier in the **Schedule Name** input field. This will be used in one or more firewall rules to associate with the following time range. The name must contain letters and can also include numbers or underscores. It must be less than 32 characters long and you can not use "WAN" or "LAN". (If editing an existing schedule which is already in use, then you cannot change the name,)

The **Description** field may be used to optionally describe this entire schedule. Additional description fields are also available to explain about the specific days and times.

The form doesn't know about years specifically, but the month calendar is based on the current year. To change the month, select it in the **Month** drop-down menu. Then in the displayed calendar, click the day of the week column header to select the day or select a specific day of the month number to add entries for the schedule. You may highlight multiple columns or days. (Note that Sunday is in the end-of-the-week seventh day column.) To unselect a day, click it again.

Then click the **Add Time** button to generate the Configured Ranges which will be displayed below.

Note

The form is a little tricky and unintuitive. If you click a day on the calendar, and then change the month and click another day, both these dates are remembered even though not shown — and when you click the **Add Time** button both dates will be added. To reset the month calendar forms (and time form fields), click the **Clear selection** button.

By default, the full day is matched from midnight to the last minute of the day. For the days you wish to have specific times, set it in the four drop-down **Time** fields: start hour, start minute, end hour, and end time. The schedule uses 24-hour clock time (aka military time) so be sure to use 13 and greater for after noon and evening hours (and *0* for midnight). The minutes choices are only 00, 15, 30, 45, and 59.

As a single schedule may have multiple days or times, you may enter explanations one at a time in the **Time range description** text field.

After adding the time range, the added days and times are displayed as non-modifiable fields. Note that the first column may have months and day of the months displayed or weekdays displayed. Multiple dates may be associated in a single entry even though not all are viewable (without clicking and scrolling). The first three fields cannot be changed, so redo them, click the corresponding **Delete** button. (But you may change the entry's description.)

To add additional days, weekdays, and time ranges for this single schedule configuration, set the month(s), click the days or weekdays, set the times again, and click the **Add Time** button again. When finished, click the **Save** button.

Again, note that this does not define a new firewall rule. That is done separately by selecting the now-defined name in the **Schedule** drop-down in the Advanced Options section (as seen in Section 16.2.2) when adding or editing a specific rule.

16.10   Virtual IPs

Virtual IPs (VIP) can be used for CARP-based high availability redundancy, OpenVPN-provided IPs, IP aliases for using additional IP address(es) on a single interface, inbound NAT mappings, gateways, and transparent subnet gateways using the technique called *Proxy ARP*.

CARP, or the Common Address Redundancy Protocol, is used so multiple hosts can share the same virtual IP address (or a set of virtual addresses). These hosts are part of a redundancy group which is identified with a Virtual Host ID (VHID). One of the hosts is the *master* and responds to ARP requests and traffic for the assigned IP address. It also periodically advertises that it is alive. If it becomes unavailable, the IP address will move to another member of the group so service can continue,

The ARP hack makes it so the pfSense gateway will respond to ARP requests for a not-directly-connected IP address that pfSense will route for.

The **Firewall** → **Virtual IPs** page shows a table of the configured virtual IP addresses. These may be IP addresses, subnets, or ranges (delimited with a dash). CARP entries will also list their VHID number. The columns list the virtual addresses' corresponding interface, type (like Proxy ARP, IP alias, CARP, or other), and an optional description for each. There are no virtual IPs configured by default.

The virtual addresses also list action icons to edit or remove the corresponding entry. Click the **Edit virtual ip** pencil icon to change its configuration (as covered in the following section).

Use the **Delete virtual ip** trash can icon to remove an entry. It will make sure you don't have any use of it with OpenVPN, CARP, inbound NAT mappings, or gateway configurations. Be careful removing it if you are unclear what may also use the address but is not reported. It will prompt you to confirm the removal. If you mistakenly later used the same IP as the main IP address in an interface configuration, this will remove the address from the interface too. (It can be restored by going the interface configuration, saving it, and then applying changes again.)

To create an IP alias or a Virtual IP address entry to be used by other pfSense features, click the **Add** button.

16.10.1 Add or Edit Virtual IPs

Depending on the Virtual IP type, various form fields may or may not be available for setting values on the **Firewall** → **Virtual IPs** → **Edit** page. The **Type** selection is required for a Virtual IP. The choices, as introduced in the previous section, are (available via a radio button): IP Alias, CARP, Proxy ARP, and Other.

All the types provide fields to define the **Interface**, **Address(es)**, and **Description**.

The **Interface** drop-down menu is used to select the network interface to assign or be associated with this virtual address. The interface often defaults to your WAN. Choices may depend on your pfSense network setup, such as WAN, LAN, OPT1, and/or localhost.

The Proxy ARP and the Other type have the **Address type** drop-down selection. This is used to select either a *Single address* (the default) or *Network*. If *Network* is selected, the upcoming subnet drop-down is available.

For the Proxy ARP type, the **Address(es)** input field is for entering the proxy ARP addresses' CIDR block. If the **Address type** is set to *Network*, then use the corresponding subnet drop-down menu. (It defaults to /128.)

The IP Alias and CARP type also has the network's subnet mask drop-down menu. Note that in this context it is not a CIDR range. (It defaults to 128.)

For Proxy ARP or Other type virtual IP, the network may be expanded into multiple IP addresses when configuring target mappings for Outbound NAT (Section 17.4.2) or destination addresses for Port Forwarding (Section 17.1.1) or 1-to-1 NAT (Section 17.2.1). (For example, 203.0.113.0/26 would list 62 IP addresses.) To disable this there, click the **Disable expansion** checkbox.

Use the **Description** field to enter a brief explanation or reminder about what this Virtual IPs configuration will be used for.

Virtual IP CARP Settings

The CARP type also enables the fields for the Virtual Host ID (VHID) and CARP advertisement.

Enter the CARP authentication group password in the **Virtual IP Password** field. (Enter it in the second field to help confirm it was entered correctly.)

Enter the redundancy group identifier in the **VHID Group** drop-down menu. Note this must be the same for all members of the group. The selections are 1 to 255 and it defaults to 1.

The **Advertising frequency** drop-down for the **Base** is how often to advertise this CARP system as a member of the redundancy group. It defaults to 1 second and longest delay is 255 seconds.

The **Skew** drop-down menu is used to define a preference for when this host may be the master CARP host. The default is 0 (zero) which is the highest preference and usually means this host is the master. The lowest preference value is 254. This same *Skew* feature is also re-purposed for DHCP failover which is covered in Section 19.4.

Click the **Save** button to save the settings. It will take you back to the **Firewall** → **Virtual IPs** page with an updated table. It may prompt you that the changes need to be applied; click the **Apply Changes** button so they will take effect.

16.10.2   CARP Failover and High Availability Status

Details about both the CARP setup and High Availability Sync can be seen via the single **Status** → **CARP** page. Commonly these two features are combined as CARP will handle the automatic failover of a pfSense firewall and the High Availability Sync (using the OpenBSD *pfsync* technology) will keep the connection state tables synchronized between the pfSense systems. That way if one pfSense firewall is unavailable and a new pfSense system takes over for the clients' traffic, the existing connections may continue uninterrupted.

A shortcut for **Related settings** goes to the **System** → **High Availability Sync** page (as covered in Chapter 36). (For the CARP configuration, go to the **Firewall** → **Virtual IPs** page as just discussed.)

If CARP is active, the **Temporarily Disable CARP** button may be used to not accept incoming CARP packets and to remove the CARP virtual IP address from the network interfaces. This does not remove the pfSense configurations for it. If the system is rebooted, the CARP will be reactivated.

CARP may be re-activated by clicking the **Enable CARP** button. This will tell the system to accept incoming CARP packets and to reconfigure the interface with the virtual IP address.

If you need to take your node down without users noticing much, click the **Enter Persistent CARP Maintenance Mode** button. This will make this pfSense host infrequently advertise it is a member of the redundancy group and have a very low preference for becoming the master CARP host, This may cause a failover while still allowing it to participate in the group.

Use the **Leave Persistent CARP Maintenance Mode** button to advertise more frequently as set in the Virtual IP CARP Settings' **Advertising frequency** as covered in the previous section.

The CARP Interfaces table lists each interface and Virtual Host ID, its associated IP address alias, and its status:

- **DISABLED** — CARP is not enabled.

- **INIT** — The CARP interface is starting up or the interface is marked down.

- **MASTER** — It is advertising its presence and forwarding traffic.

- **BACKUP** — It is listening for advertisements.

The **pfSync nodes** list shows the *creator IDs* for PF packet filter states used by *pfsync*. These IDs should uniquely identify each peer that is alive in the cluster.

16.11 Filter Reload

The **Status → Filter Reload** page may be used to regenerate and reload the various packet filter configurations. This may include aliases, gateway groups, dummynet and ALTQ Limiter rules, 1:1 and outbound NAT rules, automatic outbound rules, filter rules, bogons firewall rules, firewall limit settings (like state timeouts), setting up logging information, setting up SCRUB information, processing down interface states, setting up TFTP helper, creating uPNP rules, running plugins, and much more.

Click the **Reload Filter** button to do so.

If you have enabled synchronization of packet filter configurations for high availability (HA), you will also have a **Force Config Sync** button. It may be used to trigger this synchronization immediately. For more information, see Chapter 36.

After clicking a button, its status will soon display at the bottom of the page. This long output is basically a summary of all the steps it did; it may also mention about your custom packet filter rules that got reloaded. If you are using traffic shaping, you may also want to see the **Status → Queues** page (see Section 25.7).

16.12 Troubleshooting Rules and Firewall Failures

As seen Figure 16.2, when hovering over the counters in the *States* column in the rules view, useful per-rule statistics are available:

- **evaluations** — How many times this rule was inspected (even if this specific rule doesn't match the traffic). Also note that a stateful rule is only evaluated once for its entire connection.

- **packets** — How many packets went through that rule.

- **bytes** — The total bytes handled by this rule.

- **states** — The count of current matching states.

- **state creations** — The total states created by this rule.

The counters may be rounded to nearest millions or thousands identified with units "M" and "K". And the bytes may be rounded to "MiB" and "KiB".

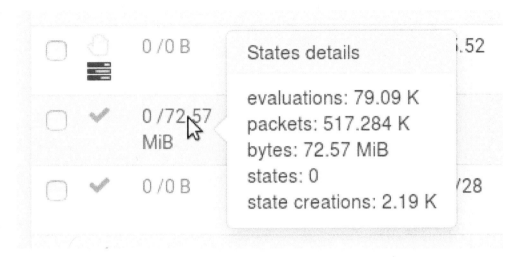

Figure 16.2: **Firewall** → **Rules** : States details

These counters may be used to evaluate ordering of the rule, such as when a rule is added, you can see the counters increase or don't increase. Greatly increasing counters may be useful for identifying lots of traffic matches which may even highlight an attack, abuse, or rule misconfigurations. Counters that no longer increase or are always zero may identify dead rules or unuseful ordering.

You may want to move valid rules with large and frequent counts earlier (higher) in the rule set for optimization and performance. In addition, for optimization, valid rules with low matching counts could be considered for a later (lower) place in the rules.

If your firewall rules don't appear to be working, the **Status** → **Filter Reload** status view may indicate what failed. (An example of not working is adding *Easy Rule* rules via the firewall logs, but the firewall logs continue to show the same for later connections.)

An example failure (as seen in the **Status** → **Filter Reload** status view):

```
There were error(s) loading the rules: /tmp/rules.debug:22:
cannot define table bogonsv6: Cannot allocate memory - The
line in question reads [22]: table  persist file "/etc/bogonsv6"
```

This particular error was caused by the downloaded IPv6 bogons table which was too large to load. This is remedied by increasing the table **Firewall Maximum Table Entries** limits on the **System** → **Advanced** → **Firewall & NAT** page (see Section 16.8).

After making rule or firewall configuration changes, you can try reloading it again with the **Reload Filter** button.

16.13 pfInfo

The PF firewall is configured for collecting packet and byte count statistics. If a LAN is defined, it is configured to collect stats for the LAN's corresponding network interface. If not, the stats will be for the interface corresponding with the WAN.

The **Diagnostics** → **pfInfo** page displays these statistics and counters for the PF packet filter for both IPv4 and IPv6. It also shows the current pool memory hard limits and global timeouts, and the interface statistics for each interface known to PF.

By default, the **Automatically refresh the output below** checkbox is selected and updated information is displayed every 2.5 seconds. Click that checkbox to disable this refresh.

The counters, as seen in Figure 16.3, include bytes in and out, packets in and out that are blocked or passed, number of entries in its state table, how often the state is used or updated, and many other counters.

The memory limits and most of the global timeouts may be set via the **System** → **Advanced** → **Firewall & NAT** page as covered in Section 16.8.

The interfaces output will usually include many interfaces (some you may not recognize) that are known to PF. It will indicate when the device counters were last cleared (or when the PF system started up) and how many states or rules reference that interface. It will also show the IPv4 and IPv6 packets and byte counts for inbound and outbound for both matching blocks and passes. These details may be several pages long to scroll through.

```

Status: Enabled for 157 days 08:37:18          Debug: Urgent

Hostid:    0x42bcc09
Checksum: 0xde29e9c4eb4af4ea140cec3d4548a9

Interface Stats for re1                IPv4              IPv6
  Bytes In                     230338562260                 0
  Bytes Out                   3823256603781                96
  Packets In
    Passed                      1330474991                 0
    Blocked                           5538                 0
  Packets Out
    Passed                      2783507412                 1
    Blocked                            466                 0

State Table                           Total              Rate
  current entries                       295
  searches                         8286183083         609.5/s
  inserts                            30362730           2.2/s
  removals                           30362435           2.2/s
Source Tracking Table
  current entries                         0
  searches                                0           0.0/s
  inserts                                 0           0.0/s
  removals                                0           0.0/s
Counters
  match                            31318637           2.3/s
  bad-offset                              0           0.0/s
  fragment                              165           0.0/s
  short                                   4           0.0/s
```

Figure 16.3: **Diagnostics** → **pfInfo**

16.14 pfTop

pfTop shows live traffic information between connected machines (aka states), and active rules and queues for the packet filter. It is available via the **Diagnostics** → **pfTop** page. This output updates every 2.5 seconds (so go to the dashboard or another page to stop this frequent job). The pfTop Configuration allows selecting the view and, if applicable, how it is sorted and the maximum count of entries it will display.

A keyboard interactive version of pfTop is also available via the text console menu. It is described in Section 37.10. Use it if you want to see peak or instantaneous speed.

The top of the output shows you the count of all the displayed entries and its total, what view it is displaying, and how it is sorted; for example the following indicates it is showing 100 entries out of 244 total:

```
pfTop: Up State 1-100/244, View: default, Order: bytes
```

The **View** drop-down menu choices are:

default

In the default view, for each connection, it shows the protocol (like TCP, UDP, or ICMP), direction (In or Out), source IP and source port number (colon delimited), destination IP and port, state, age, expiration, total packet count, and total bytes transferred in that connection. The state field details, such as FIN_WAIT_2:ESTABLISHED, are introduced in Section 16.15 and in Table 16.4. The age field may show the hours, minutes, and seconds the connection has been up. (ICMP entries may be shown in seconds.) The expiration field is for when the state expires. An example is shown in Figure 16.4.

label

The label view shows packet filter rule labels for corresponding rule numbers. It does not show state information. Rule labels are optional names or descriptions to identify firewall rules as added by pfSense. Not all rules have labels so that field may be blank. For each rule, this output shows how many packets and bytes transferred, how many times the state was matched, what the maximum concurrent states the rule can have (usually this column is blank), the action (such as pass, deny, or block), if the state establishment is logged (if it shows "Any" then all packets are logged for a connection), the direction (like in, out, or any), if the rule is a *quick* rule meaning that subsequent rules are skipped when matching (this is identified with the letter Q), the network interface the rule is specifically for (if any), the protocol (like IPV6-ICMP, TCP, or UDP), and the rule's stateful tracking option (such as *keep state*, *modulate state*, or *synproxy state*). To see the rule configurations instead of labels, use the rules view instead.

long, size, speed, state, time

The long, size, speed, state, and time views are like the default view but also adds columns for if the connection is via a different host (with port), average bytes since the rule was created, and the rule number which would have matched for that state. These five views just have the columns in different orders.

queue

This displays the pfSense system's defined ALTQ queues as covered in Chapter 25. This pfTop view is commonly empty by default. This shows the queue name, the bandwidth, the priority, the scheduler (such as *cbq*, *priq*, or *hfsc*), the count of packets transmitted, the bytes transmitted, the count of packets dropped, the bytes dropped, the qlength or qcount, CBQ borrows, CBQ delays, the packets per second, and bytes per second. (Note that some scheduler types don't provide all the details.)

rules

The rules view is like the labels view but shows the packet filter rule configurations instead (at the end of each line). This view does not show state information.

```
pfTop: Up State 1-20/20, View: default, Order: dest. addr
PR    D SRC                  DEST                   STATE   AGE   EXP  PKTS BYTES
udp   O 192.168.1.105:58801  4.4.4.4:53             1:0      21    39     1    62
udp   O 192.168.1.105:7159   4.4.4.4:53             1:0       1    59     1    62
udp   O 192.168.1.105:7159   8.8.8.8:53             2:1       1    29     2   140
udp   O 192.168.1.105:58801  8.8.8.8:53             2:1      21     9     2   140
udp   I 192.168.0.201:64939  157.56.144.215:3544    0:1       0    60     1    89
udp   O 192.168.0.201:64939  157.56.144.215:3544    1:0       0    60     1    89
udp   I 192.168.0.201:56263  192.168.0.3:53         1:2      21     9     2   152
udp   I 192.168.0.201:64071  192.168.0.3:53         1:2      21     9     2   140
udp   I 192.168.0.201:49938  192.168.0.3:53         1:2       1    29     2   152
udp   I 192.168.0.201:57155  192.168.0.3:53         1:2       5    25     2   207
udp   I 192.168.0.201:54644  192.168.0.3:53         1:2       1    29     2   140
tcp   I 192.168.0.201:51320  192.168.0.3:80         9:9     113     8   200  131K
tcp   I 192.168.0.201:51324  192.168.0.3:80         9:9      77    52   206  142K
tcp   I 192.168.0.201:51326  192.168.0.3:80         4:4      23 86400   136 94114
tcp   I 192.168.0.201:51322  192.168.0.3:80         9:9      95    31   193  133K
tcp   I 192.168.0.201:51325  192.168.0.3:80         9:9      41    75   200  141K
icmp  O 192.168.1.105:40777  192.168.1.1:0          0:0    2678    10  5300  414K
icmp  O 192.168.0.3:40777    192.168.1.15:0         0:0    2678    10  2650  207K
icmp  O 192.168.0.3:40777    192.168.1.105:0        0:0    2678    10  5300  414K
icmp  I 192.168.0.3:0        192.168.1.105:40777    0:0    2678    10  5300  414K
```

Figure 16.4: pfTop default view, sorted by destination address

The sort key for state views may be selected via the **Sort by** drop-down menu. Its options include: *None* for no ordering, *Age*, *Bytes* (the default). *Destination Address* (aka *To*), *Destination Port*, *Expiry*, *Packet*, *Source Port*, and *Source Address* (aka *From*). Some sort keys aren't useful in different views which may not have the same fields for ordering. Also note that the labels, queue, and rules views don't offer a sort key option.

The states views are limited to displaying a maximum of 100 state entries by default. Use the **Maximum # of States** drop-down menu to select a different count or *All*. The labels, queue, and rules views don't limit the number of entries displayed.

16.15 Connection States

The **Diagnostics** → **States** display is used to show the known packet filter firewall states. These are network connections that are being started, in use (or established), closing, or recently closed. A single connection commonly may be indicated with multiple states; for example, if an outbound connection originates from within the LAN, it will also have a WAN state. For an abbreviated view, see the **Diagnostics** → **States Summary** page as covered in Section 16.16.

The States display table shows the following fields. Some of the field headers can be clicked on to sort on that field or clicked on again to reverse the sorting. (Some of the fields contain data that doesn't intuitively sort.)

Interface

The interface name as used by pfSense, such as WLAN, WAN, OPT1, or other custom labels; or it may be a FreeBSD interface device name (like lo0). By default, the table shows state entries for all interfaces; to select a specific interface, use the **Interface** drop-down menu in the State Filter section covered in an upcoming paragraph.

Protocol

This is the Internet protocol, such as ICMP, TCP, and UDP.

Source (Original Source) -> Destination (Original Destination)

The IP addresses, including port numbers, of the source and targets of traffic going via the pfSense router. This uses character arrows to indicate direction. If it is an outbound state, it will show a right arrow **->** as commonly seen with WAN entries. If it is not an outbound state, then it will show a left arrow **<-** as commonly seen with LAN entries. Addresses within parentheses indicate the original source or destination address such as of a neighboring router.

State

This is the current state for both sides of this connection (delimited with a colon). It may be displayed as numbers for some protocols or using names for UDP (such as MULTIPLE:SINGLE) and TCP (like CLOSING:ESTABLISHED and ESTABLISHED:FIN_WAIT_2). See Table 16.4 for TCP state details. For UDP, the MULTIPLE state means both hosts have sent packets; SINGLE means the source has sent more than one packet, but the destination hasn't sent a packet back.

Packets

The packets in and packets out counter. This number may be formatted with a K for thousand, M for millions, G for billions, or T for trillions.

Bytes

The bytes in and out via this state, as shown in bytes through tebibytes (TiB).

The state entries also have a corresponding **Remove all state entries from ... to ...** garbage can icon. If you click this trash icon, a pop-up window will prompt to verify you are sure to remove all state entries for that source and target. Note that you may have multiple states for those same addresses (such as on different ports). If you are sure you want to remove them, click the **OK** button. Otherwise, click **Cancel**.

CLOSING	Awaiting acknowledgment that closed from the peer.
CLOSE_WAIT	Waiting for a request for connection termination locally.
ESTABLISHED	Application acknowledged the synchronization (SYN) packet; this is the normal state for most data transfer.
FIN_WAIT_1	Waiting for acknowledgment of an already sent connection termination request; or waiting for a connection termination request from the remote peer.
FIN_WAIT_2	Waiting for the remote to request connection termination.
TIME_WAIT	Waiting to make sure the other side received an acknowledgment of a connection termination request.
SYN_SENT	Sent a connection request and now waiting for matching connection request.

Table 16.4: Common TCP States

If you don't have all these columns or the trash icon, it may mean that your web browser display is too narrow; but you can scroll that table to the right to see the other content and a horizontal scroll bar may be at the bottom of the table.

This display is limited to 10,000 maximum state entries. A small home network may have around 500 state entries (which will be a long webpage), while a busy office may have tens of thousands. pfSense may be configured to not display any of the states by default unless the following filtering is used. This configuration, **Require State Filter**, is found on the **System → General Setup** page in the webConfigurator section as covered in Section 5.1.

The output can be limited by using the State Filter options available above the table. The **Interface** drop-down list may be used to select a known interface name to only display results for. The **Filter expression** text input box is used for a simple case-sensitive text comparison for the protocol, source/destination, and state fields. (It is not a regular expression.) Note that this text expression doesn't match against the interface name field (so use the previous option for that).

For example, the expression "ESTAB" will match and display the ESTABLISHED states, and the expression "192.168" would match the addresses with that. The filter expression cannot have multiple keywords for multiple fields nor match two states (like MULTIPLE:MULTIPLE).

Click the **Filter** button to gather the new states and display based on the selected interface and expression. If no states match the filter, it will indicate that. This filter menu can be collapsed by clicking the minus button on its header bar.

If the filter expression matches a complete IP address or is a subnet, you may have a new red **Kill States** button to remove all these filtered states (as displayed below on the webpage). Clicking it will followup with an additional prompt to confirm if you are sure to kill the matching states.

16.15.1 Source Tracking

If load balancing sticky connections are enabled, an additional page link **Source Tracking** is available which is used to view the current source tracking table. This feature is enabled in the Load Balancing section of the **System** → **Advanced** → **Miscellaneous** page as covered in Section 15.2.2.

The table shows the source and destination IP addresses, number of states, number of connections, and average connections per second (rate).

This table is usually empty by default. (Note you need more than one gateway defined to utilize source tracking.) But this view can display up to 1000 entries, so if it is long or if you want to reduce it, use the **Filter expression** textbox to only show the table entries containing a match to the given pattern. This can be used to enter a complete or partial IP address or other details. A source, destination, or a pair could be matched by also matching with literal space, dash, period, and space; for example: "`- . 192.168.1`". It can also search for entries matching states, rates, or connections, for example: "`states 2`", "`connections 1`", or "`rate 10`" (use a space before the number). Press Enter or the **Filter** button to use the filter expression.

All source tracking entries for a source-to-destination relationship may be removed by clicking the entry's corresponding danger icon.

16.15.2 Reset States

At the top of the **Diagnostics** → **States** and **Diagnostics** → **States** → **Source Tracking** pages is a link to **Reset States**. This will allow you to remove all the state table entries (including source tracking if you use it). Normally the state table is managed automatically by the firewall, but resetting the states may be needed after significant changes to the NAT or firewall rules.

The **Reset the firewall state table** checkbox is used to remove all the firewall state table entries. (Older versions of pfSense may have this already checked by default.) To proceed with this after checking it, click the **Reset** button. A pop-up window will prompt to confirm you want to remove these entries. Press **OK** to do so (or click **Cancel** to not remove the states).

All the open connections may be lost as this flushes the NAT and filter state table. You may not receive the "flushed successfully" message and your browser may indicate the webpage timed out or is temporarily unavailable as the firewall also lost the state for your web browser's session. Just go to your pfSense front page to re-establish it. (Within a few seconds your state table will grow, as can be seen on the **Diagnostics** → **States** view.)

If you have Load Balancing sticky connections enabled on the **System** → **Advanced** → **Miscellaneous** page, you will also have a **Source Tracking** checkbox to **Reset firewall source tracking**. (For more details, see Section 15.2.2.) The current source tracking states can be seen via the **Source Tracking** link as covered in the previous section. To remove all these existing source / destination associations, check the checkbox and press the **Reset** button.

16.16   States Summary

The display at **Diagnostics** → **States Summary** shows a quick — but usually long — view of the state table broken down by source IP, destination IP, all IPs, and IP pair. For an example, see Figure 16.5. Each of these sections contain table columns for the IP address, number of states per that IP address (or pair), its protocol (like ICMP, UDP, or TCP), number of states per each protocol for that IP, source ports count per protocol for that IP, and destination ports count per protocol for that IP. (To be clear, the first "# States" column is for the number of states per IP and the second "# States" column is the number of states per the individual protocol per IP.) The tables are sorted by IP and then by protocol.

By Destination IP					
IP	**# States**	**Protocol**	**# States**	**Source Ports**	**Dest. Ports**
8.8.8.8	2	udp	2	1	1
23.74.25.192	1	udp	1	1	1
23.235.44.143	2	tcp	2	1	1
23.246.22.144	2	tcp	2	1	1
23.246.22.155	2	tcp	2	1	1
23.246.23.143	2	tcp	2	1	1
23.246.23.164	2	tcp	2	1	1
23.246.23.177	8	tcp	8	4	1
50.112.102.155	2	tcp	2	1	1
50.112.121.39	2	tcp	2	1	1
52.40.122.66	2	tcp	2	1	1
54.85.234.190	2	tcp	2	1	1

Figure 16.5: **Diagnostics** → **States Summary** By Destination IP

Note that this summary page doesn't have any actions, does not automatically update, and the column headers are not clickable sorting buttons. To get the updated summary, refresh the webpage in your web browser.

For the traditional IP pair view with detailed state information, see Section 16.15 about **Diagnostics** → **States**.

16.17 Address Tables

As also discussed in Section 16.5, pfSense can use collections of addresses and networks — known as PF tables or pfSense aliases — for the packet filter to look up against. The feature at **Diagnostics** → **Tables** is used to show the contents of the defined tables. The **Related settings** icon link on the top right or the **Firewall** → **Aliases** menu item can be used to add or import custom tables (aliases) as described in Section 16.5. (The **Diagnostics** → **DNS Lookup** page as covered in Section 21.1 can also be used to add aliases for IP addresses.)

The default view is for the *sshguard* (login brute force detector) table which may, by default, display: "No entries exist in this table." The table to display can be changed via the **Table** drop-down list. The choices include both custom-created tables and pfSense provided tables. The webpage will automatically update when a table selection is made.

It may display the date of the last update of the table. It will also report the number of records in the table. Clicking on the information icon may provide more information about the table. The table itself is a list of IP addresses or networks. Depending on the table, it may be a very long list.

Custom tables may be emptied entirely by clicking the **Empty Table** button; it will then prompt to confirm this choice of removing all records — which can be answered with **OK** or **Cancel**. Individual entries may be removed by clicking the corresponding trash can icon. It will also prompt to confirm removing a single record.

The bogons and alias downloads list views also provide an **Update** button which may be used to re-download the table from a remote URL. (For details, see Section 16.8.1 and Section 16.5.) This does not prompt to confirm and it may take several seconds to complete. It will report that the database has been updated. (Some details about your pfSense system are disclosed to the remote download server as discussed in Section 5.4.5.)

16.18 Firewall Log Entries

On any of the **Firewall** → **Rules** pages, you can click on the **Related log entries** shortcut to get to the packet filter logs. They are also available via the **Firewall** link via the **Status** → **System Logs** page. This will open its normal view with links to the dynamic and summary views (covered in the following sections).

This shows the matched rules from when they are logged. Note that not all rules have logging enabled. The Action column shows a red X icon for packets that were blocked. The green checkmark icon is for packets that were passed (or allowed). Packet filter setups normally won't have any logs for the successful traffic. Hovering over the action icon will show "block" or "pass" and the tracker number. Clicking on it will pop-up a window showing the PF rule that triggered that action.

The entries show the network interface for the match. Normally the direction of the packet is *incoming* but that is not stated. Packets that were matched going *out* will be indicated with a right-pointer graphic. Commonly the entries only show logging for the WAN, because that is the interface that is commonly setup for rules with logging.

The source origination and destination target IPs are listed for each matching logged rule. If applicable, a port number (delimited by a colon) may also be shown. These IP addresses are prefixed by an *info* icon which when clicked will show the DNS hostname (the DNS PTR resource record data) for the address under it.

The protocol of the matched logged rule (like IGMP or UDP) is also listed. TCP protocol matches will also show the TCP flags, such as the following:

- **A** or "." (period) — ACK (Acknowledgment)

- **C** — CWR (Congestion Window Reduced)

- **E** — ECE (Explicit Congestion Notification)

- **F** — FIN (Finished)

- **P** — PSH (Push)

- **R** — RST (Reset)

- **S** — SYN (Synchronization)

- **U** — URG (Urgent)

You may click on the column headers to re-sort the log entries by that field.

16.18.1   Manage Firewall Log

A few log settings specific for packet filtering logs may also be configured on the site-wide **Status → System Logs → Settings** page (see Section 11.2). This includes logging for the implicit default allow (pass) and block rules, logging about matches for blocking bogon and private networks, and showing rule description labels for logged entries. The **Manage log** wrench icon shortcut may also be used to set these logging options (by overriding the general options). On a busy firewall, the circular logging may rotate out even the recent log messages frequently. You may need to increase the **Log file size** bytes value for your system if you are losing needed recent logs. For generic details, see Section 11.3.

For the packet filter logging matches for the default block rules are logged by default. To disable this logging, uncheck the **Log packets matched from the default block rules in the ruleset** checkbox. Note that if you have logging enabled in your firewall rules, those will still be logged when matched.

By default, the *pass* matches are not logged. If you want to log the allowed matches, check the **Log packets matched from the default pass rules put in the ruleset** checkbox.

Packet filter logging for blocked bogons and private networks is also enabled by default. To disable, uncheck the respective **Log packets blocked by 'Block Bogon Networks' rules** or **Log packets blocked by 'Block Private Networks' rules** checkboxes. (Those blocks are configured in the Reserved Networks section for the interface assignments as covered in Section 13.2.)

If you want the packet filter logs (Normal View only) to show the rule descriptions (also known as the *label*) for the matching logged messages, make a selection in the **Where to show rule descriptions** drop-down menu. By default, the rule descriptions aren't displayed. To add a new *Rule* column, select the **Display as column** choice. Or to place on a new subsequent line for each firewall log entry, choose the **Display as second row** option in the drop-down menu. (Note that the *second row* choice may break sorting.)

Note that this firewall logging view showing the labels will require a lookup of the packet filter rules and then match them for every displayed log entry. This may make the normal firewall log view slow on systems with many filter rules or logs.

Click the **Save** button to activate these firewall logging settings.

By the way, you may also remotely log the packet filter log messages by selecting **Firewall Events** checkbox in the remote logging options when enabled and configured on the **Status** → **System Logs** → **Settings** page as covered at Section 11.2.1.

16.18.2 Advanced Log Filter for Firewall Logs

The firewall log output may be searched using the **Log filter** funnel icon shortcut. See Section 11.1 for generic log filtering details.

You may use regular expressions for wildcard-type matching. If you want to negate matching, prepend a text field with the exclamation mark (!). An empty field implies *all* — it will match any value for that attribute. The fields you may search on include the time, interface, source IP address, source port, destination IP address, destination port, protocol, and TCP protocol flags.

If you want to show just allowed traffic check the **Pass** checkbox (and keep the **Block** checkbox unchecked). Or vice versa. If you don't have either checked, it defaults to showing both anyways.

You may also set the number of log entries to display in the **Quantity** number field.

Then click the **Apply Filter** button to do the search. It will reload new data from the pfSense system before displaying it.

16.18.3 Easy Rules

The **Status** → **System Logs** → **Firewall** → **Normal View** page provides a simple way to add specific packet filter rules based on previous matches. The source addresses are prefixed with a minus square icon. This may be used to add to your packet filter rules to block this IP. You will be taken to a new page when clicking it to review adding this address to a block list. (Note it is not an IP plus port combination for the block list.) Press the **Confirm** button to proceed. This will add or update a Firewall Aliases IP named *EasyRuleBlockHosts* with the interface name (like *WAN*) appended to it. A firewall rule for the corresponding interface will have a block rule using that aliases as the source. This may be later removed or managed via the **Firewall** → **Rules** pages.

Correspondingly, the destination addresses are also prefixed with a plus square icon to pass this traffic. Instead of using an alias, this will add a new rule specific for the source, destination, protocol, and port numbers if applicable. Again you will be taken to a page to confirm adding the new rule.

These rules are identified with "Easy Rule" in the description. (Note that the easy rule feature is not available in the **Dynamic View**.)

16.19   Dynamic View of Firewall Logs

For viewing automatically refreshed packet filter logs, see **Status** → **System Logs** → **Firewall** → **Dynamic View** subpage. It is updated approximately every 26 seconds. It has the same fields as the normal view and you may use the **Log filter** and **Manage log** shortcuts to search or define some log settings (as described above). But note that this dynamic view doesn't show the rules even when configured.

The column fields are not sortable. The most recent log entries are at the bottom. Also the *Easy Rule* feature is not available on this dynamic page.

16.20   Summary View Graphs

Multiple pie charts summarized from the packet filter logs are shown at the **Status** → **System Logs** → **Firewall** → **Summary View** subpage. These are for the packet filter rules that were most recently matched and logged — up to 5000 lines. The actual counts used for the pie charts are listed as data points below the corresponding graphics.

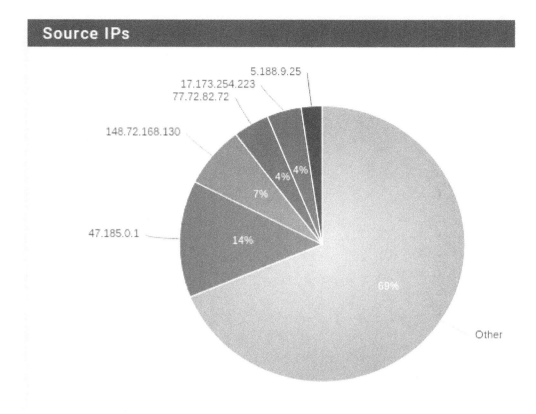

Figure 16.6: **Status → System Logs → Firewall → Summary View** Scurce IPs

The pie charts are for the packet filter rule actions (such as block and pass), interfaces (like WAN and LAN), protocols (like TCP, IGMP, IDP, and ICMP), source IPs, destination IPs, source ports, and destination ports. They are colorized and percentages are listed for the slices. (The **Lookup** button for the IP addresses takes you to the **Diagnostics → DNS Lookup** page as covered in Section 21.1.)

The pie charts only display up to the five highest data points plus *Other* for the consolidation of all the other data points (as seen in Figure 16.6).

17 Network Address Translation

The firewall can be used to map addresses to other addresses or to redirect to other addresses. As part of this, it can replace the addresses and ports on outgoing packets. This is commonly used for sharing a single public address for a range of internal hosts (that use private or reserved addresses inside). This *Network Address Translation* (NAT) makes it so the connections to the outside systems all appear to come just from the pfSense gateway. It can also replace incoming packets' addresses and ports to redirect them to different hosts or ports. Bidirectional translation is also available which is a combination of replacing addresses for both inbound and outbound packets.

These translations are done internally in the PF packet filter by tracking the stateful connections' original addresses and ports. After associated connections return, that traffic can be re-mapped back to the original addresses and ports.

Access to these NAT features are available via the **Firewall** → **NAT** page. The default view is for **Port Forward**; it is for redirecting packets. Bidirectional mappings are viewed and configured via the **1:1** subpage. The **Outbound** subpage is for the common definition of NAT — sharing public addresses for the internal network that has private addresses. The **NPt** (Network Prefix translation) subpage is also for bidirectional mappings for IPv6 prefixes. These features are covered in this chapter. This chapter also introduces the UPnP and NAT-PMP protocols services.

Various advanced configurations for the NAT firewall are available under the **System** → **Advanced** → **Firewall & NAT** page. This is discussed in this chapter in Section 17.3.

pfSense can also manage other redirections to a pool of servers via its load balancer feature. This is covered in Chapter 34.

Note

When packet filtering is turned off by checking the **Disable Firewall** checkbox, NAT will also be disabled.

If you want to disable NAT for IP sharing, but not the packet filtering rules, select the **Disable Outbound NAT rule generation** mode on the **Firewall** → **NAT** → **Outbound** page (as described in Section 17.4).

17.1 Port Forwarding

The **Firewall** → **NAT** menu item takes you to the **Port Forward** page which is mainly used to redirect traffic from the outside via the pfSense gateway into an internal system. The page shows a table of your existing firewall NAT inbound redirect configurations. pfSense doesn't have any NAT rules by default.

When enabled, the packet filter will have a translation rule for redirecting incoming connections on a specified interface to another address and possible different port that is on the pfSense system itself or to a host on a different interface. By default, a corresponding firewall rule will also be put in place to track the traffic to the new destination, so replies will be routed out the correct interface. (Automatically generated firewall rules may be seen at the **Firewall** → **Rules** page.)

The table's columns show the interface the packets will be matched on (like the WAN), the protocol (like TCP), the source address and ports, the destination address and ports, the NAT IP and ports, and an optional description for the entry. Commonly the source is not defined and the asterisks (*) imply it will come from any source. The destination address may be all addresses on a specific interface, a network, or single host, for example. The NAT IP and ports is the new target for the redirection.

At the front of each entry is a checkbox to select the rule for use with some of the buttons below the table, such as adding an entry before or after the first or last selected rule or to remove multiple rules at once. Clicking text within a rules entry may also check it. When the rule is selected it may also be highlighted in a gray background.

In the second column, there is an icon which may be clicked to toggle if the rule is enabled or disabled. If it is enabled it will show a checkmark icon. When a rule is disabled, the text for the rule in the table is displayed in a lighter color and the icon will be a cross. Note that toggling this will immediately update the pfSense configuration, but you will also need to click the **Apply Changes** button for it to take effect.

Note

If you toggle the rule to disable or enable it, it may reload the current webpage. If you have reordered rules or added (or removed) separators without saving, these changes may be lost.

There may also be one or more icons indicating the status or more details about the rule. Hover over them to see these details, such as indicating if the rule excludes NAT from a later rule (red hand icon), that traffic matching this rule is passed (play button icon), or another rule is associated with this rule (random, crossed arrows icon). Hovering over this *Linked Rule* graphic will pop up details about the firewall rule it is linked to.

Each rule also have action icons to modify, copy, or remove it. Click the **Edit rule** pencil icon to make changes. Use the **Add a new NAT based on this one** clone icon to create a new rule, populated with settings from this existing rule. The **Delete rule** trash can icon will also prompt you to confirm if you want to delete the entry.

The entries in the table may be grabbed and moved by using the mouse pointer click and drag. This is used for ordering of the NAT rules. After re-ordering rules, be sure to use the **Save** to keep your new ordering.

The **Separator** button is used to add a divider with optional explanation between sections of your rules. This is a nice way to organize, explain, and separate sets of rules. This will bring up a separator at the bottom of the table with a text field. Enter a description in it if you wish. It defaults to a light blue color; you may click one of the color balls to change the separator color. If you don't want the separator, just click the **Cancel** button to abort the addition. Click the **Save** button next to the text input field to add the separator. Then use the mouse click drag and drop to move it to where you want it in the table ordering.

Note that this separator addition is not saved yet. So also click the **Save** button at the bottom to actually store it in the configuration.

To remove multiple rules (or a single rule) you may select them to remove by clicking their checkboxes and then press the **Delete** button at the bottom of the table. This will prompt you to confirm removing the checked entries.

To add a new rule, click an existing rule's **Add a new NAT based on this one** clone icon action, or use either of the **Add** buttons at the bottom of the table. The first button (with up arrow) will add the upcoming new rule to the top of the ordering, while the second button (with down arrow) will add it to the bottom.

Adding a new rule or editing an existing rule will take you to new page with a form for adding or editing the entry, as described in the following section.

17.1.1 Add or Edit Port Forwarding

The **Firewall** → **NAT** → **Port Forward** → **Edit** form has multiple required fields depending on the selected features.

If you are editing a previously-created NAT rule, the **Rule Information** section at the bottom of the page will show the date and time when the rule was created and last updated and the administrator(s) involved.

The **Disable this rule** checkbox may be used to deactivate this port forwarding or redirection entry. (This configuration will still exist but won't be used.)

If you need this rule to specifically exclude a certain source address from redirection (because you have another larger matching redirection rule), check the **No RDR (NOT)** checkbox. (When checked, you do not need to define the redirection target IP and port.)

Normally the redirection is done on the WAN interface. If you need to match elsewhere, in the **Interface** drop-down menu select where this rule will be used. (Selecting a different interface may change the default destination.) In addition to normal interfaces, this may list other features, if enabled, like L2TP VPN, PPPoE Server, IPsec, and OpenVPN.

Commonly redirection is done for TCP traffic. You may choose an alternate in the **Protocol** drop-down menu instead as desired. The options include TCP, UDP, TCP/UDP (for either), ICMP, ESP, AH, GRE, IPV6, IGMP, PIM, and OSPF.

This port forwarding is commonly used for redirecting to another destination for any originating source. But if you need the rule to only be matched for certain sources, then click the **Display**

Advanced button for the **Source** field. This will bring up additional fields for defining the source matching. Note it defaults to **Any** for what to match.

To specific a source, select a choice from the **Type** drop-down menu. Depending on other pfSense enabled features, it may have selections like PPPoE clients, L2TP clients, and "net" networks and addresses based on your network interfaces (such as **WAN net** or **LAN address**).

To specify an address, select **Single host or alias** and then enter valid IP address or a previously created alias in the corresponding **Address** field. (Note no mask is used for a single host.)

To match on a range of sources, select **Network** in the drop-down menu and then enter both the address and mask in the corresponding fields. (Note that it will not allow you to use a network alias for the network.)

Use the **Invert match** checkbox (for the source) to reverse its meaning. This will then match for any source except for the defined source interface, address, or network.

Usually matching on a source port is not needed. But if your redirection rule needs to be defined based on a specific port, then it may be selected with one or more **Source port range** fields. By default, it is set to **Any**. The **From port** and the **To port** drop-down menus have several pre-defined selections from CVSup through VNC (by name only) as seen in Table 16.2. You may select one of these names and the second drop-down menu will change to it too. You don't need to select it twice as this is not a range. (You cannot select different ports by these names.)

To enter your own port number, select **Other** from the **From port** drop-down menu. Then you can enter the number in the corresponding **Custom** field. Or you may use a port alias as previously defined at the **Firewall → Aliases → Ports** page as covered in Section 16.5. For a range of ports, select or enter the ending port with the **To port** field(s).

The destination for port forwarding usually defaults to the **WAN address** when the interface is at its default WAN. (This default may change based on the **Interface** selection.) As described previously for the **Source Type** selections, the **Destination Type** drop-down menu has various choices. It also adds the **This Firewall (self)** option which will use all the addresses assigned to this local pfSense system's interfaces (and automatically updated whenever they change addresses). If you have Virtual IPs setup, they will also be listed in parentheses at the bottom of the drop-down menu's selections. (If this interface has many virtual IPs expanded for a network, you may use the **Disable expansion** checkbox as seen in Section 16.10.1 when editing a Virtual IP.) If using a **Type** of **Single host or alias** or **Network**, then its corresponding **Address/mask** field(s) are required.

To inverse the meaning of an interface, address, or network destination, check the **Invert match** checkbox. So in other words, when checked, it implies forwarding for any matching destination except the one defined here.

Port forwarding requires the destination port or ports to be defined in the **Destination port range** fields. The **From port** can be set to **Any** to redirect for all destination ports. See the previous explanation for the source ports for details.

The target IP address to redirect to is required. Enter it in the **Redirect target IP** field. You may also use a host alias as previously setup via **Firewall → Aliases** (see Section 16.5).

The **Redirect target port** is also required. Commonly it is the same port as listed in the previous **Destination From Port**. If it is set to **Other**, then enter a valid port number in its **Custom** field. If your **Destination port range** has a specified (different) **To port**, then pfSense will automatically figure out the target port range with your **Redirect target port** used as the beginning port of the range. You may also select a port name such as listed in Table 16.2.

Enter an explanation for this redirect rule in the **Description** text field.

Check the **No XMLRPC Sync** checkbox if you do not want to synchronize this NAT entry to another pfSense CARP-based firewall. For more details, see Section 36.2.

To help with NAT across interfaces, pfSense can run a proxy service. This feature is called *reflection* and is covered in the Section 17.3. The NAT rules default to using the system default which is to have reflection disabled. To change this system default, see the **System → Advanced → Firewall & NAT** subpage for the **NAT Reflection mode for port forwards** setting.

To set up reflection for this specific rule, use the **NAT reflection** drop-down menu. Either enable option will generate a redirect rule on all interfaces (even including pseudo interfaces like *enc0*, *l2tp*, *openvpn*, and *QinQ*). The proxy option will also startup a TCP proxy daemon (using `xinetd`) listening on the loopback interface only that will open and forward the communication with the target IP address and port, and a redirect rule will redirects to that loopback proxy. To make sure no reflection is done (regardless of the system setting), choose **Disable**. NAT still works without reflection when on a single interface.

The **Filter rule association** drop-down menu (when adding a new NAT rule) is used to setup a corresponding packet filter rule by default. A description is especially useful when you are using this automatic generated rule, so when viewing it on the **Firewall → Rules** page you can understand its context. (Note it will be limited to 62 characters.)

If you don't want the new packet filter rule to reference this NAT rule, then select **Add unassociated filter rule** instead from the drop-down menu. If you don't want any extra packet filter rule automatically generated, select **None**.

To have the packets passed without using the filter rules, select the **Pass** choice. This will only work with redirections on the interface that has your default gateway. (It will not work with a multi-WAN setup.)

If you are editing a NAT rule that already has a rule association, you can click on the "View the filter rule" link to access it. To create a new rule, check the **Filter rule association** checkbox.

Click the **Save** button when finished setting up this NAT rule. It will take you back to the table view of all your NAT entries. You can use the **Apply Changes** button to activate it or continue to organize or add other entries.

17.2   1:1 Mappings

Bidirectional one-to-one mappings are available via the **Firewall → NAT → 1:1** subpage. A common example of this is mapping an external IP address with an internal address, such as an internal web server accessible with an external IP address. This can be used for individual IPs (for single hosts) or can be for entire subnets.

No port numbers are translated. (If you want port mapping instead, see Section 17.1 about the **Firewall** → **NAT** → **Port Forward** feature instead.)

Note that because the traffic to the pfSense system is mapped to an internal machine or network instead, network services on the pfSense system previously using those same addresses will no longer work. To work around this, consider having multiple addresses assigned to your external (WAN) interface, for example, and running the 1:1 mapping and pfSense services on different IPs. Or use the port forwarding feature instead to selectively choose what is mapped to inside machines.

This 1:1 mappings table shows the configured entries with the interface it is configured on and the external and internal (source) IPs that are mapped together. If used, a destination IP will also be displayed, but normally it shows an asterisk (*) to imply that the traffic can be to or from any IP.

An icon in front of the interface may be used to toggle if the entry is active or not. (When there is a checkmark, click on it to get it disabled. Or click on the X to enable it.) The hand icon indicates that the entire mapping is negated — meaning that if it matches, later rules that match it too will not be used.

Actions are also available to edit, copy (clone), or remove the entry. You can also remove multiple entries by selecting each with their checkboxes and then clicking the red **Delete** button. (You may be prompted to confirm this removal.) The entries may also be reordered by dragging and dropping them. Then use the **Save** button to store the ordering. You may need to activate your changes by clicking the **Apply Changes** button when prompted.

To introduce a 1:1 mapping, click an **Add** button for either the beginning or end of the list.

17.2.1   Add or Edit 1:1 NAT

To setup a rule without using it, click the **Disable this rule** checkbox. When ready, you may enable it here or via the 1:1 mappings table.

To exclude this specific rule so a later more generic but still matching rule is not activated, check the **Do not perform binat for the specified address** checkbox. This will still create a NAT rule but will not continue with later 1:1 mapping evaluations if this one matches (and this one won't be used either).

Select where this 1:1 mapping will be used in the **Interfaces** drop-down menu. Commonly it would be the WAN interface. The list may also include pseudo interfaces such as L2TP VPN, PPPoE Server, IPsec, and OpenVPN.

Then enter in the required **External subnet IP** field, the starting subnet address for the external network. Usually this is on the subnet for the selected interface. The subnet mask used for this is from the following **Internal IP mask** (which is undefined by default for new mappings).

It is common to use a Proxy ARP type virtual IP address for the external interface for 1:1 translation. (See Section 16.10.1 about the **Firewall** → **Virtual IPs** → **Edit** feature.)

Warning
Mappings will make the pfSense system itself no longer handle locally the traffic for its IP addresses. That traffic is translated to an internal machine instead, so the pfSense system becomes inaccessible via the same IP addresses. Other services on the pfSense system that are listening only on the same IP addresses will stop working.

The other side of the 1:1 mapping is defined with the **Internal IP** fields. Commonly this is on the LAN subnet. By default, this will be a single host IP. To change this use the **Type** drop-down menu. The selections also include *Any*, *Network*, and predefined *net* and *address* selections for your interfaces. It may also have other predefined settings if applicable such as *PPPoE clients* and *L2TP clients*.

When it is set to the *Single host* type, you need to enter in the IP address in its **Address** field, (You cannot enter a mask which defaults to 32 behind the scenes.)

If you are using a network, then enter the subnet address and the mask in the **Address** field and **mask** menu. (If you don't enter a mask, it will default to 31.) This mask will also be used to define the external subnet.

To invert the matching for the NAT rule, check the **Not** checkbox. This means the internal-side of the mapping would match everything except what is defined here.

Generally the mappings will work for connections from or to any destination. If you need it to be more precise, set it in the **Destination** fields. It has similar settings to the previous **Internal IP** fields. The destination single host type also allows entering an alias. (If there are many virtual IPs expanded for a network, you may use the **Disable expansion** checkbox when editing a Virtual IP; see Section 16.10.1 for details.)

You may optionally enter an explanation about this mapping in the **Description** text field.

The **NAT reflection** selection is used to setup an additional redirect rule so traffic on the other network interfaces will be reflected for this mappings main interface. This defaults to use the system's default which is defined in the Network Address Translation section of the **System → Advanced → Firewall & NAT** subpage. See the **Enable NAT Reflection for 1:1 NAT** checkbox as discussed in Section 17.3.

You can override this system default by selecting **Enable** or **Disable** instead. (Note if the **No BINAT (NOT)** checkbox is selected, then the reflection is not implemented.)

To enable this 1:1 mapping, click the **Save** button and then click the **Activate Changes** button to reload the packet filter.

17.3 Advanced NAT Settings

Various customizations for the NAT setup are available via the **System → Advanced → Firewall & NAT** subpage. Scroll down to the **Network Address Translation** section on that page. Generally you won't need to use these custom settings. (The other settings on this page are covered in Section 16.8.)

The firewall can allow access to internal systems' services by using the public IP address of the pfSense system. This feature to communicate across interfaces is called NAT reflection and is enabled via the **Firewall** → **NAT** → **Port Forward** and **Firewall** → **NAT** → **1:1** pages.

The **NAT Reflection mode for port forwards** drop-down menu may be used to define how port forward behaves system-wide. (For the 1:1 bidirectional mapping mode, see the later paragraph.) Its options are *disable* to not provide the NAT reflection; *NAT + proxy* for when the interface or gateway address for the port forwarding may not be known when the firewall is loaded; or *Pure NAT* when the interface and gateway address are known. The proxy solution uses a separate daemon which only supports TCP and UDP and is limited to ranges of only 500 ports (or only a 1000 ports total for multiple port forwards). The Pure NAT solution supports all protocols and doesn't have port limits.

The NAT + Proxy mode for NAT Reflection has a default timeout of 2000 seconds for port forwarding communications. If you need to change this timeout, enter a number in seconds in the **Reflection Timeout** field.

The **Enable NAT Reflection for 1:1 NAT** checkbox is used for automatically creating NAT redirect rules for inbound 1:1 bidirectional mappings to help mappings work with traffic on the other interfaces. As covered in Section 17.2, individual 1:1 mappings also allow overriding this system setting with the **NAT reflection** selection. Note that at firewall rule load time, it must know the interface and gateway address for this communication. (For the port forwarding mode, see the earlier paragraph.)

For full use of 1:1 NAT or Pure NAT Reflection, enable the **Enable automatic outbound NAT for Reflection** checkbox to direct traffic out the same subnet it originated.

pfSense runs a proxy so internal devices can reach external TFTP servers (for firmware or VOIP phone updates, for example) through the firewall and the packets will return back to the client. (Note this is for the *Trivial* TFTP protocol and not for FTP.) If an interface (such as WAN or LAN) is selected in the **TFTP Proxy** option, a NAT rule is enabled for the redirect to the proxy. Multiple interfaces may be selected by using the Ctrl or Shift key when clicking in the menu.

17.4   Outbound NAT

By default, the pfSense firewall will setup Network Address Translation rules on your WAN interface so any packets from your internal subnets to any outside destination will share the WAN interface's IP address. When those connections receive responses, the PF packet filter's state tracking will be used to redirect the traffic back to the original source host and original source port. This feature is enabled on the **Firewall** → **NAT** → **Outbound** subpage in the **Outbound NAT Mode** section with the radio button for **Automatic outbound NAT rule generation** selected. This option also includes IPsec passthrough by not modifying the inside-originating connections with the source port of 500 (isakmp). When the default automatic mode is selected, any manually added outbound mappings will be ignored (and only the automated outbound rules used).

These automatic rules may be viewed at the bottom of the same webpage, as seen in Figure 17.1. Each row shows the interface and its source addresses (of any port) that the address translation is being done on. Note that this is done for any destination. If the destination is prefixed with an exclamation mark (!), then its meaning is reversed to imply that the NAT is only done for any destination not matching it. It rewrites the source of the outbound packet to be the (or in) the NAT address. (Or it will indicate that NAT is not being used.) Normally the source port is randomized (seen with a crossed-lines icon), but for specific needs like port 500 used for IPsec, then it uses a static port (marked with a check icon). Automatic rules are setup for each interface that can be used for outbound traffic.

	Interface	Source	Source Port	Destination	Destination Port	NAT Address	NAT Port	Static Port	Description
✔	WAN	127.0.0.0/8 172.16.1.0/28 1.2.0.0/21 192.168.100.48/30 172.16.200.0/28 172.16.76.0/27	*	*	500	WAN address	*	✔	Auto created rule for ISAKMP
✔	WAN	127.0.0.0/8 172.16.1.0/28 1.2.0.0/21 192.168.100.48/30 172.16.200.0/28 172.16.76.0/27	*	*	*	WAN address	*	⤨	Auto created rule
✔	OPT2	127.0.0.0/8 172.16.1.0/28 1.2.0.0/21 192.168.100.48/30 172.16.200.0/28 172.16.76.0/27	*	*	500	OPT2 address	*	✔	Auto created rule for ISAKMP
✔	OPT2	127.0.0.0/8 172.16.1.0/28 1.2.0.0/21 192.168.100.48/30 172.16.200.0/28 172.16.76.0/27	*	*	*	OPT2 address	*	⤨	Auto created rule

Figure 17.1: **Firewall → NAT → Outbound** : Automatic Rules for the Automatic mode

The other Outbound NAT Mode settings are hybrid, manual, and disable which can be selected instead with a radio button. The **Hybrid Outbound NAT** selection allows the admin to setup custom outbound NAT mappings which are configured in the firewall first plus the automatic outbound rules as discussed earlier. (Adding these custom mappings is described in the following section.)

The **Manual Outbound NAT** mode only uses the custom mappings and the automatic outbound NAT is not used.

To not use any outbound NAT including the default automatic WAN mappings, select the **Disable Outbound NAT** radio button. To change the mode, click the corresponding **Save** button. (If prompted, also click the **Apply Changes** button to reconfigure your firewall.)

17.4.1 Custom Outbound NAT Mappings

The middle Mappings section displays a table of any manually-defined outbound NAT rules. These are only used if the hybrid or manual mode is selected.

Like the previously-described Automatic Rules table, it lists the external interface where the address translation will be done, the source (inside) and destination (outside) addresses and ports that need to be matched, and the new source NAT address and port to be used for the outbound packet (so responses can get back). It will also identify if it will use a random port or a static port for this.

Each rule has action icons to edit (as covered in the following section), copy, or delete it. To remove multiple rules, you can select them with the checkbox at the beginning of the row and then use the red **Delete** button. You may be prompted to confirm removing rules.

You may re-order the rule entries by dragging and dropping rows. Then use its **Save** button to save that mapping order.

If you are using the automatic outbound modes or selected to disable the outbound mappings, then any manually-defined rules are ignored (and not used). Ignored or disabled rules are identified with a times icon and the row will be in a dim gray color. If you are not, then you can click on the check or times icon to toggle a specific rule to be disabled or enabled.

Use a **Add** button to configure a new mapping in front or after the list.

17.4.2   Add or Edit Advanced Outbound NAT

To setup a custom Outbound NAT rule, you will need to define the interface, address family, protocol, and the destination network. These have defaults, but it is required to define the source network.

If you later need to stop this outbound mapping but don't want to remove its configuration, check the **Disable this rule** checkbox.

The **Do not NAT** checkbox is used to exclude this defined rule from the address translation. The NAT rule still exists in the firewall. This *no* rule is used when you have an outbound mapping configured in another rule and you need to limit the same one for specific packets, such as a specific protocol type. You could create this by copying an existing advanced rule and then on the first rule setup the limitations and check this checkbox. (Normally you would never use this if it is your only mapping.)

Select the exit interface for matching in the **Interface** drop-down. It defaults to WAN. This will list the other interfaces and your virtual interfaces like L2TP Server, PPPoE Server, IPsec, and OpenVPN.

Normally the mapping is done for all protocols. If you want the outbound NAT to only apply for a specific protocol, such as TCP, UDP, TCP/UDP, ICMP, ESP, AH, GRE, IPV6, IGMP, carp, or pfsync, select it in the **Protocol** drop-down menu.

Then configure the required **Source**. Its drop-down defaults to *Network*. You can also select *Any* for any source address (even if unknown by your system) or *This Firewall (self)* to match on all addresses assigned to all interfaces even if they change.

When using the default *Network* source type, it is required that you enter the network address and the netmask (which defaults to /24) for the mapping in the corresponding fields.

When TCP or UDP or the *any* protocol was selected, you will also have a **Port or Range** field where you may enter a port number, a custom port alias name (see Section 16.5), or a range of ports (delimiting the numbers with a colon). Then the mapping rule will only match when the source packet comes from a valid port. (By default, any port will be matched.)

The **Destination** defaults to *Any* which is the common setting for outbound NAT. If you want this mapping to only happen for a specific network, then select *Network* and then enter the network address and netmask in the corresponding fields.

As with the source port, you can optionally define the port or ports for matching the destination.

The **Not** checkbox is used to invert the meaning of the destination. For example, if you have the destination defined to a network, checking this checkbox means that the mapping will match when the packet is for all destinations other than that network. Note you can not use this with *Any*, because the inverse would be *none* which would be impossible for mapping an outbound packet.

By default, the outbound NAT mappings will be for the IP address of the defined interface. The **Address** drop-down menu may be used to select or enter different addresses for the rule. If you have virtual IPs (as either subnets or ordinary IP addresses) or host aliases setup, they will be choices in the menu. (If this interface has many virtual IPs expanded for a network, this expansion may be disabled via the virtual IP **Disable expansion** checkbox as covered in Section 16.10.1.)

Or if you want to enter your own subnet, select the *Other Subnet* choice and a **Other subnet** field and corresponding netmask menu will appear. Note if your enter your own subnet, the firewall must already be routing it or each of the addresses within the subnet need to be defined as Virtual IP addresses (as covered in Section 16.10).

If you select a *Host Alias*, a Virtual IP subnet, or enter your own subnet, you will also have a **Pool options** drop-down menu. This is used to select the method for assigning the redirection address when there is more than one IP address. The choices are:

- **Round Robin** — loops through the redirection addresses. This is the default.

- **Round Robin with Sticky Address** — loops through the redirection address. Multiple connections from the same source are mapped to the same redirection address.

- **Random** — randomly uses an address within the defined block of addresses.

- **Random with Sticky Address** — randomly uses an address within the defined block of addresses. Multiple connections from the same source are mapped to the same redirection address.

- **Source hash** — ensures the redirection address is always the same for each source. It will use a random key, but if you want to optionally specify a key, enter it in the **Source Hash Key** field. You may enter any string and it will hashed to make a hexadecimal key or you may enter your own hex string that starts with "0x" and followed by 32 hexadecimal digits.

- **Bit mask** — the network portion of the redirection address is applied to the source address.

If you selected a *Host Alias*, you need to use the round robin method because it is the only pool option when there are multiple redirection addresses.

The common use of NAT is for the original source ports to be remapped to new port numbers. The default remapping range is within 1024 to 65535. To define your own range, enter the starting and ending port numbers separated by a colon in the **Port or Range** field. If you just want it to use the same port numbers, check the **Static Port** checkbox which implies that the NAT firewall will not modify the source port on the TCP and UDP packets.

If using CARP and this system is the *master*, to disable automatically synchronizing this outbound mapping to the other CARP firewalls, check the **No XMLRPC Sync** checkbox. Note that *slave* nodes may still be updated. (For more information, see Section 36.2.)

You may add a brief explanation for this mapping in the **Description** text field.

Use the **Save** button to store this advanced outbound NAT configuration. Then when prompted click the **Apply Changes** button to reconfigure your firewall with the new rule. Then you will be back at the view of the **Firewall** → **NAT** → **Outbound** mappings.

17.5   Network Prefix translation (NPt)

Network Prefix Translation (NPt) uses bidirectional mapping between internal and external address spaces (of the same size) for translating one IPv6 prefix to another. The inside IPv6 hosts have a corresponding outside address to reach them. It is stateless and ports are not mapped. (Note that Network Address Translation is generally not recommended for IPv6.)

Note

While this feature is called *Network Prefix Translation*, it doesn't necessarily provide the same algorithms or features defined by the IPv6-to-IPv6 Network Prefix Translation (NPTv6) specification (RFC 6296).

The **Firewall** → **NAT** → **NPt** subpage has a table to view and manage the current NPt mappings. Like the other NAT (and packet filter) views, entries may be selected with the front checkbox. The mapping can be disabled (or enabled) by clicking the checkmark (or disabled icon) at the front of the row. Each entry lists the interface the rule is on, the external prefix (external addresses), internal prefix (source addresses), and an optional description.

Corresponding actions may be used to edit (pencil icon), copy (clone icon), or remove (garbage can) the mapping. You can also use the **Delete** button to remove multiple selected mappings. The **Save** button may be used to save any changes to the ordering of the mappings done with dragging and dropping.

Use either of the **Add** buttons to introduce a new mapping to the top or bottom of the list. (Or use the clone action to start a new mapping based on an existing one.)

After making a change or adding a mapping, click the **Apply Changes** button when prompted.

17.5.1   Add or Edit NPt

The **Disabled** checkbox is used to keep this NPt configuration but not put it into use. Make sure it is unchecked (the default) for enabling it.

Select the interface for the NPt in the **Interface** drop-down. It defaults to the WAN which is the normal use.

Enter the required internal (or source) Unique Local IPv6 Address (ULA) and prefix in the **Address** field and **prefix size** drop-down menu (which defaults to /128 for one host).

Inverse matching of the source or internal IPv6 prefix is done by checking its **Not** checkbox (prior to the address input field).

Then enter the required Global Unicast routable IPv6 destination **Address** and prefix. If you want to invert it, use the **Not** checkbox that precedes this.

For your reference, optionally enter an explanation in the **Description** text field.

Click the **Save** button to store the settings and return to the NPt table view. Then click the **Apply Changes** button to actually load this NPt rule.

17.6 NAT Logging

The pfSense interface doesn't have any option for enabling the logging for NAT or redirect rules. Also by default, pfSense doesn't log for allowed traffic. To see the NAT or redirection connections, enable the **Log packets that are handled by this rule** checkbox in the firewall rule(s) for the LAN or other interfaces that you are doing NAT on. This is covered in Section 16.2.1.

Or see the **Status** $\rightarrow$ **System Logs** $\rightarrow$ **Settings** page (as discussed on Section 16.18.1) about logging packets for pass rules.

17.7 NAT States

The states for NAT connections can be viewed on the **Diagnostics** $\rightarrow$ **States** page as introduced in Section 16.15. To limit it to the NAT states, enter the first part of the network address in the **Filter expression** field (such as "172.16.1") and click the **Filter** button. Keep the **Interface** drop-down set to *all* since the connections will commonly be shown on both the internal and external interfaces. The complementing state entries will show the originating address and port in parentheses.

The **Diagnostics** $\rightarrow$ **States Summary** view as covered in Section 16.16 may also show summary counts for the NAT states. Manually look in the various sections for part of the IP addresses that are used for the NAT range.

By IP Pair					
				Protocol counts	
IP	# States	Protocol	# States	Source Ports	Dest. Ports
172.16.1.4 -> 17.249.60.89	2	tcp	2	1	1
172.16.1.4 -> 8.8.8.8	2	udp	2	1	1
172.16.1.4 -> 104.154.127.207	2	tcp	2	1	1
172.16.1.4 -> 216.58.193.142	2	tcp	2	1	1

Figure 17.2: **Diagnostics** $\rightarrow$ **States Summary : By IP Pair**

In the **By IP Pair** section, you can see specific NAT state connections for the internal NAT'ed addresses and their outside connections. An example is in Figure 17.2.

17.8   UPnP and NAT-PMP Port Mapping

Universal Plug and Play (UPnP) Internet Gateway Device Protocol and NAT Port Mapping Protocol (NAT-PMP) are two methods for improving Internet connectivity for gaming consoles and other devices or applications behind a NAT gateway. UPnP is commonly used by client devices to create port mappings, while NAT-PMP allows individual applications to manage their own port mappings. The **Services** → **UPnP & NAT-PMP** menu is used to enable this gateway device daemon, `miniupnpd`, and clients on the NAT'ed LAN can use it for port redirections.

This feature is only available on pfSense systems that have more than one network interface configured.

The top right of page has shortcuts to view the related status and related logs. If the daemon is enabled, icons will also be available to restart the service and stop the service,

17.8.1   UPnP & NAT-PMP Settings

Click the checkbox for **Enable UPnP & NAT-PMP** and select at least one or both of **Allow UPnP Port Mapping** or **Allow NAT-PMP Port Mapping** checkboxes to use this feature. Then click the **Save** button to activate it.

While UPnP has been associated with Microsoft systems and NAT-PMP with Apple systems, NAT-PMP is a newer and simpler standard in more common use even for Microsoft-compatible systems.

To turn on the UPnP support, check the **UPnP Port Mapping** checkbox.

To turn on the NAT-PMP support, check the **NAT-PMP Port Mapping** checkbox. Normally this is not enabled.

Select the interface to the Internet that has a public IP address in the **External Interface** drop-down menu. This defaults to the WAN.

Select one or more local network interfaces in the **Interfaces** menu. (Select multiple by pressing the Control key while clicking a selection.) The LAN interface is the default. Do not select the WAN interface as it may be a security risk. You also can not select an interface here that is the same as the previously-defined external interface.

Enter the maximum kilobits per second download and upload rates to be reported to clients in the **Download Speed** and **Upload Speed** fields. (By default, it will try to detect the interface speed.)

By default, it will use the external interface's main IP address for the Internet side. If you need to use an alternative IP address such as a virtual IP, enter it in the **Override WAN address** field.

To have the PF firewall port redirections handled by the ALTQ traffic shaper, enter the previously-created queue name in the **Traffic Shaping** field. See the **Firewall** → **Traffic Shaper** → **By Interface** or **By Queue** pages as discussed in Chapter 25.

To have the PF packet filter log matching redirection rules for debugging or analysis, check the **Log packets** checkbox. The packet filter logs may be viewed via the **Status** → **System Logs** → **Firewall** page (Section 16.18).

The protocol has a time tracking field that increments every second. It uses this to detect loss of state. By default, it uses the time of when the `miniupnpd` daemon started. To use the system's boot time instead, select the **Uptime** checkbox.

When a device is discovered, to learn more about it, it provides an XML description which includes a serial number which is the unique ID derived from the WAN interface's MAC address, the URL for your pfSense system web interface, and the pfSense version as a model number. To override the URL, enter it in the **Custom presentation URL** field. To provide your own model number, enter it in the **Custom model number** field.

17.8.2 UPnP Access Control

Click the **Default Deny** checkbox to deny all external and internal port ranges for all IP addresses by default. When using this, enter the allowed redirections in the following **ACL Entries** fields.

You may setup permission rules via the **ACL Entries** fields. It is recommended that rules be used to restrict insecure requests. Use the **Add** button to add additional ACL fields. The format is four space-delimited fields:

1. **allow or deny** — Enter `allow` or `deny` to accept or reject packages for the following ports and addresses.

2. **external port range** — This may be a single port or a range of ports using a dash for the external ports.

3. **IP/mask** — The network address must be an IP/bits format.

4. **internal port range** — Single port for the internal port or a range using a dash between the minimum or maximum port number.

The following example only allows redirection of ports greater than 1024 and has the last rule as a default deny for everything else.

```
allow 1024-65535 192.168.0.0/24 1024-65535
allow 1024-65535 192.168.1.0/24 1024-65535
allow 1024-65535 192.168.0.0/23 22
allow 12345 192.168.7.113/32 54321
deny 0-65535 0.0.0.0/0 0-65535
```

If using this, adjust the network address (with mask) to match your own internal (e.g. LAN) addresses. This final deny rule may be enabled by using the previous **Default Deny** checkbox.

You may remove an ACL field by clicking its corresponding **Delete** button.

After making changes, use the **Save** button to put them in place. If the service is already running, it will be restarted which will clear any existing sessions. Note that if the **Enable UPnP & NAT-PMP** checkbox is unchecked, this service will be turned off.

17.8.3   UPnP & NAT-PMP Status

The **Status** → **UPnP & NAT-PMP** page is used to view its packet filter entries and to clear these rules and restart the service. It will show the external redirect port, protocol, and the internal IP address and internal ports that it will redirect to. It may also have a description column which is the PF redirect rule explanation added by the service.

Note it doesn't create the entries until the clients on the internal network ask for port redirections.

There are no actions to remove individual redirections. You may use the **Clear all sessions** button which will kill the current daemon, flush all `miniupnpd`-specific firewall rules, and then restart the service.

17.8.4   UPnP & NAT-PMP Logging

The logging is available via the **Status** → **System Logs** → **System** → **Routing** log entries page. To see recent matching log entries, use the **Log filter** funnel shortcut to enter "`miniupnpd`" in the **Process** field and click the **Apply Filter** button.

18 Network Time Protocol (NTP)

pfSense uses and provides Network Time Protocol (NTP) service. Your system's time can be seen in the main dashboard's System Information widget. By default, the NTP service will have a persistent association with a remote time server to synchronize its local clock. This default server is *0.pf-sense.pool.ntp.org* which is a pool of NTP servers. By using round-robin DNS, one of these remote servers will be selected from the DNS pool. Additional servers or hardware clocks may also be used for better or consistent time. In addition to keeping your pfSense system's clock, other computers may synchronize with your pfSense time server.

The NTP server configuration is available via the **Services** → **NTP** menu item. It has links for different configurations. It defaults to the **Settings** page for its standard configurations. Access control restrictions may be configured via the **ACLs** link. A connected GPS device using the NMEA standard may be used as one of your time references; this may be configured via the **Serial GPS** page. While not preferred, Pulse Per Second radios are another time source and may be configured via the **PPS** link. These configurations are covered in this chapter.

The NTP server daemon, `ntpd`, may be restarted or stopped (or started if not running) via its corresponding actions at the **Status** → **Services** page or via those shortcuts on any of the NTP pages.

18.1 Network Time Protocol Status

The **Status** → **NTP** page shows a list of all its known time sources each with a summary of their current state. (This page will not display any details if the **Services** → **NTP** → **ACLs** settings has the **Disable ntpq and ntpdc queries (noquery)** checkbox enabled. See Section 18.4 for details.)

The status field is also called the *tally* and has the following possibilities:

Active Peer

> This is the current time source. (You need at least one active peer.)

Candidate

> This is a selected source included in the final set by the combine algorithm. (It was considered, but a better server is currently used.)

Selected

This is a backup source. (You shouldn't see this since pfSense only allows adding up to the maximum of ten time servers.)

PPS Peer

This is a selected Pulse Per Second (PPS) source.

Outlier

This source was discarded by the NTP cluster algorithm. It could be considered if you have less than three valid time sources or if its configuration is set to the **Prefer** option.

Excess Peer

This source is also not used. It was discarded as an excess candidate. It could be considered if you have less than three valid time sources or if its configuration is set to the **Prefer** option.

False Ticker

This source is currently rejected because the time may be wrong, but may be available as a candidate later.

Unreach/Pending

This source is discarded because it failed sanity checks or is not valid. It is not a candidate as it is unfit to synchronize. This status may be displayed when the server is configured with the **No Select** option. A source may also indicate it is unreachable if access control restrictions disallow it. (See the **Disable all except ntpq and ntpdc queries** or **noserve** checkboxes on the **Services** → **NTP** → **ACLs** subpage covered in Section 18.4.)

Network Time Protocol Status										
Status	Server	Ref ID	Stratum	Type	When	Poll	Reach	Delay	Offset	Jitter
Unreach/Pending	192.168.191.191	.INIT.	16	u	-	512	0	0.000	0.000	0.000
Candidate	138.68.46.177	90.187.19.113	2	u	73	128	377	40.411	-1.959	0.814
Active Peer	66.85.74.226	128.252.19.1	2	u	122	128	377	30.459	-2.891	0.598
Unreach/Pending	85.236.36.4	192.53.103.108	2	u	112	128	377	127.863	3.239	0.645
Candidate	96.126.105.86	132.246.11.231	2	u	46	64	7	40.500	-2.314	2.774
Outlier	129.6.15.27	.NIST.	1	u	45	64	7	48.021	-0.786	2.951
Candidate	74.40.74.60	66.133.129.31	2	u	126	128	377	2.647	5.443	0.682

Figure 18.1: Network Time Protocol Status

The other fields, as displayed in Figure 18.1, further summarize its current state.

Server

This is the IP address of the associated NTP server. This may show pseudo addresses for local hardware like 127.127.20.0 for GPS clock and 127.127.22.0 for PPS clock.

Ref ID

This is the association identifier or codes like "INIT" for association initialized, but not yet synchronized; "RATE" for access is temporarily denied because the client rate threshold was exceeded; "STEP" for step time change and association not yet resynchronized; "DENY" for access denied; and others.

Stratum

The stratum number is the level hierarchy for NTP servers. Stratum 1 is for primary servers directly connected via telephone, radio, or satellite to national time services. Level 2 is the secondary servers which synchronize against Level 1 servers. Many preferred public secondary servers are available as higher strata numbers which sync with lower numbered servers.

Type

The type is indicated with a single character code: **u**: unicast or manycast client; **b**: broadcast or multicast client; **l**: local reference clock; **s**: symmetric peer; **A**: manycast server; **B**: broadcast server; or **M**: multicast server.

When

The seconds (or minutes or hours) since it last received a packet from that server.

Poll

This is the interval in seconds of when your local server polls the remote server. With pfSense, this is generally between 64 and 512 seconds.

Reach

The reachability register is an octal (base 8) number which represents the valid responses for the last eight polls. Octal 377 means that it was successful the last eight times, for example in binary bits: 11111111. It is not an easy indicator to immediately understand for the other numbers. The following octal numbers indicate it was at least successful the last four times: 17, 37, 57, 77, 117, 137, 157, 177, 217, 237, 257, 277, 317, 337, 357, and 377 (all their binary numbers end with 1111). Octals 125 and 252 show it works every other time (1010101 and 10101010). Octals 200, 300, 340, and 360 indicate it has been failing the last few times.

Delay

This is the round-trip time in milliseconds to receive a reply from the remote server.

Offset

The time difference between your local server and the remote server is displayed in milliseconds. A negative number means your local time is in the future. Note that this display offset is based on the local NTP server's time and not necessarily the local clock time which it may be in the process of slowly adjusting.

Jitter

The *jitter* is a root mean square (RMS) average. It is the difference between two offset samples (that are squared). Larger numbers indicate that the offsets appear to be random and there is an uncertainty of getting the time from that system. If multiple server entries show large similar numbers like 1000 or greater, this may indicate that your local server had a time problem off by at least a few seconds.

The table updates every five seconds. Note it may not have any changed statistics during that time due to the polling scheduling.

The statistics are reset when the NTP service is restarted. If you want recorded statistics, see the **Statistics Logging** configurations on the **Services** → **NTP** → **Settings** (discussed in Section 18.3).

18.2   NTP Log Entries

For the NTP logging, see the **Status** → **System Logs** → **NTP** page. This should have various log entries from the `ntpd` daemon, such as what remote NTP servers it is listening to. It may also report the initial time setting at bootup from the `ntpdate` command.

To search or adjust this logging see Section 11.1 and Section 11.3 about the **Log filter** and **Manage log** shortcut features.

Last 50 NTP Log Entries. (Maximum 50)			
Time	Process	PID	Message
Jan 25 08:30:53	ntpd	39194	DNS 0.pfsense.pool.ntp.org -> 195.21.152.161
Jan 25 08:30:53	ntpd	39194	195.21.152.161 8011 81 mobilize assoc 3201
Jan 25 08:30:54	ntpd	39194	195.21.152.161 8024 84 reachable
Jan 25 08:30:54	ntpd	39194	DNS us.pool.ntp.org -> 129.6.15.28
Jan 25 08:30:54	ntpd	39194	129.6.15.28 8011 81 mobilize assoc 3202
Jan 25 08:30:55	ntpd	39194	DNS 2.netbsd.pool.ntp.org -> 2600:3c03::f03c:91ff:feae:82c1
Jan 25 08:30:55	ntpd	39194	2600:3c03::f03c:91ff:feae:82c1 8011 81 mobilize assoc 3203
Jan 25 08:30:55	ntpd	39194	DNS ntp01.frontier.com -> 74.40.74.60
Jan 25 08:30:55	ntpd	39194	74.40.74.60 8011 81 mobilize assoc 3204
Jan 25 08:30:56	ntpd	39194	74.40.74.60 8024 84 reachable
Jan 25 08:30:56	ntpd	39194	129.6.15.28 8024 84 reachable
Jan 25 08:31:00	ntpd	39194	195.21.152.161 903a 8a sys_peer
Jan 25 08:31:00	ntpd	39194	0.0.0.0 c61c 0c clock_step -0.662392 s
Jan 25 08:30:59	ntpd	39194	0.0.0.0 c615 05 clock_sync

Figure 18.2: **Status** → **System Logs** → **NTP**

To further troubleshoot NTP, you may enable further diagnostic messages (such as seen in Figure 18.2) on the **Services** → **NTP** → **Settings** page (as covered in the following section). If you want NTP event, statistics, and status messages, enable the **Log peer messages** and/or **Log system messages** checkboxes. You may also configure the **Statistics Logging** settings if you want recorded statistics.

18.3 NTP Settings

The **Services** → **NTP** → **Settings** page is used for the basic NTP server configuration.

The default configuration has the UDP port 123 network service listening on all your network interfaces. Use the **Interface** selector to choose to serve on only specific interfaces. You may select multiple interfaces. Note that if no interfaces is highlighted, then all interfaces — possibly even those not listed — will be serving NTP.

Note

Your firewall rules may need to be adjusted to lock out or allow access for your clients to NTP as expected.

To change the default remote NTP server to synchronize with, update the **Time Servers** text field with a new DNS name.

The server daemon doesn't use all entries from a single DNS round-robin but only a single IP address — so you may want to define multiple time servers. Up to ten servers may be configured by clicking the **Add** button. This will bring up an additional text input field to enter another server name (or IP address). When you have multiple servers, they all may be considered, but the best server will be actively used. (This may be seen via the **Status** → **NTP** page.)

When you have multiple time server choices, it will have a **Delete** button available to remove its corresponding entry. If you don't have any time server defined, it will fall back to use from the pool of NTP servers via the *pool.ntp.org* DNS name. For details on available public NTP servers for different continents and countries, see the NTP Pool Project at `http://www.pool.ntp.org/en/use.html`.

For each time server, the **Prefer** checkbox means the associated server is preferred over other servers (if added). To not use the server but still keep its configuration and collect its stats, use its **No Select** checkbox. (Then the status will indicate the server as "Unreach/Pending.")

When providing NTP service to others and your server becomes isolated from other outside clocks, it will report its stratum level as 12 as an orphan. This implies that its orphan clients will use lower numbered stratums instead (if available). This type of service option may be changed in the **Orphan Mode** field. Enter a number from 1 to 15.

As described in Section 28.2, various NTP statistics about the state of your clock may be collected and then visualized via the **Status** → **Monitoring** page. This includes the combined offset of the server (where less than 1 millisecond is good and should always be less than 128 ms), the combined system jitter (which should be less than 1 millisecond), the clock jitter in milliseconds (which should be less than 1 ms), the clock frequency wander in parts per million (which should be less than 1 PPM), the frequency offset relative to hardware clock in PPM (smaller the number the better), and the total dispersion to the primary reference clock (which should be 9 ms or less). To be able to later see these historical details, enable the **NTP Graphs** checkbox.

Additional logging can be enabled by checking the **Log peer messages** and **Log system messages** checkboxes. These would log additional informational, event, statistics, and status messages for the peers or the system, respectively. (See Section 18.2 for details about the **Status** → **System Logs** → **NTP** page.)

Additional log files may be created under the /var/log/ntp/ directory (as available via the Unix shell). To access this configuration, click the **Display Advanced** button for **Statistics Logging**. Three checkboxes are available for enabling writing of statistics records for the clock driver; loop filter (**Log clock discipline statistics**) for the time offset, frequency offset, root mean square (RMS) jitter, Allan deviation (ADEV), and the time constant; and peer information, including a delay and dispersion. If you don't have a local clock driver in use, its statistics file won't be created. Note these statistics files will grow over time and won't be managed by circular logging or log rotation.

Leap seconds are periodically added at the end of December or end of June to keep the difference between the irregular astronomical (aka solar) time (UT1) and the atomic clock-based UTC to be less than 0.9 seconds. If you want your local system's NTP server to gracefully handle leap seconds itself instead of waiting for your time server sources, see the **Leap seconds** section on the page. Use the **Display Advanced** button to view its fields. Either paste in the leap seconds file or upload it via your web browser's file upload feature there. A version of the file is published by the U.S. National Institute of Standards and Technology (NIST) which is available at ftp://ftp.nist.gov/pub/time/ or https://www.ietf.org/timezones/data/leap-seconds.list. In normal use, this local NTP leap seconds handling is not needed.

Use the **Save** button to immediately put your changes into use. It will restart your *ntpd* server.

18.4   NTP Access Restrictions

Additional NTP server configurations for access control are available via the **Services** → **NTP** → **ACLs** subpage. The default restrictions for all IPv4 and IPv6 client access are defined in the top section. Per-host or by network restrictions can be setup in the bottom section.

When the **Kiss-o'-Death** checkbox is enabled (the default), a "KoD" packet is returned to let the client know it was denied service. It will also respond indicating if the rate limit is exceeded. (If this is unchecked, NTP packets that are restricted get silently dropped.)

Run-time change configuration (such as by a control program) are ignored when the **Modifications** (nomodify) feature is checked. Only queries to return information are allowed. This is the recommended and default behavior.

By default, pfSense allows others to get details about your NTP server version and the operating system version. If you don't want anyone to query your NTP server's status, check the **Queries** (noquery) checkbox.

Note

If the **Disable ntpq and ntpdc queries (noquery)** checkbox is checked, then the **Status** → **NTP** page won't provide any status details.

By default, time packets are allowed. To block time packets, check the **Service** (noserve) checkbox. (Some NTP admins may want to allow monitoring or remote configurations even though not serving the time.)

Note

Disabling all using the **noserve** checkbox will also stop synchronization with other peers. You won't be able to serve the time unless it can communicate with at least one peer.

Checking the **Peer Association** (nopeer) checkbox will allow providing time service to polling hosts, but doesn't allocate peer memory resources for them. (New associations are denied.) This is the default.

The NTP server provides a feature (NTP Control Message mode 6) which may be used for NTP monitoring and remote event logging. The NTP server won't provide this by default. To allow remote event logging, uncheck the **Trap Service** (notrap) checkbox. (Responding when a peer randomly becomes unreachable is called a *trap*.)

The above settings are used for setting the server's defaults. To further restrict or open access for individual clients or networks, use the Custom Access Restrictions section. For example, you could restrict everything with defaults, then open up per host or network; but note this may not easily work as intended, because if you are only using remote network peers for synchronization, you will then need to allow them access too.

Enter the client or network address in the **Network** field. Then in the **Mask** drop-down menu, select its network mask. (For a single IPv4 client, enter 32 as the mask.)

Then check the checkboxes to enable the restrictions (aka flags) as described previously. Unchecked means it is allowed. When no flags are checked, free access is opened up for that host or network. Be careful with these settings as they are all unchecked and override the defaults.

Click the **Add** button for additional host or network access controls. **Delete** buttons become available for each per-network configuration after adding a second one. To delete the first one, blank out the network field and uncheck all its corresponding checkboxes.

The NTP service is restarted and these access control configurations are put into place immediately when saving.

18.5 Serial GPS

You can use a locally-attached GPS receiver using the NMEA protocol as a reference clock for your time server. (NMEA is defined by the National Marine Electronics Association for marine electronics communication.) For advanced details about the NTP Generic NMEA GPS Receiver driver, see `http://doc.ntp.org/current-stable/drivers/driver20.html`.

This is configured for a single serial-connected device via the **Services** → **NTP** → **Serial GPS** subpage. It is recommended to have at least one other clock source when using GPS. To enable it, you will need at least to set the serial port.

Select the hardware, such as Garmin, MediaTek, SiRF, U-Blox, and SureGPS, in the **GPS Type** drop-down menu. Depending on the selection, this will preset some following values like a time calibration offset, baud rate for the serial connection, initialization commands sent to the GPS device, and/or flags for the NTP clock driver. You will also have different option based on this type selection. pfSense recommends not using the default option, but setting it to **Generic** if you need a default. If you need to define some of your own settings, select the **Custom** choice.

If you have a `/dev/cua` serial port device, you will have a **Serial Port** drop-down menu to select where your GPS is connected. This defaults to *None*.

The default input and output baud rate for the device is 4800. If you selected the SureGPS type, it sets it to 9600. Select what your GPS hardware supports in the corresponding drop-down menu from also 19200, 38400, 57600, and 115200.

A NMEA sentence defines how data is transmitted from the GPS clock. This is encoded in a special format not covered in this book. See your GPS manufacturer's documentation to provide these details for the upcoming **GPS Initialization** textbox. To automatically assign this, select a standard from the **NMEA Sentences** selection menu. These include:

All
> Process all supported sentences. (This is the default.)

RMC
> Recommended minimum data with position, velocity, and time.

GGA
> Essential fix information, 3D location, and accuracy data.

GLL
> Geographic latitude, longitude, and time.

ZDA or ZDG
> Date, Zulu (UTC) time, and time to destination.

If using the custom or Garmin type, you will have a **Process PGRMF** checkbox to only use the Garmin-proprietary Position Fix Sentence. When selected then other sentences will be ignored.

The PPS time offset calibration factor is set in fractional seconds in the **Fudge Time 1** field. By default, this is set to 0.155. If Garmin type is selected, then it is set to 0.600.

The **Fudge Time 2** field set in fractional seconds is used to compensate for delays. It is the offset to the actual time. This fudge time can be estimated by manually comparing its time against other clocks by setting it to 0 (zero). This is unset by default. If the Garmin type is selected, then it is set to 0.600. For Generic, MediaTek, and U-Blox types, it is 0.400. For SiRF type it is 0.704. And SureGPS defaults to 0.407.

Enter the stratum number for this clock in the **Stratum (0-16)** field. This is a number from 0 to 15. Entering 16 means it is unsynchronized.

To use this clock for synchronization (among other clock sources), make sure the **Prefer this clock** checkbox is selected. (This is the default.) Instead, if you just want to display results from this GPS clock, click the **Do not use this clock** checkbox. Note you cannot not use both of these settings at the same time, and selecting one will toggle the other off.

The following four flags are used for customizing clock drivers. By default, the NMEA driver will use PPS processing. To turn that off, uncheck the **Enable PPS signal processing** checkbox.

It will use the assert (rising) edge of the PPS signal by default. This can be set to use the clear pulse edge by checking the **Enable falling edge PPS signal processing** checkbox.

The kernel PPS discipline is enabled by default. To disable it, uncheck the **Enable kernel PPS clock discipline** checkbox.

To obscure the GPS location in the timecode, select the **Obscure location in timestamp** checkbox.

For clock statistics, the sub-second fraction of time can be recorded by enabling the **Log the sub-second fraction of the received time stamp** checkbox. This may cause lots of extra logs. (See the **Log reference clock statistics** checkbox in the **Statistics Logging** section under the **Services → NTP → Settings** page (Section 18.3.)

By default, the **Status → NTP** page will show extra details (like global positioning data) when using GPGSV (detailed satellite data) or GPGGA (fix data) with the initialization commands. This non-clock-related status may be disabled by unchecking the **Display extended GPS status** checkbox.

Specify the driver reference identifier string in the **Clock ID** field. This will be used for logging and stats. It can be up to four characters long. If unset, it will default to "GPS."

The **GPS Initialization** data is written directly to the serial port to initialize the GPS. Be careful with what you send to it. Click the **Display Advanced** button to expand additional settings to define this.

The **Auto correct malformed initialization commands** checkbox may be used to trim lines, prefix and append required characters, and add a computed checksum. Each NMEA sentence line ends with a checksum.

The **NMEA Checksum Calculator** may be used to generate a checksum for the input (which is the data between the $ and * characters) by pressing the **Calculate** button. The result will be in the corresponding field.

Use the **Save** button to restart the NTP service with these GPS settings. Go to the **Status → NTP** page to see it. When this is use, the status page will identify the GPS clock with the 127.127.20.0 pseudo IP address.

To disable it, just set the **Serial Port** option back to **None** (and save).

18.6   Pulse Per Second Configuration

You may use a radio clock, cesium clock, GPS device, or other Pulse Per Second (PPS) output device connected to your serial port as another precision source. Configure this via the **Services** → **NTP** → **PPS** subpage.

   Warning
Note another preferred peer source with a complete timestamp should be defined because PPS only indicates when a second changes and not which second it is.

To enable use of a PPS device, select where it is connected (such as `cuau0`) in the **Serial Port** drop-down menu. To disable this PPS reference, simply set it to **None** (the default).

In the **Fudge Time** field, enter the fractional seconds for the time offset calibration. (It defaults to 0.0 seconds.)

This defaults to use a stratum number of 0 (as a reference clock). The **Stratum** field may be used to lower the priority usage of this clock. Enter a number within 0 to 15.

Three **Flags** checkboxes are available for further configurations. By default, PPS capture is on the rising (assert) pulse edge. To use the falling (clear) pulse edge, enable that checkbox. Kernel PPS discipline is disabled by default. It can be enabled too. To record a timestamp once for each second, check its corresponding checkbox.

To set a custom reference clock identifier (for stats and logging) enter it in the **ClockID** text field. This is limited to four characters. If not set, it will use ".PPS." as the identifier.

Clicking the **Save** button will store the settings and restart NTP server. It will stay on the same PPS form page. View the **Status** → **NTP** page. Note it will show the server IP as 127.127.22.0 which virtually represents the PPS reference clock. It is in use when the status is not unreachable or pending and the reach shows 377, for example.

19 DHCP Services

DHCP, or the Dynamic Host Configuration Protocol, is a standard method for managing and providing configuration information to other devices on a network. The common usage is for the DHCP client to request an IP address to use, but it may also learn about the default gateway router, name servers, and other networking services or details to use. pfSense can run a central DHCP server that maintains a list of IP addresses to be allocated — or leased — to local clients as well as serving these other details.

In addition, pfSense also provides DHCP version 6 (DHCPv6) and IPv6 Stateless Address Autoconfiguration (SLAAC) service. These are covered in the following chapter.

This chapter covers providing DHCP services for IPv4. If your pfSense system uses DHCP to get its networking details from a different DHCP server, this is configured per interface as discussed in Section 13.2.3.

The DHCP service can be enabled and configured under the **Services** → **DHCP Server** menu.

Note

You must have an interface configured with a static IPv4 address to enable a DHCP server. In addition, the subnet for the interface needs to be larger (smaller number) than a CIDR mask of /31 so there will be enough addresses to serve to clients. Also the DHCP server can not be enabled if a DHCP Relay is already enabled on any interface.

Near the top of the page one or more links for interfaces will be listed to select the interface to configure a DHCP server on. The default view will be for the first interface that already has a DHCP server enabled; else if you have a LAN interface it will be selected by default. If you have multiple choices, select the interface you want to configure. (If your desired interface is not there, then check its properties to make sure it has a static IP address and that it has a large enough subnet.)

At the top right of the page are icons to restart the DHCP server, temporarily stop it from running, view the list of current leases provided (Section 19.6), and for DHCP logging (Section 19.8).

19.1   DHCP Server General Options

To actually run a DHCP server for the selected network interface, the **Enable DHCP server** checkbox must be selected.

Legacy BOOTP queries are allowed by default. To not respond to them, check the **Ignore BOOTP queries** checkbox.

Unknown clients are those that don't identify themselves with a hostname. By default, they are allowed to get a dynamic address assignment. But if you don't want them to, check the **Deny unknown clients** checkbox. If you don't want your DHCP server to even respond to these unknown clients, check the following **Ignore denied clients** checkbox.

Some DHCP clients send a client identifier or a UID which may be used to acquire a lease and is recorded. Check the **Ignore client identifiers** checkbox if you don't want the UIDs for clients recorded.

The DHCP server configuration form will also show the current subnet and its mask and the range of IPv4 addresses that are available within that subnet. For example, it may show an available range of 172.16.1.1 through 172.16.1.14 within the subnet of 172.16.1.0 with a mask of 255.255.255.240.

Enter the start and end of the IPv4 address range which your DHCP server will dynamically assign addresses to its clients in the **From** and **To** fields.

19.2   DHCP Server Additional Pools

A *pool* in DHCP is a way to have different configurations or different DHCP options for different assigned addresses, even when they are on the same network. Use the **Add pool** button to add a new pool which implies an additional configuration. Note that a few configurations are global to all pools and they cannot be configured specific to a pool. A new page will open to add and configure the new pool. It will have most of the same setting options (described in this chapter) with a few minor differences. To get back to the main DHCP settings (without adding the pool), click on the interface names link at the top.

The **Additional Pools** section of the form won't be there (as you won't have a pool within a pool). The available range details will also show the DHCP pool ranges which are already in-use. To save the new pool-specific options, you will need to enter the **Range** fields for **From** and **To**. Also consider entering a pool-specific explanation in the **Pool Description** field.

Adding a new pool also doesn't provide the global settings for failover peer IP, static ARP, logging leases using local timezone, nor enabling statistics graphs. Those are all set in the main DHCP configuration. The Client ID column in the static mappings table also is not displayed.

When one or more pools are defined, its main configuration's pool table will show the starting and ending IPv4 addresses with an optional description for each pool. If you double-click on the pool entry, it will take you its pool-specific page to update its configurations. Each pool will also have corresponding action icons to edit or remove it.

19.3 Servers (DHCP Options)

You may enter one or two WINS (NetBIOS Name Service or NBNS) name servers in the **WINS Server** fields. This only accepts IPv4 addresses for them. This detail will be provided to the DHCP client to use if it needs them. (Note that it will use the NetBIOS Hybrid mode node type option where the client may try a direct server query first for resolving names, and then fallback to IP broadcast messages.)

If you want your DHCP clients to use domain name resolvers of your choice, enter them in the **DNS Server** fields. These are IPv4 addresses for the DNS servers that will handle recursive requests for your clients. If this is not set and you are using the built-in resolver (Unbound), it will define your pfSense system's IP address instead for clients to use it. Or as a final fallback, it will assign the DNS server IP addresses that your pfSense system knows about, like configured via **System → General Settings** (Section 5.1.2).

19.4 Other DHCP Server Options

Normally the DHCP server tells the DHCP clients that the router for them to use is your pfSense system. If you need the clients to use a different router as their default, enter its IPv4 address in the **Gateway** field. Note that the router should be available on the client's subnet. You may enter the word "**none**" if you don't want to provide any router definition to the DHCP client.

For the client's DNS lookups for short names, it may append your pfSense system's domain name to get answers for a fully-qualified domain name. (This is *localdomain* in default installs of pfSense and can be changed for pfSense on the **System → General Settings** page as described in Section 5.1.2.) To offer to the DHCP clients a different domain name to append, enter it in the **Domain name** field.

The **Domain search list** is similar to the previous option, but instead of a single domain you may enter multiple domain names to append to the not-fully-qualified names. Use a semicolon or space to separate each domain name. Note that some DNS resolvers have a limit, such as six domains or 1024 total characters in this DNS search list.

A dynamically-assigned address (the lease) will be valid for two hours (7200 seconds) by default. This can be changed by entering the seconds in the **Default lease time** field. A common setting is 43200 seconds for half of a day. This must be at least 60 seconds.

If the DHCP client does ask for a specific lease time, it will be capped to one day maximum (86400 seconds). This expiration may be changed in the **Maximum lease time** field which must be longer than the previous default lease time.

The pfSense server's DHCP for IPv4 offers failover functionality and DHCP load balancing. This can only use two compatible DHCP servers which synchronize with each other and serve from a common address pool.

This means you will need to setup another DHCP server within the network running the recommended same version of ISC DHCP server, with similar configurations without mixed pools, and a complementing failover setup. Another pfSense system in the subnet may be used for the other DHCP failover server. (Configuring another ISC DHCP server without pfSense is outside the scope of this book, but pfSense's DHCP failover implementation uses the common 519 and 520 ports for failover communications.)

To enable on the pfSense system, enter the other DHCP failover server's IP address in the **Failover peer IP** field. (This is a global option and is not available for specific pools. If using address pools, they should be identical in both failover server configurations.) In addition, each failover server will only allocate about half of the total IP address range, so be sure to plan for that also.

pfSense recommends using the CARP-style virtual IP setup for further redundancy. See the **Firewall → Virtual IPs** page as covered in Section 16.10 for more details. The Virtual IP's **Skew** setting (Section 16.10.1) may be used to help define if your pfSense system is the primary or secondary DHCP failover peer. Note that this defaults to 0 (zero) which means it will be the primary failover, but if you set the skew to above 10, it will be the secondary.

When configured as the *primary* failover peer, the pfSense system has a reasonable 50-percent load-balancing split and will only allocate new leases for 10 minutes if the DHCP failover peers cannot synchronize their leases.

Normally, the pfSense system will send out Address Resolution Protocol requests and listen to ARP replies. When DHCP static maps are setup (as in the upcoming Section 19.5), ARP entries are created for each static entry. When the global **Static ARP** checkbox is selected, the system will not send Address Resolution Protocol requests and will only reply to ARP requests for its own addresses.

The **Status → DHCP Leases** page (Section 19.6) shows the current lease times using the UTC timezone. To have these displayed in the pfSense system's configured timezone, check the **Time format change** global option checkbox. (The system's timezone can be set on the **System → General Settings** page as seen in Section 5.1.3.)

To be able to view historical details about how many leases have been used, number of static leases, and the size the of DHCP range, enable the global option **Statistics graphs** checkbox. This will enable minutely collection of this data which may be presented via the **Status → Monitoring** page. See Section 28.2 for details.

19.4.1   Dynamic DNS (DHCP Options)

The DHCP server can use DNS dynamic updates to tell an authoritative DNS server about the IP addresses associated with the DHCP clients' hostnames. This may be enabled by checking the **Enable registration of DHCP client names in DNS** checkbox and configuring the following settings. This DNS update is authenticated using TSIG technology which requires a working clock, and a shared key name, shared secret, and same algorithm on both systems. These will be provided by your DNS administrator.

Enter the domain name (like "example.com" to be updated in the **DDNS Domain** field. The DHCP client's hostname (like "texas") will be prepended to it to form the full-qualified domain name (such as *texas.example.com*). The DNS server will have a DNS zone configuration for that domain which is enabled for dynamic DNS updates using the following settings.

If using static maps (as configured in Section 19.5), you may choose to provide their predefined-static names instead of what is detected via DHCP, by checking the **DDNS Hostnames** checkbox.

Enter the IPv4 address for the authoritative DNS server in the **Primary DDNS address** field.

For the TSIG authentication, enter the key name in the **DNS Domain key** field. (Normally it looks like a DNS domain name.) Then select the algorithm which must also match the DNS server in the **Key algorithm** drop-down menu. The default is HMAC-MD5, but commonly HMAC-SHA256 is used on DNS servers. The other choices include HMAC-SHA1, HMAC-SHA224, HMAC-SHA384, and HMAC-SHA512.

The TSIG shared secret is entered in the **DNS Domain key secret** field. (It may look something like "pRP5FapFoJ95JEL06sv4PQ==".)

Some DHCP clients can manage their own dynamic DNS updates and may indicate this to your DHCP server. By default this is allowed. It uses what is called an *interim update scheme* where the DHCP server keeps track if it did a DNS update for the same before. If you don't want your DHCP server to do dynamic updates for the address (A) records, select *Ignore* from the **DDNS Client Updates** drop-down menu. Or to tell the DHCP client to not do its own updates, select *Deny*.

19.4.2 MAC Address Control

When using a pool, you can control address allocation based on the client's MAC addresses. Enter comma-separated client MAC addresses to allow allocation from the pool in the **MAC Allow** field.

To prevent allocation for specific clients, enter their MAC addresses, also comma-separated, in the **MAC Deny** field. If you have **Ignore denied clients** checked (and you aren't using DHCP Failover), this will silently ignore the listed clients.

19.4.3 NTP Option (DHCP)

To tell the DHCP client where a Network Time Protocol server is at, enter its IP address in the **NTP Server 1** field. You may also provide a secondary NTP server IP in the **NTP Server 2** field.

19.4.4 TFTP Option (DHCP)

To tell the DHCP client about a local TFTP server (commonly used for network booting), enter its IP address in the **TFTP Server** field.

19.4.5   LDAP Option (DHCP)

Some clients (such as Apple devices) may be able to use LDAP after getting its details from DHCP. To indicate this, enter a complete LDAP URL in the **LDAP Server URI** field. This would include the *ldap::// * scheme, address, optional port, and various LDAP entries and attributes.

19.4.6   Network Booting Options (DHCP Server)

To provide DHCP options about network booting, select the **Enable** checkbox and configure the following. The actual implementation and setup of the boot files and environment and the PXE (Preboot eXecution Environment) clients is beyond the focus of this book.

For networking booting, enter the IP address of the server where the boot file will be loaded from in the **Next Server** field.

Then enter the pathname of the initial boot file that the network client will load in the **Default BIOS file name** field. The download server would have this file available there at that pathname.

The DHCP client may indicate to the DHCP server about its architecture, so you can provide compatible PXE boot files. For booting 32-bit x86 Extensible Firmware Interface (EFI) based systems, enter the pathname in the **UEFI 32 bit file name** field. Or for booting 64-bit x86 EFI-based systems, enter the pathname for the boot program in the **UEFI 64 bit file name** field.

Then enter the location (such as "10.0.1.4:/var/tmp/rootfs") that the network boot client will use for its root (main) disk in the **Root path** field.

19.4.7   Additional BOOTP/DHCP Options

You may provide additional information to DHCP clients with custom DHCP options. This may be used for existing standard options or to define your own new options. Each option has a code number and a structured value. Enter your desired code in the **Number** field. Numbers in 224 to 254 may be used for your local private use. Be careful using other codes which may already be used.

The data then assigned to that option may be a simple structure as defined in the **Type** drop-down menu. It defaults to *Text*. You may also choose *String, Boolean, Unsigned 8-bit integer, Unsigned 16-bit integer, Unsigned 32-bit integer, Signed 8-bit integer, Signed 16-bit integer, Signed 32-bit integer*, or *IP address or host*.

Then enter the data (for that type) in the **Value** field. A boolean option can be defined as *on, true, off,* or *false*. If using a hostname for an IP address, make sure it only resolves to a single IPv4 address.

Using the **Add** button will bring up additional fields. To remove one of the custom options, click its corresponding **Delete** button.

Click the **Save** button to store and automatically start the DHCP server with the new settings. Note it will also restart any existing IPv4 DHCP service.

19.5   Static DHCP Mappings

At the bottom of a **Services** → **DHCP Server** page configuration is a table showing the DHCP Static Mappings for the interface. These are for defining a specific, non-changing IP address, a hostname, and several other optional attributes for a device requesting this via DHCP. This feature may be used to override the server settings for a specific DHCP client.

The first column will have a checkmark if a static ARP entry is also created for the MAC and IP address pair. The table also lists the static DHCP entry's MAC address, client identifier (if it exists), IP address, hostname, and optional description. Corresponding actions icons allow editing the static mapping or removing the entry. By default, there are no static mappings so the table is empty.

A static mapping can be added by clicking the **Add** button (in the **DHCP Static Mappings for this Interface** section). This will take you to a new page.

Or to conveniently add a static mapping for an existing DHCP lease, follow the **Related status** shortcut or go to the **Status** → **DHCP Leases** page and click a lease's corresponding **Add static mapping** plus icon action. (See Section 19.6 for details.)

19.5.1   Add or Edit Static DHCP Mappings

The form for adding or editing the static DHCP mapping has many fields, but only the MAC address or Client identifier is required. A *Client identifier* is a unique key for associating a device to a DHCP lease. Some sites use a manufacturer's serial number to associate a lease with specific hardware. Some use a DNS hostname to not be device specific. Enter a MAC address or client identifier in the appropriate field.

If your web browser is within the DHCP subnet and you want that same system to have a static DHCP mapping, click the **Copy My Mac** button. This will enter the detected MAC address in that field. Note if you have intermediate devices between you and the pfSense system, the MAC address of the device closest to the pfSense system will be inserted.

You only need to configure the other following settings if you need this one specific static mapping to have different options. These are documented in detail in the previous sections.

The common reason for using a static mapping is to define a specific IPv4 address for the DHCP client. This may be entered in the **IP Address** field.

You can also provide a hostname for the client in the **Hostname** field. For this, use a non-fully-qualified short name, but note that most DHCP clients do not use this provided hostname.

For your own reference or reminder about this static mapping, enter an explanation in the optional **Description** text field.

The form has several additional options which may be used to override the DHCP server's settings for this mapping, including for network booting (if enabled for the server), permanent ARP entry, Net-BIOS name servers (WINS), DNS servers, default gateway router, local domain name and search list for resolver hostname lookups, default and maximum lease expiration times, dynamic DNS updates, NTP servers, and TFTP server.

Click the **Save** button to store the single static mapping configuration (for the DHCP server for the interface). You will be taken back to the DHCP server configuration page with the static mappings table at the bottom showing the new entry. To reload the DHCP server with the configuration changes, click the **Apply Changes** button.

19.6 DHCP Leases

The **Status** → **DHCP Leases** page is used to list the systems that are currently assigned an address from your DHCP server. For each, it will show the IP address, MAC address, and hostname. It may optionally show a Client ID (CID) and a description. For each lease, it will have the start and end (expiration) day and time, and indicate if it is online (per ARP). The lease type column is for the binding: active, expired (for free), reserved (for backup); or if it is static.

The lease times are shown in the UTC timezone. If you want this to show the times in your pfSense system's configured timezone, select the **Time format change** option in the DHCP server configuration.

The entries may have corresponding action icons: **Add static mapping** or **Edit static mapping** (see Section 19.5.1); **Add WOL mapping** or **Send WOL packet** (if offline); and **Delete lease**. (For details on WOL aka Wake-on-LAN, see Section 13.9). The **Delete lease** (trash can icon) is used to remove an offline entry from the leases database.

By default, the leases table only shows the active and static leases. At the bottom of the page is a button to **Show all configured leases**; click it to see offline or expired leases, for example.

The page also provides a table to summarize with the count of leases in use for each pool. (Note this count will adjust based on if all configured leases are displayed or not.)

For further details, click the **Related log entries** shortcut icon to see the latest DHCP-related logging.

Other historical stats about the lease usage is available via the **Status** → **Monitoring** page, but only if the **Statistics graphs** option is checked (see Section 19.4).

19.7 DHCP Relay

The **Services** → **DHCP Relay** feature may be useful if you need your DHCP clients and DHCP server(s) on different networks, or if you want to use a single DHCP server but it is on a different network. The DHCP Relay will listen for the DHCP client queries and then forward them on to one or more DHCP servers. It will then send back replies to the source of the original DHCP request. (As an alternative, based on your needs, you could configure a DHCP server for each subnet, as covered previously.)

Note
The DHCP Relay cannot be enabled when the DHCP server is already in use (on any interface).

The icons on the titlebar may be used to restart the DHCP service, stop the DHCP service, configure the DHCP Server, view the available lease pools and the leases in use, and view the latest DHCP log entries. These are for the DHCP server in general and not specific to the DHCP Relay.

Click the **Enable** checkbox to display the DHCP Relay configurations.

Select one or more network interfaces that you want to run the DHCP Relay Agent on in the **Interface(s)** menu. (This will only list your interfaces that have an IPv4 address assigned.)

If needed, click the **Append circuit ID and agent ID to requests** checkbox to replace the existing agent option field of incoming DHCP packets with the name of the interface.

In the **Destination server** field, enter the target IPv4 address where the DHCP requests will be relayed to. You may have multiple server addresses, by clicking the **Add server** button and entering additional IPv4 addresses in each new field. Use the **Delete** button to remove one of the destination servers.

Click the **Save** button to run the DHCP Relay Agent daemon. To stop the server, disable it with the first checkbox and save.

19.8 DHCP Log Entries

Logging for the DHCP server (`dhcpd`), IPv4 DHCP client (`dhclient`), and the DHCP relay (`dhc relay`) can be viewed via the **Status → System Logs → DHCP** page. The IPv6 DHCP services are also logged there. The logging may be very verbose and frequent — especially if you have many devices requesting DHCP details. (An example is in Figure 19.1.)

Last 50 DHCP Log Entries. (Maximum 50)			
Time	Process	PID	Message
Jan 31 01:30:26	dhcpd		Wrote 2 leases to leases file.
Jan 31 01:30:26	dhcpd		DHCPREQUEST for 172.16.1.4 from 00:7f:28:35:b7:ad (Wireless_Broadband_Router) via rl1
Jan 31 01:30:26	dhcpd		DHCPACK on 172.16.1.4 to 00:7f:28:35:b7:ad (Wireless_Broadband_Router) via rl1
Jan 31 01:30:53	dhclient		RENEW
Jan 31 01:30:53	dhclient		Creating resolv.conf

Figure 19.1: **Status → System Logs → DHCP**

For details on using the advanced log filter or to override the general logging options for the logs, see Section 11.1 and Section 11.3, respectively.

20 DHCPv6 and Router Advertisement

pfSense can provide both IPv6 stateless address autoconfigurations (aka SLAAC) using *Router Advertisements* (RA) and stateful address autoconfiguration using DHCPv6, the Dynamic Host Configuration Protocol for IPv6. SLAAC can be used for autoconfiguring a unique local address based on a combination of information advertised by an IPv6 router and local information. (Even without a router, a device can generate a *link-local* address which may be used to communicate with other IPv6 devices on the same link.) SLAAC can also provide other parameters, like DNS settings. The DHCPv6 complements this by sharing other information or to actually track (using leases) the exact addresses that IPv6 clients should use for accountability. They can both be used at the same time as explained in this chapter.

Note while the naming and the overall features are similar, DHCPv6 is very different from DHCP for IPv4. For DHCP for IPv4, see the previous chapter. For example, DHCPv6 does not support options to set routers or gateways. (That is handled via Router Advertisements instead.) It is common for DHCPv6 clients to only do DHCPv6 when instructed per an IPv6 Router Advertisement.

If your pfSense system uses SLAAC or DHCPv6 to get its networking details from a different Router Advertisements or DHCPv6 server, this client configuration is setup per interface as discussed in Chapter 14.

The **Services** → **DHCPv6 Server & RA** menu link takes you to the pages for configuring a DHCPv6 server or Router Advertisement (RA) daemon. One or more tabs (links) near the top of the page will list the available interfaces to configure for DHCPv6 or Router Advertisements. Commonly it will just default to LAN. Select the interface you want to configure the server on.

Note

Your desired interface must be configured with a static IPv6 address to enable a DHCPv6 server or for Router Advertisements. (To setup the IPv6 interface, see Section 14.1.)

Below the interface selection(s) are two more links for selecting the configuration view of either DHCPv6 Server (the default) or Router Advertisements.

20.1   Router Advertisements

The **Services** → **DHCPv6 Server & RA** → **Router Advertisements** subpage is used to configure a Router Advertisement (RA) daemon for IPv6. The pfSense router can advertise itself and the IPv6 network it is supporting by listening to router solicitations and sending router advertisements. This provides *Neighbor Discovery* so IPv6 hosts can automatically configure their interfaces and other parameters, like the router willing to forward for them and DNS servers to use.

Address autoconfiguration via Router Advertisements is stateless. For accountability and tracking of assignments, both DHCPv6 (which uses leases) and RA may be offered at the same time. RA offers *managed* and *other* modes to use the stateful DHCPv6 for address or non-address information autoconfiguration (in addition to RA's stateless address autoconfiguration). This is covered in the following **Router mode** configuration.

Note

To configure Router Advertisements, you must have an interface configured with a static IPv6 address with a prefix length of 64.

If you have multiple capable interfaces, be sure to select the correct interface. Link tabs near the top will allow you select the interface to configure RA on. It commonly defaults to LAN. (Below the interface tab, it has a link to change to the page to setup a DHCPv6 server.)

The RA configuration is done in two sections: **Advertisements** and **DNS Configuration**. The only required setting is to change the following **Router mode** from its default disabled setting.

20.1.1   Router Advertisement Settings

There are several choices to make for running the Router Advertisement service and how it advertises. The **Router mode** drop-down menu has the following choices:

- **Router Only** — DHCPv6 is not used to supplement this for either addresses or other configuration information.

- **Unmanaged** — DHCPv6 is not used to supplement this for either addresses or other configuration information. The prefix may be used for an automatic-generated address and for determining whether it is on the same link so doesn't need a router.

- **Managed** — DHCPv6 will be used for address autoconfiguration and stateless autoconfiguration parameters (like DNS settings). The prefix may be used for determining whether another address shares the same link to know if it needs a router.

- **Assisted** — DHCPv6 will be used for address autoconfiguration and stateless autoconfiguration parameters (like DNS settings). The prefix may be used for automatic address generation and for determining whether it is on the same link so doesn't need a router.

- **Stateless DHCP** — DHCPv6 is not used for address autoconfiguration, but DHCP may be used for other stateless configuration parameters (like DNS settings). The prefix may be used for automatic address generation and for determining whether it is on the same link so doesn't need a router.

- **Disabled** — Select this to not run the Router Advertisement service. (This is the default mode.)

A Router Advertisement message can communicate default router preferences to help hosts pick an appropriate router. The *Normal* preference is the medium priority. You may change this in the **Router priority** menu to either *Low* or *High*.

If you have a CARP interface enabled, you may use it for the Router Advertisement service. Select the CARP interface in the **RA Interface** drop-down menu. If this interface is the master CARP host, this assumes you have more than one pfSense system running an Router Advertisement service. (See Section 16.10 for an introduction to CARP.)

By default, the prefix is valid for one day after the message is sent. (When it expires, the address is invalid.) You can change this in the **Default valid lifetime** number field. The maximum allowed in pfSense is 655350 seconds (7.5 days). Note that the IPv6 Stateless Address Autoconfiguration RFC 4862 specifies that a valid lifetime less than two hours is ignored.

Generated addresses remain preferred for 14400 seconds (4 hours). This may be changed in the **Default preferred lifetime** field by entering the number of seconds. It is suggested to set this to 604800 seconds (7 days). Note this value must not be longer than the previous **Default valid lifetime** setting.

The minimum time between sending unsolicited Router Advertisements is 5 seconds. To change this, enter the seconds in the **Minimum RA interval** number field. The minimum allowed value is 3 and the maximum is 1350. A common setting is 198 seconds. Note this minimum time should not be longer that 75% of the following **Maximum RA interval** time setting.

The maximum time between sending unsolicited multicast Router Advertisements is 20 seconds (unless using Track Interfaces which is 10 seconds). To change this, enter the seconds in the **Maximum RA interval** number field. The minimum allowed input is 4 seconds and the maximum is 1800 seconds (for 30 minutes). A common setting is 600 seconds (for 5 minutes).

By default, the pfSense system advertises it is useful for three times the **Maximum RA interval** time. If that is unset, then it is only 60 seconds. This may be changed by entering the seconds in the **Router lifetime** number field. A common recommendation is 1800 seconds. The maximum allowed input is 9000 seconds (for 2.5 hours). The number 0 (zero) means it should not be used as a default router.

The Router Advertisement service will advertise for the IPv6 subnet for the selected network interface (at the top of the webpage). To add additional prefixes, enter the IPv6 address in the first **RA Subnets** field and its subnet bits in the corresponding drop-down menu. Use the **Add** button to add another RA Subnet. (And use the **Delete** button, after one is added, to remove an entry.)

20.1.2 Router Advertisements DNS Configuration

The Router Advertisement service provides options for DNS configuration. You may enter up to three DNS server IPv6 addresses in the **Server** fields that the IPv6 host may use for recursive

DNS service. Note that the DNS servers must be IPv6 addresses (such as Google's public DNS at 2001:4860:4860::8888) or they won't be used. If this is not set, it will use the local DNS forwarder or resolver if enabled and listening on IPv6 (Chapter 21). Or it will provide the pfSense system's detected or defined DNS server selections if they are IPv6 (Section 5.1.2).

It will provide pfSense's local domain name for the host to append if needed for DNS lookups. The **Domain search list** field may be used to optionally add additional domain names.

Clicking the **Use same settings as DHCPv6 server** checkbox will use the DNS server settings as configured for the DHCPv6 server (Section 20.2).

Use the **Save** button to start the Router Advertisements daemon with these settings. Its logging may be viewed on the **Status** → **System Logs** → **System Routing** subpage for the `radvd` process.

20.2   DHCPv6 Server Configuration

When the **DHCPv6 Server** tab is selected, at the top right of the page are icons to view the list of current leases provided (Section 20.4) and for DHCPv6 logging (Section 20.6).

There are several DHCPv6 server configurations in the DHCPv6 Options section. To run the service (after it is configured), first check the **Enable DHCPv6 server** checkbox.

This page will indicate the interface name that is being configured. It will display the IPv6 subnet (or if it is using Prefix Delegation), its mask size in bits, and the available range for handing out IPv6 addresses within your subnet. You may need to adjust the default range or enter your desired values in the required **Range** fields, enter both the lowest **From** and the highest **To** IPv6 addresses. Note it cannot have a slash in the address. You cannot have a virtual IPv6 address within this same range. Nor can any static DHCPv6 mappings be in this same range.

For automated delegation of IPv6 prefixes, enter the lowest and the highest IPv6 address (within the following size) in the **Prefix Delegation Range From** and **To** fields, respectively. The assigned prefixes will be assigned with the bit length selected in the **Prefix Delegation Size** menu. The allowed choices are 48, 52, 56, 59, 60, 61, 62, 63, and 64. It defaults to 48 bits.

By default, the IPv6 address for your pfSense system's known DNS server is provided to the DHCPv6 clients for their DNS lookups. If you want to share custom DNS server addresses instead, enter one to four IPv6 addresses in the **DNS Servers** fields.

The server will also provide the default domain name that the DHCPv6 clients may use for resolving non-fully-qualified domain names in DNS. By default, it just provides the domain name defined on the local pfSense system. (In a default install, this is just "localdomain".) To provide a different value, enter the valid name in the **Domain name** field.

The **Domain search list** field is like the previous option, but instead of being a single domain for completing names for DNS lookups, it is a space-separated list of domains to append (the client resolver tries one at a time).

The **Default lease time** is the amount of time in seconds that a lease may be assigned to a client. This is its valid lifetime. The minimum allowed is 60 seconds. The default is two hours (7200 seconds).

The maximum length in seconds that a lease may be assigned is defined in the **Max lease time** field. When set, this must be higher than the previous default lease time. The default is one day (86400 seconds).

The lease times are recorded in the UTC timezone. If you need it tracked using your pfSense system's local timezone instead, click the **Time Format Change** checkbox. For example, visit the **Status** → **DHCPv6 Leases** page as explained in Section 20.4.

Then the configuration has several categories for advanced DHCPv6 server settings. Click a corresponding **Display Advanced** button to show these additional options as covered in the following sections.

Click the **Save** button to store the settings which will automatically enable or restart the DHCPv6 server daemon. (Be sure to have the enable checkbox marked.)

20.2.1   Dynamic DNS (DDNS) Options for DHCPv6

To have your DHCPv6 server dynamically update a DNS server hosting a DNS zone with the assigned address details, check the **DHCP Registration** checkbox. When this enabled, the following domain key name and secret must be provided for the TSIG authentication for communicating with the DNS server.

Enter the domain name that will be updated in the **DDNS Domain** field. A fully-qualified domain name is created by appending this to the client's hostname.

By default, the hostnames for the clients come from the client via DHCP. Clicking the **DDNS Hostnames** checkbox, means it will use the hostnames as defined in the static maps as configured in the following Section 20.3.

Enter the IP address of the DNS nameserver hosting the zone to be updated via Dynamic DNS in the **DDNS Server IP** field. Note that even though this is for DHCPv6, this primary address must be IPv4.

Enter the TSIG key name used for the DNS authentication in the **DDNS Domain Key name** field. This is commonly in domain name format.

pfSense defaults to use the legacy default HMAC-MD5 algorithm for the TSIG key. Commonly DNS servers use HMAC-SHA256. To change this to match your DNS server, make your selection from the **Key algorithm** menu, which also includes HMAC-SHA1, HMAC-SHA224, HMAC-SHA384, and HMAC-SHA512 (which is considered most secure).

Usually the shared secret (and the key and algorithm) is provided by the DNS server administrator. Enter in the **DDNS Domain Key secret** field. (It may look something like "pRP5FoJ95J06sv4PQ==".)

A DHCPv6 client may indicate back to the server that it will do its own dynamic DNS updates. If so, the server won't trigger an update for the address record (but it may still do a PTR record reverse lookup update in DNS). The **DDNS Client Updates** menu is used to change this from this default *allow* behavior. The other choices are *deny* for the server to tell the DHCPv6 client that it should not do its own DNS updates; and *ignore* for the server to tell the client that it may optionally do its own DNS updates.

To also have your server request a DNS update for the reverse lookup of address, check the **DDNS Reverse** checkbox. This is for PTR record lookups under the ARPA domain name which has a DNS label for every digit in a reversed IPv6 address, such as fdc8:d48b:f546:6a99:: becomes a long domain name with 32 labels: *0.0.0.0.0.0.0.0.0.0.0.0.0.0.0.9.9.a.6.6.4.5.f.b.8.4.d.8.c.d.f.ip6.arpa.*

(This book doesn't cover the setup or the delegation of DNS zones and updates. For fun, read RFC 8501 *Reverse DNS in IPv6 for Internet Service Providers*: "ISPs will often delegate an IPv6 prefix to their customers. Since 2^^80 possible addresses could be configured in a single /48 zone alone, it is impractical to write a zone with every possible address entered, even with automation. If 1000 entries could be written per second, the zone would still not be complete after 38 trillion years.")

20.2.2   Time Servers for DHCPv6 Clients

You may provide a list of Simple Network Time Protocol servers to the client to use for time synchronization by entering the SNTP IPv6 addresses in the **NTP Server 1** and **NTP Server 2** fields.

20.2.3   LDAP Option for DHCPv6

The **LDAP URI** field is used to provide the LDAP URL to a DHCPv6 client to help it lookup information from that LDAP server. An example is: "ldaps://host.example.com/dc=example,dc=com". Note this is an experimental option from 2006 which never became a standard. This may not work.

20.2.4   Network Booting Options for DHCPv6

The **Enable Network Booting** checkbox is for enabling a DHCPv6 option for passing configuration information to network clients (RFC 5970).

Enter the HTTP or TFTP URL for a boot file in the **Bootfile URL** field. This would point to a boot loader or operating system kernel, for example. Note if the hostname in the URL is an IPv6 address, the IPv6 address part needs to be enclosed in [and] square bracket characters.

20.2.5   Additional BOOTP/DHCP Options for DHCPv6

DHCPv6 provides various *options* for providing details or asking a DHCPv6 client for some values. You may define your own options using numbers and corresponding value using text strings.

In the **Number** input field enter an option code within 1 to 65535 for the custom option. Then enter the data in the **Value** field. Note this option is a *text* type only.

Use the **Add Option** button to get additional fields for more custom options. Or to remove one custom option, click its corresponding **Delete** button.

Behind the scenes, it will generate its own numbered custom option names, such as *custom-opt1-0* with the middle term from the interface name for the DHCPv6 server configuration.

20.3 Static DHCPv6 Mappings

At the bottom of the **DHCPv6 Server** page is a section for setting up DHCPv6 static mappings. This is for assigning a specific IPv6 address and/or hostname over DHCPv6. (Note this feature doesn't have all the assignable attributes like seen for non-IPv6 DHCP as covered in Section 19.5.1.)

No DHCPv6 static mappings exist by default. When added, the table will show the DUID, an optional IPv6 address, hostname, and optional description. It will also have action icons to edit or delete the corresponding static mapping.

Click the **Add** button to add a new one. Note that this static mapping configuration is specific to the DHCPv6 running on one interface. Be sure you are on the correct interface as displayed near the top of the webpage. (If you aren't on an interface, the same page will just reload.)

20.3.1 Static DHCPv6 Mapping Configuration

To setup a DHCPv6 static mapping, you need a valid DHCP Unique Identifier (DUID). The DHCP server uses DUIDs to identify clients to select configuration parameters to provide to them. Enter it in the **DUID** field.

To assign a specific (fixed) address to the identified DHCPv6 client, enter it in the **IPv6 address** field. (If this is left blank, the DHCPv6 server will just provide one from its pool.)

If you want a hostname assigned to the DHCPv6 client, enter it in the **Hostname** field. This is a short name and doesn't include the domain part. (pfSense won't allow a period in this hostname.) Note that DHCP clients often completely ignore the provided hostname.

You may optionally describe this mapping in the **Description** field.

If the DHCPv6 server (for the same interface) has the **Network booting** feature enabled, then the static mappings configuration will have additional input fields to override the server's netboot defaults. Enter the file name for the client to load as its initial boot file in the **Netboot filename** field. If you need to set the location for the DHCPv6 client's root disk, enter it in the **Root path** field.

Click the **Save** button to store the static mapping details.

20.4   DHCPv6 Leases

Tables showing the DHCPv6 leases and delegated prefixes are available at **Status → DHCPv6 Leases**. The leases table entries are identified with an icon to show if it is a static mapping, an active DHCPv6 lease, or if it is expired. It has the following columns: IPv6 address, IAID, DUID, MAC address, Hostname, Start and End (expiration) times (if it is not static), Online, and Lease Type, like if the binding is active, expired (for free), reserved, or released.

If you want the start and end times to be displayed using your pfSense system's configured timezone instead of UTC, select the **Time Format Change** option in the DHCPv6 server configuration.

In addition, the entries may have corresponding actions with icons for adding a static mapping (see Section 20.3), adding a Wake-on-Lan (WOL) mapping (see Section 13.9), and deleting a lease. Clicking the **Delete Lease** action icon will stop the DHCPv6 service, remove the offline entry from the database, and then restart service.

By default, the tables will show the active and static leases only. Click the **Show all configured leases** button at the bottom of the page to see offline or recently expired leases also.

The Delegated Prefixes table identifies with an icon prefixes that are active, expired, or static. It lists the IPv6 Prefix (and if applicable what DUID it is routed to), IAID, DUID, Start and End times (if not static), and the current State.

20.5   DHCPv6 Relay

Similar to the DHCP Relay, the **Services → DHCPv6 Relay** feature may be used to listen for DHCPv6 queries on one or more interfaces and pass them along to other DHCPv6 servers (using IPv6). When it gets a DHCPv6 reply, it will send it to the original downstream source. Note that DHCPv6 is an entirely different protocol than DHCP for IPv4.

Note
This relay can not be enabled if a DHCPv6 server is already running on any interface.

Enable the DHCPv6 Relay service with the **Enable** checkbox. This will expand its configurations.

In the **Interface(s)** menu, select one or more network interfaces that the relay agent will receive DHCPv6 queries. This will only list your interfaces that have an IPv6 address assigned. It will be empty if you don't have any IPv6 addresses.

(If your form has a checkbox for appending IDs, ignore it. That feature is not in the DHCPv6 mode of the relay agent.)

Enter the target IPv6 address where the DHCPv6 queries will be forwarded to in the **Destination server** field. Click the **Add server** button to enter additional IPv6 addresses for target DHCPv6 servers. (Use the **Delete** button to remove one of the destination servers.)

Click the **Save** button to start the DHCPv6 Relay Agent.

To turn it off later, simply uncheck the enable checkbox and save again. Or to stop it temporarily, turn off the *dhcrelay6* service via the **Status** → **Services** page (Section 7.7).

20.6 DHCPv6 and RA Log Entries

Logging for the DHCPv6 server (`dhcpd`), the IPv6 DHCP relay (`dhcrelay`), and the IPv6 DHCP client (`dhcp6c`) can be viewed via the **Status** → **System Logs** → **DHCP** page. (It also includes the logging for the IPv4 DHCP services.) The logging may be very verbose and frequent — especially if you have many devices requesting DHCP or DHCPv6 details.

To identify the DHCPv6 Relay Agent in the logs, the entries will show *dhcrelay* as the process name and "Bound to *:547" in the log message.

Logging for the Router Advertisement daemon (`radvd`) will be on the **Status** → **System Logs** → **System Routing** subpage.

For information about using the advanced log filter and overriding the general logging options for these logs, see Section 11.1 and Section 11.3.

21 DNS

The Domain Name System, or DNS, is a distributed database commonly used for matching hostnames with Internet addresses. The database is also used to store other information, such as defining where mail servers may be found to route email. A database key and its values are known as a resource record set. The resource record data is defined and served via authoritative servers which either have the final answers or provide pointers (NS records) that tell what servers should be asked next. Clients iteratively query starting at a root server to child servers to get answers. Usually the details are cached so commonly-repeated queries don't have to be frequently re-looked-up. The resource record data has an associated time-to-live (TTL) value so caches know when to expire the data. Shared DNS caches, also called recursive caching resolvers, are commonly provided by Internet Service Providers (and assigned via DHCP) to provide DNS lookups for their customers. (The authoritative servers and caching resolvers are known as *nameservers*.)

pfSense provides tools to perform DNS lookups for troubleshooting or testing and a server for a local shared recursive caching resolver. It can also be configured to serve some of your own authoritative data. pfSense can also be configured to utilize the nameserver(s) as provided via DHCP or to share nameserver details to IPv6 neighbors and to its own DHCP, PPPoE, IPsec, and OpenVPN clients.

pfSense provides a full-featured, iterative, validating, caching DNS resolver (`unbound`) which is running by default, and a simple caching DNS server (`dnsmasq`) as an alternative solution. These are described in Section 21.2 and Section 21.3 respectively.

pfSense doesn't provide a full-featured authoritative DNS server (with zone transfers and DNSSEC signing, for example) in the base system. Nevertheless, the DNS Resolver and the DNS Forwarder may be configured using *overrides* to serve some authoritative data from local configurations or from external authoritative DNS servers. Also the full-featured BIND suite can be installed and managed in pfSense using the *bind* package. (See Section 35.2 about installing packages.)

21.1 DNS Lookup

To test DNS resolution, you can use the **Diagnostics** → **DNS Lookup** feature. It provides a simple form to do DNS queries. Enter the hostname or IP address to lookup in the field and press the **Lookup** button. (An example is shown in Figure 21.1.)

If it is an IP address to lookup, it will perform a PTR lookup for reverse DNS. Otherwise it will do an A (address) record lookup. It will display the answer in the results section. It will also display the query timings for each nameserver that provided answers. (This example has the local name server, 127.0.0.1, and two other external caching resolvers as provided by an upstream ISP that was offered via DHCP.)

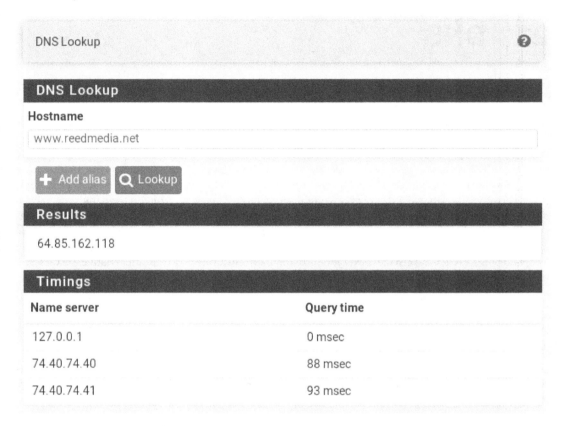

Figure 21.1: **Diagnostics → DNS Lookup**

After the lookup, the page will add a new button **Add alias** (or **Update alias** if the alias already exists). This may be used to add the name and its address to the packet filter's convenience aliases as covered in Section 16.5. (Note this is not a DNS alias known as a CNAME.)

The page also provides links to the pfSense **Diagnostics → Ping** (Section 27.2) and **Diagnostics → Traceroute** (Section 27.5) features passing along the same query for additional details. (Older versions of pfSense also linked to the external DNS Stuff website (www.dnsstuff.com) for further research about the IP address.)

The **Diagnostics → DNS Lookup** is very simple in regards to DNS. The advanced DNS command-line tools, `dig`, `drill`, and `delv` are all available via the text console (see Section 37.9). This book doesn't cover these tools, but as an easy example at the shell, just type the command name (`dig`, `drill`, or `delv`) followed by the domain name to lookup and press Enter, for example:

```
[2.3-RELEASE][admin@pfSense.office]/root: delv www.reedmedia.net
; fully validated
www.reedmedia.net.       86400    IN      A       64.85.162.118
www.reedmedia.net.       86400    IN      RRSIG   A 5 3 86400   ←
   20160905030004 20160806030004 24291 reedmedia.net. GVGRMoDsR ←
   +L9nN+Tn2dgJ/jC2MTgNwhqkKzgrQY8+T4wgQLm3DsYA9hp   ←
   yKy0iSSb7MoEx1+RDJczFxA9UVOOymdQAdLMkmtKrG628Kj/5BaJGmkR 9 ←
   hF1qSbFrRgoZZJX5hvpL3hAzzMD3Wo9w5hpiW2S0ZqKXmsZdc2YayoE YtM=
```

21.2 DNS Resolver (Unbound)

The **Services** → **DNS Resolver** page has three submenu pages, for **General Settings** (the main view), **Advanced Settings**, and **Access Lists**. Each of these views have action icons in the top right to restart the DNS resolver, stop it, and to show the related log entries (which also shows logs for other DNS services).

This DNS resolver, `unbound`, is enabled by default. To disable it, uncheck the **Enable DNS resolver** checkbox.

DNS uses the Internet standard port 53 for TCP and UDP. If you need to run an alternate setup (such as port forwarding incoming DNS traffic to a different port), set a number in the **Listen Port** field.

To provide an encrypted DNS over TLS service, check the **Enable SSL/TLS Service** checkbox. This requires a certificate to be used which may be selected in the **SSL/TLS Certificate** form. You can introduce a certificate for this DNS over TLS use via the **System** → **Certificate Manager** → **Certificates** subpage (Section 12.2.1). By default, DNS over TLS listens on TCP and UDP port 853. A custom DNS over TLS port may be entered in the **SSL/TLS Listen Port** number field. (The DNS over TLS feature was introduced in pfSense version 2.4.4.)

The DNS resolver by default will listen for DNS queries (and answer to its clients) on all IPv4 and IPv6 interfaces. Use the **Network Interfaces** selection list if you need it to only listen on specific networks, such as the WAN, LAN, or only the Localhost.

If you need to define what networks the resolver's iterative outgoing DNS lookups go through, use the **Outgoing Network Interfaces** selection list to specify the interfaces such as the WAN or LAN.

When the DNS Resolver is configured with Host Overrides (see Section 21.2.3) to also provide authoritative answers, the **System Domain Local Zone Type** drop-down menu may be used to define how it will behave if there is no match to the query in the local data. The choices are:

Deny
   to not attempt to resolve it and also don't respond.

Refuse
   to not attempt to resolve it but just answer with DNS return code REFUSED.

Static

> to act as an authoritative server only so if the answer doesn't exist don't attempt to resolve it and return the DNS return code NODATA or NXDOMAIN as appropriate.

Transparent

> to attempt to resolve it if the name doesn't exist in the local data. (Default behavior)

Type Transparent

> to attempt to resolve it if the name doesn't exist in the local data or has a different DNS Type.

Redirect

> is used to override all subdomains.

Inform

> is used to log the specific client query for troubleshooting or analysis.

Inform Deny

> to not respond but still log the client query for analysis.

No Default

> to turn off serving reverse lookups for private and reserved addresses (also known as AS112).

DNSSEC provides a way to prove that DNS data came from where it was expected to come from and that the data wasn't modified. (It also proves that negative responses really don't exist.) It uses a cryptographic chain of trust starting with the DNS roots plus signatures for the record data. This DNSSEC service is enabled by default. It includes an automatically-maintained trust anchor that starts the chain of trust and validation is enabled. If you do not want to do DNSSEC validation, uncheck the **Enable DNSSEC Support** checkbox.

Instead of having the resolver do its own iteration to find answers it can forward its queries on to upstream resolvers. To enable this for all lookups, check the **DNS Query Forwarding** checkbox. Note that this uses the system's configured nameservers. See the **DNS Server Settings** on the **System → General Setup** display. To use the DNS servers(s) assigned by DHCP (or PPP) instead check the **Allow DNS server list to be overridden by DHCP/PPP on WAN** checkbox. These are explained in Section 5.1.2.

By default, the resolver has internal IP ranges defined (10.0.0.0/8, 172.16.0.0/12, 169.254.0.0/16, 192.168.0.0/16, fd00::/8, and fe80::/10) which are not allowed to be returned in DNS answers unless listed in Host Overrides (Section 21.2.3) or Domain Overrides (Section 21.2.4). This helps protect against DNS Rebinding attacks where a website can access internal networks by using internal IP addresses (via DNS). If you need to turn this off, check the **Disable DNS Rebinding Checks** checkbox on the **System → Advanced → Admin Access** page (Section 5.3.1).

If you want to use DNS over TLS for all DNS forwarding, then check the **Use SSL/TLS for outgoing DNS Queries to Forwarding Servers** checkbox. This means all your DNS servers that you may forward queries to must support DNS over TLS on port 853. (This DNS over TLS feature was added in pfSense 2.4.4.)

When running a DHCP server and the **DHCP Registration** checkbox is checked, pfSense will watch the DHCP leases database to maintain a list of authoritative address and reverse lookup records served over DNS.

If you have static DHCP mappings setup and you want to have those hostnames in your DNS, check the **Register DHCP static mappings in the DNS Resolver** checkbox.

The DNS Resolver, *unbound*, has many other tunables. To set your own options, click the **Display Custom Options** button and then enter them in the **Custom options** text box. Documentation for the many options are listed in its manual at https://www.unbound.net/documentation/unbound.conf.html. Note that other options are tunable via the **Services** → **DNS Resolver** → **Advanced Settings** display as covered in Section 21.2.1

Below the general DNS resolver options, are two tables listing the Host Overrides and Domain Overrides. (They are empty by default.) These are used to serve authoritative data from a local configuration and to utilize external authoritative DNS servers. These are covered in Section 21.2.3 and Section 21.2.4.

21.2.1 DNS Resolver Advanced Settings

The webConfigurator has many additional tunables for the *unbound* DNS server controllable via the **Services** → **DNS Resolver** → **Advanced Settings** display.

Query name minimization is a DNS feature that will trim part of the domain name to lookup when doing DNS queries to root and parent nameservers. This is not an optimization technique, but it is an attempt to increase privacy in lookups. This may be enabled when using the **Query Name Minimization** checkbox. When enabled, if a non-DNSSEC-signed query response fails, it will try again with the full name. If you don't want it to try again meaning you may have more DNS failures, check the **Strict Query Name Minimization** checkbox. (This feature was introduce into pfSense in version 2.4.4.)

To allow the DNS Resolver to identify the pfSense systems hostname over DNS, uncheck the default **id.server and hostname.bind queries are refused** checkbox. Uncheck the **version.server and version.bind queries are refused** checkbox to allow the DNS Resolver to identify its software version over DNS,

Prefetch is a technique to query for records in the cache before they timeout so they can be quickly served to others. To enable this, check the **Message cache elements are prefetched before they expire to help keep the cache up to date** checkbox.

When using DNSSEC, the validator can also lookup corresponding cryptographic key data earlier. Enable this prefetching by checking the **DNSKEYs are fetched earlier in the validation process when a Delegation signer is encountered** checkbox.

When DNSSEC is in use (the default), if DNSSEC data is missing for domains marked as DNSSEC signed via the trust anchor chain, then queries will purposely fail. This is the default behavior. If you want to make your system insecure or DNSSEC isn't working because an intermediate firewall is stripping the related DNS records, then uncheck **DNSSEC data is required for trust-anchored zone** checkbox to disable this standard feature.

The size of the message cache (for response codes and validation status) is limited to 4 MB. To set it to a larger size because you have a busy DNS resolver, increase it using the **Message Cache Size** drop-down menu. (This is in megabytes.) Note this also tunes the resource record cache to twice that size.

By default, the DNS Resolver allocates 10 TCP buffers for outgoing queries and 10 TCP buffers for incoming connections per thread. (The number of threads depends on how many CPUs or Hyper-Threading processors are detected.) For busy DNS needs, you may need to increase these limits (up to 50) using the **Outgoing TCP Buffers** and **Incoming TCP Buffers** drop-down menus. If the outgoing is set to 0 (zero), it will not use TCP for outbound queries. If the incoming is set to 0 (zero), it will not accept any incoming queries over TCP. (Most DNS traffic uses UDP.)

The EDNS (Extension mechanisms for DNS) feature advertises its UDP buffer size to peers to the standard 4096 bytes. If you have timeouts dues to problems with fragmentation reassembly, you can set it to 1480 in the **EDNS Buffer Size** drop-down menu. Setting it to 512 may fix path MTU problems, but usually increases TCP traffic (so you may also need to increase the **Outgoing TCP Buffers** value above).

The number of DNS queries that every thread can handle at the same time are defined with the **Number of Queries per Thread** drop-down menu.

When the DNS Resolver is very busy, i.e., the queue of resolver jobs is full, it will timeout half of the queries. This helps protect against denial of service for other queries due to high query rates or slow query processing. The default timeout time is 200 milliseconds which is a common normal resolution time. To adjust this time use the **Jostle Timeout** drop-down menu.

In DNS, cached records are cleared out when their time-to-live (TTL) expires (as provided from their external authoritative DNS). This DNS Resolver forces long TTLs to be capped to its one day (86400 seconds) default. If you want to set a different cap, enter the seconds in the **Maximum TTL for RRsets and Messages** field. Note that if you set the max too low, it may cause the server to lookup commonly-used records too often making the server extra busy. If you set the max too high, it may use more memory, but will still remove the records per their own TTL or this setting (which ever is less).

If TTLs for frequently-requested records are very low (like 0 or 1 seconds), the system may need to look them up often over the Internet. The **Minimum TTL for RRsets and Messages** field may be used to restrict how quickly these records expire in seconds. Note this is considered by some to be against Internet standards as it may cause use of records that are stale, i.e., have wrong data. The default is 0 which means it will not override any TTL.

The resolver keeps track internally for its own use about EDNS support details, lameness (authoritative servers that should have answers but don't), and round-trip times for DNS servers it communicates with. By default, it will keep track of up to 10,000 DNS servers with the individual details timing out in 15 minutes. If you need to tune this to a shorter time (down to one minute), use the **TTL for Host Cache Entries** drop-down menu. To keep track of fewer or more DNS servers, adjust the amount using the **Number of Hosts to Cache** drop-down menu.

The DNS Resolver has a feature to flush the cache if there are too many unwanted DNS replies which may be an indication of DNS cache poisoning attempts. It is disabled by default. If you want to enable this defense, set a value in the **Unwanted Reply Threshold** drop-down menu. A suggested value is 10 million.

The **Log Level** drop-down menu may be used to define how much the *unbound* server logs. Higher numbers increase the amount of logging. The choices are 0 for errors only, 1 (default) for operational information also, 2 for further operational details, 3 for queries, 4 internal algorithms, and 5 for cache misses. The most recent logging can be seen via the **Status → System Logs → System → DNS Resolver** display as covered in Section 21.6.

Normally, DNS Resolvers are only accessible for customers and friendly networks. This is to stop potential abuse with cache poisoning and malicious or accidental denial of service attacks. pfSense auto-configures the DNS Resolver to allow recursion for clients within the networks for pfSense's interfaces. To disable this access control and refuse to do DNS except for the localhost, check the **Disable the automatically-added access control entries** checkbox. If you need to open up the DNS Resolver for other clients outside of your network, see the upcoming Section 21.2.2.

DNS caches can be poisoned, that is some malicious party can inject their own data into the cache so unknowing users of it can be led to wrong websites or have emails redirected to wrong mail servers, for example. One technique adds randomness to the DNS transaction by mixing up the case of DNS labels (such as *wWW.aBcHiNa.cOm*) in queries and checking that the returning answer matches. This feature, considered experimental, is off by default. To enable it, check the **Use 0x20 encoded random bits in the DNS query to foil spoofing attempts** checkbox.

After using the **Save** button, click **Apply Changes** to reload the DNS server with the new configurations.

21.2.2   DNS Resolver Access Lists

The **Services → DNS Resolver → Access Lists** display is used to allow outside DNS clients and networks to use pfSense's DNS Resolver. As discussed in Section 21.2.1, the networks for the internal interfaces are allowed. The display provides a table listing the additional DNS access rules. Note that this table view does not list the network address details. For the access list entries, it provides an **Edit ACL** action icon and a **Delete ACL** action icon to modify or remove the DNS Resolver rule.

By default, no additional external networks are configured for DNS access. To add a new access list, click the **Add** button. Note that you don't need to open this access unless you specifically want to allow friendly known networks to use your DNS resolver.

When adding or editing a DNS access list, the **Action List Name** is used to as an identifier for you to recognize this rule. Optionally, use the **Description** field to include an additional explanation for your own use.

The **Action** choices are **Allow** to allow the DNS queries, **Deny** to stop queries, **Refuse** to stop queries and send a DNS return code of REFUSED, and **Allow Snoop** also allows DNS queries including for non-recursive queries.

The **Networks** setting is required. Enter the network address and its corresponding subnet mask. You may optionally add another description per network to identify or explain its purpose. If you want multiple networks for the same access list name and action, click the **Add Network** button. (Use the **Delete** button to delete any network entries you don't need. At least one is required if using this.)

Click the **Save** button to save the DNS Resolver access list entry. Then you will need to click the **Apply Changes** button for it to take effect.

Note

This is for the DNS Resolver configuration only. You may need to configure a packet filter firewall rule to allow incoming DNS and outgoing DNS for the corresponding network too. An example of this DNS packet filter rule is described in Section 16.3.

21.2.3 Host Overrides (Unbound)

The Host Overrides feature allows the admin to configure the *unbound* DNS server with local DNS address (A and AAAA) and reverse lookup (PTR) records. It may be used to locally change DNS for custom replies or publish your own simple DNS for your network.

The middle section of the **Services** → **DNS Resolver** → **General Settings** page lists the Host Overrides. The table columns for an entry show the hostname, domain name, IP address, and optional description. If the *IP* field says "Alias for" this means you have additional names associated with a single configuration's address.

The rows also have actions to allow editing or removing the single entry. Use the **Add** button there to create a Host Override entry or click an entry's pencil icon to edit it. This will take you to a new page. (Note that an *alias* entry won't have a trash can icon — to remove it, edit it and then choose its corresponding **Delete** button.)

Enter the hostname in the **Host** field. This implementation wants this to be the short name or single label without any period delimiter. The domain part (or final label) is entered in the required **Domain** text field. This field may contain periods and multiple labels. (You may choose to leave the **Host** entry blank and place the entire DNS name in the **Domain** field.)

Then enter the IPv4 or IPv6 address in the required **IP Address** field.

Optionally, an explanation for this override entry may be entered in the **Description** text field.

You may also have other names that provide the same IP address. In the **Additional Names for this Host** section, you can add another hostname, domain name, and description. To add even more names, click the **Add Host Name** button and more fields will pop up. (Note that these additional names will not be returned with a DNS PTR lookup.) To remove one of the additional names, simply click its **Delete** button.

After saving the entry, click the **Apply Changes** to activate it. Then you can do a DNS query against the pfSense server to test it (such as using the **Diagnostics** → **DNS Lookup** page).

Note it will also create one pointer record per IP address for a reverse lookup IP address query to return the fully-qualified hostname,

21.2.4 Domain Overrides (Unbound)

Domain Overrides provides a way to provide DNS answers without finding them via standard DNS resolution. It will not attempt to iterate to resolve the query, but will forward the query on to a specifically configured server that will provide an authoritative answer for it. This feature may be used to override real DNS.

Note

The *unbound* DNS Resolver's Domain Override feature provides normal resolver responses. It will refuse queries that don't set the recursion desired (RD) bit. If you need authoritative answers, see the *dnsmasq* **Services** → **DNS Forwarder** → **Domain Override** implementation instead in Section 21.5.

In the **Domain** field, enter the domain name or specific hostname you want to manage. It will also cover any names under that domain. The **IP Address** field is used to set to where a DNS server will answer for queries authoritatively within that domain. (That server doesn't need to be known via the public DNS.)

To forward the DNS queries for this domain using DNS over TLS service, click the **TLS Queries** checkbox. Note that this will use TCP port 853. (This DNS over TLS feature was added in pfSense 2.4.4.)

Optionally, enter a valid hostname for checking the TLS authentication certificate when forwarding over TLS in the **TLS Hostname** text field. (This configuration was introduced in pfSense 2.4.4-p3.)

The optional **Description** field may be used to describe the purpose of this Domain Override.

Note

When DNS rebind checking is active (the default), these override domains (and subdomains) can contain private addresses and they are marked as DNSSEC *insecure* meaning its chain of trust is ignored.

Click the **Save** button and then on the new display the **Apply Changes** button to activate the change.

21.2.5 DNS Resolver Status (Unbound)

The **Status** → **DNS Resolver** page provides *unbound* statistics for its infrastructure cache when the service is enabled. This status page was introduced in pfSense 2.4.4.

The details are listed in two tables each organized by the remote DNS server IP addresses used for a specific DNS zone. The Cache Speed table (as seen in Figure 21.2) shows the time-to-live for the entry in seconds; ping time; variance; round trip time; retransmission timeout; and counts of timeouts for A, AAAA, and other DNS record types for each zone and server.

The Cache Stats table provides further information about the nameservers for specific zones. The table columns indicate:

- if EDNS queries or replies are dropped (1 means EDNS is not dropped);

- the EDNS version (or -1 if EDNS is not supported);

- the time in seconds when probing restarts;

- if the server doesn't serve DNSSEC data;

- if the server is not authoritative (but is just a recursor);

- if the server is not authoritative for address (A) records;

- or if the server is not authoritative for other DNS record types.

Status / DNS Resolver   C ⊙ ≑ └ ▤ ❷

DNS Resolver Infrastructure Cache Speed							
Server	**Zone**	**TTL**	**Ping**	**Var**	**RTT**	**RTO**	**Timeout A**
2001:503:231d::2:30	com.	858	0	94	376	752	1
208.94.149.2	dnsmadeeasy.com.	859	1	74	297	297	0
2a01:8840:a1::17	io.	859	0	94	376	752	0
2600:9000:5304:a000::1	awsdns-32.com.	894	0	94	376	752	0
2.22.230.67	akam.net.	896	4	80	324	324	0
184.85.248.67	akam.net.	896	2	58	234	234	0
2001:503:a83e::2:30	com.	859	0	94	376	752	1
17.253.200.1	apple.com.	896	1	73	293	293	0
213.248.216.1	uk.	860	9	71	293	293	0
204.19.119.1	apple.com.	896	3	78	315	315	0
199.233.217.200	netbsd.org.	893	10	92	378	378	0
65.22.161.17	io.	859	26	100	426	426	0
2001:500:1::53	.	464	0	94	376	752	1
2a02:26f0:67::41	whitehouse.gov.	895	0	94	376	1504	2
2600:1480:1::43	akam.net.	894	0	94	376	752	1

Figure 21.2: **Diagnostics → DNS Resolver**

These details will include all known servers it currently knows about in the cache, even if they aren't being used. For example, if you don't have IPv6 access, it will probably still show IPv6 nameservers with zero ping times and with timeout counts.

Note that a busy resolver can have hundreds to thousands of cache statistic entries so this page may be quite long.

21.3 DNS Forwarder (dnsmasq)

The **Services** → **DNS Forwarder** page is used to enable and configure the alternative simple caching server. It uses the local system resolver configuration to know what upstream DNS resolvers to use. It will cache forwarded responses, up to 10,000 names, for later quicker responses. This pfSense resolver is not capable of iteratively finding unknown answers starting at the root servers, but instead, as a resolver, it forwards the requests on.

It can also be used as an authoritative server and configured with address (A and AAAA records if you have them) and reverse-lookup PTR records as listed in the local host name database. You may optionally setup local authoritative DNS answers using Host Overrides or point to specific external authoritative servers using Domain Overrides; these are covered in Section 21.4 and Section 21.5.

Its action icons near the top right allow restarting and stopping the service. The **Related log entries** icon links to the **Status** → **System Logs** → **System** → **DNS Resolver** view — this will display the most recent DNS log entries; see Section 21.6 for details.

Note

pfSense by default already runs a full-featured caching DNS resolver. To use this DNS Forwarder instead, disable the DNS Resolver first. This is covered in Section 21.2.

To enable the DNS forwarder, check the **Enable DNS forwarder** checkbox. Then the DHCP server, if enabled, will provide the LAN IP address as a DNS server to DHCP clients so they will use this DNS forwarder.

Check the **Register DHCP leases in DNS forwarder** checkbox, to include hostnames from other local systems in your DNS. (This is for systems requesting a DHCP lease that send their own hostname.) Note for non-fully-qualified domain names you may need the **Domain** defined in the **System** → **General Setup** menu (Section 5.1.1).

To include the static mapped hostnames from pfSense's served DHCP and DHCPv6 leases, check the **Register DHCP static mappings in DNS forwarder** checkbox. Again, make sure that your **Domain** is defined in the **System** → **General Setup** menu (Section 5.1.1).

For reverse lookups (PTR), by default, it will return names from the hostnames known via DHCP. If you prefer to use the hosts overrides first, check the **Resolve DHCP mappings first** checkbox.

By default, for forwarding DNS queries, it will send to all defined nameservers in parallel and use the first reply. If you want it to send to each nameserver one at a time in order, check the **Query DNS servers sequentially** checkbox. By default, the configuration for the list of nameservers is in the **DNS Server Settings** on the **System** → **General Setup** page. As an alternative, make sure the

Allow DNS server list to be overridden by DHCP/PPP on WAN checkbox is checked to use the DNS server(s) assigned by DHCP or PPP. These are covered in Section 5.1.2.

If you don't want pfSense to forward on DNS address queries (that it cannot answer locally) that don't contain a dot (that is no domain name), then check the **Require domain** checkbox.

If you don't want reverse lookups for private IPv4 addresses (like PTR records for 10.in-addr.arpa, 168.192.in-addr.arpa, 16.172.in-addr.arpa) to be forwarded on, check the **Do not forward private reverse lookups** checkbox. Note you can override this behavior by specifically listing the in-addr.arpa entries and their corresponding authoritative servers in the Domain Overrides (as discussed in the following section).

By default, it also has rebind protection and it will reject responses from upstream nameservers that use private IP addresses (other than 127.0.0.0/8 addresses commonly used by DNS real-time black lists). This can be turned off using the **Disable DNS Rebinding Checks** checkbox on the **System** → **Advanced** → **Admin Access** page. See Section 5.3.1 for more details.

The **Listen Port** selection may be used to set an alternative TCP/UDP port. (Port 53 is the Internet standard default for DNS.) The DNS Forwarder cannot be used when the standard DNS Resolver (covered in Section 21.2) is running, because they both listen on the same TCP and UDP port 53. If you need to run both, you can workaround by setting a different **Listen Port** number and possibly use packet filter port forwarding to redirect port 53 as appropriate to your custom port.

By default, this server listens for DNS queries on all available interfaces. If you want to have it only respond on specific interfaces, select them in the **Interfaces** menu. (It will then discard queries on other interfaces.)

If you only want it to listen on the above defined interfaces, also check the **Strict interface binding** checkbox. Note that this doesn't work with IPv6.

The forwarding DNS server is `dnsmasq`. If you want to further configure this server with additional custom command-line arguments, enter them in the **Custom options** text box. For more details, see its manual at `http://www.thekelleys.org.uk/dnsmasq/docs/dnsmasq-man.html`.

Click the **Save** button to save the general DNS Forwarder settings. It will then prompt on the new page that the changes need to be applied — so click the **Apply Changes** button so they will take effect.

At the bottom of the page are two tables showing the Host and Domain Overrides. These are for configuring authoritative DNS data or using specific authoritative servers. These are covered in the following Section 21.4 and Section 21.5.

Note
The overrides will not be in use until the `dnsmasq` service is enabled by setting the **Enable DNS forwarder** checkbox.

21.4   Host Overrides (dnsmasq)

The host overrides is used to add hostname and corresponding IP address entries to the system's local /etc/hosts database. Normally, this is used for local hostname lookups on a single system, but pfSense can be configured to serve this information as authoritative DNS data. Instead of going out to the defined forwarders to ask the DNS question, it uses these local answers. If the table near the bottom of the **Services → DNS Forwarder** lists any entries, you may use the edit icon to update that specific entry or the delete icon to remove it. (Note if you delete an entry and it has entries identified as an *Alias* that it will delete them too.) You may click the **Add** button to add an entry.

On the **Edit Host Override** page (also used to add a new entry), you can enter the hostname, domain name, and its IP or IPv6 address. Note that this hostname is just the first label and doesn't include the period, and the domain name is required. You may also include an optional description which may be used as a reminder of its purpose.

If the address has additional hostnames, add it to the **Additional Names for this Host** section. (This is also called an *hostname alias*.) If you have more than two hostnames (for the same address), then click the **Add Host Name** button to add an additional name. Click the **Delete** button (which only appears if you have additional names) to delete one. (To delete the first alias, just blank out its settings.)

After clicking the **Save** button, the parent DNS Forwarders page will reload and will indicate that the DNS forwarder configuration has been changed but not applied. The Host Overrides table lower on the page should show the new entries. Click the green **Apply Changes** button. And if the DNS Forwarder is enabled, the hostnames or addresses can then be looked up against that DNS server.

21.5   Domain Overrides (dnsmasq)

The Domain Override table at the bottom of the **Services → DNS Forwarder** page lists authoritative DNS servers to use for some specific domains. This is used to force the queries for any name under that domain to go to the specified servers. (Also, it will exclude DNS rebind rejections for any returned answers from there.) If there are any entries, they can be edited or removed using the corresponding action icons.

To add an entry, click its corresponding **Add** button.

The **Edit Domain Override** page (also used to add a new entry) has two required fields: **Domain** and **IP Address**. For the domain, enter a single label or multi-label (separated by dots) domain name. (This doesn't have to be a name known in the public DNS.) Then list the IP address of the DNS server that will authoritatively answer for queries within that domain.

If you need to allow some names within the domain to be forwarded as usual, add an additional Domain Overrides entry for the specific domain name but use an "#" (pound sign) for the **IP Address**. Or if you don't want to forward for that domain at all, use a "!" (exclamation mark) in that field.

If you need to have the DNS queries originate from a specific IP address on the pfSense system (such as if you are using a VPN), list the IP address in the optional **Source IP** field.

Optionally, you may also add a description for this entry for your tracking purposes.

Click the **Save** button to begin using the details. It will take you back to the original DNS Forwarder page that shows the Domain Overrides table at the bottom.

21.6 DNS Service Log Entries

The logging for the default full-featured DNS resolver (`unbound`) and the simple caching forwarder (`dnsmasq`) are available via the **Status** → **System Logs** → **System** → **DNS Resolver** subpage. The `unbound` DNS resolver's verbosity is defined with the **Log Level** value on the **Services** → **DNS Resolver** → **Advanced Settings** page. In addition, the *Inform* values for **System Domain Local Zone Type** may be used to log queries. See Section 21.2.1 for details.

Logging for the hostname aliases lookups is identified with `filterdns`. (See Section 16.5 for details.) In addition, if you have the `bind` DNS server package installed, its logging is identified with the `named` process name.

This log output may be searched or adjusted using the **Log filter** and **Manage log** shortcuts as covered in Section 11.1 and Section 11.3.

22 Dynamic DNS

The pfSense dynamic DNS features provide a way for external DNS servers to publish a DNS address resource record containing your pfSense system's public IP address. These DNS settings can be updated automatically to reflect IP address changes. This is useful in environments where the pfSense system's IP address periodically changes and you want an external DNS authoritative server to publish an updated record to refer to the new address. By using dynamic DNS, you can use a DNS hostname instead of an IP address to access or see the system.

pfSense provides multiple techniques for sharing the IP address changes by using web-based methods to third-party dynamic DNS services or by using the RFC 2136 Dynamic DNS UPDATE protocol to make the change using DNS itself. These are covered in this chapter.

22.1 Dynamic DNS Clients

Several commercial and free dynamic DNS providers offer an web-based interface to upload dynamic DNS information. The **Services** → **Dynamic DNS** page is for displaying the Dynamic DNS Clients using an HTTP interface. If your provider is not listed, the **Services** → **Dynamic DNS** → **RFC 2136 Clients** page is for providers who use the standard RFC 2136 DNS Updates protocol for making changes (Section 22.2).

By default, dynamic DNS is not setup and the Dynamic DNS Clients table is empty. Click the **Add** button to display the page to setup a Dynamic DNS Client (which is covered in the following section). When a client exists, the table fields will contain the interface name (such as WAN or LAN), the service which is the organization that provides the dynamic DNS service, the hostname hosted by that service, the cached IP address of your interface that hostname now refers to, a brief description of this client entry, and action buttons for editing, disabling (or enabling), and removing this specific dynamic DNS client service.

If the cached IP address is displayed in green color, then it is up-to-date with the service provider. If the entire client entry is displayed in light gray or lighter font, then that dynamic update client is disabled (and you may click the **Enable service** action icon or use the edit page to enable it). If you need to update the provider because it has an old IP, click the **Edit service** action icon and then scroll down to the **Save & Force Update** button and click it. You may have multiple dynamic DNS clients configured and enabled, but that is not common usage.

22.1.1   Add or Edit a Dynamic DNS Client

The **Edit** page is used to add a new dynamic DNS client or to edit an existing one.

By default the new client will be enabled; to keep the configuration but to not use it, check the **Disable** checkbox. It can also be disabled via the action icon on the previous page's table view.

The **Service Type** drop-down menu is used to select the dynamic DNS provider as listed in Table 22.1. These providers use web-based interfaces to upload dynamic DNS information. If your provider uses standard RFC 2136 DNS Updates, see the **Services** → **Dynamic DNS** → **RFC 2136 Clients** page instead as explained in Section 22.2.

The **Service Type** menu also includes **Custom** and **Custom (v6)** which may be used to use your own or a different dynamic DNS provider. The form on this page will reflect the options available for the selected service provider type.

Note

Some of the dynamic DNS code for interacting with these providers has never been tested by the developers and some hasn't been used in over a decade. This book's author successfully used the No-IP service for this feature.

The IP address is from the interface selected using the **Interface to monitor** drop-down menu. It will list your interface names, such as WAN and LAN. A Gateway Group (identified with "GW Group") may also be selected if previously defined via the **System** → **Routing** → **Gateway Groups** subpage (see Section 15.2). If you need to do the update from a different interface, use the **Interface to send update from** drop-down menu to select the interface name.

The DNS label to be set and served by the provider is set in the **Hostname** field. This is a complete fully-qualified domain name. If you are using HE.net Tunnelbroker (as selected as the **Service Type**) then enter your tunnel ID. If you are using GleSYS, then enter your record ID. If you are using DNSimple, only enter the domain name (in the Hostname text box).

If you are using Namecheap, an additional field for the domain name is available; enter the domain or subdomain zone as served by Namecheap.

If you also have a MX record and your dynamic DNS provider supports updating this corresponding record, enter the desired static mail server name in the **MX** text field.

Some providers support DNS wildcards. This is so any name under a subdomain name will be matched to provide the address record. If you want to set this catch-all up, check the **Enable Wildcard** checkbox.

To log additional details about the dynamic DNS setup, check the **Enable verbose logging** checkbox.

To only use IPv4 (even if IPv6 is available) for the HTTP interface connection, check the **Force IPv4 DNS Resolution** checkbox for **HTTP API DNS Options**. If you want it to check the authenticity of the peer's TLS/SSL certificate trust chain when negotiating its connection, check the **Verify SSL Certificate Trust** checkbox. (In older versions, these were in a CURL options section.)

A username is required for most providers. For custom entries, this is the HTTP Authentication username. If using Route 53, enter your access key ID. For GleSYS, enter the API user.

Azure DNS	azure.microsoft.com
City Network	citynetwork.se
Cloudflare	www.cloudflare.com
DigitalOcean	digitalocean.com
DNSexit	dnsexit.com
DNSimple	dnsimple.com
DNS Made Easy	www.dnsmadeeasy.com
DNS-O-Matic	dnsomatic.com
DynDNS (dynamic, static, custom)	dyndns.org
easyDNS	easydns.com
Euro Dns	eurodns.com
freeDNS	freedns.afraid.org
GleSYS	glesys.com
Google Domains	domains.google.com
GratisDNS	gratisdns.dk
HE.net (and v6)	dns.he.net
HE.net Tunnelbroker	ipv4.tunnelbroker.net
Loopia	loopia.se
Namecheap	namecheap.com
No-IP (including free)	no-ip.com
ODS.org	ods.org
OpenDNS	opendns.com
OVH DynHOST	www.ovh.com
Route 53	aws.amazon.com
SelfHost	selfhost.de
SPDNS (and v6)	spdns.de
ZoneEdit	zoneedit.com

Table 22.1: Dynamic DNS Providers

The **Username** has a corresponding **Password** field. It has two password text boxes used to confirm you enter it correctly (same in both fields). If using FreeDNS, enter its Authentication Token here. For Route 53, enter your Secret Access Key. If using GleSYS, enter the API key. For DNSimple, enter the API token.

Using the DNSimple and Route 53 providers, you will have a **Zone ID** text field. Use your corresponding Zone ID provided by Route 53 or the Record ID provided by DNSimple.

Custom entries also offer a **Update URL** text field. It is used to define a custom URI using an HTTP interface to update the dynamic DNS. For example, maybe your custom provider wants you to pass the account and other details as part of the URI. Use the special *%IP%* macro (literal "I" and "P" within percent signs) to represent the new IP address to be embedded in the URL.

If you want pfSense to check if the provider indicates success, use the **Result Match** text area input. If the provider returns some details that matches this text, then it will indicate it worked. Leave it blank if you don't want to check the results. Note that carriage returns (^M), newlines (^J), and tab characters at the beginning or end of the results returned from the HTTP interface are removed prior to comparing the text. If you want to compare against multiple possible results, separate the text with a vertical bar (|). If you need to match a literal vertical bar, escape it with a slash (\|). To match the new IP, use *%IP%* (literal "I" and "P" within percent signs).

If you can set the DNS time-to-live for the DNS record, enter the value in the **TTL** text field. Normally, the TTL is a number defined in seconds that represents when DNS caches will drop it and look it up again (when queried). Commonly it is capped at 604800 seconds (7 days). If, for example, your IP changes every day and you expect frequent lookups for your DNS name, then you may want to set it to 30 so caches will only get 30 seconds behind at the latest. Note that some providers may have different syntax for representing the time.

The optional **Description** text field is used to briefly describe its purpose for your own administrative reasons in the table view of your clients.

After filling out the needed dynamic DNS settings, click the **Save** button. If you have any fields with invalid settings or you still require details, these errors will be indicated at the top of the page. If saving a client for the first time, the DNS dynamic update will be performed immediately (instead of waiting for the configured interface's next change).

If editing an existing entry, an additional button, **Save & Force Update**, is available to also immediately trigger the dynamic DNS update.

After saving the client details, you will be taken back to the table view of configured clients.

22.2   RFC 2136 DNS Updates

The **RFC 2136 Clients** page via the link from **Services** → **Dynamic DNS** is used to do dynamic DNS using the standard DNS UPDATE protocol as defined in RFC 2136, Dynamic Updates in the Domain Name System. A remote DNS server will need to be pre-configured with an authentication method and to allow dynamically updating a DNS zone using this method. pfSense will use the `nsupdate` utility to submit the DNS UPDATE request.

This page has a table for each entry showing the interface to be monitored, the optional server to send the dynamic update request to, the DNS hostname to update with the new IP address, the cached IP which is the IP and/or IPv6 address that was most recently registered, and the description which is an internal explanation only used by the pfSense admin. (It does not have any configurations by default.)

In addition, the table entries will have the following actions: **Edit client** (pencil icon) to modify and update the settings; **Enable client** (checkbox icon) or **Disable client** to activate or deactivate its DNS settings; and **Delete client** (trash can icon) to remove the corresponding entry.

22.2.1 RFC 2136 Settings

To add or update dynamic DNS using DNS UPDATE, click the **Add** button or for an existing entry, click its **Edit client** pencil icon. This will take you to a new page with a form with several fields.

To activate the following dynamic DNS configuration, check the **Enable** checkbox. (Or use the enable/disable action toggle buttons on the previous page.)

Select the interface (like WAN or LAN) to monitor for IP address changes (for updating the DNS entry), in the **Interface** drop-down menu. Any options identified with "GW Group") were previously defined via the **System** → **Routing** → **Gateway Groups** subpage as covered in Section 15.2.

If you have multiple interfaces that you want dynamic DNS for, create multiple *RFC 2136 Clients* configuration entries (or also use the external Dynamic DNS providers as configured in Section 22.1).

Dynamic DNS is used to update a DNS label for an address record. Enter that label name in the required **Hostname** text field. Note this is a complete DNS name with the hostname and domain name parts.

The DNS time-to-live is required in the **TTL** counter field. This is the number of seconds this DNS record will be cached by various DNS resolvers. If you expect your interface's IP address to change frequently, then have a low number. But even if your IP changes rarely, you won't want your old address cached for a long time. Commonly this is set to a 60 seconds or a few minutes (like 300 seconds).

Enter the key name setting as known on the remote DNS UPDATE server in the required **Key name** field.

Using a HMAC shared secret to authenticate with the remote DNS server is a best practice and pfSense requires this setup here. pfSense uses HMAC-MD5 (algorithm 157) for this. Note that newer BIND tools generate HMAC-SHA256 by default.

Enter the HMAC-MD5 key as known by the remote DNS UPDATE server in the required **Key** field. This is also known as the secret, shared secret, or public key. It is commonly a string of characters that looks like "vuN2PvNN/wkk6cDPMwFq+w==".

In normal usage the `nsupdate` command will send the update to the master DNS server as identified in the hostname's zone's SOA MNAME field. If you need to override this to update the zone on a different DNS server, enter its IP address or hostname in the **Server** field.

Normally UDP is used for small DNS UPDATE requests. If you need a TCP connection instead, check the **Protocol** checkbox.

If the monitored interface has an internal or private-use address, but is accessible from the Internet with a public address, check the **Use public IP** checkbox. This will use the feature discussed in the following Section 22.3 to try to detect its public IP address.

By default, if you have them, both IPv4 DNS A and IPv6 DNS AAAA address records will be updated for the defined DNS hostname. If you only want one of these updated or known, select it in the **Record Type** radio list.

You may also enter an explanation about this RFC 2136 client configuration in the **Description** text field for your own local use.

Use the **Save** button when finished with the form. If you are editing an existing entry and want the DNS to be updated even if the interface's address did not change, use the button, **Save & Force Update**. After saving, you will be taken back to the table listing the your RFC 2136 settings. Note if you don't have the enable checkbox selected, the new changes won't be used.

If your dynamic DNS updates aren't working, look in the general logs at **Status** → **System Logs**. Use the **Log filter** feature (as covered in Section 11.1) to look for "rfc2136". If a log entry indicates a "TSIG error" with "NOTAUTH(BADKEY)", you may be using a different algorithm on the server side or the wrong key (secret), for example.

22.3   Use Public IP

If the **Use public IP** checkbox is enabled for a RFC 2136 Clients configuration and its corresponding local interface is assigned a private-use IP address, a simple HTTP page request is done to a remote web-based service for it to return the real IP address in use. This check IP feature is not needed for the (non-RFC 2136) Dynamic DNS Clients because those remote services can already detect their peer (your pfSense) IP address.

By default, it uses `http://checkip.dyndns.org` (when the feature is enabled). If you need to use an alternate service, the configuration is found via the **Services** → **Dynamic DNS** → **Check IP Services** subpage. The page has a table listing the remote web services to use for this. Entries that are disabled may be displayed in a lighter font. Only the first enabled entry in the table will be used.

The default service may be deactivated by clicking its corresponding **Disable service** action icon in the table.

To add a check IP web service, click the **Add** button. This will take you to a new page to add it. An identifying name and the URL field is required.

Note
The check IP web service must return output containing the IP address string in the format: "Current IP Address: a.b.c.d".

Check the **Enable** checkbox. The service will only be used if it is enabled (and is the first service in the list).

Enter a name to identify the web service in the **Name** field. It may only contain letters, digits, or underscore.

Enter its web address in the **URL** field. Be sure to include the *http://* or *https://* URI scheme.

If the remote service uses HTTP authentication, enter the credentials in the **User name** and **Password** fields. Also enter the password a second time in the **Confirm** field.

If using a HTTPS service, you may have it verify the authenticity of its TLS/SSL certificate to make sure it is communicating with the correct end-point by checking the **Verify SSL Peer** checkbox.

As desired enter an explanation for the IP check service in the **Description** field.

Click the **Save** button to store the configuration. This will return you back to the table view of the services.

To modify an entry's settings, click on the **Edit service** pencil icon in the actions list. To remove an entry, click its **Delete service** trash can icon in the actions list. The entries may be activated or deactivated by clicking the **Enable service** or **Disable service** action icon.

23 Wireless Networking

This chapter covers setting up a wireless interface for the pfSense system to join a wireless network to gain Internet access, connecting to neighboring peers, and using pfSense to provide wireless access for others. Its capabilities — known as operating modes — depend on what your wireless hardware supports. This chapter also shows how to review your current wireless network and see your nearby peers.

Infrastructure / BSS (using an Access Point)

To have your pfSense system act as a wireless client and connect to an access point, the mode should be set to Infrastructure (also known as BSS). BSS or Basic Service Set is the standard method of communicating to other wireless devices indirectly through a central access point (like a wireless router). Using an access point (also known as a BSS master) is common for permanent wireless networks and it may provide a wider range for connecting to various devices.

With this you will need at least an IPv4 or IPv6 configuration type such as DHCP. You will also need to define the SSID name and its corresponding authentication details to connect to.

Ad-hoc / IBSS (peer-to-peer)

For a simple point-to-point connection for two machines, use the Ad-hoc mode (also known as IBSS). wireless devices to connect directly (wirelessly) to each other, peer-to-peer, without using an access point. Other ad-hoc nodes will forward data for each other based on connectivity and routing algorithms — so it may not have a single point of failure. The system will need to keep connections for every device it is communicating with and is generally used for devices that are close to each other. Many wireless devices do not support the ad-hoc mode due to its limitations.

For this you would normally use a static IPv4 configuration type and then define the IPv4 address. (Or you may use static IPv6.) The other machine in the ad-hoc mode would also be configured for IBSS and with a different static address.

Access Point

To run your own wireless network, use the Access Point mode. If your wireless hardware supports it, your pfSense system can be configured as a base station or hub for the various BSS clients to communicate with each other — and as a gateway so they can access other networks, such as your LAN or the Internet via your WAN. (This is powered by the `hostapd` daemon.)

An SSID must be set to identify your wireless network. When running an Access Point, a specific, non-auto, channel number must be defined. Access points commonly use DHCP to provide IP addressing and other network details to their wireless clients.

Note again that some wireless adapters do not have the hardware functionality to be used as an access point. If it is not supported, the Interfaces view on the dashboard may show it is down with a red "x" graphic (meaning it is disabled). In addition, the **Status** → **Interfaces** page may show the interface with the status of "down."

23.1   Wireless Interfaces

In pfSense versions 2.4 and later, the wireless devices are not immediately available for interface assignments. They must be created first via the **Interfaces** → **Assignments** → **Wireless** subpage.

To setup the wireless device, go to the **Interfaces** → **Assignments** page and then follow the **Wireless** link. If you already had wireless devices created, this table would list them by name with their operating mode (and an optional description). Corresponding action icons may be used to edit the entry or to remove it.

To create the wireless interface, click the **Add** button. This will take you to a new page to select the hardware, covered in the following section.

Note while the interface is listed on the **Interfaces** → **Wireless** subpage, it is not configured or used for anything until it is assigned as described in Section 23.3.

23.2   Wireless Interface Configuration

The Wireless Interface Configuration page only lets you choose the hardware device, its wireless mode, and a brief description for its use. This short menu is available via the **Interfaces** → **Assignments** → **Wireless** subpage by clicking the **Add** button or the pencil icon action to edit an existing wireless interface.

The many other specific settings for an already-defined wireless interface are available once it is assigned (Section 23.3) or later via the main **Interfaces** menu (by clicking on its interface name). This is covered in Section 23.4.

FreeBSD supports a wide range of wireless adapters from many different chipset manufacturers and device vendors ranging from Aironet to ZyDAS. The **Parent Interface** drop-down menu will list only the recognized wireless devices that are detected and supported by FreeBSD. These are listed by device name (and number) and its detected vendor description. The wireless driver names may include the following: an, ath, ath_hal, bwi, bwn, ipw, iwi, iwn, malo, mwl, ral, rsu, rum, run, uath, upgt, ural, urtw, urtwn, wi, wl, wpi, and zyd. (Note that some vendors may offer devices that are supported by different drivers.)

Only certain hardware is capable to operate as an access point. This may include various Cisco, D-Link, HP, Linksys, Netgear, Proxim, or other cards supported by the ath (Atheros) driver; the ipw Intel PRO/Wireless 2100 driver; the iwi Intel PRO/Wireless 2200BG/2915ABG/2225BG driver;

A-Link, Amigo, AMIT, AOpen, ASUS, Belkin, Canyon, CNet, Compex, Conceptronic, Digitus, E-Tech, Edimax, Eminent, Encore, Fibreline, Gigabyte, Hawking, iNexQ, JAHT, LevelOne, Linksys, Micronet, Minitar, MSI, OvisLink, PheeNet, Pro-Nets, Repotec, SATech, Sitecom, Surecom, Sweex, TekComm, Unex, Zinwell, Zonet, and other cards supported by the `ral` Ralink Technology RT2500 driver; Buffalo, Hercules, KCORP LifeStyle, SerComm, SparkLAN, Tonze, and other USB devices supported by the `ural` Ralink Technology RT2500USB driver; and 3Com AirConnect, Corega, Dlink, Intersil, NDC/Sohoware, Netgear, and SMC devices supported by the `wi` Intersil PRISM driver. (Note this list is not exhaustive and some of the devices for listed vendors may not work as access points.)

Usually there would only be one wireless device, so you can just keep this default selection. But if you have multiple wireless devices, select your desired device in the **Parent Interface** drop-down menu.

Later you will see that the wireless interface name will be changed by appending "_wlan" and a number (starting with 0) to the FreeBSD device name (for example: `ath0_wlan0`).

The operating mode (as introduced earlier) defaults to **Infrastructure (BSS)**. The other choices are **Ad-hoc (IBSS)** and **Access Point**. Make your selection in the **Mode** drop-down menu.

You may enter an explanation for this wireless interface in the **Description** text field. This will be shown in other sections to help identify the network interface. (You may also want to enter the description from the above parentheses from your **Parent Interface** selection here to better identify it.)

When editing an existing configuration, you can not change the parent interface nor its operating mode if it is already in use. To change the mode (after it is first saved), use its specific network interface configuration page (as seen in Section 23.4.3).

Click the **Save** button when finished. This will take you back to the previous page with the interface listed in the table.

23.3   Assigning a Wireless Interface

To further configure a new wireless network interface, click **Assignments** in the **Interfaces** drop-down menu. An existing interface may be configured by clicking on its interface name in the left column. The middle **Network port** column will better identify the hardware by its FreeBSD cloned device name with your custom description in parentheses. (Older versions of pfSense will list it by its FreeBSD driver name and number and a MAC address.)

Adding a new wireless interface is done in the *Available network ports* section by selecting the desired wireless device in the **Network port** drop-down menu (as discussed in Section 13.1), (Note that since pfSense 2.4, you will need to create the wireless interface first via the **Interfaces** → **Wireless** subpage as discussed previously.) Then click its corresponding **Add** button.

After adding the interface, the page will reload with a new pfSense interface name listed. By default, it would have a *OPT* name and number. It is disabled by default. Click on this new pfSense interface name to configure it as covered in the following section.

23.4   Wireless Configurations

Follow the basic steps to enable the interface as discussed in Section 13.2. This will include the General Configuration at the top and Reserved Networks at the bottom. The page may also include Static IPv4 Configuration and other choices based on enabled options. You may want to change the automatic *OPT* name to "WIFI," for example, in the **Description** field. Your settings will depend on how you want to use (or provide) your wifi. The page will also have multiple sections for wireless-specific settings as covered in following sections.

A wireless interface assignment may also be removed via the **Interface** → **Assignments** page. Click on the **Delete** button corresponding to the pfSense interface name (and FreeBSD wireless interface name and your optional description) to remove it. You will be prompted to confirm this deletion.

23.4.1   Common Wireless Configuration

When adding (or later re-configuring) a wireless interface, the interface's configuration offers some additional choices related to wireless networking. Scroll down to the **Common Wireless Configuration** section.

These *common* settings are applicable all the wireless networks on this specific network interface. (This menu header will list the interface name, such as ath0.) To keep these few settings for use for other wireless configurations even if you delete or reassign this interface, click the **Persist common settings** checkbox.

For wireless devices that support multiple operating modes (or bands), you may use the **Standard** drop-down menu to force it to operate at specific mode, such as 802.11a, 802.11b, or 802.11g. The default is 802.11ng. To have the driver select this, choose the *Auto* choice. Note this may limit the frequencies (or channels) which may be considered.

If your wireless interface supports 802.11g, it will provide a **802.11g OFDM Protection Mode** drop-down menu. This is used to protect the newer protocol from 802.11b by preventing collisions or lowering data rates in a mixed mode network. It defaults to *Off* which would be fine in a 802.11g-only network. The other choices are *CTS to self* (Clear to Send) and *RTS and CTS* (Request to Send and Clear to Send sequences). (Note that not all devices support CTS.)

Use the **Channel** drop-down menu to select the wireless channel to use. It will list the standard numbers as detected and the channel number. It may also show the frequency at the maximum transmit power and maximum regulation transmit power (in dBM). While some channels may be listed, it still may not be supported by your card (and regulatory region). For your wireless client to scan for a channel to operate on, select the *Auto* choice. Note if you are setting up an Access Point, you must define a specific channel.

If you have a Atheros device that supports CTS and ACK timeouts, you will have a **Distance setting (meters)** field for tuning these timers. Set it to an integer number for meters for the distance between your system and another station. Based on this distance, pfSense will define some recommended values for Inter Frame Spacing (IFS) for collision avoidance for multiple stations and timeouts for point-to-point communication.

23.4.2 Regulatory Settings

Commonly network devices are restrained based on government rules to help prevent wireless interference at various frequencies. Some devices allow changing their default settings which may include maximum transmit power and the available channels. If you want to use what your hardware assumes for your location, keep the following Regulatory Settings set to *Default*.

If you need to adjust for your actual location or government policies, use one or more of the following selections to calculate the regulatory constraints. Note that when changing this, your existing wireless pairings will be dropped.

Select a SKU from the **Regulatory domain** drop-down list. The *DEBUG* option will expose all device channels with no limitations. The region codes include:

APAC
> Asia Pacific

APAC2
> Asia Pacific with DFS on mid-band

APAC3
> Asia Pacific without ISM band

ETSI
> Europe

ETSI2
> Europe without HT40 in 5 GHz

ETSI3
> Europe and others

FCC
> United States

FCC3
> United States with 5470 band, 11h, DFS

FCC4
> United States 2.4 GHz with Public Safety Band (PSB)

JAPAN
> Japan

KOREA
> Korea

NONE
> Region Free (but still has defined constraints)

ROW
> China/Taiwan and Rest of the World

Included in this regulatory domains list may be some private codes too:

GZ901
    Zcomax GZ-901 (900 MHz GSM)

SR9
    Ubiquiti SR9 (900 MHz GSM)

XC900M
    Zcomax GZ-901 (900 MHz GSM)

XR9
    Ubiquiti XR9 (900 MHz GSM)

To override the regulatory domain for a specific country or region, you may use the **Country** drop-down menu. This will map choices like Albania to NONE, Brazil to FCC, and Viet Nam to APAC2, for example.

Some of the regulatory constraints vary based on if you are operating your wireless indoors or outdoors. To specifically select this, choose from the **Location** drop-down list. The *Anywhere* choice implies the constraints will be defined.

 Warning
Some settings may not be available and may disable or constrain your wireless network device differently than expected. Be sure to use supported values.

23.4.3 Network-Specific Wireless Configuration

Generally the operating mode is already defined when the interface is first added, but you may change it here in the **Mode** drop-down menu. The choices are: *Infrastructure (BSS)*, *Ad-hoc (BSS)*, and *Access Point*. The default Infrastructure or optional Ad-hoc modes will connect to other available network, or you can run your own network access point.

- The Infrastructure mode will need at least a **IPv4** or **IPv6 Configuration Type** such as DHCP (as defined in the General Configuration section at the top of the page). You will also need to define the **SSID** name and its corresponding authentication details (covered in the following sections) to connect to.

- For the Ad-hoc mode you would normally select a Static IPv4 in the **IPv4 Configuration Type** in the General Configuration section and then define the **IPv4 Address**. Or you may select and define a static IPv6 address. (The peer system would also use IBSS Ad-hoc mode with its own static IP address.)

- When running an Access Point, an SSID must be set — enter your desired SSID to identify your wireless network in the following field. A specific channel number for your access point must be set and not just *Auto* (as described in the previous common wireless configuration section). In addition, a Wireless Standard 802.11n (or 802.11ng) selection with an access point requires Wireless Media Extensions (WME). This provides support for some quality of service mechanisms including traffic classes for voice, video, background, and best effort. So check that **Enable WME** checkbox to enable it. Normally DHCP is used to provide IP addressing and network details to the access point's clients.

If you are setting up an access point, then enter your required desired service set identifier in the **SSID** input field. While SSID can contain any type of characters, some devices don't work well with spaces or special characters.

The **SSID** field is for the remote access point's name if using Infrastructure mode. If it is blank, your wireless device may connect to any available access point, or for Ad-hoc mode, any available station.

if you are using 802.11ng or 802.11na, you will have a **Minimum wireless standard** menu for defining what standards are allowed to associate with your access point. Select *802.11n* to only allow High Throughput (HT) capable stations to connect and legacy stations will not be allowed. Select *802.11g* to only allow 802.11g-capable stations to associate (and 802.11b systems are not allowed). Or select *Any* (the default) to allow both HT and legacy systems to associate.

Or you may have a **802.11g only** checkbox. When checked only 802.11g stations are allowed to associate with your access point and 802.11b stations are not permitted. This is unchecked by default, implying that both are allowed.

To pass packets directly between wireless clients as an access point, check the **Allow intra-BSS communication** checkbox. This internal bridging may be useful to isolate wireless traffic. The default (unchecked) is to have the packets pass through the pfSense system so you can configure packet filter rules for them as needed.

To use Wireless Multimedia Extensions on supported hardware, check the **Enable WME** checkbox. This helps prioritize traffic for background, best effort, video, and voice. (Note that 802.11n requires WME to be enabled.)

By default, the access point SSID is included when answering undirected probe request frames and in beacon frames. To not broadcast it, check the **Hide SSID** checkbox. Note this may cause problems for some clients and the SSID may still be discovered.

23.4.4 WPA

Most modern wireless networks use WPA (or Wi-Fi Protected Access) or WPA2 to provide security. Make sure the **Enable WPA** checkbox is checked.

Then enter the passphrase or shared key in the **WPA Pre-Shared Key** field. This will be displayed as typed. It must be at least 8 characters long and the maximum is 63 characters. (This is required when selecting *Pre-Shared Key* for the upcoming **WPA Key Management Mode** setting.)

Normally, the newer WPA2 (802.11i/RSN) protocol is used. To use WPA (802.11i/D3.0) select it in the **WPA Mode** menu. Or if you need to support either, select *Both*.

To define the accepted key management algorithm, use the **WPA Key Management Mode** drop-down menu. The choices are: *Pre-Shared Key* (WPA-PSK for WPA or WPA2 Personal), *Extensible Authentication Protocol* (WPA-EAP for WPA or WPA2 Enterprise), or *Both*. When using the default pre-shared key mode be sure to also set the passphrase in the previous **WPA Pre-Shared Key** field.

The **WPA Pairwise** drop-down menu is to choose the cipher for generating the secret key used after the authentication. It defaults to the recommended *AES* (CCMP-128 Counter mode with CBC-MAC). The other choices are *TKIP* (Temporal Key Integrity Protocol) or *Both*. Note that TKIP is not considered secure. This cipher is also used for the following group multicast rekeying.

The WPA protocol automatically changes its encryption keys, known as rekeying, for increased security. The **Group Key Rotation** number input field is used to set the time interval in seconds for rekeying the random Group Temporal Key (GTK) for broadcast/multicast data. While it is common to use 600 seconds (once every ten minutes) or 86400 seconds (once per day), this defaults to 60 seconds. The **Group Master Key Regeneration** field is used for the interval time for rekeying the auxiliary key used to derive the GTK. It defaults to 3600 seconds (or one hour). This master rekey interval must be greater than the previous group interval time. The accepted inputs are from 1 to 9999.

In addition to the timed interval, to have your access point rekey the GTK when any station using it leaves, check the **Strict Key Regeneration** checkbox.

23.4.5   802.1x RADIUS Options

Your access point can have multiple users with their own passwords that are authenticated from a centralized server. Users may be added or removed without interrupting your wireless service for others. This authenticator feature is supported using the 802.1X standard for network access control and typically the authentication is powered by a RADIUS server. To use this, check the **Enable IEEE802.1X Authentication** checkbox. These 802.1x RADIUS options are only used if you are defining the Access Point mode and have WPA enabled (as seen previously).

Enter the IP address and shared secret for the RADIUS authentication server in the first and last **Primary 802.1X server** fields. This shared secret is the passphrase known to the RADIUS server so you may use it. It is not the passphrase for a specific user. RADIUS uses port 1812. If yours uses a different port, enter it in the middle port number field.

If you have an additional RADIUS authentication server, enter its details in the **Secondary 802.1X server** fields. This secondary server will only be used for failover if the primary server does not respond.

Wireless clients may be able to authenticate to multiple access points even if they are only associated to one AP. This allows quicker roaming between access points. To allow your access point on this interface to accept authentication for possible future AP use (also known as preauthentication), click the **Authentication Roaming Preauth** checkbox.

Note again that after clicking **Save**, the changes aren't immediately activated — so click **Apply Changes** when prompted.

23.5   Firewall Notes

Firewall rules may be required for your wireless network. Via the **Firewall** → **Rules** page, select the tab for the interface (like *WIFI*) and click a **Add** button to introduce or edit rules as needed. See Chapter 16 for details.

If you are using your pfSense system as an access point and sharing an IP address using NAT, check your **Firewall** → **NAT** → **Outbound** subpage settings. If you are using automatic outbound address translation rules, the source should already include your wireless network's assigned IP address block as part of the **Source** entry. But if you are using a manual mapping, you can select your wireless interface and define the source. For more information, see Section 17.4.

23.6   DHCP Notes

When using DHCP to provide networking details to access point clients, after adding an access point you will need to set up the DHCP Server. As described in Chapter 19, when you have additional local networks, the **Services** → **DHCP Server** page will have an additional tab to configure it. Select that tab (like *WIFI*) and click the checkbox to enable the DHCP server on that wireless interface. If your wireless interface tab does not exist, make sure the interface has a static IPv4 address and its subnet mask allows a network of at least two hosts (/30).

Set your DHCP Server's **Available range** settings as needed. Note you don't need to have the range include the wireless interface's own IP too.

(If you are using IPv6, see Chapter 20 instead.)

23.7   Wireless Status

When you have a wireless interface defined, your menu will have a link for **Status** → **Wireless**. This page lists the access points and ad-hoc peers that are detected in your vicinity by your wireless network device(s). It will also list what wireless peers your network is currently associated with. If you have multiple wireless interfaces, use the interface links near the top to select the interface to view the status for.

Click the green **Rescan** button at the bottom to scan for nearby access points. This may take about ten seconds, so reload the same webpage if necessary to display its findings.

The *nearby* table lists the following attributes. These field headers may be clicked on to sort (or again to reverse sort) the list by that attribute. By default, it is sorted by the receive signal strength (RSSI field).

- **SSID** — The network name (or Mesh ID). Note that the displayed name may be abbreviated.

- **BSSID** — Its unique MAC address.

- **CHAN** — The channel it is on. For b/g protocols, channels 1, 6, and 11 don't have overlapping frequencies.

- **RATE** — Its maximum frame transmit rate, generally specified in megabits per second.

- **RSSI** — This is the receive signal strength and the background noise (separated by a colon), both indicated in -dBm units. For reference, -1 dBm signal strength is significantly stronger and cleaner than -100 dBm. Signal strength in -80 to -100 dBm is unlikely to be usable. The second number for noise is reversed. Noise near 0 is a high noise level with degraded strength and performance. Noise near -100 dBm has less interference. Generally the noise level may be the same for all the entries.

- **INT** — The time interval between beacons announcing its wireless presence. 100 ms is often the defined interval.

- **CAPS** — The capabilities captured from the neighboring station. This describes some of the features it supports. The first character string may be flags. See the following lists for details.

The possible *nearby peers* flags are:

- **A** — Channel Agility allows channel switching or frequency hopping.

- **B** — Packet Binary Convolutional Code (PBCC) mode provides error correction to help improve performance. Nevertheless, newer technologies have faster rates.

- **c** — Contention-free (CF) pollable uses Point coordination function (PCF) and is able to participate in its QoS.

- **C** — CF Pollable Request.

- **D** — This 802.11g feature provides both direct-sequence spread spectrum (DSSS) and Orthogonal frequency-division multiplexing (OFDM) methods.

- **E** — Extended Service Set (ESS). Infrastructure mode providing an Access Point where devices can communicate with each other. (It may have more than one AP for roaming.)

- **I** — Independent Basic Service Set (IBBS) is an ad-hoc network with no access point. (It can only connect to one station at a time.)

- **P** — Wired Equivalent Privacy (WEP). This is weak security that has been superseded by WPA.

- **R** — Robust Security Network (RSN) encrypts the whole frame. This is WPA2.

- **s** — Short Slot Times reduce retransmission delay after collisions to increase throughput.

- **S** — Short Preambles have reduced packet headers to improve performance. Old devices require long preambles. This is a 802.11g feature.

The capabilities may include:

- **WME** — Wireless Multimedia Extensions for QoS

- **WPA** — Wi-Fi Protected Access

- **WPS** — Wi-Fi Protected Setup

- **RSN** — 802.11i Robust Security Network (aka WPA2)

- **HTCAP** — 802.11n High Throughput capabilities

- **ATH** — Atheros protocol extensions

- **VEN** — Unknown vendor-specific extension

The *associated* table shows the following. These table headers may also be used to sort the data.

- **ADDR** — This is the MAC address of the associated peer. The ADDR field may show the BSSID address as seen in the above nearby list.

- **AID** — This is the association ID. (The peer was granted network access by your pfSense access point.)

- **CHAN** — The channel used for the association.

- **RATE** — The current transfer rate in megabytes per second.

- **RSSI** — The receive signal strength.

- **IDLE** — Your access point has an inactivity timer and it will purge old associated peers that have been idle.

- **TXSEQ** — The transmit sequence number.

- **RXSEQ** — The receive sequence number.

- **CAPS** — This lists the single character capabilities.

- **ERP** — This lists the single character state flags, information elements data, and, if it exists, multiple-input and multiple-output (MIMO) signal strength and noise. (This table field should be called "Flags."

Historical and recent wireless information about associated stations for the Infrastructure (BSS) mode only is available via the **Status → Monitoring** page. Other graphs about quality, packets, and other traffic counters for the wireless interfaces are also available. See Section 28.2 for details.

The **Status → Traffic Graph** webpage (Section 28.1) is also useful to visualize real-time activity for a wireless interface, including current bandwidth usage for specific wireless clients.

23.8   Wireless Log Entries

Logging for your wireless access points are available via the **Status** → **System Logs** → **System** → **Wireless** subpage. This includes the verbose logging with debugging, informational messages, notifications, and warnings for all the *hostapd* server modules, such as WPA, IEEE 802.11, IEEE 802.1X, RADIUS, and MLME. They all should be identified with a FreeBSD network interface name such as ath0_wlan0. Separate access points may be on different interfaces.

You may search or adjust this log output with the **Log filter** and **Manage log** shortcuts as covered in Section 11.1 and Section 11.3.

24 Tunneling

This chapter covers the interfaces for the tunneling technologies available via the subpages linked from the **Interfaces** → **Assignments** page. These include: QinQ stacking VLAN, GRE, GIF, and client-side PPP, PPPoE, PPTP, and L2TP. By themselves, these tunneling technologies are not encrypted. Additional tunnel technologies and server-side VPN setups are described in later chapters.

24.1 QinQ Interfaces

QinQ (IEEE 802.1ad) tunneling is used to create Layer 2 Ethernet connections between different sites. Also known as double VLAN or stacking VLAN (like 802.11Q in 802.1Q), QinQ encapsulates the VLAN tag with an inner tag for the private network and an outer tag for the public network. This allows expanding the VLAN numbering up to 16777216 numbers by using 1 through 4096 for both the inner and outer tags (but see the upcoming warning). For normal tagged VLANs, see Section 13.6. Behind the scenes, the QinQ setup is powered by FreeBSD's *Netgraph* networking system.

The QinQ feature is managed via the **Interfaces** → **QinQs** subpage available via the **Assignments** menu entry. None are defined by default, but when they are setup, the table shows the network interface the VLAN is associated with, its first tag number (the outer or *service* VLAN), the range of second tags or *members* (the inner or customer VLANs), and the optional description. The action icons may be used to edit the existing QinQ configuration or to remove it.

Click the **Add** button to set it up.

24.1.1 QinQ Configuration

To complete the configuration, the first level tag and one member tag is needed.

In the **Parent interface** drop-down menu select the network interface (which is listed by FreeBSD interface name and its hardware MAC address) to create QinQ interfaces for. This drop-down will only offer the hardware interfaces on your pfSense system that have the needed capabilities. (These network devices are capable for the software tagging mode without decreasing the MTU under 1500 bytes and capable of jumbo frames which means they can cope with frames larger than the Ethernet specification.)

Enter a single tag number in the required **First level tag** field. The other tag numbers added below are stacked on this. Allowed numbers are 1 through 4094.

To simplify firewall rules, you can have a QinQ interface group with this and other QinQ interfaces. Enable this with the **Adds interface to QinQ interface groups** checkbox. This will add it to the **Interface Groups** feature as covered in Section 16.4.

The optional **Description** text field may be used to enter an explanation of this QinQ interface for the pfSense administrators.

Enter a member tag number in the required **Tag(s)** field. (This is a number between 1 and 4094.) You may also enter a range of numbers delimited with a colon (:) or a dash (-), such as "2-3". To add more tag numbers, click the **Add Tag** button and another input field will appear. When saved, each member will be created as a separate virtual network interface. You can also remove a tag field by clicking its corresponding **Delete** button.

Warning

Too many QinQ members (or too large of a range) may cause your pfSense system's networking to be limited due to running out of buffer space. Access to the pfSense webConfigurator or to its text console via ssh may be lost. The pfSense system may also reboot and continually restart back up into the unstable state.

Click the **Save** button to create the QinQ interfaces.

Then back at the **Interfaces → Interface Assignments** page, see the network port drop-down list for adding a pfSense interface will have the new QinQ devices listed. Each will be identified with the member tag first then the service tag number and the FreeBSD network device name (and number), such as *QinQ 11 on VLAN 10 on re0*. (If you defined several members or a large range, you will have separate entries for all of them.) See Section 13.1 about assigning a QinQ interface. Then you may configure it with an IP address and use it in various places in pfSense. Other devices may use the same tag numbers for matching the VLAN traffic.

24.2 Point-to-Point Interfaces

The pfSense system can be setup with the Point-to-Point Protocol (PPP) to directly connect it with another physical node. It can be used with various asynchronous serial devices, such as ISDN terminal adapters, null modems ("cross-over" cable), and modems. In addition to standard PPP, pfSense also provides support for the PPP-over-Ethernet (PPPoE) protocol, Point-to-Point Tunneling Protocol (PPTP), and its successor, the Layer 2 Tunneling Protocol (L2TP).

While pfSense can connect to an ISP using PPTP, note that it has various vulnerabilities and is not recommended for secure, private communication. (For more information, also see VPN → PPTP.)

This section covers the client-side configurations. See Chapter 31 to setup pfSense as a PPPoE server and see Chapter 32 for serving L2TP.

To setup or view the client PPP interfaces select the **PPPs** link at the top of the page via the **Interfaces** → **Assignments** menu. (None are setup by default.)

When setup, the table will display the Point-to-Point interface name, its interface or serial device details, an optional description, and actions to edit or delete its configuration.

Click the **Add** button to setup a Point-to-Point interface. Note that many of these configurations are redundant and are also available when configuring an interface as discussed in Section 13.2.

24.2.1   Add or Edit PPP Configuration

There are many PPP configurations based on the type: PPP (modem), PPPoE, PPTP, or L2TP. Select one of these from the required **Link Type** option list. Then the configuration form may update based on the options available for that type. (See the following sections for details.) The common attributes are to select the link interface, description, username, and password. There is also a button for generic advanced options and additional type-specific options (as covered in following sections).

Select one or more devices or interfaces in the **Link Interface(s)** menu field. For the PPP link type, this will show your detected serial devices used for connecting with a modem for example. A common device name on FreeBSD is /dev/cuau0 as the first dial-out serial device. For PPP, select only one device.

For the PPPoE, PPTP, or L2TP link types, the **Link Interface(s)** menu will list the available capable network interfaces by their FreeBSD device name and number and MAC address in parentheses, followed by the pfSense-defined interface name. These all support multilink connections (MLPPP), so choose two interfaces if using that (with shift-click).

An explanation for this configuration may be entered in the **Description** field.

Also enter the authentication login name and password for the peer to authenticate your client, in the **Username** and **Password** fields. (Enter the password twice to confirm it was typed correctly.) A username and password are required for PPPoE, L2TP, and PPTP link types.

After making or entering your selections, click the **Save** button to store the new settings.

Generic Advanced PPP Options

Clicking the **Display Advanced** button will popup multiple additional options for any of the link types. (Also clicking it will bring up some additional options above that which are documented in following sections.)

Outgoing traffic can trigger an automatic reconnection for a virtual full-time connection. Enable this by clicking the **Dial On Demand** checkbox.

If no packets in either direction are on the Point-to-Point connection, after a defined time period, the connection is stopped. You can set this amount of time in seconds in the **Idle Timeout** field. It defaults to 0 (zero) which disables this.

By default, Van Jacobson TCP header compression is used with the IP Control Protocol (IPCP) layer to save some bytes for every TCP packet. To turn this off, click the **Disable Compression** checkbox.

By default with pfSense, the *mpd* daemon will attempt to make it so the maximum segment size (MSS) is not larger than the interface's MTU. This is to help it so packets aren't dropped. If you don't want this, check the **Disable TCPmssFix** checkbox.

When using multilink PPP, multilink fragment headers are not allowed to save two bytes on every frame. If you need these headers, click the **Disable ShortSeq** checkbox.

By default, address and control field (ACF) compression is done to reduce two bytes for each frame. If you don't want this, check the **Disable ACF compression** checkbox.

By default, one byte per most frames is saved using protocol field compression. If you don't need this, check the **Disable Protocol compression** checkbox.

Prior to pfSense version 2.4.4, it configured multilink automatically if there was more than one port. There is now a **Multilink over single link** checkbox to enable it.

To override the MTU with a detected higher value, check the **Force MTU** checkbox. Note this is not done if using multilink over single link. (This option was introduced in pfSense version 2.4.4.)

When the link interface is selected (at the top of the configuration), you will have one or more **Link Parameters** fields (for each interface). The fields include:

- **Bandwidth** — Used for multilink PPP to distribute bytes evenly over each of the links. Enter the bits-per-second number here for the interface so it can chop up the fragments appropriately.

- **MTU** — Set this to the largest PPP frame size (without the header) that this link can send for the maximum transmit unit (MTU) size. It must be at least 576 bytes. (For PPPoE, if it is larger than 1492 butes, it uses the RFC 4638 *PPP-Max-Payload* tag.)

- **MRU** — Set this to the largest PPP frame size (without the header) that this link can *receive* for the maximum receive unit (MRU) size. It must be at least 576 bytes.

- **MRRU** — Multilink PPP allows PPP frames to be fragmented, so MTU and MRU aren't important. Set this to the maximum size of bytes a PPP frame can be for multilink.

PPP (Modem) Specific Configurations

pfSense comes with a database of Internet Service Providers and their plans for many countries which may be used to preset a username, password, a phone number for GSM and CDMA networks or other modem dialup, and/or an access point name (APN).

Use the **Country** drop-down menu to pick a location from Afghanistan through Zimbabwe. For example, selecting *United States* as the country will populate the **Provider** menu with several Internet Server Provider companies, such as Leap Wireless and Mid Rivers Cellular.

After selecting the country and provider, make a selection in the **Plan** menu. Note you do not need to use these fields, but they may be a convenience for some.

For the modem dialup connection enter a phone number in the **Phone number** field. Commonly, CDMA networks use *#777* and GSM networks use **99#*.

Use the **Display Advanced** button to access the following PPP-specific advanced options.

pfSense has a comprehensive chat script with modem commands to help dialup and connect with various dialup networks. For those that use an access point hostname (such as "ufone.mms") for 3G connections, enter it in the **Access Point Name (APN)** field. Then enter the optional APN number in the following field.

If it is necessary to send a password or code to the modem device before it can be operated, enter it in the **SIMPIN** field. If your modem connection needs to wait for the SIM to connect to the network after the above PIN is entered, enter a time in seconds in the **SIM PIN wait** field. It is zero (0) by default.

If you need a custom modem setup by sending an initialization string, enter it in the **Init string** field. This does not start with the "AT" Hayes command.

If there is no response for 45 seconds from the modem after dialing, the connection attempt will abort. To override this timeout, enter the number of seconds in the **Connection Timeout** field.

Clicking the **Uptime logging** checkbox will enable tracking of the accumulated uptime for the PPP connection. This may be viewed via the **Status → Interfaces** page for the PPP interface at the *Uptime* field. (See Section 13.3.) If this is unchecked, the historical tracking is lost.

PPPoE Specific Configurations

To connect only to a PPPoE with an allowed *service-name*, enter it in the field for **Service name**. Or you may use the **Configure NULL service name** checkbox to use a blank service name. (Don't enter a value and check it at the same time. But even if the field is empty, a blank service name will be configured.)

Click the **Display Advanced** button to access a **Periodic Reset** option. This drop-down menu is used to reload the PPPoE interface on a schedule. The choices are *Disabled*, *Custom* to enter a time and date, and *Pre-set* to use a pre-defined schedule. When custom is selected, fields will be available to set the hour and minute for the daily reset time. Or to reset on a specific day (at that time), enter the month, day, and year (mm/dd/yyyy) in the **Specific date** field.

Or to reload the interface at a preset scheduled time, radio button selections will be available to do the reset at this time on this on-going date. The choices shown with `cron` syntax are: *Monthly* (first minute of first day of every month), *Weekly* (first minute of every Sunday), *Daily* (first minute of every day), and *Hourly* (first minute of every hour).

PPTP/L2TP Advanced Options

For PPTP or L2TP link types, when a link interface is selected, expanding the **Advanced Options** will expand **IP/Gateway** settings for setting the local IP address and the peer IP address (for each interface).

Enter the local IP address and its subnet in the drop-down field. Then enter the remote peer's IP address or a hostname in the **Gateway IP or Hostname** field.

24.2.2 PPP Log Entries

The **Status → System Logs → PPP** page is for logging messages from the *mpd5* PPP daemon for your assigned PPP client interfaces. This may include logs about using the PPPoE dial-on-demand mode, PPP IPCP (Internet Protocol Control Protocol) requests, CHAP authentications, and more.

See Section 11.1 and Section 11.3 for details on using the advanced log filter or to override the general logging options for viewing these logs.

Note if you are running your own PPPoE or L2TP service, its login and service logs are available instead via the **Status → System Logs → VPN** page for PPPoE (Section 31.2 and Section 31.3) and for L2TP (Section 32.3 and Section 32.4).

24.3 GRE Interfaces

The Generic Routing Encapsulation protocol (GRE) is a tunneling technology for transporting packets through a network. Basically, it allows a payload — the packet to be delivered — to be encapsulated in a GRE packet and then forwarded on. When the GRE packet is received at the GRE endpoint, the payload is extracted and then routed again to its final destination address. It is commonly used to tunnel protocols other than IP.

The GRE interface is setup with an IP address of the local tunnel end (the source) and an IP address for the remote tunnel end (the destination), It also has the IP addresses for the real source (your network interface) and destination (the remote system also configured with GRE). The destination, like a Cisco router, is configured on its side to be a *source* endpoint.

These GRE tunnels may be managed by clicking on the **Interfaces → Assignments** menu item and then going to the **GREs** subpage. This page has a table showing the interface, the remote address of the tunnel, and an optional description for each GRE tunnel. No GRE tunnels are configured by default. The GRE tunnel entries will also have corresponding action icons to edit or delete the GRE interface.

To add a GRE interface, click the **Add** button.

24.3.1 GRE Configuration

The GRE configuration page has several fields. IP addresses for the local and remote endpoints are required. First select the network interface (such as WAN or LAN) for the local end of the GRE tunnel in the **Parent Interface** drop-down menu. This will define the local address for the tunnel.

Then enter the IPv4 or IPv6 address for the peer in the **GRE Remote Address** field.

The tunnel also requires a local address and remote addresses to use for the tunnel's actual endpoints. Enter these IP addresses in the **GRE tunnel local address** field and **GRE tunnel remote address** fields. The **GRE tunnel subnet** drop-down menu is used to define the network itself that is to be tunneled.

To add a static route for that remote tunnel network, click the **Add Static Route** checkbox.

You may optionally explain the purpose of the GRE tunnel in the **Description** text field.

Click the **Save** button when done. This will immediately setup the interface and routing rules.

When a packet from the pfSense system is sent to an address defined in the and **GRE tunnel subnet**, for the **GRE tunnel remote address** it will be encapsulated in a new GRE packet which will be sent to the address defined in the **GRE Remote Address** field. There it will be de-encapsulated and forwarded on to the final tunnel destination.

24.4 GIF Interfaces

GIF is generic tunneling system which can even tunnel IPv6 over IPv4. It has physical addresses for the source and destination in the outer header. This outer packet encapsulates an inner packet that has tunnel endpoint addresses in its header.

This feature is managed via the **Interfaces** → **GIFs** subpage (found via the **Assignments** menu entry). The table will show the interface used for the local end of the GIF tunnel, the IP address for its peer, and an optional description. To edit a GIF configuration, click its **Edit GIF interface** action pencil icon. The corresponding trash can icon may be used to remove a GIF interface.

No GIF interfaces are setup by default in pfSense. Use the **Add** button to introduce a new GIF interface.

24.4.1 GIF Configuration

The GIF interface requires valid IP addresses for the remote address where the packets are sent and for the local and remote tunnel endpoints. To get started, select the interface (such as the LAN) to use for the local address in the **Parent Interface** drop-down menu.

Enter the destination (outer packet) address for the GIF's peer in the required **GIF Remote Address** field.

Then enter the tunnel (inner packet) endpoint addresses in the **GIF tunnel local address** and **GIF tunnel remote address** fields. Traffic for an entire virtual network at the inner destination can be routed. Select the subnet in the **GIF tunnel subnet** drop-down menu. (When using an IPv4 address, select a number from 1 to 32.)

Explicit Congestion Notification (ECN) uses optional header bits to help supported network infrastructures to be notified about network congestion. These bits conflict with tunnel endpoint processing. By default, GIF turns off the outer TOS bit on ingress and drops it on egress. If you need ECN, click the **ECN friendly behavior** checkbox and it will attempt to copy and enable these bits. Note that the other peer will also need to be configured to understand this.

By default, GIF drops incoming packets that don't appear to be from the remote end. This filtering may be turned off by checking the **Outer Source Filtering** checkbox.

You may enter details about your GIF usage in the **Description** text field.

Press the **Save** button to activate the changes.

To use the GIF tunnel, the peer (like a Cisco device) needs to be setup with the corresponding GIF configuration. And your pfSense firewall needs to allow the traffic for both the external traffic (outer IPs) and the encapsulated traffic (inner IPs). (The outer traffic protocol is either IPv4 or IPv6.)

To setup firewall rules for the inner IPs, you need to first create a pfSense-style network interface. Go to the **Interfaces** → **Assignments** page and then select the your new available *gif* network port (aka device) and click the **Add** button. Then its configuration, check the enable checkbox and save the interface configuration. (You don't need to make other changes there, but you could use a custom name if you wish.) Then apply those changes. (For details on creating the new interface, see Section 13.1.)

At the **Firewall** → **Rules** page, you should see the new interface name in the top list. Select it to get to its rules (which should be empty). Use a **Add** button to set it up for the inner tunnel IPs. (See Section 16.2 for generic information.)

If you have enough firewall logging enabled, you may be able to use the Easy Pass feature to add a pass rule for the inner IPs directly from the **Status** → **System Logs** → **Firewall** page (as covered at Section 16.18.3). Note you will need the new pfSense interface name for it (like *OPT1*) as using the FreeBSD device name (like "gif0") will fail.

25 Traffic Shaping

Traffic shaping is a way to solve the problem of competing use cases on a network, for example, from interactive games, video conferencing and command-line sessions having too little responsiveness and too much latency due to Youtube uploads, iTunes downloads, and other bulk traffic. A goal of traffic shaping is to reduce the impact of heavy users, often with a goal to improve speeds or *Quality of Service* (QoS) for other uses. pfSense provides a queueing mechanism that retains some excess outbound packets in a queue and then schedules them out for later transmission for a smoothed output rate.

The traffic shaping is powered by the PF packet filter and its ALTQ (Alternative Queueing) bandwidth control system. Note that some network drivers do not support ALTQ. You may notice this later as reported in the **Notices** popup (Section 4.5).

This is managed with *queues* which are associated with a specific interface, define the maximum bandwidth (or bitrate) on the interface, and define a scheduler technology to use, also called a *type* or *discipline*, which decides if packets are sent immediately, dropped, or delayed. Other options or choices depend on the selected scheduler. The scheduler algorithms supported by pfSense include:

CBQ

> the *Class Based Queueing* discipline. This is organized with child queues which can borrow excess bandwidth. This also allows defining a priority from 0 to 7 related to the time that packets take to get sent.

CODELQ

> the *Controlled Delay* (CoDel) discipline. It was designed to overcome bufferbloat. Behind the scenes it has a good queue for no bufferbloat and low delays and a bad queue which may drop packets when delayed over 5 milliseconds. This discipline does not allow child queues nor does it offer other options — implying it is easy to configure. (CoDel may also be used as a parameter for the FAIRQ, HFSC, CBQ, and PRIQ schedulers.)

FAIRQ

> the *Fair Queueing* discipline. Its child queues may use a *hogs* setting to allow bandwidths less than this to burst. It also offers defining priorities.

HFSC

> the *Hierarchical Packet Scheduler* discipline. This may be used to define a tree of child queues with priorities and minimum and maximum bandwidths for guaranteed real-time service. This is the default for new queues.

PRIQ
> the *Priority Queueing* discipline. It allows one level of child queues where each queue is configured with a unique priority from 0 to 15. This does not feature bandwidth limits for child queues.

When a child queue is enabled or when using CODELQ (which does not support subqueues), the traffic shaping takes effect for the firewall. No additional firewall rules are needed. You may also have specific packet filter rules which reference these queues to limit bandwidth or prioritize traffic for matching traffic. For example, you could provide more bandwidth for one office network and define a higher priority for video conferencing and lower priority for gaming traffic.

Enabling this ALTQ-based traffic shaping is done via the **Firewall** → **Traffic Shaper** menu. This page provides four views. The **By Interface** (which is displayed by default), **By Queue**, and the **Wizards** pages are for setting up or managing the ALTQ-based traffic shaper.

The **Related status** shortcut icon or the **Status** → **Queues** menu item leads to a view of the traffic shaping queues, as covered at the end of this chapter.

In addition to shaping, pfSense provides policing using the **Limiters** feature to drop excess packets or to limit bandwidth. This is explained in detail in Chapter 26.

25.1 By Interface

The default **Firewall** → **Traffic Shaper** view lists the available network interfaces (such as WAN and LAN). The list is sorted to have the interfaces with configured shapers at the top. Click on the interface name or icon in the list (or tree view) to bring up a form to enable and configure its settings.

Check the **Enable/Disable** checkbox to enable this queue. (It is unchecked by default.) Checking this, depending on the type, may allow you to create child (or subqueues) for sharing the traffic shaping settings. (If this is not checked and you later attempt to add a child queue, the child queue configuration may not get saved.)

For a top-level queue, the **Name** identifies the interface (such as *lan* or *opt1*) and cannot be changed.

The **Schedule Type** drop-down options include the HFSC, CBQ, FAIRQ, CODELQ, and PRIQ algorithms as explained previously. The default is HFSC.

Note
Changing the scheduler type changes the available options, so previous child queue settings may be lost.

The **Bandwidth** field is a numerical input to select the maximum bitrate on the interface. The corresponding drop-down list selects the measurement type; it defaults to kilobits per second (Kbits/s) with other options of Mbits/s, Gbits/s, Bits/s, and % to use a percentage. This bandwidth must be set. If you don't have a preference, set it to your interface's known bandwidth rate. If you set it to some rate greater than your interface's speed, behind the scenes it will adjust to configure it using the detected maximum speed. Note if you set the bandwidth to a slow rate, that interface may become nearly unusable.

The **Queue Limit** is the maximum number of packets that may be queued at a time. This is unset by default, which implies a system default of 50.

The **TBR Size** is the Token Bucket Regulator size, measured in bytes. This defines how many bytes may be dequeued at once. It is unset by default implying the system will determine this size.

Click the **Save** button to save the configurations. You will then be prompted for the changes to take effect, so press the **Apply Changes** button.

A **Remove Shaper** button will be introduced to left side after saving. This is used to remove all queue settings. Clicking it will popup a confirmation window to proceed with removing all the ALTQ traffic shapers.

To remove a single queue, use the **Delete this queue** button at the bottom. If a queue is undefined, instead it will show a **Disable shaper on interface** button. Using this will do the same thing to unset this configuration.

If the discipline type is not CODELQ, your queue can have children queues — and a **Add new Queue** button at bottom will be available.

25.1.1 Add Queue

Click the **Add new Queue** button to add a child or subqueue for the already configured scheduler. It must have the **Enable/disable discipline and its children** checkbox checked to provide this button. If you press this button prior to saving any new changes, those changes will be lost as it loads the new form webpage. Note that the CODELQ scheduler type does not use child queues so doesn't offer this button.

The options available on this form vary based on the parent queue's schedule type. All of the child queues are identified by entering a single unique keyword in the **Name** field. This is limited to 15 alphanumeric characters or hyphen (-) or underscore (_). Use a name that helps explain its purpose, such as "std," "http," "employees," "developers," "ssh," "ssh_interactive," and "ssh_bulk."

The CBQ. FAIRQ, and PRIQ types have a **Priority** number input field. For CBQ and FAIRQ, the range is 0 (lowest) to 7 (highest) and the default is 1. For PRIQ, the number needs to be unique within 0 (lowest) to 15 (highest).

The maximum number of packets allowed to be in a queue is set in the **Queue Limit** field. If not set, it defaults to 50 packets.

The common scheduler options have checkboxes for the following:

Default Queue
 Packets not matched by the following. At least one of the child queues must have this selected.

Random Early Detection (RED)
 Drops packets based on average queue size and statistical probabilities.

Random Early Detection In and Out

Like RED, but checks for *in* packets and *out* packets as marked by QoS.

Explicit Congestion Notification (ECN)

Uses the RED method for detection and notifies ECN-enabled end-points about the network congestion so they can reduce their transmission rates.

Codel Active Queue

Uses the Controlled-Delay Active Queue Management algorithm to drop packets.

You may further explain this child queue's purpose in the **Description** text field.

The HFSC, CBQ, and FAIRQ types have a **Bandwidth** input and corresponding measurement type drop-down menu which is used to define the rate for this specific child. Note that the total of all the children's bandwidths cannot be higher than the parent's defined bandwidth. (For the PRIQ type, the second-level queues do not support their own bandwidth limits or sharing. (The PRIQ type doesn't support bandwidth limits or sharing, but the ALTQ does do the bandwidth throttling as defined on the parent queue.)

The CBQ type has a **Borrow from other queues when available** checkbox. This means this child can borrow bandwidth (if there is excess) from the parent. It is not checked by default.

The FAIRQ type uses a round-robin with packets managed in *buckets* with low-bandwidth (not *hogs*) to get priority. It defaults to 256 buckets. You can tune this in the **Number of buckets available** field. Its maximum is 2048. The **Bandwidth limit for hosts to not saturate link** field is used to define the hogs limit. You may enter a number with an immediate string (no space) for the rate in seconds like "1Kb" for one kilobit (per second).

The HFSC scheduler has additional options which use service curve specifications:

m1

initial bandwidth (within first milliseconds). It is defined using a number immediately followed by rate string or percentage, such as "100Kb", "2Mb", "1Gb", or "50%". This must be smaller than the *m2* bandwidth. When used, this field is required.

d

first milliseconds to use initial bandwidth. This field is also required.

m2

bandwidth assigned to the queue (after the first milliseconds). This is written using a bandwidth string or percentage. If this is defined, it must be larger than *m1*.

These combined bandwidths cannot be greater than 80% of the defined parent queue bandwidth.

To define the maximum allowed bandwidth for the queue, enable the **Upper Limit** checkbox and enter service curve values in the **m1, d**, and **m2** fields.

Use the **Real Time** checkbox and set the corresponding fields to define the minimum required bandwidth for the queue.

Check the **Link Share** checkbox and fill out the service curve fields to define the bandwidth (B/W) share of a backlogged queue.

There are no PRIQ specific options.

Click the **Save** button to save the new child queue configuration. It will then prompt you to **Apply Changes** too. (Note that the **Delete this queue** button will delete the parent queue if this child queue is not saved yet.)

These new queues are also listed in the **Firewall** → **Traffic Shaper** → **By Queue** page.

25.2 By Queue

The **By Queue** page (via the **Firewall** → **Traffic Shaper** page) is just another way to display and manage the enabled queues. They are listed on the left side. When one is clicked on, all the interfaces will be listed with some brief shaper details (if any) and buttons to either copy a shaper or to delete a queue. By default, the page will be empty with no queue configured or selected.

This only displays queues that have been added in the earlier Section 25.1.1 (**Add new Queue**) step and enabled with the checkbox or added using a wizard.

When a queue is selected, for each interface, it shows the scheduler type (like CBQ), the shaper's configured bandwidth, if the priority is on, and if it is the default.

The **Clone Shaper to this interface** button is available for interfaces that don't have an associated queue. Clicking it will copy the selected queue to that interface. Note if the interface doesn't already have a scheduler type defined, it will be configured with the same scheduler type but the bandwidth, queue limit, and the token bucket regulator sizes are not defined.

Use the **Delete Queue from this interface** button to remove the selected queue from corresponding interface. It will prompt you to confirm this action. Then it will take you back to the starting **By Queue** display.

Clicking on an interface name will take you to its corresponding **By Interface** configuration form as covered in the previous section.

25.3 Using Queues with Packet Filter Rules

Traffic shaping is enabled for a network interface immediately when using CODELQ or when adding a child queue to any of the other scheduler types. You may also use **Firewall** → **Rules** so packets may be assigned to your defined queues. This is configured when adding or editing a rule via Advanced Options section with the **Ackqueue / Queue** drop-down menus (see Section 16.2.2). By default, no queues are used and these are set to *none*.

Queues may be associated with any type of rule, but are commonly used with the *match* type as available with *Floating* rules. When a queue is specified for a *block* rule, it is used for queueing the resulting TCP RST or ICMP packets.

Use the **Ackqueue** drop-down menu to select one of your previously-defined queues for TCP ACK (acknowledge) packets that have no data payload and have a type of service field (ToS) requesting *low-delay*. For interactive sessions, commonly this would be used with a queue that has a higher priority or better advantage so TCP acknowledgements are sent back quickly, so the other system can send packets at an optimum rate. Or if you want to purposely slow down the sender, then slow down the TCP ACKs. When ACKs are delayed, the sender's next packets get delayed. This queue may only be selected when the following is also defined.

The **Default Queue** menu is used to select the queue to be assigned for the non-low-delay, non-TCP ACK packets. Note that pfSense requires that you must choose different queues if setting both of these.

After saving, be sure to accept the changes so the firewall rules are loaded.

New traffic shaper rules will only work for connections created after the new rules are put in place. Note that this feature is mostly about quality of service and not specific restrictions. In other words, if you try to use this ALTQ traffic shaper to limit bandwidth for a specific network service or addresses, you may not notice any complete effect due to algorithms sharing resources. (It may not be noticeable unless other queues are using up all the bandwidth or have heavy congestion.) If you want more reliable limits, see the **Firewall** → **Traffic Shaper** → **Limiters** feature as discussed in the following chapter.

Rules that use these ALTQ queues may be identified via the **Firewall** → **Rules** pages in the *Queue* column. Auto-generated rules from the traffic shaper wizards may have explanations in the *Description* column to help identify them.

Note
Removing a shaper or a queue does not also remove its corresponding queue configuration in the PF packet filter rules. While it won't actually do any traffic shaping, the rules can be cluttered with old unused settings.

25.4   Traffic Shaper Wizards

The wizards features provides a step-by-step way to configure and enable traffic shaping and corresponding firewall rules. They provide a convenient way to prioritize traffic based on various networking protocols and services, such as online games and Voice over IP. The **Firewall** → **Traffic Shaper** → **Wizards** subpage offers two different wizards — for multiple networks or for dedicated links. To exit a wizard without completing it, just click the pfSense logo to go to the dashboard or go to another page. Restarting a wizard may have some fields or choices set based on your previous selections.

Note
Using a wizard may reset previous settings even if were created by a different wizard.

25.5 Multiple Lan/Wan Traffic Shaper Wizard

The first wizard prompt for multiple WAN/LAN traffic shaping is to enter the number of WAN connections you have. It will list how many WANs your pfSense system has configured that support ALTQ and have a gateway. (Normally this will be 1.) The number of ALTQ-supporting interfaces that don't have a gateway is listed in the following field for the number of LAN-type interfaces. Change these numbers as needed.

Then click the **Next** button to proceed. This will generate a form for the counts defined — for each LAN and then each WAN. You must select a unique interface in each associated **Interface** drop-down menu.

Then select the **Scheduler** queueing discipline. The choices are: PRIQ (the default), HFSC, and CBQ.

Some of the interfaces also allow entering the download and upload rates in the corresponding fields. It defaults to kilobits per second, but you may change that to megabits per second or gigabits per second in the drop-down menu.

Note

The bandwidths defined on this step or other wizard steps should not be more than 30% of the associated interface's or its link's bandwidth.

Click the **Next** button to proceed in the wizard.

The next wizard pages are for defining queues and firewall rules for specific network services. This step starts with prioritizing Voice over IP (VOIP) traffic. Enabling the checkbox will allow configuring this. You can select the provider or list the address of your remote PBX or SIP trunk. The **Provider** choices include VoicePulse, Asterisk/Vonage, and PanasonicTDA. Select *Generic (lowdelay)* if your provider is not available — or instead of using the provider, you may enter an IP address or existing Alias (Section 16.5) for a SIP Trunk or PBX to prioritize in the **Upstream SUP Server** field. If you enable VOIP prioritization, you will also set the VOIP upload rates for the WAN connections and download rates for the LAN connections.

Click **Next** to continue.

The Penalty Box feature is used to limit the bandwidth for a specific system. Click the checkbox to enable this and enter the desired IP address or Alias in the **Address** field.

When enabled, enter a number in the required **Bandwidth** field. This can be a percentage between 2% and 15% or a rate. The following drop-down menu is used to select a percentage (the default) or the units for a rate such as bits per second through gigabits per second. Then continue in the wizard.

If you want to lower the priority for Peer-to-Peer (P2P) traffic, check the **Enable** checkbox. The **p2pCatchAll** checkbox is used to use the following limits for all traffic that is not categorized. Enter the bandwidth for the P2P traffic in the following fields as a percentage or amount of bits per second. You can also select to limit specific P2P protocols; check the checkboxes as desired for the following:

- Aimster

- BitTorrent (or Torrent)

- BuddyShare

- CuteMX

- DCplusplus

- IRC DCC

- DirectConnect

- DirectFileExpress

- eDonkey2000

- FastTrack

- Gnutella

- grouper

- hotComm

- HotlineConnect

- iMesh

- Napster

- OpenNap

- Scour

- Shareaza

- SongSpy

- WinMX

The next wizard page is for prioritizing network gaming traffic. Instead of limiting priority (or lowering), this is used for raising game traffic to be higher than most other traffic. To use this, check the **Enable** checkbox. You can then select the specific game consoles or game services to raise priority for my checking the desired checkboxes:

- Battle.net (Blizzard Entertainment)

- EA Origin Client

- GameForWindowsLive

- Windows Live games

- PlayStation

- Steam

- Wii and DS

- Xbox

In addition, many specific games can be selected to improve their priority on the network:

- ARMA 2

- ARMA 3

- Battlefield 2 [1]

- Battlefield 3 and 4 [1]

- Battlefield: Bad Company 2

- Borderlands

- Call Of Duty (United Offensive)

- Counterstrike

- Crysis 2

- Crysis 3

- Dead Space 2 [1]

- Dead Space 3

- Delta Force

- Dirt 3

- DOOM3

- Dragon Age 2

- Empire Earth

- EVE Online

- Everquest [1]

- Everquest II

- Far Cry

- Far Cry 2

- Far Cry 3

- GunZ Online

---

[1] This network game and some others may use a large port range and may need manual adjustment of the generated rules to correctly prioritize other traffic possibly using same ports.

- Half-Life
- League of Legends [1]
- Lineage II
- Mass Effect 3
- MechWarrior: Online [1]
- Minecraft
- PlanetSide
- PlanetSide 2
- Operation Flashpoint: Dragon Rising
- Quake III
- Quake IV
- StarWars: The Old Republic [1]
- Tiger Woods 2004 for PS2
- Tribes Ascend
- Unreal Tournament Series
- Wolfenstein Enemy Territory
- World of Warcraft

Use the **Next** button to continue in this wizard.

The sixth step of the wizard allows you to define a higher or lower priority for various other network-using software and specific services, such as remote desktops, messengers, VPNs, multimedia streaming, web traffic, email, and many more:

- AIM
- APNS
- Apple MobileSync
- Apple Remote Desktop
- BattleNet Downloader
- CrashPlan
- CVSUP
- DNS

- Facetime

- Git

- Google Hangouts

- HBCI

- HTTP

- ICMP

- ICQ

- IMAP

- IPSEC

- IRC

- iTunes Radio

- Jabber

- Lotus Notes

- Microsoft RemoteDesktop (MSRDP)

- MSN

- MySQL Server

- NNTP

- PC Anywhere

- POP3

- PPTP

- RTMP

- RTSP

- Slingbox

- SMB

- SMTP

- SNMP

- Steam Downloader

- Streaming MP3

- Subversion

- Teamspeak3

- Teamspeak

- Ventrilo

- VNC

Enable the checkbox to configure this. Then use the corresponding drop-down menus to change from the default priority. Note this only has a lower or higher choice so you cannot rank the many applications.

Then continue in the wizard to the page to configure the system with these settings. Click the **Finish** button to do this. If services were selected, new *Float* rules will be created. This will reload basically all the pfSense network services as seen on the **Status** → **Filter Reload** page (Section 16.11).

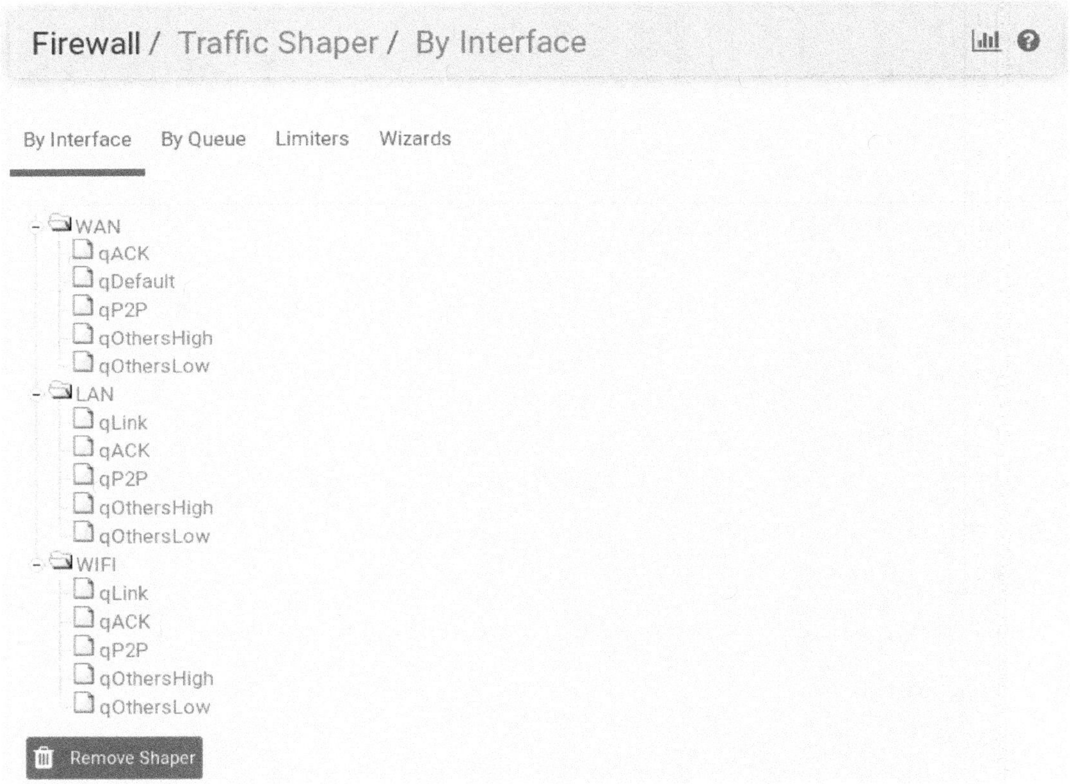

Figure 25.1: **Firewall** → **Traffic Shaper** → **By Interface** (after multi wizard)

After completed, you can go back to the **Firewall** → **Traffic Shaper** page to see all the links to the various ALTQ settings. For example, see Figure 25.1. Following these will allow you to edit them for more detailed ALTQ configurations as covered in the beginning of this chapter.

25.6 Dedicated Links Traffic Shaper Wizard

For more details about some of the following choices, see the previous section. The first wizard prompt for dedicated links traffic shaping is to enter the number of WAN connections you have. The default is 1. Enter your choice and click the **Next** button to proceed.

The next page is for the shaper configuration for Connection #1. It provides the following parameters which may be set. The **Local interface** name (such as LAN) and its scheduler type (which defaults to HFSC). The **WAN Interface** name and its scheduler type (which also defaults to HFSC). The **Upload** speed and measurement (which defaults to kilobits per second). The **Download** speed and measurement. Use the drop-down fields as desired and enter the required upload and download speeds and then click **Next**.

The next wizard page lets you enable to prioritize Voice over IP (VOIP) traffic. Check that checkbox if desired. (This will allow you to configure the following options.) You can select the provider or list the address of your remote PBX or SIP trunk. The **Provider** choices include VoicePulse, Asterisk/Vonage, and PanasonicTDA. Select *Generic (lowdelay)* if your provider is not available — or instead of using the provider, you may enter an IP address or existing Alias (Section 16.5) for a SIP Trunk or PBX to prioritize in the **Upstream SUP Server** field. If you enable VOIP prioritization, you will also set the VOIP upload and download rates (like on the previous page). Click **Next** to go to the next wizard page.

The Penalty Box wizard page is used to enable lowering the priority of traffic. The options can only be modified if the **Penalize IP or Alias** checkbox is checked. Enter the IP address or the Firewall Alias (see Section 16.5) of the system to penalize. The bandwidth rate or percentage is required. The **Units** defaults to % (percent), but you can also select bit rates instead. Click the **Next** button to continue.

The Peer-to-Peer (P2P) networking wizard page is used to lower the priority of P2P traffic below all other traffic. Check the **Enable** checkbox to configure it. The **p2pCatchAll** checkbox is used to handle the uncategorized traffic through the queue. For this uncategorized traffic, you also select the bandwidth rate or percentage. You can also select to limit specific P2P protocols with checkboxes from *Aimster* through *WinMX*. Click **Next** to continue.

The following wizard form is used to prioritize the traffic for known gaming consoles, gaming services, and even specific games, such as *Battle.net* and *Minecraft*. A long list of checkboxes are available to select these.

The wizard also has page for lowering or raising the priority of many other protocols, such as for remote service and terminal emulation, messengers, VPN, multimedia and streaming, web, mail, game downloaders, and other miscellaneous protocols. Click the checkbox for enabling other networking protocols to access the many drop-down menus, for *AIM* through *VNC*. They are all set to *Default priority*, but can be set as desired to *Higher priority* or *Lower priority*. After making your selections, press **Next** to continue in the wizard.

The final page of the Traffic Shaper wizard will prompt you to press the **Finish** button to create new rules, as applicable, and load the new settings (which may take a few seconds).

25.7 Queue Stats

When you have traffic shaping enabled, the **Status** → **Queues** page will show your queues (which are also identified with the interface), with the following details averaged every second:

- Packets per second (PPS)

- Bits per second (Bandwidth)

- Child borrowing excess bandwidth from parent class (Borrows)

- Packets delayed due to overlimits (Suspends)

- Dropped packets due to overlimits (Drops)

- Current queue counts over the defined queue limit (Length)

(Some scheduler types may not provide the corresponding features, so values may display "NaN.")

Some queues with child classes may have their statistics accumulated. Clicking on a queue name will take you to the form to view or edit its settings.

It may take a few seconds for the stats to get generated the first time. Use the **Refresh rate** drop-down menu to change the time period for the displayed values and how frequently the stats are updated on this page. The fastest choice is 0.5 seconds and the slowest is five seconds.

A progress bar will move back and forth to help visualize this activity. By default it represents packets per second. Use the **Statistics** drop-down menu to change it to *Bandwidth* to have the progress bar update based on bits per second.

26 Limiters for Traffic Shaping

In addition to the traffic shaping powered by PF's ALTQ as covered in the previous chapter, pfSense offers bandwidth limiting, artificial delays, and instrumented packet loss using FreeBSD's IPFW *dummynet* technology. It supports this on multiple WANs and can shape the traffic bidirectionally on single interfaces. This involves setting up a virtual *pipe* — an emulated link — with a defined bandwidth, delay, and packet loss rate. It may be used to simulate problematic networks and connections. Optionally, child *queues* may be added for packet scheduling and to share the pipe's bandwidth for different packet flows. In pfSense terminology, this technology is also called a *limiter*. Then a PF packet filter rule is configured to use one or two *dummynet* pipes or queues. (This is a pfSense-custom PF feature which is not in FreeBSD. This IPFW technology is also used for the captive portal feature described in Chapter 29.)

This is setup in two parts — first via the **Firewall** → **Traffic Shaper** → **Limiters** subpage to configure the IPFW dummynet pipe (and optional queues) and then via the **Firewall** → **Rules** configuration for the **In / Out pipe** in the advanced options to use it.

26.1 Configuring Limiters

To get started with this, from the **Firewall** → **Traffic Shaper** → **Limiters** subpage, click the **New Limiter** button. This will bring up a form to add the new configuration. (By default, no limiters are defined.)

The first option is a checkbox to enable it and its children. Check that when you are ready to use it.

Then enter a single word to identify your limiter configuration (such as "uploads" or "downloads") in the **Name** field. It must begin with a letter or digit and it may contain an underscore (_) or dash (-). (It defaults to "new".) A better longer description may be set in an upcoming field.

The maximum bandwidth must be specified. In the **Bandwidth** number field, enter (or select) an integer of 1 or larger. By default, the units are kilobits per second. This may be changed in the **Bw type** drop-down menu to megabits per second or bits per second.

Use the **Schedule** drop-down menu to select a day/time range for when this bandwidth rule is applicable. It defaults to *none* meaning this bandwidth setting is for all the time. When this is defined to an existing schedule, then the bandwidth is set to unlimited when the pfSense clock time is not within that schedule time. Otherwise when the schedule matches the current time, this configured bandwidth is put into use. No schedules are setup by default. They are defined via the **Firewall** → **Schedules** page. See Section 16.9 for more details.

Note

Don't get confused about this **Schedule** terminology. This is about the date- and time-based pf-Sense firewall scheduler and not the IPFW *dummynet* scheduling algorithm type.

Use the **Add Schedule** button to introduce additional schedule-based bandwidth limiters for this same configuration. This only makes sense if you are actually using different day- or time-based limits. To remove one of them, use its corresponding **Delete** button.

You may configure limiters for specific systems or networks using the **Mask** feature. The limiter definition will be used for all traffic with its default setting of *None*. In the drop-down you may choose *Source addresses* or *Destination addresses* to match originating or target IPs or networks. Use the **IPv4** and **IPv6 mask bits** drop-down menus to define networks for matching. They default to 32 and 128, respectively, to indicate that they match single hosts only. (The mask bits fields are only selectable when a mask other than none is selected.) When this is set, this limiter's rule will only be used when the packets source or destination IP address(es) match.

The **Description** text input field may optionally used to enter an explanation for this limiter for the pfSense admin's reference.

26.1.1   Queue

Multiple algorithms are available for configuring the *queue* which temporarily stores packets and the *scheduler* which arbitrates how these packets are sequenced. There are different policies for dropping packets and controlling bottlenecks.

The Active Queue Management (AQM) method is selected in the **Queue Management Algorithm** form. These algorithms may or may not support Explicit Congestion Notification (ECN) which may be used to mark packets instead of dropping them. These choices also may have additional customizable parameters for its queue management. To access the additional parameters, click the **Save** button after selecting the algorithm and then check below the **Queue Management Algorithm** setting for new fields. The parameter tunings are beyond this book's focus. The defaults are sane. (The algorithm, scheduler, and ECN options for limiters were introduced in pfSense 2.4.4.)

The AQM choices are:

Tail Drop

> Tail Drop is the traditional simple algorithm that drops the most recent incoming packets when the queue is full (i.e., that it can't buffer). Tail Drop has no parameters and does not support ECN marking. This is the default algorithm, but isn't really an active queue management method.

Controlled Delay (CoDel)

Controlled Delay drops (or marks) packets based on the time in the queue. The minimum allowed queue delay is 5 milliseconds. This can be set in the **target** parameter. CoDel waits 100 milliseconds before dropping a delayed packet. This can be changed in the **interval** parameter. The maximums are 5000 milliseconds. CoDel supports ECN.

Proportional Integral controller Enhanced (PIE)

PIE was designed to address bufferbloat. It drops (or marks) incoming packets based on the rate of change of the queueing latency. Experiences shows that PIE can achieve high link utilization and ensure low latency during congestion. The latency delay is 15 milliseconds. This can be changed in the **target** parameter with a maximum of 5000 milliseconds. The rate of change interval (or update) is every 15 milliseconds. This can be set in the **tupdate** parameter with a max of 5000 milliseconds. The drop probability calculations can be tuned in the **alpha** and **beta** parameters. The **max_burst** allowance is for when PIE is not dropping (or marking) packets. PIE supports ECN. The **max_ecnth** parameter is the maximum ECN marking threshold.

Random Early Detection (RED)

RED, also known as random early discard, probabilistically drops (or marks) packets. As the queue builds, it drops more packets. It has four parameters: weight **w_q**, minimum threshold **min_th**, maximum threshold **max_th**, and maximum drop probability **max_p**. RED supports ECN.

Gentle Random Early Detection (GRED)

GRED is based on RED, but has a more linear drop probability versus RED's abrupt design. In high-load FTP traffic examples, GRED performs significantly better. GRED has the same parameters as RED and supports ECN.

The Queue Scheduler configuration is in the **Scheduler** drop-down menu. Some of the choices have additional parameters which may be set after saving this page.

Worst-case Weighted Fair Queueing (WF2Q+)

WF2Q+ allows sharing bandwidth between different queues according to their weights. WF2Q+ does not have any parameters and doesn't offer ECN support. It is the default scheduler.

First-in-First-out (FIFO)

FIFO, also known as first come first served, is the simplest scheduler. All packets are stored in the same queue. FIFO doesn't have any parameters and doesn't support ECN.

Quick Fair Queueing (QFQ)

QFQ is a fast variant of WF2Q+ with near-optimal guarantees. QFQ doesn't have any parameters and does not have ECN support.

Deficit Round Robin (RR)

Deficit Round Robin (DDR) uses time slots and is one of the fastest schedulers, but has poor service guarantees. This scheduler has no parameters and doesn't provide ECN support.

PRIO

The PRIO scheduler tracks priorities and packets are dequeued from highest priority queues. PRIO has no parameters and doesn't offer ECN.

FlowQueue Controlled Delay (FQ_CODEL)

This is a hybrid of CoDel AQM per queues for dropping (or marking) packets, a modified DDR scheduling to share between queues, and the *FlowQueue* scheme to hash the flows into queues. FQ_CODEL provides **target** and **interval** parameters like the CoDel AQM has for its minimum allowed queue delay and delay before dropping. The **quantum** parameter defaults to 1514 bytes and is the number of bytes served before moving to the end of an old queues list. The **limit** parameter is the limit in packets in all queues than can managed. It defaults to 10240 packets. The **flows** parameter defaults to 1024 subqueues and is the number of subqueues that the scheduler creates and manages. FQ_CODEL offers ECN marking support.

Fair Queue Proportional Integral controller Enhanced (FQ_PIE)

FQ_PIE is also a hybrid scheme based on the previous FQ_CODEL but uses the PIE AQM algorithm for 1024 subqueues. Its hard size limit for all queues is 10240 packets. It has the same parameters as PIE as described previously. FQ_PIE also offers ECN support.

The *dummynet* limiter queues up packets before any simulated delay. If the queue is not large enough, packets may be dropped; while too large of a queue may introduce a delay. The **Queue length** value is used to define this as a number of packets. Normally this number input field is not set and pfSense defaults to 50 slots. On slow links you may want to consider using a smaller queue. As an example, 100 slots can queue an hundred 1500-byte Ethernet packets which is 1.2 megabits; if on a 1 megabit per second connection, this would be around 1.2 seconds of queue delay. pfSense recommends not setting this, but a common value is 50 slots (which would drop the delay to half a second for the same example). Too high of a queue size may cause the system's network buffers to be exhausted. (Prior to pfSense 2.4.4 this field was called **Queue size (slots)**.)

By default, Explicit Congestion Notification marking for ECN-enabled TCP flows is disabled (even if an algorithm supports it). Use the **Enable ECN** checkbox to enable it for supported algorithms. Note that if the selected queue management algorithm or scheduler algorithm doesn't support ECN, then this won't be used.

26.1.2   Advanced Options

It simulate a delay in the speed of signal — or propagation delay — enter a value in milliseconds in the **Delay (ms)** field. For example, this can increase a packet's round-trip time. It defaults to zero for no delay.

To simulate a lossy link, enter a fractional number using a decimal point between zero for no loss and one for 100% packet loss in the **Packet Loss Rate** field. For example, the value "0.5" will randomly only allow half the packets and "0.1" will lose 10%. The smallest allowed non-zero number is 0.001 for one in a thousand packets dropped. The largest is 0.999 for 999 out of a thousand dropped.

The queues are stored using a hash table. Its size defaults to 256. To change this, enter a number within 16 and 65535 in the **Bucket size (slots)** field.

Be sure to have the **Enable** checkbox checked if you want to use this limiter. Click the **Save** button when finished. After saving a new limiter configuration, its name will be listed on the left side on the **Limiters** page. When prompted, press the **Apply Changes** button to reload the firewall rules. Or you may wait to do this after your have setup corresponding packet filter rules using this new limiter (pipe) configuration. You may want to create separate limiter configurations for uploads versus downloads (for bandwidth limits), for example.

Note

These limiter configurations do nothing until they are used by a firewall rule as covered in the upcoming Section 26.3.

26.2 Enabling Child Queues

Each limiter configuration may also have child queues defined with it. To create a child queue, click the **Add new Queue** button at the bottom of a specific limiter's configuration. This will bring up a similar form like just described for defining it. Use a different name than its parent. It does not have a **Bandwidth, Scheduler**, nor **Delay** settings. because the children share the parent pipe's bandwidth and scheduling.

It adds a **Weight** input field. This is used to assign a percentage of the share of bandwidth of the parent pipe. You can enter a value within 1 to 100. Children with the same weights will get the same amount of the pipe's bandwidth. The weight doesn't change the priority. Even if a higher weight child is backlogged, a lower weight child will still get its (weight) share of the bandwidth. It defaults to 1 which may imply to mean unimportant traffic. But if other children under the same pipe aren't getting traffic, then even a *weight 1* queue will use all the bandwidth.

For the other settings, see the explanations in the previous section. (Note that the **Packet Loss Rate** option currently does nothing with child queues.)

Click the **Save** button to save the child queue. Be sure that the **Enable** checkbox is checked. Use the **Apply Changes** button when ready. Then to use the child queue, configure a firewall rule to use it as explained in the following section.

26.3 Using Pipes in Firewall Rules

To use a limiter, you need a corresponding packet filter rule that references it. Go to the **Firewall** → **Rules** page. This may default to the WAN rules view. Select the interface or other view you want to use the limiter with. Then edit an existing rule or add a new rule. Make sure that the new rule is above any default allow rules or it won't be matched (the limiter rule won't be used). For details on rule configurations, see Section 16.2.

In the rule configuration, scroll to the end of the Extra Options section and click the **Display Advanced** button to expand the advanced options (as discussed in Section 16.2.2).

Near the bottom of these options, see the **In / Out pipe** configuration. It has two drop-down menus which will contain the limiter names previously setup and enabled in the previous section. The first (left) is for selecting the limiter to use for incoming upload traffic from the external network in via the interface. The second (right) drop-down menu is for selecting a different limiter for outgoing download traffic via pfSense out the network interface. Both are set to *none* by default.

The outgoing pipe is not required, but only define it for a bidirectional rule if the incoming pipe is also defined. A pipe must be selected for the In direction (left field) before selecting one for Out (right field) too.

Note

For Floating rules with an *Out* direction, the **In / Out pipe** configuration meanings are reversed so the left menu is for outgoing and the right is for incoming.

Be sure to save your rule configuration. Use the **Apply Changes** button after saving when you are ready to reload the firewall.

On your firewall rules view, an asterisk (or star) icon next to the rule means it has an advanced setting. Hovering over it may show that it is a "limiter" and its pipe name(s).

Note

Your limiters are only used when it is for the last matched PF rule. The firewall usually evaluates all rules and acts on the last matching rule. But you may have custom rules or various pfSense built-in rules which act immediately by using the *quick* option. You may need to reorder your rules or adjust a later rule for your limiters for it to even be used.

A common way to add a rule for traffic that is blocked is to search for it via the **Status → System Logs** page and click the corresponding **Easy Rule: Pass this traffic** plus icon in the Destination column. (See Section 16.18 for details.) Then in the new rule's advanced options setup the **In / Out pipe**.

For limiters to be effective, you may need to use static IPs. To limit for DHCP clients, find the client's hardware MAC address using the **Status → DHCP Leases** page. Use the **Add static mapping** (plus icon) action for a known IP address as discussed in Section 19.5.1. (Consider entering a description of the device.)

26.4 Limiter Configuration

The **Firewall → Traffic Shaper → Limiters** feature will list the created limiters in the left column (above the button to create a limiter and to the left of the configuration form if displayed). Children queues may be listed there nested under their parent pipe. Click the name of the limiter (or the icon in front of it) to bring up the form for its configuration (as explained earlier).

26.5   Removing a Limiter

When deleting a limiter, if filter rules reference the same queue name, it will need to be manually removed from there first. There is not a link to the specific rule, so go to your **Firewall** → **Rules** page and look for a rule in the table with an asterisk (or star) in first column (before the States column) indicating it has advanced options. Hover over it to see if it is for the same limiter name. Then remove the rule or edit it so it doesn't have this limiter use. Note you may need to look in different rules views to find it.

Press the **Delete Limiter** button at the bottom of its specific limiter configuration. Then okay that deletion in the pop-up dialog. It will take you back to the main Limiters view page and that now-old limiter name should no longer be listed. Then click the **Apply Changes** button at the top of the page when you are ready to reload your firewall without that limiter.

Deleting a parent pipe will remove all of its queue children (if any). Or you may delete a specific child, by going to the child's configuration and clicking the **Delete this queue** button at the bottom.

26.6   Limiter Information

Details about your limiters may be seen via the **Diagnostics** → **Limiter Info** page. (This is also linked from the **Related status** shortcut in the top right of the topic header of the main limiters page.) By default, no limiters are configured. But when they are, this page will show the details about the configured bandwidth limiters and how packets are grouped for sharing available bandwidth. (Some installs may show some default unlimited limiters configured in the status output, but they aren't used.) The information, like the following, is updated every 2.5 seconds.

```
Limiters:
00001: 111.000 Kbit/s     0 ms burst 0
q131073  50 sl. 0 flows (1 buckets) sched 65537 weight 0 lmax 0  ↵
    pri 0 droptail
  sched 65537 type FIFO flags 0x0 0 buckets 0 active
00002: 200.000 Mbit/s     2 ms burst 0
q131074  50 sl.plr 0.001000 0 flows (1 buckets) sched 65538  ↵
    weight 0 lmax 0 pri 0 droptail
  sched 65538 type FIFO flags 0x1 256 buckets 0 active
    mask:  0x00 0xfffffffe/0x0000 -> 0x00000000/0x0000


Queues:
q00001  50 sl. 0 flows (1 buckets) sched 1 weight 1 lmax 0 pri 0  ↵
    droptail
q00002  50 sl. 0 flows (1 buckets) sched 2 weight 50 lmax 0 pri  ↵
    0 droptail
```

The output here is very verbose. The pipes are defined with a number such as "00001:" and "00002:" as seen in this example. This is followed by the pipe's bandwidth and delay time. The next line starting with "q" is the default generated queue settings for the pipe, such as 50 slots and 0.001 packet loss rate (plr).

The "Queues" section is only displayed when child queues are enabled. This may be used to see the weights assigned. The output may show some parameters like "burst" and "flows" which are currently not configurable by pfSense.

Since pfSense version 2.4.4-p1, it will also show the packet scheduler stats.

26.7   Limiter Examples

You can check your incoming or outgoing speed locally using the **Status** → **Traffic Graph** page as covered in Section 28.1.

Historical minimum, maximum, 95th-percentile, and average rates may also be viewed and analyzed via the **Status** → **Monitoring** page by choosing *Traffic* as a graphing axis (Section 28.2). Or choose *Quality* as an axis to see packet loss and delays on a graph. (Note that these are for entire interfaces.)

You can also measure and compare your current download and upload speeds from a third-party web-based service, like http://Speedtest.net/ or https://www.backblaze.com/speedtest/, by connecting to it via a system within your limiter-using pfSense network.

You may also use *ping* or the **Diagnostics** → **Ping** feature (Section 27.2) to see it in use. For example, with a Packet Loss Rate of 0.5:

```
10 packets transmitted, 5 packets received, 50.0% packet loss
round-trip min/avg/max/stddev =  ↵
    42.659659/43.057040/44.112780/0.601052 ms
```

Or round-trip results for a configured Delay of 500 milliseconds:

```
round-trip min/avg/max/stddev =  ↵
    541.636502/541.902603/542.279824/0.187495 ms
```

27 Network Diagnostics

pfSense provides several tools to troubleshoot or otherwise understand your network. This chapter introduces the snooping or watching traffic at the packet level, testing TCP ports, using $ping$, doing traceroutes, and viewing socket connections.

This chapter also introduces the SNMP service which may be used for sharing diagnostics and statistics.

27.1 Packet Capture

The **Diagnostics** → **Packet Capture** feature may be used to snoop on network traffic seen at your network interfaces. Behind the scenes, it uses the $tcpdump$ tool to capture and save all or matching traffic.

The quickest way to try it using defaults is to scroll down below the options and click the **Start** button. The page will reload and then it should display "Packet capture is running" at the bottom and a **Stop** button now provided.

The page will not automatically reload on its own to show the captured packets even when completed. Either visit the page later or press the **Stop** to view the packets. If you wait long enough (and don't reopen the page), it may be completed even though it indicates it is running.

When the capture is completed and you go back to the **Diagnostics** → **Packet Capture** page, it will provide new buttons at the bottom (of the options) for **View Capture** and **Download Capture**. Above that it will display the date and time of this last capture.

Clicking the **Download Capture** button will allow you to save a raw file to your local system. This little-endian pcap (Packet Capture) file may be analyzed with a local program such as Wireshark, WinDump, or Microsoft Message Analyzer. You may also use $tcpdump$ on many platforms to read, filter, and present the data.

Click the **View Capture** button to just view the results at the bottom of the same pfSense webpage. Note that the output may be way too long to display in a web browser. Since pfSense 2.4.4-p3, it is limited to 50 MB. If the packet capture is too large, then download it with the **Download Capture** button instead.

Or you may use the text console (Section 37.9) to analyze the raw packets data file; for example:

```
tcpdump -vv -e -r /root/packetcapture.cap | less
```

The Packet Capture Options at the top of the webpage may be used to limit the capturing and to improve its output (when viewing here on the webpage).

The **Interface** drop-down menu may be used to select a different network interface on the pfSense system to sniff on. By default, it may be your WAN interface which sees packets going to and from the outside network that hit that device.

Many network cards offer a promiscuous mode which will pass all traffic allowing the system to read frames intended for other network devices or other computers. Use the **Enable promiscuous mode** checkbox to enable this mode to also snoop on others' traffic. Note that this feature is not required to see traffic that is specifically already sent from or to the desired interface, so this is disabled by default.

By default, any type of packet may be captured. To restrict it to only IPv4 or IPv6 Internet packets, use the **Address Family** drop-down selection.

This interface may also be used to filter based on some transport, Internet, or link layer protocols. By default, it will capture any. Use the **Protocol** drop-down menu to restrict its filtering for Any, ICMP, ICMPv6, TCP, UDP, ARP, CARP, pfsync, or ESP. (Note that you cannot select ICMPv6 when doing only IPv4 nor ICMP or ARP with IPv6.) From the same drop-down menu, you may select to *Exclude* a protocol from the packet capturing which means it will match all protocols except that selection. (This menu doesn't allow selecting multiple choices.)

The **Host Address** text field is used to enter an IP address or subnet (using CIDR) to match either the source or destination. Leave the field blank for capturing packets from or to anywhere (that are seen via the interface). Use the exclamation mark "!" to prefix the value to reverse the matching to capture packets that do not match that address. Use pipe characters "|" to separate multiple values for boolean *OR*. For boolean *AND* use commas "," between the multiple required addresses. For example, to see traffic to and from Google's public IPv4 DNS servers use:

```
8.8.4.4 | 8.8.8.8
```

The **Port** field will be used to match the source or destination port. Leave this field empty to not filter by a port. You may enter a valid port number or valid port name (like *https* or *ssh*).

By default, it will capture up to 65535 bytes of data for each packet. It is recommended to limit this *snap length* to the smallest number for the protocol information you want to capture to be more efficient so packets aren't potentially lost. Use the **Packet Length** input field for this. Common recommendations include 68 bytes for minimal IPv4 packets and 96 bytes for IPv6 packets. When viewing locally, extra large numbers don't matter since it may not display all the packet content anyways, but you may want at least 512 or more for the *tcpdump* to display decoding for DNS, NFS, and SMB for example. Setting it to 0 (zero) sets the full default which is useful for downloading for outside analysis of the full content.

The packet capturing will collect up to 100 packets by default. Use the **Count** field to enter a positive integer for it to receive that many packets. Note that pressing the **Stop** button may cause it to capture less than this count.

Use the **Level of detail** drop-down menu to provide more detail. Note that this setting does not change what data is filtered and saved (or downloaded), but is for the local display purpose only. Click the **View Capture** button to update the Packets Captured display.

The following four examples show the same two UDP DNS query and answer packets for each of the detail levels.

When viewing the captured packet details locally, for each packet it will show a timestamp with microseconds resolution, the address family (like IP), the source IP and port (delimited with a period), the destination IP and port, and the protocol (like UDP and length or ICMP echo request with its id and sequence numbers and length). This is the *Normal* quiet or quick view when displaying the results.

```
10:20:54.512918 IP 172.16.1.4.38719 > 8.8.4.4.53: UDP, length 42
10:20:54.559401 IP 8.8.4.4.53 > 172.16.1.4.38719: UDP, length  ↩
   231
```

The *Medium* selection adds IP packet details, such as time to live, IP identification value, total (header and data) length, and flags. It will also show TCP flags, window size, checksums, options, and many other attributes. Depending on the packet it may do some decoding; for this example, it explains part of the DNS exchange. Other packets understood by `tcpdump` for decoding include SMB/CIFS, NFS. AFS, KIP AppleTalk DDP, NBP, and ATP.

```
10:20:54.512918 IP (tos 0x0, ttl 63, id 31835, offset 0, flags [  ↩
   none], proto UDP (17), length 70)
    172.16.1.4.38719 > 8.8.4.4.53: 57834+ [1au] A? reedmedia.net  ↩
    . (42)
10:20:54.559401 IP (tos 0x0, ttl 58, id 393, offset 0, flags [  ↩
   none], proto UDP (17), length 259)
    8.8.4.4.53 > 172.16.1.4.38719: 57834 2/0/1 reedmedia.net. A  ↩
       64.85.162.118, reedmedia.net. RRSIG (231)
```

Additional details such as TCP sequence numbers, wireless power management, ICMP6 hop limits, or more decoding fields may be provided with the *High* selection.

```
10:20:54.512918 IP (tos 0x0, ttl 63, id 31835, offset 0, flags [  ↩
   none], proto UDP (17), length 70)
    172.16.1.4.38719 > 8.8.4.4.53: [udp sum ok] 57834+ [1au] A?  ↩
       reedmedia.net. ar: . OPT UDPsize=4096 OK (42)
10:20:54.559401 IP (tos 0x0, ttl 58, id 393, offset 0, flags [  ↩
   none], proto UDP (17), length 259)
    8.8.4.4.53 > 172.16.1.4.38719: [udp sum ok] 57834 q: A?  ↩
       reedmedia.net. 2/0/1 reedmedia.net. A 64.85.162.118,  ↩
       reedmedia.net. RRSIG ar: . OPT UDPsize=512 OK (231)
```

The *Full* selection will also display the link-level header, which includes MAC addresses, wireless fields, and Ethernet frame lengths.

```
10:20:54.512918 00:7f:28:35:b7:ad > 00:e0:18:79:29:39, ethertype  ↩
    IPv4 (0x0800), length 84: (tos 0x0, ttl 63, id 31835,  ↩
    offset 0, flags [none], proto UDP (17), length 70)
```

```
     172.16.1.4.38719 > 8.8.4.4.53: [udp sum ok] 57834+ [1au] A?  ↩
          reedmedia.net. ar: . OPT UDPsize=4096 OK (42)
10:20:54.559401 00:e0:18:79:29:39 > 00:7f:28:35:b7:ad, ethertype ↩
     IPv4 (0x0800), length 273: (tos 0x0, ttl 58, id 393, offset ↩
     0, flags [none], proto UDP (17), length 259)
     8.8.4.4.53 > 172.16.1.4.38719: [udp sum ok] 57834 q: A?  ↩
          reedmedia.net. 2/0/1 reedmedia.net. A 64.85.162.118,  ↩
          reedmedia.net. RRSIG ar: . OPT UDPsize=512 OK (231)
```

When viewing the results, by default, addresses and ports will be displayed as numbers. Use the **Reverse DNS Lookup** checkbox to attempt to display addresses and ports using their names. This may also use names as applicable for some decoding types. Note that this option may cause delays when viewing large packet captures that contain many unique addresses to lookup.

Don't mistakenly press the **Start** button to redisplay the previously captured packets as that will overwrite the saved data. Use the **View Capture** button instead.

27.2 Ping

The **Diagnostics** → **Ping** feature is used to get a response from a remote host for basic network troubleshooting. The common usage is to enter an IP address or hostname in the **Hostname** field and then click the **Ping** button. It will return the results from the Unix `ping` command (as shown in Figure 27.1) including the byte size in the response and the time for each packet to return (usually in milliseconds). It will also provide a summary showing the percentage of packet loss and round trip times statistics.

This may be used to indicate if a host or network is down or if there is network congestion. If a hostname cannot be resolved (via DNS) it may immediately return indicating this as an error. Or if the host is not responding, the results may indicate it with 100.0% packet loss or "Destination Net Unreachable" reported. Note that some responses may take several seconds.

For fault isolation, you can first ping the local network interfaces, and then ping hosts and gateways further away one at a time. Note that packet filter rules may restrict the ICMP ECHO_REQUEST, ICMP6_ECHO_REQUEST, ECHO_RESPONSE, or ICMP6_ECHO_REPLY packets. You may need to adjust local firewall rules to allow sending or receiving these messages.

Note that some systems block the ICMP ECHO_REQUEST/ECHO_RESPONSE traffic; you may want to try using TCP using the **Diagnostics** → **Test Port** feature as covered in Section 27.4.

The other options are: **IP Protocol** to choose IPv6 (instead of default IPv4), **Source address** to optionally force the source address (such as the LAN or WAN IPv6 Link-Local) to be something other than the default IP address of the interface the probe packet will be sent on, and **Maximum number of pings** to set the count of packets — up to ten — it will send (instead of three).

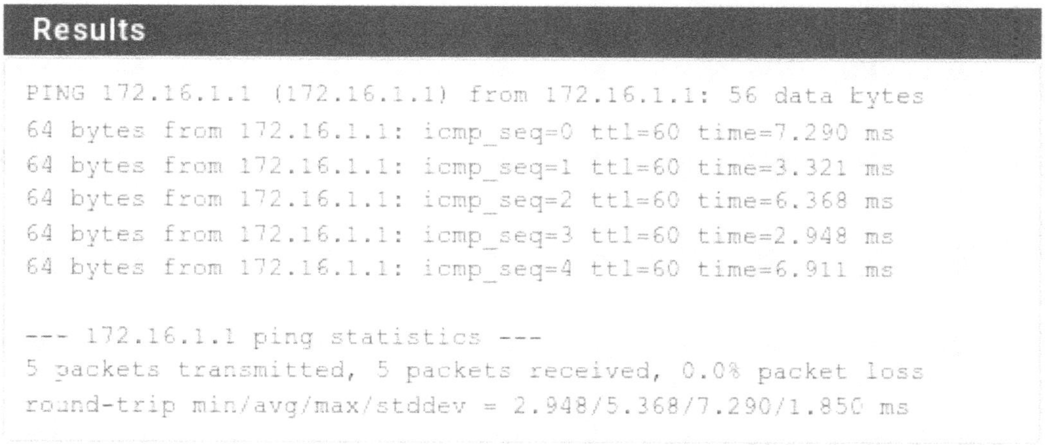

```
Results

PING 172.16.1.1 (172.16.1.1) from 172.16.1.1: 56 data bytes
64 bytes from 172.16.1.1: icmp_seq=0 ttl=60 time=7.290 ms
64 bytes from 172.16.1.1: icmp_seq=1 ttl=60 time=3.321 ms
64 bytes from 172.16.1.1: icmp_seq=2 ttl=60 time=6.368 ms
64 bytes from 172.16.1.1: icmp_seq=3 ttl=60 time=2.948 ms
64 bytes from 172.16.1.1: icmp_seq=4 ttl=60 time=6.911 ms

--- 172.16.1.1 ping statistics ---
5 packets transmitted, 5 packets received, 0.0% packet loss
round-trip min/avg/max/stddev = 2.948/5.368/7.290/1.850 ms
```

Figure 27.1: **Diagnostics** → **Ping** results

A ping feature is also available via the text console menu; see Section 37.8 for details.

27.3 Sockets

The **Diagnostics** → **Sockets** feature shows open or connected Internet end-points as known to the local pfSense system. Formerly known as sockets, they contain an IP address and port number. Note that this page does not show the connections that are going through the pfSense system, but only those that the actual origination or destination is the pfSense system itself. (To see states of connections going through the pfSense box, see **Diagnostics** → **States** and **Diagnostics** → **States Summary** in Section 16.15 and Section 16.16.) This feature is useful to see what the pfSense system is offering and if there are any current connections to (such as the web interface) or from it (such as a DNS lookup).

The display contains two tables: IPv4 first and IPv6 at the bottom. The output can be sorted (and sorted in reverse) by clicking once (or twice) on any of the following field headers:

USER
The local user ID to whom the process belongs. A common user is the *root* superuser, but many processes also run as dedicated users, such as user *unbound* and user *dhcpd*

COMMAND
The name of the Unix command running on the pfSense system associated with the network process, such as running server like *nginx*, *ntpd*, *syslogd*, or *xinetd* or a local client like *ssh* or *wget*.

PID

The process ID number of the locally running command. While PIDs are unique, a process may have multiple sockets.

FD

The process's own file descriptor number associated to the socket. (Each process has its own file descriptor numbering, so same numbers for different processes is irrelevant.)

PROTO

The transport protocol, such as UDP or TCP. It is listed with trailing *4* or *6* to indicate if is IPv4 or IPv6.

LOCAL

The local IP address (on the pfSense system) including port number. The address and the port are delimited with a colon. If the address is an asterisk (*), it means that it is binding to — listening on — any local address that system has. (If a local address is within 127.0.0.0/8 or ::1, then this indicates it is for use locally on the pfSense system only.)

FOREIGN

The remote IP address including port number of the socket pair — also known as the peer. A foreign wildcard address of "*.*" indicates this is a listening service. When there is a real address that means there is a connection.

Sockets   ❓

🔘 Show only listening sockets

IPv4 System Socket Information

USER	COMMAND	PID	FD	PROTO	LOCAL	FOREIGN
root	php-fpm	67467	5	udp4	*:*	*:*
root	php-fpm	53621	5	udp4	*:*	*:*
root	php-fpm	26492	5	udp4	*:*	*:*
root	sshd	73959	5	tcp4	172.16.1.1:22	172.16.1.4:41403
dhcpd	dhcpd	4815	8	udp4	*:67	*:*
dhcpd	dhcpd	4815	20	udp4	*:2826	*:*
unbound	unbound	337	6	udp4	*:53	*:*
unbound	unbound	337	7	tcp4	*:53	*:*

Figure 27.2: **Diagnostics → Sockets → Show all socket connections**

The default view only displays the local listening sockets — local servers are waiting for (more) remote clients. This can be toggled by pressing the button on the top left. The **Show all socket connections** button will have the tables also display the connected sockets — where a client is communicating with a server (as seen in Figure 27.2). This can be local clients connecting to remote servers, or remote clients (like a web browser) connecting to a local server. Alternatively, the **Show only listening sockets** button will go back to the default view which excludes the already connected sockets.

The webpage does not refresh automatically and won't indicate when the socket information has changed. You can use the view button or reload the page to get updated details.

27.4 Test Port

To verify that a host is accepting connections on a TCP port, the **Diagnostics** → **Test Port** feature can be used. As an alternative, to determine if a host is up via ICMP, use **Diagnostics** → **Ping** as covered in Section 27.2

To quickly use the connection test, enter a valid hostname or IPv4 address in the **Hostname** text input box, enter a valid TCP port number (1 - 65535) in the **Port** field, and click the **Test** button. The other choices on the form are optional.

The response may be immediate or may take a few seconds. (It has final timeout of 10 seconds.) If it cannot look up the hostname, can't route to the host, or doesn't receive a valid response, it will simply output "Connection failed" at the top of the page.

When the connection works, it will output that the port test was "successful."

The **Source port** field may be used to set a valid source port for the connection to originate and any response to return to.

The **Show remote text** checkbox, when checked, will display any output from the successful connection to the Received Remote Text section at the bottom of this webpage. Note that some connections, like HTTP port 80, do not have any initial output, while some, like SSH port 22 and SMTP port 25, do have an identification banner.

The **Source address** drop-down menu is used to select a network interface, such as WAN or LAN, for the connection. This can be used to do a TCP test from different networks (different IPs). It defaults to *Any* which implies it will automatically select the IP of the best interface.

The **IP Protocol** drop-down allows selecting IPv4 (the default) or IPv6. When using an IP address (and not a hostname) in the **Hostname** field, the TCP test will force using IPv4 or selected IPv6. When using an IPv6 address, you must set the protocol to IPv6.

After each run of the **Test Port**, the fields continue to be defined so you may test again or make adjustments.

27.5 Traceroute

A *traceroute* attempts to trace the route that an IP packet would follow to a host. The **Diagnostics** →
Traceroute tool is useful in network analysis to see if any hops (intermediate systems) are down or to
see round-trip times to each hop. It is also an alternative to ping or TCP probes to see if a destination
host is up.

The only required field is the **Hostname** — enter an IP or hostname as the target for the trace. Then
click the **Traceroute** button.

Note

While usually the output is returned quickly, a standard *traceroute* run could take several minutes
when there are problems. This may result in a web browser receiving an HTTP 504 Gateway Timeout error (instead of a pfSense webpage). This pfSense interface's default is for 18 hops and when
failing it may take approximately one to two minutes.

The results will be displayed at the bottom of the page below the form, as in the following. Three
probes are sent for each hop. In the output, each hop is numbered followed by its address. (If a
number has multiple addresses, then it received a response from them all, up to three.) The time
for the round trip of each probe is displayed in milliseconds. If the round-trip time is longer than 5
seconds, it is timed out and an asterisk (*) is displayed.

```
1   71.97.37.1   24.462 ms   24.786 ms   4.939 ms
2   172.102.50.214   7.336 ms   7.436 ms
    172.102.52.28   9.921 ms
3   74.40.3.17   4.913 ms   4.863 ms   4.903 ms
4   74.40.4.14   4.902 ms   4.904 ms
    74.40.1.82   7.402 ms
5   4.15.44.125   1802.506 ms   1457.462 ms   1665.044 ms
6   * * *
7   4.68.70.2   7.216 ms   7.464 ms   *
8   4.68.70.2   7.231 ms
    67.17.68.33   47.468 ms   82.470 ms
```

The **IP Protocol** drop-down defaults to IPv4. If diagnosing IPv6, select it instead.

The **Source Address** drop-down menu allows selecting the network interface, such as the WAN or
LAN, for the trace to originate from. It defaults to *Any* for automatic standard behavior. If it attempts
to access the target path using the wrong source address (over the wrong interface), it may not have
any results (or all results timed out). For example, it may attempt to access some target over the
wrong network, so use this selection to choose a specific network interface for the trace.

The **Maximum number of hops** drop-down list allows selecting the maximum number of hops to
trace. (This hop limit is called the Time to Live in IPv4.) It defaults here to 18 and can be set from 1
to 64 (which is the FreeBSD default).

The default trace doesn't do reverse DNS lookups (PTR) for the IPs along the path and only displays the numeric IP addresses. Check the **Reverse Address Lookup** checkbox to provide the resolved hostnames. Note that slow DNS lookups may slow down the trace.

The trace uses UDP by default which may be blocked by some systems. If you wish to use ICMP or ICMP6 ECHO instead, check the **Use ICMP** checkbox.

If you don't receive any usable results, you may be restricted by your firewall rules. Review and adjust your packet filter rules as needed. The traceroute may show loops, extra large round-trip times, and other issues that are outside of the scope of your network.

27.6 SNMP

pfSense can provide statistics and other diagnostic information about your system via SNMP, the Simple Network Management Protocol. It can be enabled as an SNMP agent via the **Services →** **SNMP** page.

To turn on the SNMP daemon, `bsnmpd`, check the **Enable the SNMP Daemon and its controls** checkbox. Then click the **Save** button.

> ⚠ **Warning**
> The default SNMP service (when enabled) is accessible using a standard public community string and will disclose a lot of information about your pfSense system.

You may want to restrict its access to your own management stations using your PF packet filter at the **Firewall → Rules** page. The SNMP service listens on UDP port 161. For it to accept polling events on a different port, enter the number in the **Polling Port** field.

The SNMP *sysLocation* value is empty by default. You can set a physical location for your pfSense device (which is being monitored) in the **System Location** text field, such as "telephone closet, 3rd floor" or more specific like rack, room, building, city, country, or street, city, state, and zip.

Note that the pound sign (#) is not allowed in the SNMP strings.

The *sysContact* value is also not set. You may identify the contact person along with the contact information (such as "Your Name <your@email.address>") for who is responsible for your pfSense system in the **System Contact** field,

The read community string, *begemotSnmpdCommunityString.0.1* is set to "public" by default. This is common configuration value and really implies it is open. It is recommended that this be changed in the **Read Community String** field to help restrict access. (The write community string is not set by pfSense.)

27.6.1 SNMP Traps

The SNMP Service information is available by remote clients doing polling requests. SNMP traps are for sending information without polling. To have the pfSense system send unrequested information to a network management system, check the **Enable the SNMP Trap and its controls** checkbox. When this is selected, additional options will be available (and be required).

To send traps, set the target hostname in the **Trap server** text field. UDP port 162 is the standard port for receiving SMTP traps; if that system is listening for these traps on a different UDP port, set it in the **Trap Server Port** field.

The **SNMP Trap String** field is also required when using traps. Enter the SNMP community name for authenticating with the trap receiver.

27.6.2 SNMP Modules

When using SNMP, several modules are enabled by default. These may be disabled (or re-enabled) by using the corresponding checkboxes. These modules include:

MibII
> Provides details about the networking by implementing parts of the MIB-2 Internet standard.

Netgraph
> Enables remote access to the FreeBSD netgraph subsystem.

PF
> Provides details about the PF packet filter, including counters, states, limits, timeouts, tables, ALTQ, and more.

Host Resources
> This implements the standardized RFC 2790 Host Resources MIB, which includes details about storage, devices, and file systems.

UCD
> This provides memory, load average, CPU usage, and other system statistics by implementing parts of the UCD-SNMP-MIB.

Regex
> This is used to make your own custom SNMP values and counters from log files or other files. This book doesn't cover this module's configuration; see `http://thewalter.net/stef/software/bsnmp-regex/` for details.

If you want the SNMP Service to listen on a specific network interface, such as WAN, LAN, or Localhost, select it in the **BIND Interface** drop-down menu. By default, it is available via all interfaces.

After making changes, click the **Save** button to immediately activate this new SNMP Service configuration.

The *bsnmpd* SNMP Service daemon can be restarted and stopped (or started) via the **Status** $\rightarrow$ **Services** page (see Section 7.7).

Its logging is available via the **Status** $\rightarrow$ **System Logs** $\rightarrow$ **System** $\rightarrow$ **General** log entries page. To see recent matching log entries, use the **Log filter** funnel shortcut to enter "**snmpd**" in the **Process** field and click the **Apply Filter** button.

28 Monitoring and Graphs

pfSense provides various ways to monitor its system and network. This chapter covers real-time graphing of its network interfaces and snapshot graphs and summaries of its networking, packet loss, system load, memory usage, captive portal usage, and more. These may be used to visually detect and understand the health of your system and the network it provides.

28.1 Traffic Graph

The **Status** → **Traffic Graph** page provides a real-time animated descriptive graph and other live traffic diagnostics about an interface on the pfSense system. The graph shows bandwidth in (dark blue spikes going up) and out (light spikes going down) in bits, kilobits, or megabits per second. Updated every second, the graph (as seen in Figure 28.1) shows the last two minutes. Hovering over the graph with the mouse pointer will provide the details for that point in time.

The table at the right of the graph shows the top ten bandwidth uses per IP address. This is updated every three seconds. It lists the host, incoming bandwidth, and outgoing bandwidth.

By default, the details are for the WAN device if it exists. Use the **Interface** drop-down menu in the Graph Settings above to select a different interface (such as the LAN) to visualize. (This can also be used to see IPSec or OpenVPN usage.)

The **Sort by** form can be used to change the default sort ordering for the bandwidth table (with the highest shown first). It defaults to Bandwidth In and may be changed to Bandwidth Out.

The default table shows only the *Local* hosts as known by pfSense. Use the **Filter** drop-down to change this. The other two choices are **Remote** to only show outside hosts (and not the IPs within the pfSense network) and **All** to consider connections with any host (including local) in the whole 0.0.0.0/0 Internet.

Figure 28.1: Traffic Graph

The hosts are shown with just the IP address by default. To be more descriptive use the **Display** form to select **Host Name** to show just the first label from a DNS reverse lookup (or local configuration), **Description** to use a local identification as configured into pfSense if available[1], or **FQDN** to show the full name returned from a DNS reverse lookup (or local configuration). Note that long names may be cropped to the column width. If no alternative is found, just the IP address is displayed.

The graph won't be updated if this pfSense webpage is open on an inactive browser tab. In this case when not visible, the graphs are cleared. If you want the graphs to be up-to-date when you go back to the web browser tab, choose the **Keep graphs updated on inactive tab** option in the **Background updates** drop-down. Note this may increase the CPU usage as it frequently retrieves the network stats. (Use **Clear graphs when not visible** to go back to the default.)

28.2   Status Monitoring and Graphs

The **Status → Monitoring** page shows one or more graphs based on recorded diagnostic snapshots. The default view is for a single graph about the system processor. By default, every 60 seconds, the system records the percentage of time for the user, nice, system, and interrupt CPU states and a count of the running processes. The graph, as seen in Figure 28.2, shows this utilization displayed as percentages as a line graph over the last 24 hours. Note that the graph also has the process count at the top of the graph (as it displays two different data types).

---

[1]The local hostname description configurations are explained in Section 21.2.2, Section 21.4, and Section 21.5.

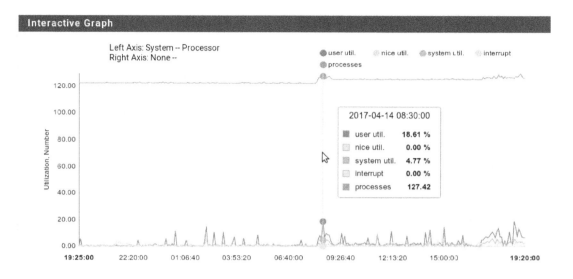

Figure 28.2: Interactive Graph (**Status** → **Monitoring**)

The graphs are interactive. A color key is labeled at the top of the graph. You may click on a label to hide it from the graph; click it again to display it again. The graph may redraw as the scale changes. By selecting a single data, you may better see its changes. Double-click on a label to only show that specific data (and hide the rest); click again to again show all the data.

You may also hover the mouse pointer over the graph to pop-up the stats for a specific point (like a timestamp). Note that the time of the day will be for your system's defined timezone. (It defaults to UTC. See Section 5.1 to change it.)

Below the graph is a table (such as Figure 28.3) with a summary of the data with the minimum, average, maximum, and last (most recently recorded) values for each recorded data type. Some data may also be reflected in the 95th percentile column. This is so infrequent peaks are ignored by cutting off the top five percent.

Data Summary

	Minimum	Average	Maximum	Last	95th Percentile
user util.	0.00 %	2.31 %	19.02 %	6.59 %	
nice util.	0.00 %	0.03 %	0.34 %	0.00 %	
system util.	0.00 %	1.25 %	9.53 %	2.35 %	
interrupt	0.00 %	0.72 %	7.05 %	0.89 %	
processes	122.00	123.70	129.38	126.00	

Figure 28.3: Data Summary (**Status** → **Monitoring**)

To reload and redisplay the graph and summary, click the **Refresh Graph** shortcut.

You may be able to identify problems by noticing spikes or drops or other anomalies that aren't easily explained by time of day or other known pfSense usage. Note that some graphs may have different data types represented in same graph with the axis representing both types. This may cause visible confusion like displaying percentage and milliseconds charts together.

 Warning
Old data that is no longer updated won't show the dates but only the times in the normal graph views. This may be misleading as the graph may be for long ago.

The **Export Graph** shortcut is used to download the data as a CSV spreadsheet file. Note your web browser may prevent viewing this. You may need to allow this pop-up window.

28.2.1   Graph Categories

The following graphs may be available for display, but it may vary by what has been recorded on your system. Normally the system collects and records the data every 60 seconds. (The graphs don't refresh by default.)

- **System**

    - **MBuf Clusters** — The network memory buffer clusters (for storing packets) currently in use, the cache size, the total size, and the maximum limit.

    - **Memory** — The percentage of memory for active (recently referenced or currently used), inactive (already freed, but still cached, is available for use), free (fully available for allocation), cache (almost available for allocation, backed by swap or mmap), and wire (used by kernel and networking and cannot be swapped out).

    - **Processor** — user, nice, system, and interrupt CPU states and a count of the running processes. (This is the default view.)

    - **States** — This is the PF packet filter's state statistics. This includes the inserts and removals per second to the state table (state changes), the count of known connections that are recorded in the state table (filter states), the total unique source IP addresses and unique destination IP addresses in the state table.

    (Some of most-recent memory and CPU details may be seen in near real-time via the **Diagnostics** → **System Activity** page as covered at Section 7.5.)

- **Traffic** — Interface statistics for the inbound and outbound PF packet filter pass and block counters and totals (including IPv6) in bits per second for IPsec, OpenVPN, and your network interfaces (like LAN and WAN). The negative numbers in the graph axis are for outbound traffic (when the **Inverse** option is on as discussed in the following section).

- **Packets** — Interface statistics for the inbound and outbound PF packet filter pass and block counters and totals (including IPv6) in packets per second for IPsec, OpenVPN, and your network interfaces (like LAN and WAN). The negative numbers in the graph axis are for outbound packets.

- **Quality** — This has the delay (latency average) and, delay standard deviation (latency std. dev.) in milliseconds and the packet loss percentage for the monitored gateway(s). (See Chapter 15 for details about *dpinger* which is the gateway monitoring tool.)

- **Captive Portal** — The number of concurrent and logged in users for the captive portal system.

- **NTP** — This graph is only available when the NTP Server settings has the **NTP Graphs** checkbox enabled. This shows the NTP's offset, system jitter (sjit), clock jitter (cjit), wander, frequency, and root dispersion (disp). See Section 18.3 for more details.

- **Queues** — The bytes per second statistics for the configured ALTQ queues per network interface (like LAN).

- **Queuedrops** — The dropped packets per second for the configured ALTQ queues per network interface (like LAN).

- **DHCP** — This shows the count of th DHCP server's leases and static leases in comparison with its available DHCP range. This graph is only available when the DHCP Server settings has the **Statistics graphs** enabled; see Section 19.4 for details. Note that you need to enable this for every DHCP server instance for every interface you want to record and see these details for,

- **VPN Users** — The count of OpenVPN users (CLIENT_LIST).

- **Cellular** — This view shows the signal strength (rssi), upstream bandwidth, and downstream bandwidth for the corresponding 3G PPP interface. This graph may not be available. Some 3G devices like Huawei modems may provide stats.

- **Wireless** — This provides channel numbers, rates, and the signal strengths in dBm for the stations associated with a pfSense wireless interface. This data collection (and resulting graphs) are available for the wireless *bss* mode.

- **None** — Don't generate a graph. This is used when you only select one view for the two axis capability.

The graphs to display are defined in the Settings section.

28.2.2 Graph Settings

Click on the **Settings** shortcut link (wrench icon) on the top right of the page to toggle the Settings form. Or the settings panel may be viewed by default by enabling the **Monitoring Settings** checkbox on the **System → General Setup** page (Section 5.1.4).

The main category for the graph is defined in the **Left Axis** drop-down menu. The options are the categories previously listed. The specific graph for that category may be selected in its adjacent **Graph** drop-down menu.

To redisplay the current graph view and summary data with that graph instead, click the **Update Graphs** button. Or use that button at any time to try the other settings.

This page's graph can also display two different graphs in the same chart. Select the second graph in the **Right Axis Category** and **Graph** drop-down menus. This will provide the key for all the fields on the same chart (the second graph's labels will say "right axis"). The left side will have the first graph's axis explanations and the right side will be for the second graph. As you may imagine this can be confusing when viewing very different data sets. But it may also be useful to comparing different datasets which may have corresponding meanings. For example, you can view *Traffic — WAN* and *Packets — WAN* at the same time for a very comparable graph. As an interesting example, try both *Traffic — WAN* and *Traffic — LAN* axis as seen in Figure 28.4.

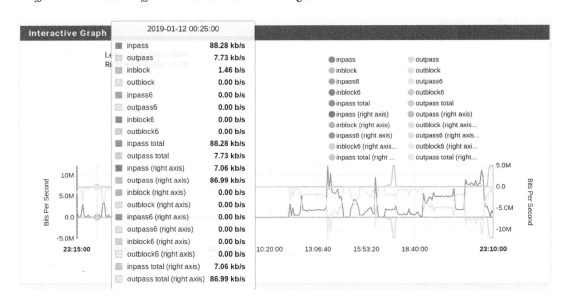

Figure 28.4: WAN and LAN Traffic Interactive Graph (**Status → Monitoring**)

The displayed graph defaults to show the data for the previous 24 hours. Use the **Time Period** drop-down to select a larger date range (like one year or four years) or to be more specific for recent activity (like one hour).

On some pfSense systems, you may also choose *Custom*. This will bring up fields to define the graph's start date, start hour, end date, and end hour. The date fields provide a calendar widget for selection or you may enter manually using the *MM/DD/YYYY* format. The hours are 0 midnight to 23 (11 p.m.).

The preciseness of the graph depends on its time period. The default one day time period, defaults to plotting for every five minutes. The four year period defaults to every day. And an hour period defaults to the highest granularity of per minute. Use the **Resolution** drop-down to adjust this. Note that some resolutions may not be applicable or useful, so won't be available for some time periods. (If using a custom time period, it will just automatically use the highest available resolution.)

This feature uses line graphs by default. It can also display its data in bar charts and area graphs to represent accumulations. The charting style may be selected in the **Graph Type** menu.

To reverse direction to show the most recent activity on the left side of the graphs, change the **Inverse** from *Off* to *On*.

The graphs are static. For periodically updated graphs, change the **Refresh Interval** setting from *Never* to one, five, or ten minutes. To have it automatically update, this setting must be saved as described in the following. Else you can just refresh the graph each time you desire by clicking the **Update Graphs** button. Note if you use your browser to refresh the webpage, it may not redisplay based on your temporary settings.

28.2.3 Advanced Graph Settings

To save your settings or for a few other features, press the **Display Advanced** button. This will expose a few additional buttons.

Initially there is only a single view (showing the processor details in a line graph). You may store settings for multiple desired graphs (so you don't need to redo these settings each time). Click the **Add View** button to create another graphing view. This will prompt you for a name to use to describe this view. Then the top of the **Status** → **Monitoring** page will have additional tabs for each view. (Your new view name will be highlighted.) Consider selecting your setting changes before doing the add view step.

The **Save View** button saves the settings for the current view (which is "Default" when you only have one). This means when you change the default settings, when you later visit this page, you will reuse your settings. Be sure to change to your desired view before saving the changes.

To delete one of your views (except the default view), select it, and then click the **Settings** shortcut, and then click the **Display Advanced** button and then click the **Remove View** button. The page will refresh and display the default view (and the now-deleted view won't be listed).

Behind the scenes, data related to your enabled services and features is collected every minute into several files under the /var/db/rrd/ directory. To stop all this collection, click the advanced **Disable Graphing** button. It will ask you to confirm to stop this work. Note once it is disabled, the old data is not lost, but this page won't display the old data regardless. This includes all custom views too. (To restart this collection, click the advanced **Enable Graphing** button.)

The advanced **Reset Data** button may be used to actually delete all this historical collection. It will ask you to confirm this action. Then all the graphs's earliest times will be from the time it was reset.

29 Captive Portal

A captive portal is a feature where users need to authenticate or otherwise have permission prior to gaining full Internet access. Commonly a packet filter limits their access and redirects disallowed web usage to a pfSense-served login *portal* webpage. There may be a timeout scheduled for how long the user has network access. This is a common setup in hotels and wifi hotspots.

pfSense can manage multiple different captive portals. These are called *zones*. Each zone can have a different configuration such as authenticating using a different user database, have different webpages, and have different rules for timeouts, reconnecting, and bandwidth usage, for example. A network interface can only be used once, so if you need multiple (different) zones, you will need multiple interfaces that the customers get access through.

The ways a user (or device) may use the captive portal-based network are by:

- Authenticating with a username and password;

- Using a pre-generated *voucher* (or token) to permit service;

- The device has a pre-allowed MAC address;

- The device has a pre-allowed IP address (including specified using a DNS hostname);

- Or the destination is at a pre-defined IP address (or hostname) or on a pre-defined network.

When the customer attempts to open a webpage in their web browser and they haven't been already allowed access, that access will be blocked. For example, with the Firefox web browser, a pop-up at the top of webpage may display: "You must log in to this network before you can access the Internet." (An example is shown in Figure 29.1. This screenshot example is for a captive portal zone configured with vouchers support.) The customer can click the corresponding button **Open Network Login Page** to get access via the pfSense Captive Portal login page if not displayed in the browser window itself.

In normal usage, a webpage displays a welcome message from pfSense with Username/Password login prompts. If voucher support is enabled for the zone, a prompt to enter that token alternatively is also displayed.

If a wrong username, password, or voucher is submitted, it will display "Invalid Credentials Specified" with the login authentication fields again. Note that it may be difficult to see on a small phone device.

Note

The username is case sensitive. If your web browser auto-capitalizes the first character of the username, be sure to adjust this as needed.

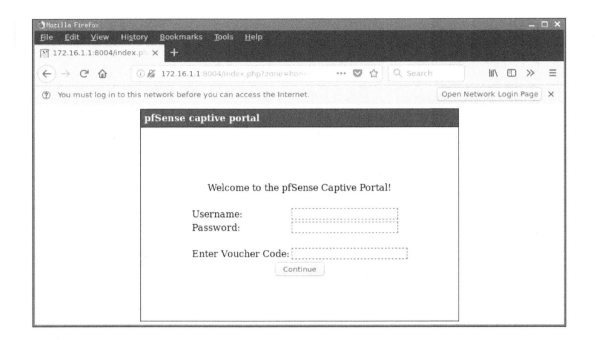

Figure 29.1: Captive Portal login (with vouchers support)

29.1   Captive Portal Zones

The captive portal zone configurations may be viewed or setup via the **Services** → **Captive Portal** menu item.

A table lists the configured Captive Portal Zones. (It is empty by default.) Zones can be added via the **Add** button below the table. When one or more captive portal configurations exist, they will be listed by name, the interfaces they are capturing, the number of current visitors using them, and an optional description about the captive portal.

The corresponding Actions column provides icons for **Edit zone** and **Delete zone**. Editing the zone will take you to its many possible configurations as covered in Section 29.3 and other sections in this chapter. You can remove a specific captive portal's entire configuration with the trash can icon which should prompt you to proceed.

29.2   Add Captive Portal Zone

Adding a new zone is done using a two page form. You may have multiple zones to represent different configurations, such as having different captive portals controlling different network interfaces or some using RADIUS, LDAP or local user database for authentication, some using hardware device MAC addresses, and others using pre-generated voucher tokens, for example.

Enter a unique captive portal name in the **Zone name** field. It can only be based on letters, numbers, and underscores — and you cannot start the name with a number. This is used as a reference and configuration file identification if you have multiple different captive portals.

The **Zone description** field is optional. It is used just for the administrator's explanation about this specific captive portal configuration.

Click the **Save & Continue** to go to the next step.

The next configuration page will include the new zone name in the title and header. Check the **Enable Captive Portal** checkbox and then the multiple configuration options will display as covered in the next section.

29.3   Captive Portal Configurations

These settings for adding a new zone or editing an existing zone are the same. To edit an existing zone's configuration, click its corresponding **Edit zone** (pencil icon) action in the zones table. This will bring up its configurations and link to further settings for allowed access and custom webpages in the captive portal. The links at the top for **MACS**, **Allowed IP Addresses**, **Allowed Hostnames**, **Vouchers**, and **File Manager** are covered in the upcoming sections.

To access the configurations to edit or add them, make sure the **Enable Captive Portal** checkbox is checked.

You may optionally enter an explanation or purpose for this captive portal in the **Description** text field.

Use the **Interface** selection to choose what network, such as LAN, your captive portal should be on, You may make multiple selections. This configuration is required. Note that you cannot use the same interface for multiple captive portal zones.

To restrict how many connections to the captive portal login webpage per IP address at a single time use the **Maximum concurrent connections** selection. It accepts numbers 0 through 100. If it is blank it will default to 10. Note this does not restrict how many users can be logged in.

It is a common administration practice for captive portals to either close connections when they are not being used or if the captive portal is simply connected for a long time. It is a good idea to use a timeout to prevent it from being used for too long. But also don't make timeouts too short so users aren't bothered. You can choose to close connections when they are inactive. Set the **Idle timeout**

(Minutes) selection field. If it is blank, then there is no inactivity timeout. A suggested minimum is 3 minutes. (Note that when using RADIUS, this may be set via the *Idle-Timeout* attribute.

If you want the user to be logged out regardless of their activity, use the **Hard timeout (Minutes)** selection field. Note that in either timeout case, the user may log back in again. Also, when using DHCP for your visitors, consider using a default lease time that is longer than these timeouts.

If you want the visitor's connection to be terminated when their combined input and output bytes exceeds a quota, enter it in megabytes in the **Traffic quota (Megabytes)** number field. If set, it must be 1 MB or larger. By default it is blank and no quota is defined. Note if this is set, it may be overridden by a RADIUS value; see the following **Use RADIUS pfSense-Max-Total-Octets attribute** checkbox if you are using RADIUS.

If you want to allow previously-authenticated users to reconnect to the captive portal when using the same hardware, use the **Pass-through credits per MAC address** selection field. The number entered is used to choose how many times they may later reconnect via the same device without re-authenticating. Consider also configuring an idle timeout or hard timeout when using these pass-through credits. A visitor's pass-through credit will decrement every time they attempt to connect via the captive portal login form.

The **Waiting period to restore pass-through credits (Hours)** selection field may be used to reset these pass-through credits after a certain amount of hours. For example, you can set it to 24 (hours) for all pass-through credits to be available the next day. It is unset by default.

The **Enable waiting period reset on attempted access** checkbox is used so a visitor's waiting period gets extended when they are out of pass-through credits. This may stop some abusers by delaying their access. This implies that if they are on their final credit they cannot try to reconnect early — the visitor will need to wait the entire waiting period.

The **Enable logout popup window** checkbox is used to have the visitor's web browser open a new window (or tab) with a button to submit to disconnect the captive portal session. (To create a custom webpage for this, see the **Logout page contents** feature.)

Normally, the visitor is redirected after successful login to where they first attempted to visit (that triggered the captive portal login). If you want to encourage the visitor to go to your own webpage after they login to the captive portal, set its location in the **Pre-authentication redirect URL** text field. If the URL fields don't begin with protocol, like *http://*, then it may assume it is a local file in the pfSense web server file system — so use a complete URI.

To force users to visit a webpage after they get authenticated, enter the website address in the **After authentication Redirection URL** text field. Be sure to use the full URI, such as *https://example.org/*. This will even override any *redirurl* setting embedded in the login form, including the previous **Pre-authentication redirect URL** setting. If using RADIUS and it provides a RADIUS vendor attribute for a welcome or redirection URL, it will be used instead.

Normally when the captive portal has been configured to block devices based on their hardware MAC address, it will return a "This MAC address has been blocked" error message to a blocked visitor. If you want the visitor to be automatically redirected to a webpage of your choosing, enter its full address in the **Blocked MAC address redirect URL** text field. (See Section 29.4 for more about MAC filtering.)

To disable the same user from making multiple connections using the same username, check the **Disable Concurrent user logins** checkbox. Note that it may be difficult for users to log out (such as disconnect pop-up not appearing), so using this restriction may cause problems for users who need to use a different device.

By default, authenticated visitors are also allowed via their hardware MAC addresses. In some cases, pfSense cannot detect it or there are routers or other devices between the visitor that hide it. Use the **Disable MAC filtering** checkbox to not check by the MAC address too. (The visitor could do a concurrent login reusing an old session.) Note that when this is enabled, RADIUS-based MAC authentication won't work.

The **Enable Pass-through MAC automatic additions** checkbox is used to automatically allow devices that have been authenticated. Once authenticated they are allowed to pass-through forever using the same device (as identified by the MAC). This may be useful in networks where frequent logins aren't wanted. With this, the username may be identified as "unauthenticated" in the captive portal logging.

Note

These MAC pass-through features will not work with RADIUS-based MAC authentication.

MAC-based pass-through visitors aren't listed on the **Status** → **Captive Portal** page as logged in nor in the number of users counter on the zone's page even if they have working captive portal connectivity. The auto-added MAC entries may be viewed and managed via the **MACs** page (for a specific zone) as covered in Section 29.4. That MAC view may be used to delete the auto-added entry.

The captive portal can set hard limits on the bandwidth used by the visitor's session. To allow using the following defaults, enable the **Enable per-user bandwidth restriction** checkbox.

Note

The upcoming MAC- and IP-based captive portal configurations also have bandwidth settings which override these defaults. In addition, if using RADIUS for authentication, the RADIUS server may provide bandwidth-related attributes for the maximum up and down rates when the **Per-user bandwidth restrictions** checkbox is enabled which will be used instead. If no limits are provided or defined, then there are no limits restricted by the captive portal by default.

To set a bandwidth limitation for the visitor's downloads, enter a number in kilobits per second in the **Default download (Kbit/s)** input field. The **Default upload (Kbit/s)** number input field is used for the visitor's uploads also in kilobits per second.

29.3.1 Captive Portal Login Page

pfSense provides a simple webpage for the captive portal visitors to use to login. Since pfSense version 2.4.4, it includes a pfSense-branded logo, and it can be customized with graphical images and with some text content. When the **Use custom captive portal page** checkbox is enabled, this

Captive Portal Login Page form is not available and instead you can upload your own custom captive portal webpages as covered in the upcoming section.

To add your own logo to the default login webpage, check the **Enable to use a custom uploaded logo** checkbox and click your web browser's **Browse** feature for the **Logo Image** to upload a graphical PNG, JPG, or SVG image. Note that the image may be resized.

You may also have a graphical background by selecting the **Enable to use a custom uploaded background image** checkbox and uploading it.

Optionally enter instructions or policies for the portal visitor to read and acknowledge on the webpage in the **Terms and Conditions** text input box. Note that this should be plain text as any HTML tags will be stripped out. When this is entered, the login page will have a checkbox for the visitor to acknowledge it.

29.3.2 Custom Captive Portal Webpages

The following settings are for the HTML webpages' contents for when the **Use custom captive portal page** checkbox is checked.

The standard captive portal login webpage shows it is the "pfSense captive portal" with form fields prompting for the username and password and optionally for the voucher code. The **Portal page contents** file selection field may be used to upload a custom webpage in HTML or PHP to use instead.

For the authentication to work, it must have a POST form with the action using a special $PORTA L_ACTION$ macro with a submit button with the name *accept*, and input names for the *auth_user* (username) and *auth_pass* (password) or *auth_voucher* (voucher string). (Behind the scenes, the CGI action points to a captive portal index.php script ran by the pfSense web server.)

So the captive portal knows where to redirect the visitor to on a successful login, also include a hidden input named *redirurl* with the value of the target URL. If you want it to redirect to the page defined previously or the webpage the visitor initially attempted, used the special macro $PORTAL_REDIR URL$ for the value.

Other macros are $PORTAL_MESSAGE$ to output an internal error or context message from the pfSense captive portal; $PORTAL_ZONE$ to display the zone name (identifier); $CLIENT_IP$ to display the visitor's IP address; and $CLIENT_MAC$ to display the visitor's device's MAC address.

A simple sample HTML template follows (which includes voucher support):

```
<html>
<body>
<h2>Captive Portal</h2>
<p><font color="red" size="+2">$PORTAL_MESSAGE$</font></p>
<form method="post" action="$PORTAL_ACTION$">
<input name="redirurl" type="hidden" value="$PORTAL_REDIRURL$">
Username: <input name="auth_user" type="text">
Password: <input name="auth_pass" type="password">
```

```
<br />
Enter Voucher Code:
<input name="auth_voucher" type="text">
<br />
<input name="accept" type="submit" value="Login">
</form>
</body>
</html>
```

When using a **Secondary Authentication Server** (defined in the upcoming section) and a custom webpage, you will also need to provide HTML CGI form inputs for the *auth_user2* and *auth_pass2* names; for example:

```
<h3>Second Authentication Method</h3>
Username: <input type="text" name="auth_user2">
Password: <input type="password" name="auth_pass2">
```

When a custom webpage is uploaded (and after saving and back to next visit to this configuration page), you should have additional buttons for the **Current Portal Page**. You can use the previous file selector to replace the existing template.

The **Live View** button may be used to see generated HTML webpage after parsing the macros. Clicking the button on the view could be used to verify that login credentials work. It will just reload the login page, but if you have $PORTAL_MESSAGE$ macro in your template and there is a login error, you will see it. Also if the **Live View** login works, your captive portal status (Section 29.9) may show that tested user logged in.

The **View Page Contents** button shows the HTML webpage without replacing the macros. (Using its form submit button should fail with a HTTP 404 error since it is normally the unreplaced macro.) You can also use the **Download** button to have your web browser download the template file to save to your local system (where you may modify it and then reupload it).

To go back to using pfSense's own login webpage for the captive portal, click the **Restore Default Page** button. This will prompt to confirm and then will reload the zone's configuration webpage.

If using a custom login page, you will probably want a custom webpage for any errors, such as "Invalid credentials specified", "System reached maximum login capacity", "MAC address has been blocked", "voucher expired", or even custom messages. This is handled via the **Auth error page contents** section. You can upload the template HTML file, or view, download, or revert back to just use the pfSense default error webpage like with the previous settings.

Note

Some of the special macros in the HTML file are not replaced with content for the various types of error messages.

If the previous **Enable logout popup window** checkbox is enabled, when the visitor logs in successfully, two webpages are loaded for the user: one quickly redirects to the original page they tried to visit or the defined default *redirection* webpage (as defined previously); and a pop-up webpage which may be used to disconnect from the captive portal session. To override both webpages, you may upload a single custom webpage via the **Logout page contents** file selector. While this feature is called *Logout*, this webpage is really displayed first when the login is successful.

Note that this logout template is not used with the macro replacements.

Like with the other uploaded templates, you will later have buttons to view or download the custom logout template, or to restore to the default template.

29.3.3 Authentication

Then select the **Authentication Method**. It defaults to use an authentication backend so the users will need to login using vouchers or username and password. The other choices are *None* to don't do authentication or use RADIUS MAC authentication to bypass a login based on the specific devices' hardware MAC addresses. The following form changes based on the selected method. (Older versions prior to pfSense 2.4.4 had this as a radio button choices with the default of **No Authentication** which implies that the visitor does not need any credentials to login.)

If you are not using authentication for the captive portal visitors, you won't have any other authentication options to configure and you can jump forward to the following section.

Note

If you have visitors connect without credentials and then you later change the method to require authentication, the captive portal state may be confused. It may see a concurrent login from a same device and reuse an old session — while forcing the visitor to the login page repeatecly. To fix this manually, disconnect the users via the **Status** → **Captive Portal** page (Section 29.9).

The *Use an Authentication backend* choice allows you to authenticate visitors using accounts configured in pfSense, using pre-defined vouchers, or to authenticate against an LDAP or RADIUS service. The selections are defined in the **Authentication Server** list. The default is the *Local Database* entry. LDAP and RADIUS servers need to be identified first via the **System** → **User Manager** → **Authentication Servers** subpage as explained in Section 6.6. This field will allow you to select multiple servers or backends, but normally only a single backend is used.

The **Secondary authentication server** may be used to provide additional authentication methods, like against the local user database, LDAP, or RADIUS. For example, you may also use a different server or backend for authenticating with potentially different usernames (and passwords). Normally these secondary choices can be left unselected, but if using this and a custom login webpage form, the HTML must have input fields for submitting the *auth_user2* and *auth_pass2* values as described in the previous section. This menu will also allow multiple servers or backends to be selected.

29.3.4 Local Database

To use accounts configured in pfSense (or pre-defined vouchers), select the default *Use an Authentication backend* choice and select the *Local Database* entry in the **Authentication Server** list. (Or on older versions select the **Local User Manager / Vouchers** radio button.)

When using the *Local Database* authentication backend for local users, it will authenticate against your existing pfSense user accounts. The users may be viewed via the **System** → **User Manager** page. To add a user account, see Section 6.2.

An additional checkbox will be available: **Allow only users/groups with "Captive portal login" privilege set**. It is enabled by default. Then each user (or the group they are a member of) allowed to use the captive portal needs to have the *User - Services: Captive Portal login* privilege. For details, see Section 6.2.4

⚠ **Warning**
Changing this privilege option or removing a previously authenticated user's captive portal login privilege can put the captive portal in a confused state. Connections may timeout or hang as it doesn't provide the login page. A workaround may be for the visitor to reload or clear the cache on their web browser.

If using vouchers, the login codes may be pre-generated, viewed, or downloaded via the **Vouchers** link as covered in the upcoming Section 29.7. You may do that step after completing and saving the zone configuration first.

As a technique to disconnect visitors, you can enable the **Reauthenticate connected users every minute** checkbox. Then it will check against the authentication method every minute and if the user no longer authenticates, the user will lose network access through the captive portal. If the user needs to have seemless use, they will needed their credentials cached.

29.3.5   LDAP for Captive Portal Authentication

To use an external LDAP server for captive portal visitor authentication, select a previously-defined LDAP server in the **Authentication Server** list (when using the default *Use an Authentication backend* choice). If you don't have an LDAP server choice, add it first using the **System** → **User Manager** → **Authentication Servers** subpage (Section 6.6).

There are no other authentication configurations when using just LDAP, so you can skip the next section.

29.3.6   RADIUS for Captive Portal Authentication

To use an external RADIUS server for user logins, select the default *Use an Authentication backend* choice and then select a previously-defined RADIUS server in the **Authentication Server** list. If no RADIUS selection is there, add it via the **System** → **User Manager** → **Authentication Servers** subpage (Section 6.6). (Older versions of pfSense allowed defining the IP address, custom port number, and shared secret key for connecting for each RADIUS server here instead.)

It is not required to use RADIUS to run a captive portal, but it may provide a convenient way to manage users for multiple locations, track visitors' network usage, and also optionally provide some captive portal configurations via RADIUS attributes.

When a RADIUS server is selected, additional options are listed.

The pfSense server identifies itself to the RADIUS server when requesting access. The default indicates it is a captive portal for your custom zone name (but older versions used your hostname). To override this, enter a value in the **NAS Identifier** text field. Commonly, a fully-qualified domain name is used.

As discussed previously, the **Reauthenticate connected users every minute** checkbox is used to check against RADIUS minutely and if the user no longer authenticates, the user will lose network access through the captive portal. This is useful for disconnecting visitors via RADIUS.

The RADIUS server may send the maximum seconds the visitor is allowed network service in the RADIUS *Session-Timeout* attribute. To terminate the captive portal's connectivity for the visitor based on this, enable the **Use RADIUS Session-Timeout attribute** checkbox.

To limit the user to a maximum combined input and output traffic based on a RADIUS attribute called *pfSense-Max-Total-Octets* (which is defined in bytes), check the **Use RADIUS pfSense-Max-Total-Octets attribute** checkbox. (Note that this RADIUS attribute will supersede any amount entered in the **Traffic quota (Megabytes)** option.)

When the **Per-user bandwidth restrictions** checkbox is enabled, RADIUS attributes *pfSense-Bandwidth-Max-Up* and *pfSense-Bandwidth-Max-Down* may be used to restrict the upload and download bandwidths. Note that this will override any **Enable per-user bandwidth restriction** option settings.

If the RADIUS server expects the MAC address in a specific style (including for the *station ID*), select it in the **MAC address format** selection drop-box. The choices are: *Default* to use the common colon-delimited way; *Single dash* to use one dash (-) in the middle of the MAC; *IETF* to use dashes (-) between every octet (two hexadecimal digits); *Cisco* to use a period (.) between every pair of octets (every four hexadecimal digits); and *Unformatted* which has hexadecimal digits only and no separators.

29.3.7   RADIUS MAC Authentication

The RADIUS server can be configured to allow access based on visitor's MAC address. This uses the RADIUS *Calling-Station-Id* (or for Cisco *Called-Station-Id*) attribute.

To have the captive portal device get authenticated by matching its hardware MAC address as stored in RADIUS, select the *Use RADIUS MAC Authentication* choice in the **Authentication Method** drop-down menu. This implies that pfSense's captive portal will first try to use this before sending the visitor to the captive portal login webpage. Then select your RADIUS server in the **Authentication Server** form and you will have a few of the same settings as in the earlier sections, plus two more options. See the previous sections for the other options' details.

Enter its corresponding RADIUS password in the **RADIUS MAC secret** text field. (This is not a per-user password.)

If the visitor's MAC address (with standard password) fails to get authenticated via this RADIUS MAC authentication, the captive portal login page will be displayed. As of pfSense version 2.4.4-p1, this can be disabled by unchecking the **Login page Fallback** checkbox.

29.3.8 RADIUS Accounting

RADIUS accounting is used for collecting information about the centralized users including their current online status. To enable it, check the **Send RADIUS accounting packets to the primary RADIUS server** checkbox. This will make some additional fields available.

Then select the previously-defined RADIUS server in the **Accounting Server** menu.

pfSense can periodically update the RADIUS accounting server to record the captive portal time used by a visitor. This time can be sent by setting the **Send accounting updates** radio button choice. It defaults to **No updates** which implies that the time is not sent periodically, but still may be recorded when old sessions are closed. The **Stop/Start** selection is for sending an accounting stop message and indicate how many seconds the user had service for — and then it restarts the accounting (so basically it is periodic reauthentication). This happens approximately every 60 seconds and should be more accurate. The **Stop/Start (FreeRADIUS)** choice uses a different method of doing the same but for compatibility with FreeRADIUS server implementations. If the accounting server becomes unaccessible, it may be difficult to record these sessions. The **Interim** selection is for using the RADIUS Interim Accounting Record Extension; pfSense will continue to track the cumulative session time and update the RADIUS accounting server as it can.

When RADIUS accounting is enabled (see checkbox), the number of packets and bytes received and sent for the visitor's captive portal session (as seen by the IPFW firewall) are provided to the RADIUS accounting server. Normally, this is recorded from the pfSense server's upload and download perspective (uploads are inputs and downloads are outputs). Clicking the **Invert Acct-Input-Octets and Acct-Output-Octets** checkbox reverses it (uploads are outputs and downloads are inputs) to be from the client's perspective. In addition to *Octets*, note this is also for the RADIUS accounting *Acct-Input-Packets*, *Acct-Output-Packets*, *Acct-Input-Gigawords*, and *Acct-Output-Gigawords* attributes. (Gigawords is for how many times the bytes passed an approximate 4 Giga counter for long-running or high-use sessions.)

When a visitor's connection is terminated due to being idle for too long, the accounting will record the stop time at the current time of the termination. To record instead the last activity time (as the stop time), click the **Idle time accounting** checkbox. (Note that this time may be the login time.)

29.3.9 HTTPS Options

The captive portal webpages are served by plain HTTP by default. To use HTTP over TLS so the username and password cannot be sniffed, click the **Enable HTTPS login** checkbox. This should be the default, so check it. The following fields are only available when this is enabled.

Enter the hostname for the captive portal's webpage in the **HTTPS server name** text field. This is required if the HTTPS login is enabled.

The **SSL Certificate** selection field lists your known certificates (like the webConfigurator default shown with a hash identifier in parenthesis). This is required when using HTTPS — so select one to be used for the captive portal's HTTPS server. To create or import a certificate, see the **System → Cert. Manager** page (as explained in Section 12.2).

By default when using the HTTPS login, the captive portal's packet filter will transparently forward any TCP traffic destined to HTTP port 443 to the captive portal's defined TCP port instead. If you don't want to override other HTTPS attempts to your portal's login page, disable this automatic forwarding of TCP port 443 by checking the **Disable HTTPS Forwards** checkbox.

Note

If this **Disable HTTPS Forwards** option is checked, the common HTTPS traffic will be simply blocked prior to authentication. No captive portal login page will be displayed until the visitor tries to browse a webpage over TCP port 80 (plain HTTP).

At the bottom of the many configurations is the **Save** button. This will start the captive portal.

Generally, DNS lookups are allowed by visitors without advance authentication. (This is so their web browser can even attempt the webpage lookup that triggers the captive portal login.) So make sure your DNS forwarder or resolver is enabled and the firewall allows access to it. In addition, it is common to use DHCP service for the captive portal visitors, so enable and configure it as needed.

29.4   MAC Access

To allow access — bypassing the login portal — for specific devices by their hardware MAC addresses (without using RADIUS as discussed previously), use the **MACs** page (via the zone configuration). This feature may also be used to restrict access for specified MAC addresses.

The page lists the configured MAC rules. (None are defined by default.) A *Pass* entry means the device with the MAC address is not captured by the portal and no login authentication page is needed.

A *Block* rule cannot be bypassed for the MAC address. The captive portal always restricts and while the login page is displayed, it always shows "This MAC address has been blocked."

 Warning
MAC address rule mistakes may cause you to get locked out even from the pfSense web-Configurator portal. If this happens to you, look at Section 37.16 about using the console to revert to a previous configuration.

Click the **Add** button to add a MAC address rule. You may also click a rule's **Edit MAC address** action link (pencil icon) to modify an existing rule. To remove a rule, use its **Delete MAC address** action link (trash can icon).

29.4.1 MAC Address Rules

Selecting to add or edit will take you to a new Edit MAC Address Rules page with a few fields. The MAC address field is required.

The **Action** drop-down menu is to define whether the captive portal should allow or reject packets from the MAC address. As described earlier, the default *Pass* mode will bypass the login requirement and the *Block* mode will always display the login which cannot be bypassed.

Enter the hardware address of the device in the **MAC Address** field. It must be entered using the common format of six hexadecimal octets separated by colons. You may press the **Copy My MAC** button to have it automatically enter the hardware address of your device, but note if you have a router between you and your pfSense it will enter the MAC for the device closest to the pfSense system.

The optional **Description** field may be used to explain or name this MAC address rule entry for display in the table of configured rules.

You may restrict the maximum transfers in kilobits per second for uploads and downloads by entering the kilobits (per second) in the **Bandwidth up** and **Bandwidth down** respective fields. These are used to override the default limits, if set, on the zone's configuration. (See its **Default download (Kbit/s)** and **Default upload (Kbit/s)** input fields.)

Click the **Save** button to store the settings.

Note if the captive portal zone is not configured, the MAC address rules will not be used to block packets or do bandwidth limits. (Enable the zone using the checkbox and then save on the **Configuration** page.)

29.5 Allowed IP Addresses

The **Allowed IP Addresses** feature (linked from the zone's configuration) is used to define destination networks and specific addresses that the captive portal user may access without authentication. For example, you may allow unknown visitors to access your organization's marketing webpages without authenticating first. In addition, it may be used to allow known source IPs to route through your pfSense system without authenticating with the portal. (You may use hostnames instead as documented in the upcoming Section 29.6.)

No IP address rules are defined by default. When they are added, the table will have arrows showing what is allowed for the IP address or network. The left arrow is for allowing connections from an originating network or IP. The right arrow is for allowing connections to a destination network or IP. And the graphic for both arrows allows to and from.

Note

For connections *from* an IP address, this feature checks the source IP address of the last hop and may not necessarily be the IP address of the device. You won't be able to specifically allow different devices behind another router.

There is not a block rule for specific IP addresses with the captive portal. If you want to block for specific IPs, use the packet filter as covered in Chapter 16.

In the table, the corresponding action icons may be used to modify or remove the rule.

Click the **Add** button to add the IP address or network to allow.

29.5.1   Add or Edit IP Rules

The **IP Address** field is required. Enter the IP address there. If this is a subnet, change the drop-down menu (which defaults to /32) to the subnet mask you need.

Optionally enter an explanation or identifier for your own recognition in the **Description** field.

The **Direction** drop-down menu is used to select how access is allowed for this IP address or network. It defaults to *Both*. Selecting **From** will open the captive portal for devices coming in via that IP address or network. To allow access out to locations on the Internet without authentication, select **To** in the menu. The address for the *To* may be the final destination address or the address of the next hop router.

The **Bandwidth up** and **Bandwidth down** fields may be used to restrict the bytes transferred in kilobits per second specifically for this configured IP or network rule. The defaults may be defined in the main configuration for the zone. (Bandwidth limits may also be set based on MAC addresses and the allowed hostnames as covered in the previous and following sections.)

Click the **Save** button to store the settings.

Note that the captive portal zone needs to be enabled for the IP rules to make any sense.

29.6   Allowed Hostnames

Like the previous section's feature, you may allow specified source or destination addresses access without being captured by the portal for authentication first. Instead of defining this using an IP address, you may use DNS hostnames via the **Allowed Hostname** link from the configuration page.

No rules are defined by default. To introduce a rule based on a hostname, click the **Add** button.

When added, the table will indicate the rule direction with an arrow. The **Edit hostname** action (pencil) icon may be used to modify the rule. To remove a rule, click its **Delete hostname** action (trash can) icon.

Connections *to* an allowed hostname may not work as expected. For example, if you use this to allow access through the captive portal (without authentication) to fetch your corporate webpage, some content externally referenced from that page may be at different URIs. In addition, this target webpage may be hosted on a content delivery network or load balanced, so pfSense may allow one target where your captive portal customer may be attempting to download it from a different address (with the same hostname). To workaround these problems, use a target webpage that only is hosted in one place and has any external objects (like graphics) downloaded via same hostname, add all the multiple hostnames, or also add wider ranges by allowing IP networks using the **Allowed IP Addresses** feature (as covered in the previous section).

29.6.1 Allowed Hostname Settings

In the form page to add or edit the allowed hostname, the first option is the **Direction** drop-down menu. It defaults to *Both*. Selecting either **From** or **To** has similar behavior. Allowing access to destination also opens up access from it, and vice-versa.

To override the zone's default bandwidth limits (if set) By default, no bandwidth limits are defined. Zone-wide defaults may be set in its main configuration. Or you may configure it here specific for the allowed hostname by entering the kilobits (per second) in the **Bandwidth up** and/or **Bandwidth down** fields.

Use the **Save** button to store these allowed hostname settings. This will take you back to the previous view listing these rules.

Again, the zone must be enabled for these rules to take affect.

29.7 Captive Portal Vouchers

A voucher is a token (also known as a code or ticket) that is pre-generated so a user may get Internet access without the administrator setting up a user account in advance. This is useful for temporary customers or permitting almost anonymous access. For example, a hotel receptionist or a customer service representative at a cybercafé may give out a single voucher to a guest. This contains a code the user may type in at the Captive Portal login webpage's **Enter Voucher Code** field when attempting to use their network access.

In normal use, one voucher would be given to one customer for their single visit. While a specific single voucher could be used by many customers (and even over many visits) that could defeat auditing purposes or make the time allowed access difficult to limit.

The vouchers are organized or recorded in a *roll*. A roll is the list or record of the available codes that customers may use. The organization (or pfSense admin) may choose to have multiple rolls so they may define different allowed access time limits for types of customers (such as two hours for a restaurant customer or 18 hours for an overnight guest) or for different auditing purposes (like who assigned the vouchers). You need at least one roll assigned in pfSense to enable the voucher support.

To use this method of captive portal access, go to the **Vouchers** page linked from the configuration page via the **Edit zone** (pencil icon) action in the zones table. No vouchers are available in a default new install of pfSense. When added, this page will list them in the top table which shows the roll number, how many minutes a ticket is valid for, the number of tickets in a roll, and an optional explanation.

The actions column only exists when the voucher's checkbox is enabled. The actions include the **Edit voucher roll** pencil icon, the **Delete voucher roll** trash can icon to remove all the tokens in a roll, and the **Export vouchers for this roll to a .csv file** action.

Use this export feature to download the list of tokens. The file will be named with the captive portal zone name and the roll number, such as `vouchers_office_roll7.csv`. The file will have some comments at the top to explain what roll number it is for and how it was generated. Then each line will have a unique token. Your office may choose to import this list into a database program, ordering system, or other customer interface for printing or otherwise providing the customer with their temporary voucher.

Rolls cannot be added (and vouchers cannot be created) until the feature is enabled. Click the checkbox to **Enable the creation, generation, and activation of rolls with vouchers**. This will bring up an additional form for creating and using rolls. You may use the defaults, so click the **Save** button at the bottom. This will reload the page and now an **Add** button will appear.

29.7.1 Voucher Configurations

The vouchers will be strings (like "MNpUnYxkYam") which were generated based on a defined public/private RSA key pair. The following settings may be used to adjust how they are generated.

 Warning
Previously-generated vouchers will become invalid when modifying these settings.

First enter 64-bit or smaller valid RSA keys in PEM format in the two **Voucher Public Key** and **Voucher Private Key** text input boxes. The public key ("BEGIN PUBLIC KEY") will be used to decrypt vouchers used by visitors and the private key ("BEGIN RSA PRIVATE KEY") is used to encrypt the vouchers. A private key is not required if the vouchers are generated elsewhere.

A button **Generate new keys** may be used to generate a 64-bit RSA private key and its corresponding public key which will be automatically inserted here.

The **Character set** text input field may be used to limit to what characters the vouchers can be made of. Notice this default doesn't have some letters (l, o, and O) and digits (0 and 1) which may be confusing when a visitor reads and inputs them. This set should be at least two characters. But note that smaller the set, the longer the generated voucher strings will be. With the default settings, the vouchers are 11 characters long, but when using only two characters in this character set, the generated voucher strings are 64 characters long (made up of those two characters), for example:

`JJjjjjjJjjJJJjJJJjjjjJJjJjJjJjJJjJjJjJjJjjjJJJjJjjjjjjJjjJjjJJj`

The **# of Roll bits** field is the number of bits for storing the Roll ID in each voucher. This defaults to 16 bits. The **# of Ticket bits** input is for the number of bits for the Ticket ID in each voucher. It defaults to 10 bits. Using 16 bits means the roll can have 65535 vouchers. The **# of Checksum bits** input is the number of bits used to store a checksum over both of these IDs. It defaults to 5. The ticket bits needs to be within 1 and 16 and the other bit numbers in 1 to 31. If the RSA key is small, then these bit sizes need to be smaller. The sum of these bit sizes needs to be at least one less than the RSA's key size.

The **Magic number** is a random initializer number used so the generated vouchers are unique. The more bits free allows more of this magic to be stored. You may enter your own random number if you wish.

When a voucher used by a visitor is not valid and not expired, the default response message is "Voucher invalid." To offer your own failure message, enter it in the **Invalid voucher message** text field.

You may also have your failure response for when the voucher is valid but is expired in the **Expired voucher message** text input. Its default is "Voucher expired."

If using a custom captive portal error page template (like described in Section 29.3.2), these errors will be displayed via the $PORTAL_MESSAGE$ macro.

The **Voucher Database Synchronization** section is used to configure this pfSense as a captive portal slave node to fetch the voucher database or voucher settings from a different master pfSense captive portal system. It uses an XMLRPC web service and this master cannot be your same system. When using this synchronization, the master's voucher configurations will be used and the voucher configurations on this webpage will not be used.

To use this, enter a valid IP address for the master server in the **Synchronize Voucher Database IP** text field and the TCP port for its pfSense *webConfigurator* service in the **Voucher sync port** field. (It is normally port 443.)

The user on the master server needs to be the admin user or a user who has privileges via the XML-RPC, like *System - HA node sync*. (See Section 6.2.4 for details.) Enter the username in the **Voucher sync username** field and the password twice in the **Voucher sync password** fields (to verify it).

Use the **Save** button to continue. If you are using the voucher synchronization, it will attempt to fetch these details and will report that the "Voucher database has been synchronized."

The actual vouchers based on these local or fetched settings are generated after the roll is added and that roll's vouchers are downloaded as covered in the following section.

29.7.2 Add or Edit Roll of Vouchers

To add a new roll of vouchers click the **Add** button (after it has been enabled). Or to edit an existing roll in the table, click its corresponding **Edit voucher roll** action (pencil icon).

Note you cannot actually edit the roll of vouchers. You can not change, insert, or remove your own codes.

Enter a number (between zero and 65535) in the **Roll #** field. This is required and is used to identify the list of codes. You may not reuse an existing roll number. You may want to simply start with the number "1."

All the users using the roll have their own amount of allowed access time. Enter the time in minutes, such as "120" to allow two hours of usage, in the required **Minutes per ticket** field. The minimum is one minute. Note it is not accumulated by all users. The time is also not stopped and restarted when the customer stops using the Internet or relogs in (if needed). The customer's time allotment countdown begins the first time the voucher is used.

You may generate between one and 1023 vouchers in one roll. Enter your desired voucher amount in the **Count** field. This field is also required. (For example, if your minutes is 60 and you have a count of 10, then you will be generating ten different one hour vouchers for a total of 10 hours of access time.)

Warning
If you change this count for an existing roll, the previous vouchers in the roll will be reset as unused. So customers may get more access minutes or otherwise reuse their voucher a later time.

The **Comment** field is simply used for the pfSense admin's internal use to explain or name the roll. The admin could enter the date when it was created there for example or the name of the receptionist who will distribute them.

Click the **Save** button to add (generate new tokens) or make the changes for the roll. It will take you back to the table view of all the rolls — the main captive portal page for the zone. Use the **Export vouchers for this roll to a .csv file** action icon there to download the generated tokens (as described earlier).

29.7.3   Active Vouchers

The voucher status, test, and expiration pages are only available for captive portal zones that have vouchers enabled.

To view vouchers in use, go to the **Status → Captive Portal** page and select the zone (with vouchers support) in the **Display Zone** drop-down menu. This will bring up links for the voucher status and to access the voucher features. (The default status view is for the **Active Users**; this is covered in Section 29.9.)

Click on the **Active Vouchers** link to view the vouchers in use. Its table header will show a total count number. The table columns list the voucher code, what roll number it is in, the date and time it was first activated, when it expires in relative time (like "29min"), and the date and time it expires. PfSense versions since 2.4.4 also show the authentication method types. The column fields may be clicked on to sort the table by that column.

29.7.4 Voucher Rolls

The **Voucher Rolls** page (via **Status** → **Captive Portal**) gives a quick summary about each of your rolls. The table may be sorted by clicking on a column header.

For each roll number, it displays the defined minutes allowed per voucher, the number of vouchers (tickets) in the roll, the optional description (comment), how many vouchers in the roll have been used, how many have current active sessions, and how many vouchers are left and ready to use.

29.7.5 Testing Vouchers

To test a voucher or to see its current status, use the **Test Vouchers** page (for the selected zone) via **Status** → **Captive Portal** menu item.

You may enter one or more voucher codes (separated by spaces or on different lines) in the **Vouchers** textbox. Then click the **Test** button. At the top of the page, it will then display details about each token indicating how many minutes left for each token. The tokens will be listed with numbers in parentheses like (7/6) which means it is the sixth voucher in roll number seven. The total minutes for all the tokens listed is also displayed.

It will also indicate if the voucher has already been used and is expired. Invalid tokens are also reported. It will indicate if a listed token is too short, has illegal characters, or has bad magic, Customers attempting to use expired or invalid tokens would get their access denied.

29.7.6 Expiring Vouchers

Vouchers may be disabled by expiring them. Use the **Voucher Rolls** page (via **Status** → **Captive Portal**). Enter the voucher codes one per line or separated by spaces and then click the **Expire** button.

You can see the counts reduced in the *used* and *ready* fields on the **Voucher Rolls** table as covered in a previous section. You may also use the **Test Vouchers** feature to verify a specific voucher is expired.

29.8 Captive Portal File Manager

In addition to the custom login, authentication error, and logout pages, you may choose to have other webpages or files — like an image file referenced from your custom pages or the `favicon.ico` web icon — available via the captive portal. Executable PHP webpages may also be uploaded for dynamic use. The files are available via the captive portal's web root.

To add or list the uploaded files, use the zone's **Edit zone** pencil icon at the **Services** → **Captive Portal** page and then click on the **File Manager** link.

The table listing the files (none by default) will show the file name and its size in bytes. A corresponding **Delete file** trash can icon to delete the file from the captive portal web downloads.

To add a file, click the **Add** button at the bottom of the table. This will bring up a brief form near the top of the page to upload a new file. Use your web browser's **Browse** feature to select a local file from your system and then click the **Upload** button. If the file is not named "favicon.ico", it will be renamed to be prefixed with "captiveportal-". The list of installed files will be updated.

Note that the total limit for all the uploaded files is one megabyte.

29.9   Captive Portal Status

To see the users currently logged in via the captive portal, visit the **Status** → **Captive Portal** page. Then, in the **Display Zone** drop-down menu, select the zone to view the *Active Users* and to access the voucher features (as described in Section 29.7.3).

The display shows the list of users who authenticated via the captive portal and have current sessions. The table header shows the total count of the logged in users in the parentheses. The table lists these users with their assigned IP address, MAC address, username, and the date and time of when their most recent session started. If the session was authenticated using a voucher, then the voucher (token) is displayed in the username field.

Hover over the highlighted username to see further session details, including the duration and time left (in hours, minutes, and seconds) and the bytes sent and received. Note these numbers don't update dynamically so reload the page to get the current session details.

If a recent session timed-out, it will not be displayed in the table. Also see the logging (covered in the following section) for details about recent captive portal entries.

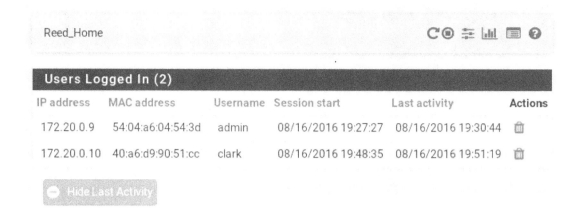

Figure 29.2: **Status** → **Captive Portal** (with **Last Activity**)

Each entry also has an **Disconnect this User** trash can action icon. If you click this icon, a pop-up window will prompt to verify this action. Click **OK** to disconnect the corresponding user.

If you want to see the date and time of the last activity associated with the connected users, click the **Show Last Activity** button below the table. The table will rewrite with a new field listing each entry's last activity date and time as seen in Figure 29.2. The **Hide Last Activity** button will toggle this view back off.

Each of the column headers may be clicked on to sort the table by that column.

Below the table, a button **Disconnect All Users** is used to remove all the current sessions and reinitialize the captive portal firewall. Clicking it will prompt to confirm this action.

Warning

The **Disconnect All Users** feature may open up the Internet access for devices to use it without captive portal authentication. If this happens, you can *re-enable* the captive portal by unchecking the **Enable** checkbox and saving the portal configuration, followed by rechecking the checkbox and saving it again.

---

pfSense also provides graphs about past and near-real-time captive portal usage via the **Status** → **Monitoring** feature. Within its tools, select *Captive Portal* as one or both of the **Axis** menus and data to see with the **Graph** menus, such as concurrent logins for each zone. For information on this monitoring, see Section 28.2.

29.10 Captive Portal Logs

The log output from the captive portal systems can be seen via the **Status** → **System Logs** → **Captive Portal Auth** page. It will display up to the last 50 log entries (per its default log settings). For details about logging, see Chapter 11.

The startup of a captive portal zone will indicate its zone name and log "Reconfiguring captive portal." New logins and terminated sessions will both be logged with the username (if known) and the MAC and IP addresses used. Rejected user authentication and disabling of a captive portal zone are not logged.

The captive portal logging may contain diagnostic or informational details about when existing voucher rolls are modified and old vouchers are marked unused, when vouchers are manually expired, if vouchers are invalid, or when there are problems creating voucher databases, etc. Note that the **Test Vouchers** feature can also log about problems.

30 IPsec

IPsec is the security architecture for the Internet Protocol that utilizes the IPv4 and IPv6 extension headers — the Authentication Header (AH) for integrity and the IP Encapsulating Security Payload (ESP) header for confidentiality. These are implemented in the kernel to authenticate and encrypt packets.

The Internet Key Exchange protocol (IKEv2) provides a way to secretly share and renegotiate keys between the hosts for the authentication and encryption of packets. This has a two-phase negotiation process which is how the IPsec configuration in pfSense is setup. Phase 1 is used to authenticate peers and setup master keys. It needs a pre-shared key or user certificate. Various authentication methods are available including *Xauth* (Extended Authentication) which provides login/password-based authentication secured by the Phase 1 and *Hybrid* authentication where a server-side certificate is authenticated by the client,

The second phase is used to negotiate parameters with the peers and periodically rekey and renegotiate its security association. Phase 1 is handled by the `charon` daemon, while Phase 2 is directly in the FreeBSD kernel.

There is a native IKEv2 client for Windows, MacOS X, iOS (iPads and iPhones), Android, Linux, NetBSD, and other systems which may be used to peer with the pfSense VPN.

Note

The remote IPsec peers need to configured with the same protocol and encryption algorithm as the pfSense system.

IPsec has two modes of operation: tunnel and transport. The tunnel mode is used to encapsulate packets into new IP packets for VPN gateways. For example, it could be used to connect machines from two different private networks with secure traffic between them. The transport mode is for host-to-host (or peer-to-peer) encrypted communication.

30.1 IPsec Tunnels

The IPsec features are accessed via the **VPN** → **IPsec** page. It displays the configured IPsec tunnels. It has links at the top to **VPN** → **IPsec** → **Tunnels** (this same main page), **VPN** → **IPsec** → **Mobile**

Clients for setting up secure connections from remote systems (see Section 30.4), **VPN → IPsec →
Pre-Shared Keys** for managing the shared secrets (Section 30.5), and **VPN → IPsec → Advanced
Settings** for logging and custom configurations (Section 30.6).

The shortcuts link to related status and related log entries (as discussed in the following Section 30.2
and Section 30.3).

The tunnels table lists the Phase 1 details: the IKE version (V1, V2, or Auto); the network interface
and remote gateway (or it will indicate it is a *Mobile Client* configuration); the IKE mode; the encryption algorithm(s) and key length bits; the hash algorithms (*P1 Transforms*); the Diffie-Hellman
(DH) group, and its description. (These are explained in further detail in this chapter.)

At the front of each column a button may be used to disable or enable the Phase 1 entry. In addition,
there are action icons for the corresponding entries to edit or delete the Phase 1 entry. Note that
removing the Phase 1 entry will also remove its Phase 2 entries. If this Phase 1 entry is not for a
Mobile Client, it will also have a copy action (clone icon) which will open up the **Edit** page with the
previous settings copied over to create a new Phase 1 entry.

The anchor icon (in the actions column) may be used to reorder selected Phase 1 entries. Check the
entries you want to move and then click the anchor icon to move them there.

Below each tunnel entry in the table is a **Show Phase 2 Entries** button. The button also shows a count
of the existing Phase 2 configurations associated with the Phase 1 entry. (There are no Phase 2 configurations by default, so this will show zero for the corresponding new Phase 1 entry.) Click it to expand
the table to show the Phase 2 columns: mode, local subnet, remote subnet, protocol, transforms, authentication methods, and actions for the corresponding entry. To add a Phase 2 configuration, click
the **Show Phase 2 Entries** followed by the **Add P2** button (which is not visible by default). (For
details, see Section 30.8.) To edit, copy, or delete a Phase 2 entry click the corresponding entry's
action icon.

The Phase 2 entries may be reordered by checking them and then clicking an anchor icon to move
them to there.

No IPsec tunnels are configured by default by pfSense. Click the **Add P1** button to start adding them.

Use the **Delete P1s** button to remove the selected Phase 1 entries. (Click the checkbox in front of
an entry to select it.) This button is not available until a tunnel has been configured. Note that you
cannot delete nor disable an entry that is using a *Routed (VTI)* mode until its interface is unassigned.
(To remove it, see Section 13.1.2.) You will need to click the **Apply Changes** button too.

30.2 IPsec Status

The **Status → IPsec** page provides an overview of the IPsec connections, and links to display the mobile users (leases), the Security Association Database entries (SADs), and Security Policy Database
entries (SPDs). The details are displayed in sortable tables. Use the column headers to re-sort the
data based on that field. Click the same header twice to change the order based on the same field.

The **Status → IPsec → Overview** table shows rows for each connection with:

Description

   The reference label for identifying in pfSense.

Local ID

   The local IKE identity.

Local IP

   The local IKE endpoint address; if using NAT Traversal, it will also show "NAT-T."

Remote ID

   The remote IKE identify; and if applicable this may also show the remote XAuth identity and the remote EAP identity.

Remote IP

   The remote IKE endpoint address (and will also indicate if is NAT-T).

Role

   The IKE version (1 or 2) and indicates if is an initiator or responder of the IKE security association.

Reauth

   The time before the security association gets re-authenticated displayed in seconds and also in days, hours, minutes, and seconds.

Algo

   The IKE encryption algorithm, integrity algorithm, pseudo random function, and Diffie-Hellman group.

Status

   If the security association state is established, it will show the established time in seconds and again in days, hours, minutes, and seconds.

The final column is for actions to click on. If the state is established, it will provide a trash icon **Disconnect VPN** action. Or if not established, it will have a sign-in icon **Connect VPN** action.

If the SAs for the ESP and/or AH are setup, the table will show a plus icon action to show child SA entries. Click it to display an additional table listing the following:

Unique ID

   The IPsec ID for the child.

Local subnets

   The list of local traffic selectors (networks).

Local SPI(s)

   The local and/or remote hex-encoded inbound or outbound Security Parameter Indexes (aka *cookies* used as a connection identifier).

Remote subnets

   The list of remote traffic selectors.

Times

Time before this child security association gets rekeyed, time before it expires (Life), and the time it has been installed. These are displayed in seconds (and days, hours, minutes, and seconds).

Algo

This lists the ESP encryption algorithm, ESP or AH integrity algorithm, pseudo random function (if set), and PFS rekeying DH group (if set). If using extended sequence numbers (ESN), it will indicate it with a number 1.

Stats

Number of input bytes and input packets processed, and output bytes and output packets processed.

It will also provide an icon to click to disconnect the Child SA.

30.2.1 Status of IPsec Leases

The **Status** → **IPsec** → **Leases** subpage provides some details about all your current mobile user connections. This is only displayed if support for IPsec Mobile Clients is enabled (see Section 30.4). The table shows the pool name (the network), how many have used it (usage), and how many are currently online. If there are leases in the pool, the ID, IP address (host), and if it is online or offline (status) are displayed for each.

You may click the column headers to sort the data. As with the other IPsec status pages, shortcuts are available to restart and stop (or start) the IPsec service and to view its configurations and logs.

30.2.2 Status of IPsec Security Associations

The **Status** → **IPsec** → **SADs** page shows the Security Association Database (SAD) such as in Figure 30.1.

Figure 30.1: **Status → IPsec → SADs**

The table shows the sources and destination as IPv4 or IPv6 addresses; the protocol such as ESP, AH, IPComp, or TCP-MD5; the Security Parameter Index (SPI); the encoding and authentication algorithms; and how many bytes have been processed for this security association.

The corresponding trash can icon may be used to delete that security association.

30.2.3 Status of IPsec Security Policies

The **Status → IPsec → SPDs** page shows the Security Policy Database (SPD), like seen in Figure 30.2.

Status / IPsec / SPDs   ⇄ ⅷ 🗔 ❷

Overview   Leases   SADs   SPDs

Source	Destination	Direction	Protocol	Tunnel endpoints
10.1.0.0/16	10.0.0.0/16	▶ Outbound	ESP	62.149.40.78 -> 83.56.124.167
10.1.0.0/16	10.0.0.0/16	◀ Inbound	ESP	62.149.40.78 -> 83.56.124.167
10.0.0.0/16	10.1.0.0/16	▶ Outbound	ESP	83.56.124.167 -> 62.149.40.78

Figure 30.2: **Status** → **IPsec** → **SPDs**

The table shows the source and destination networks; the direction with left or right arrows showing inbound or outbound direction of the policy; the protocol; and the tunnel endpoints.

30.3   IPsec Logging

The latest log entries can be read via the **Status** → **System Logs** → **IPsec** page. You can also get to it from the other IPsec pages by clicking the **Related log entries** shortcut icon. It will show log entries from the `charon` (the IKE daemon) and `ipsec_starter` processes.

To search or adjust this logging see the **Log filter** and **Manage log** shortcut features described in Section 11.1 and Section 11.3.

The **Restart Service** icon (half circle arrow) shortcut may be used to restart the IPsec services. It will show a turning engine graphic there and won't go to a different page. When completed it will reload the view of the last IPsec log entries.

30.3.1   IPsec Logging Controls

By default, IPsec will log about errors and generic flow control. It may have less logging or extra logging for troubleshooting as fine-tuned on the **VPN** → **IPsec** → **Advanced Settings** page (see Section 30.6). The first advanced configurations are for the Logging Controls which lists several IPsec subsystems that have logging:

• Daemon

- SA Manager

- IKE SA

- IKE Child SA

- Job Processing

- Configuration backend

- Kernel Interface

- Networking

- ASN encoding

- Message encoding

- Integrity checker

- Integrity Verifier

- Platform Trust Service

- TLS handler

- IPsec traffic

- StrongSwan Lib

(All these subsystems are beyond the context of this book. Consult the strongSwan documentation for further information.)

Each has a drop-down menu to define how it logs:

Silent
> absolutely no logs for the subsystem

Audit
> only has very basic auditing output

Control
> error output and generic control flow details (the default)

Diag
> diagnostic details

Raw
> data dumps in hexadecimal

Highest
> dumps that include keys and sensitive data

Use the **Save** button to use your desired logging controls (on the **Advanced IPsec Settings** page).

30.4   IPsec Mobile Clients

The **VPN** → **IPsec** → **Mobile Clients** subpage is used to configure IPsec so remote users can securely connect to your pfSense internal networks. When setup, the Mobile Client mode is also identified in the Remote Gateway table column on the **Tunnels** page.

To use this feature, make sure the **Enable IPsec Mobile Client Support** checkbox is selected. Note to use this feature, you will need a Phase 1 definition specific for Mobile Clients support. After saving this page, it will prompt you with a green **Create Phase 1** button if it is missing. Click it to go to the **VPN** → **IPsec** → **Mobile Clients** → **Edit Phase 1** page as covered in Section 30.7. Note that the Phase 1 options are slightly different versus the non-mobile mode, so be sure to use this link to set it up correctly.

Then setup the Extended Authentication (Xauth) by selecting one or more LDAP, RADIUS, or *Local Database* methods in the required **User Authentication** options menu. These choices are defined via the **System** → **User Manager** → **Authentication Servers** subpage as covered in Section 6.6. The Local Database option is used for local authentication with a pfSense user account who has the *VPN: IPsec xauth Dialin* privilege. (The privilege is added by editing an existing user.) See Section 6.2.4 for details.

The **Group Authentication** defaults to *none* for no group-based authentication. The other option is *system*.

The **Client Configuration (mode-cfg)** section provides several configuration items that may be securely exchanged via an ISAKMP method to the client. This includes some IKE attributes and some Cisco Unity extensions. Several of these configurations are checkboxes and when enabled, additional fields are available to provide further details. None of these client configurations are enabled by default.

You may choose to provide a virtual IP or IPv6 address to the IPsec mobile client. When the **Virtual Address Pool** checkbox is checked, it will allow entering the network address and network mask for defining the available range. (The subnet defaults to /24.)

If you use IPv6, then you can do the same thing for the **Virtual IPv6 Address Pool**. (Its IPv6 netmask defaults to /120.)

Click the **Provide a list of accessible networks to clients** checkbox to send the RFC 7296 IKEv2 INTERNAL_IP4_SUBNET attribute which can define what traffic allowed through the gateway, and the Cisco Unity UNITY_SPLIT_INCLUDE extension for IKEv1 which will list the subnets to tunnel.

To indicate that the client may save the Xauth password in local storage, check the **Save Xauth Password** checkbox. This provides the Cisco Unity UNITY_SAVE_PASSWD extension for IKEv1.

Use the **DNS Default Domain** checkbox to enter in a domain name to be used as the default search domain that is appended to unqualified hostnames to look them up. This is the Cisco Unity UNITY_DEF_DOMAIN extension for IKEv1.

Use the **Split DNS** checkbox to provide Cisco Unity UNITY_SPLITDNS_NAME extension for IKEv1. In the additional field, enter one or more domain names, separated by spaces, that the client should use for private networks. (It is reported that Mac OS X clients will only use the first domain name in the list.)

Click the **DNS Servers** checkbox to add up to four DNS servers' IP addresses which the clients may use for lookups. At least one must be defined when this is enabled.

To provide WINS (aka NBNS) servers to the client to use, click the **WINS Servers** checkbox and enter at least one WINS server IP address.

To provide the Cisco Unity ALT_PFS attribute to override the Diffie-Hellman group, click the **Phase2 PFS Group** checkbox and select the choice in the drop-down menu. See the **PFS key group** option in Section 30.8 for details.

To provide a message that some clients may display after login, check the **Login Banner** checkbox and enter the string in the field. This is for the Cisco Unity UNITY_BANNER extension for IKEv1.

After saving these mobile client settings, also use the apply button to restart IPsec.

30.5 IPsec Pre-Shared Keys

Shared secrets, including for EAP secure phase 1 conversation, are managed via the **VPN** → **IPsec** → **Pre-Shared Keys** subpage. This displays any existing keys with their associated identifier name. This includes both pre-shared IPsec keys defined for pfSense system users and for identities defined via this page.

An identifier named "any" will match any other peer.

The pfSense interface displays the original secret (and not the hashed version which is stored internally). This is so you may visually compare this shared string with the other peer's settings.

Each table entry will have an edit action (pencil icon). If it is a key for a system user, clicking it will take you to that user's specific **System** → **User Manager** → **Users** → **Edit** page. See the **Keys** section there (Section 6.2.3).

If the key is just for an IPsec identity defined here, editing is explained in the following. For IPsec identities, you will also have a **Delete key** (trash can icon) action to remove this identity.

Use the **Add** button to add a new, non-system user identity with a pre-shared key,

30.5.1 Add or Edit the Pre-Shared Secret

Enter a unique email address, fully-qualified domain name, or IP address in the **Identifier** field. This only allows alphabet characters, digits, at-sign (@), period, or a dash. Use "any" to be a wildcard to represent any identity.

Note that this cannot match an existing user name. If you need a key for a pfSense system user, see Section 6.2.3 about setting it via the **System** → **User Manager** page instead.

Select the type of key in the **Secret type** drop-down menu. It defaults to PSK or you can choose EAP.

Then enter the known key in the **Pre-Shared Key** field.

You may optional enter its type in the **Identifier type** form. This is empty by default and the choices are *E-mail address* and *User Fully Qualified Domain Name*. (This option and the following two options were introduced in version 2.4.4.)

For the **Virtual Address Pool** you may optionally enter the IPv4 address and subnet bits associated with this identifier. If this is unset, it will use the value from the **VPN** → **IPsec** → **Mobile Clients** configuration (Section 30.4).

You may also optionally enter an IPv4 address for the available DNS resolver in the **DNS Server** field. Again if this is not set, it will use the **Mobile Clients** DNS setting.

Click the **Save** button to store these settings. When prompted, click the **Apply Changes** button to activate it.

30.6   IPsec Advanced Settings

The **VPN** → **IPsec** → **Advanced Settings** page may be used to customize your IPsec system. This includes configurations for logging and various IPsec behaviors. See Section 30.3.1 for the advanced settings for logging controls.

Only one IPsec client with an identical certificate or username and password can connect at a time. This can be changed with the **Configure Unique IDs as** drop-down menu. Its choices are: *YES* (the default) means that any new client with the same identity will replace any existing connection; *NO* means it will replace an existing client if it asserts it is the only currently active identify; *NEVER* means multiple clients can connect using the same username and password or certificate; and *KEEP* means that any new client with same identity will be rejected and the old one will be kept.

If the **Enable IP Compression** checkbox is checked, it will propose the *IPComp* IP Payload Compression Protocol and accept its use to reduce the amount of sent data. If unchecked (the default), it will prevent the IPsec service from using compression.

The IPsec key daemon `charon` listens on all network interfaces. The **Enable strict interface binding** checkbox is used to specifically define it to only use the VPN interfaces (and to ignore any other network interfaces). This feature may not work with interfaces with dynamic IP addresses.

The **Accept unencrypted ID and HASH payloads in IKEv1 Main Mode** checkbox may be used to tell the key daemon to accept unencrypted data, such as for some SonicWall boxes. It is recommended that this stay unchecked since an attacker may brute force the Pre-Shared Key based on sniffed data.

The **Enable MSS clamping on VPN traffic** checkbox allows you to set the Maximum Segment Size for TCP sessions. This may be used to workaround problems with PMTU Discovery for IPsec. The **Maximum MSS** field may be used to enter a number within 576 and 65535. It defaults to 1400. (Regular, non-IPsec network interfaces can also have MSS clamping as defined in an interface's general configuration; see Section 13.2.1.)

The **Enable Unity Plugin** checkbox is used to provide some support for the IKEv1 Cisco Unity Extensions. This provides split tunneling for supported clients. Note that Cisco Unity has been officially unsupported by Cisco since early 2015.

The **Enable strict Certificate Revocation List checking** checkbox means that a peer's certificate will not be accepted if this pfSense system doesn't know the CRL. This is disabled (unchecked) by default.

Overlapping Security Associations can be handled with the **Initiate IKEv2 reauthentication with a make-before-break** checkbox. This can help with avoiding connectivity drops when reauthenticating.

The **Enable bypass for LAN interface IP** checkbox is used to prevent any security authentication or IPsec processing with peers on the LAN. This is enabled by default.

The **Asynchronous Cryptography** checkbox may be used to speed up cryptographic work by doing the operations on different processors or threads. Note that on a heavy use system this may cause a performance decrease. (This option was introduced in pfSense 2.4.4.)

Click the **Save** button to reconfigure your IPsec service with your customizations.

30.7 IPsec Tunnels Phase 1

As explained previously, the Phase 1 is for the secure encrypted channel setup with the peer by exchanging credentials, identifying each other, negotiating modes, and agreeing on parameters. Instead of using local and right terminology, this implementation uses *left* and *right* terms. But commonly left is for your local side and right for remote end.

This initial setup is done via the **Add P1** button at the bottom of the **VPN** → **IPsec** → **Tunnels** page or modifying an existing Phase 1 by clicking the **Edit phase1 entry** pencil icon action. This will take you to this **VPN** → **IPsec** → **Tunnels** → **Edit Phase 1** page.

Note
The form for Mobile Clients support has slightly different features and defaults. When creating (or editing) a Phase 1 for Mobile Clients, this page will be titled **VPN** → **IPsec** → **Mobile Clients** → **Edit Phase 1**.

Depending on some settings below, you may have some additional required settings For example, if using the *Mutual PSK + Xauth* authentication method a Pre-Shared Key is also required. A remote gateway must be defined when using *Mutual RSA* or *Mutual PSK*. Or if using *Mutual RSA* or *Mutual RSA + Xauth* a Certificate Authority and certificate are both required. These are all explained below.

30.7.1 General Information (IPsec Tunnel Phase 1)

Click the **Disabled** checkbox if you don't want to currently use this Phase 1 configuration. This may be useful for testing.

The **Key Exchange version** drop-down is for selecting the protocol used for initializing the connection. It defaults to IKEv1 for support with older IPsec implementations. The other choices are IKEv2 or Auto. The Auto option will use IKEv2 as an initiator and as a responder can accept IKEv1 or IKEv2.

The protocol defaults to IPv4. It must match with the address used for the following **Remote Gateway** address and also must match with the Phase 2 tunnel. To change it to IPv6 use the **Internet Protocol** menu.

The default interface for the local Phase 1 endpoint is the WAN. Use the **Interface** menu to select a different endpoint interface such as LAN. A Gateway Group (identified with "GW Group") may also be selected if previously defined via the **System** → **Routing** → **Gateway Groups** subpage (Chapter 15).

The other endpoint of the connection is entered as a hostname or IP address in the **Remote Gateway** field. This field is required for setting up a non-Mobile Clients tunnel. This is not available when editing a Mobile Clients Phase 1 configuration. This address must be the same protocol as selected previously. Note that this needs to be unique — don't use the same remote gateway for another Phase 1 configuration.

Enter some keyword or identifier in the **Description** field to help explain its purpose in the table of Phase 1 configurations.

30.7.2   Phase 1 Proposal (Authentication)

The method of authentication must match the remote end. By default, it uses a non-mobile pre-shared key which is often considered the quickest and easiest configuration. To select a different method use the **Authentication Method** menu. The standard choices are *Mutual RSA* and *Mutual PSK* (the default). The Mobile Clients setup also has additional choices: *Hybrid RSA + Xauth*, *Mutual RSA + Xauth*, *Mutual PSK + Xauth*, *EAP-TLS*, *EAP-RADIUS*, and *EAP-MSChapv2*. (The EAP options are only allowed for the IKEv2 Key Exchange version as selected previously.)

When using the IKEv1 or the *Auto* key exchange version, you will have a **Negotiation mode** selection menu. The choices are *Main* which uses multiple encrypted exchanges and *Aggressive* which uses a single Phase 1 message and the authentication is not encrypted. The aggressive mode is commonly used for remote VPNs. It is the default when configuring for mobile clients.

The **My identifier** drop-down menu is used to select how your local side of the IPsec is defined for authentication. The choices include: *My IP address* (the default), *IP address*, *Distinguished name*, *User distinguished name*, *ASN.1 distinguished Name*, *KeyID tag*, and *Dynamic DNS*. Depending on your selection, you may have a corresponding input field that is required to provide details. The distinguished name fields use a fully-qualified domain name. The *User* distinguished name also has the user name with at-sign, like "user@my.domain.com".

Similar to the previous setting, the **Peer Identifier** drop-down menu allows how the peer is defined. The choices include: *Any*, *Peer IP address*, *IP address*, *Distinguished name*, *User distinguished name*, *ASN.1 distinguished Name*, and *KeyID tag*. Again, depending on its selection, you may have a corresponding field which requires input.

When the **Authentication Method** is set to *Mutual PSK*, you will have a required **Pre-Shared Key** text input field. Enter a string that matches for both sides of the IPsec tunnel configuration. You can use the **Generate new Pre-Shared Key** button (since pfSense 2.4.4) to have it create and insert a random 56-character string into this field.

When using the *Mutual RSA* method of authentication, you will have drop-down menus for **My Certificate** and **Peer Certificate Authority**. (These options are not listed when using the pre-shared key mode.) Choose the certificate that was already setup in the **My Certificate** menu. Then choose the CA which was also already setup in the **Peer Certificate Authority** menu. The CA is only used with a EAP-TLS, Mutual RSA + Xauth, or Mutual RSA authentication mode. For more details about adding and managing certificates in pfSense, see Chapter 12.

30.7.3 Phase 1 Proposal (Algorithms)

The IPsec service will restrict the connection to a specific cipher suite, identified with an encryption algorithm, integrity algorithm, and the Diffie-Hellman key group as set in the next three options. These must be the same settings as used on the remote end.

The default encryption algorithm is 256-bit AES-CBC as identified as *AES* and *256* in the two fields. Use the **Encryption Algorithm** selector to alternatively select *AES128-GCM*, *AES192-GCM*, *Blowfish*, *3DES*, and *CAST128*. Some of the available choices have a corresponding drop-down menu for the bits size. A common setting is *AES* and *128* for 128 bit AES-CBC. Note that the Blowfish and 3DES encryption algorithms have been shown that they could be exploited.

The **Hash Algorithm** is used to set the Message Authentication Code (MAC). It defaults to HMAC SHA1, but commonly SHA256 is used. The other options are MD5 (which is considered a less secure algorithm), SHA384, SHA512, and AES-XCBC.

The Diffie-Hellman method is used for securely sharing the encryption key. It uses a pre-defined group of prime numbers. The **DH Group** drop-down menu is used to select this. It defaults to the *2 (1024 bit)* regular group. It provides several choices including Modulo Prime Groups with Prime Order Subgroup (*sub*), NIST Elliptic Curve Groups, and Brainpool Elliptic Curve Groups. This must be the same as on the remote side. Common settings include *15 (3072 bit)*, *14 (2048 bit)*, and *5 (1536 bit)* regular groups.

The Security Associations (SA) between the peers will expire by default at 28800 seconds (or 8 hours). Then it will renegotiate its channel. To change this, enter an integer number for the seconds in the **Lifetime (Seconds)** number field. 10800 seconds (3 hours) and 86400 seconds (one day) are common settings. Note that this should be longer than the Phase 2 lifetime set later.

30.7.4 Advanced Options (IPsec Tunnel Phase 1)

By default, the IPsec connection will renegotiate prior to expiring. Check the **Disable rekey** checkbox to not request this renegotiation. Note that this needs to be disabled on both ends to be effective.

When an IKE SA is rekeyed, the peer is also reauthenticated. IKEv2 can be configured to not uninstall the IPsec Security Associations by checking the **Disable Reauth** checkbox. (This setting is only available when IKEv2 is selected for the key exchange protocol.)

By default, it will make sure that the tunnel is up when it sees related traffic. Check the **Responder Only** checkbox to only start connections manually — it will listen and wait for the remote end to initiate a connection.

Some NAT firewalls or internal networks may not route IPsec packets. The service will attempt to detect NAT and workaround this by encapsulating the packets in UDP. If NAT is not detected, but the packets are restricted (such as in the Amazon cloud), you can always use the UDP encapsulation by changing the **NAT Traversal** form from *Auto* (the default) to *Force*. (This setting is only available for IKEv1.)

The IKEv2 Mobility and Multihoming Protocol, also known as MOBIKE, allows changing IP addresses or moving traffic to a different interface while keeping the VPN connection active. This feature is off by default and can be enabled when using IKEv2 by selecting *Enable* in the **MOBIKE** menu.

The **Split connections** checkbox is used to create separate tunnel configurations which may be needed if an endpoint doesn't support multiple selectors. This setting is only available for IKEv2 (and not auto).

Phase 2 rekeying may cause tunnels to be destroyed if the remote IPsec peer is not online. Dead Peer Detection (DPD) is used to periodically check for communication with the peers. When enabled (the default), all connections are restarted if no activity is detected. If you do not want it to probe with the DPD messages, uncheck the **Enable DPD** checkbox and the following corresponding fields will disappear. The **Delay** number field is used to set the seconds to periodically check (when no other traffic is being sent). This defaults to 10 seconds. The **Max failures** number field is used to define a timeout for when connections are deleted for being inactive (the periodic check fails multiple times). This defaults to 5.

Press the **Save** button when finished. This will take you back to the **VPN → IPsec → Tunnels** table view. Note that the new configuration is not in place, so click the **Apply Changes** button as prompted.

30.8   IPsec Phase 2 Configuration

An IPsec *tunnel* encapsulates the original packet with another IP header. The setup of the tunnel by establishing the security associations by deriving keys and regularly rekeying for exchanging IPsec traffic is done in Phase 2.

A *transport* mode for IPsec does not encrypt the IP header of the original packet, but the payload (packet content) is encrypted. The transport mode is usually used in combination with another protocol like GRE or L2TP to tunnel the packets.

This tunnel or transport configuration is available after a Phase 1 is setup via the **VPN → IPsec** page (covered in Section 30.1). Phase 1 entries will have a **Show Phase 2 Entries** which when clicked will expand to list them if available (with corresponding actions) and show a **Add P2** button. Editing an existing entry or copying or adding a new one will take you to the **VPN** → **IPsec** → **Tunnels** → **Edit Phase 2** page. (If the Phase 1 is a Mobile Client, it will indicate that instead.)

The form has several fields. For a tunnel, it is required to provide the remote network address. Note you can only have one Phase 2 configuration with the same combined local and remote network setup. For the Mobile Clients Phase 2 configuration, a local network address is required and you can only define the same local network once for a mobile client.

30.8.1 General Information (IPsec Phase 2)

Click the **Disabled** checkbox to keep this Phase 2 configuration but to not use it.

The **Mode** drop-down menu is used to choose the type of connection. It defaults to *Tunnel IPv4* for a subnet-to-subnet tunnel, host-to-subnet tunnel, or host-to-host tunnel over IPv4. You can alternatively choose *Tunnel IPv6* for IPv6, *Transport* (original IP headers) mode for host-to-host transport mode, or *Routed (VTI)* for route-based VPNs which can tunnel IPv4 over IPv6 and vice versa.

Note that you cannot disable this Phase 2 configuration nor change its mode from *Routed (VTI)* if an IPsec virtual tunneling interface is assigned. (See Section 13.1.2.)

If you choose *Transport*, the following network and address fields are not available. To be used, the Transport mode needs to be enabled on both hosts.

The *Routed (VTI)* mode uses the IPsec virtual tunneling interface. You cannot use this mode with Mobile IPsec. This support was introduced in pfSense version 2.4.4. When this Phase 2 mode is saved, a new available network port will be seen at the **Interfaces** → **Interface Assignments** page. This means you can create a pfSense network interface for this IPsec VTI interface. It can have routing table entries and you can use the interface in various places in pfSense as if it was a normal interface, but used as an IPsec tunnel. To assign it, click the corresponding **Add** button on the **Interfaces** → **Interface Assignments** page as discussed in Section 13.1. Once it is assigned as a network interface, you cannot disable nor delete this IPsec Phase 2 Routed VTI configuration until that network assignment is removed. (Also via the same **Interface Assignments** page.)

The **Local Network** fields are used to select the local side of the IPsec VPN. If you have a LAN interface enabled, the default type is *LAN subnet*. The other choices are *Address*, *Network*, and subnets for your other interfaces (like WAN and WIFI). If you select *Address*, then enter the IP address. If you select *Network*, enter the network address and the network (which defaults to /24).

If you need network address translation, specify the address or network to be translated in the **NAT/BI-NAT translation** fields. Like the previous configuration, it also has choices for your interface subnets, *Address*, or *Network* which is used with a PF firewall translation rule to replace the source address for IPsec packets between the local and remote network. It defaults to *None* for no PF rule. (This field is not available for the *Transport* or *Routed (VTI)* modes.)

If this is a Mobile Client Phase 2 configuration or if using the *Routed (VTI)* mode, you will have fields for the **Remote Network**. This is the remote side of the IPsec VPN. It defaults to the *Network* type. You may choose *Address* instead. (The *Routed (VTI)* mode requires a remote address.) Fill out the corresponding address field(s) for this.

Optionally enter an explanation for this Phase 2 configuration in the **Description** text field.

30.8.2   Phase 2 Proposal (SA/Key Exchange)

The **Protocol** menu allows selecting *ESP* (Encapsulating Security Payload) for encryption for data confidentiality; or *AH* (Authentication Header) for authentication and data integrity. ESP is the default.

The **Encryption Algorithms** checkboxes and corresponding bits size drop-down menus are used to select the ESP encryption algorithm and its key length. These options are only available when the **Protocol** is set to *ESP*. The default is AES with the key length default of **Auto**. Blowfish is fast for software-based encryption. 3DES is recommended for when using a crypto accelerator hardware or for compatibility. The other choices are AES128-GCM, AES192-GCM, AES256-GCM, and CAST128. Multiple algorithms may be used and at least one is required. The key length choices depend on the algorithm and may range from 64 bits to 256 bits, for example.

The **Hash Algorithms** checkboxes are used for the integrity algorithm for the ESP or AH connection. The choices include AES-XCBC, MD5, SHA1 (the default), SHA256, SHA384, and SHA512. Multiple algorithms may be selected. At least one is required. SHA1 and SHA256 are common choices.

The **PFS key group** drop-down menu is used to optionally select a Diffie-Hellman group for the connection's ESP encryption/authentication algorithm's perfect forward secrecy. It defaults to *off* (and is not used). The choices are: Regular Diffie-Hellman groups: 1 (768 bit), 2 (1024 bit), 5 (1536 bit), 14 (2048 bit), 15 (3072 bit), 16 (4096 bit), 17 (6144 bit), and 18 (8192 bit); NIST Elliptic Curve Groups: 19 (nist ecp256), 20 (nist ecp384), and 21 (nist ecp521); Modulo Prime Groups with Prime Order Subgroup: 22 (1024(sub 160) bit), 23 (2048(sub 224) bit), and 24 (2048(sub 256) bit); and Brainpool Elliptic Curve Groups: 28 (brainpool ecp256), 29 (brainpool ecp384), and 30 (brainpool ecp512). (Note that the 1, 2, 5, 22, 23, and 24 choices are considered weak and not recommended.)

Enter the number of seconds the connection should last in the **Lifetime** field. It defaults to 3600 seconds (one hour). The maximum is 86400 seconds (one day). (Note that the IKE Phase 1 lifetime should be greater than this field.)

30.8.3   Advanced Configuration (IPsec Phase 2)

If you need keep-alive traffic to keep a tunnel active and open, you can try the **Automatically ping host** feature. In the field, enter a destination IP address within the target IPsec network. It will ping every four minutes from each of your local interface's IPs.

Press the **Save** button when finished. This will take you back to the main IPsec page. If prompted, click the **Apply Changes** button to restart the IPsec service with the new settings. When the Phase 2 negotiation is finished, the IPsec connection should be ready to use. To see the new (or changed) Phase 2 entry, click the corresponding **Show Phase 2 Entries** button.

31 Point-to-Point Protocol over Ethernet (PPPoE)

Some ISPs may manage their customers' Internet access using Point-to-Point Protocol over Ethernet (PPPoE) because it is similar to using standard PPP with the convenience of Ethernet. This network protocol is commonly used with DSL service with the support included in the DSL-provided modem or router.

pfSense can be used to offer your own PPPoE service. The implementation in pfSense is powered by *mpd* which is used to help remote peers discover Ethernet addresses. It will not initiate any PPPoE connections. When enabled, it accepts incoming PPPoE connections for any ISP name or quality service tag.

pfSense can also be used as a PPPoE client. This may have been setup during the initial configuration using the setup wizard (as discussed in Chapter 3). It can also be setup via the **PPPs** page via **Interfaces** → **Assignments** menu as explained in Section 24.2.

31.1 PPPoE Server Configuration

The PPPoE configuration is accessed via the **Services** → **PPPoE Server** menu item. When configured, the table columns show the interface the PPPoE connections will be handled on, the local IP address that the PPPoE clients will use as their gateway, the max allowed simultaneous PPPoE users, and an optional description.

Note that this *local* IP address is not configured on your interface, even though it does represent your pfSense server.

The entries have corresponding actions to modify or remove a PPPoE configuration. Use the **Edit PPPoE instance** pencil icon to make changes. Click the **Delete PPPoE instance** trash can icon to remove it. (Be sure to use the **Apply Changes** button to activate any changes.)

The **Related log entries** shortcut icon will take you to the **Status** → **System Logs** → VPN → PPPoE **Logins** page as introduced in Section 31.2. Follow the **PPPoE Service** link there to see debugging details for the server.

To enable the PPPoE service, click the **Add** button. This will bring up a new page (covered in the following section) to configure it. Click the checkbox for **Enable PPPoE Server** to start enabling it.

31.1.1   Add or Edit PPPoE Server

When the **Enable** checkbox is selected, a form will be available to configure the PPPoE service. It has many options, but only the **Server Address, Remote Address Range**, and **Subnet mask** fields are required.

First select the Ethernet interface to use in the **Interface** drop-down menu. Note that the normal use of the interface is not affected by PPPoE.

When not using a RADIUS authentication backend to provide an IP address, a dynamic IP address can be provided from an address pool (which starts with the address assigned in the upcoming **Remote Address Range** field). By default, only one address is available in the pool — so only one user may connect using PPPoE at a time. To increase the address range and allow more simultaneous users, change the **Total User Count** drop down to choose up to 255 addresses.

By default, a user can only have one login at the same time. To allow the same username to have multiple concurrent logins, choose up to 255 in the **User Max Logins** drop-down menu.

Enter an unused IP address for this pfSense local end of the PPPoE link in the **Server Address** field. This will be provided to the clients to use as the gateway. Commonly this is an IP near the client range as set in the following setting. (pfSense will not allow you to use the local interface's assigned IP address nor allow it to be within the remote subnet defined via the upcoming **Subnet mask** field.)

When not using **RADIUS Issued IP Addresses**, the remote (client) end of the link is assigned an address from a pool. Set the first IP address in the pool in the **Remote Address Range** field. (Also see the earlier **Total User Count** selection to increase the pool size.)

Select the **Subnet mask** number (from 0 to 32) for the client IP addresses. (For example, 25 is a netmask of 255.255.255.128.) Do not leave it at its default of 0 which implies and will replace the **Remote Address Range** with 0.0.0.0 which may cause any specified server address to fail because it will be in that remote subnet. (This is not used by the remote end of the link, but by pfSense to configure its firewall.)

Enter an optional summary or identification of this PPPoE configuration in the **Description** text field. This will displayed in the list of PPPoE services on the **Services → PPPoE Server** page.

The remote PPPoE peer can request DNS server information to do DNS lookups on its behalf. By default, if you are running a local DNS resolver or forwarder (as described in Chapter 21), your local LAN IP address is provided to use it for DNS. The pfSense system's first configured remote DNS server is also provided (if set). (See Section 5.1.2 for details.) To optionally provide different DNS services for the PPPoE clients to use, provide one or two valid DNS server IP addresses in the **DNS Servers** fields.

By default, the PPPoE service will use the local user database for authentication. To use RADIUS instead, select the **Use RADIUS Authentication** checkbox and fill out the related following settings. At the minimum, the RADIUS server address and shared secret is required. The RADIUS settings in this form are only available when this is checked.

If you want to enable per link accounting via RADIUS, check the **Use RADIUS Accounting** checkbox.

If you have a secondary RADIUS server, click the **Use a Backup RADIUS Authentication Server** checkbox. This will allow entering the secondary server's details below.

Normally, RADIUS servers uses the source IP address to track RADIUS requests and for accounting. You can enter an arbitrary IP address in the **NAS IP Address** field, if you want to use the same address for multiple pfSense systems connecting to the same RADIUS service. (This sets the RADIUS attribute 4, *NAS-IP-Address*.)

The **RADIUS Accounting Update** field is used to set periodic accounting updates in seconds.

To have your RADIUS server provide the IP addresses to be used for the remote links, check the **RADIUS Issued IP Addresses** checkbox. (The IP address then comes from the RADIUS *Framed-Pool* attribute.)

When using RADIUS, enter the required IP address for the **Primary RADIUS Server**. Additional fields may be used to enter custom authentication port and accounting port numbers (instead of the standard 1812 and 1813 port numbers).

Then enter its required **Primary RADIUS Server Shared Secret** in the passphrase field. Enter it twice (in a second field) to confirm you entered it correctly.

To configure a backup RADIUS server, also enter its details in the **Secondary RADIUS Server** and **Secondary RADIUS Server Shared Secret** fields. (These are only available if the earlier **Use a Backup RADIUS Authentication Server** checkbox is enabled.)

The **User table** is used to setup local authentication (versus using RADIUS). Enter the login username and its required password in the fields. To restrict or assign the IP address for a PPPoE user, set it in the optional IP address field. (This will be within the range specified earlier.)

To add a second or more users, click the **Add user** button. If you have more than one user, there will be a corresponding **Delete** button to remove the user entry.

Click the **Save** button when finished with the settings. This will take you back to the table view which will list your configuration. To tell the `mpd` server to use your new configuration, click the **Apply Changes** button.

You may need to adjust your PF packet filter rules to allow traffic for your PPPoE clients.

31.2 PPPoE Logins Log Entries

The PPPoE logins and logouts can be seen on the **Status → System Logs → VPN → PPPoE Logins** page. Each entry will show the remote IP address and the authentication login name (the *User*),

This log output may be searched using the **Log filter** shortcut as covered in Section 11.1. This advanced log filter provides fields to search by Action (either "login" or "logout"), User, and IP Address.

The log output may also be adjusted using the **Manage log** shortcut as explained in Section 11.3.

31.3   PPPoE Service Log Entries

The *mpd* Multilink PPP daemon's logs for PPPoE are available via the **Status** → **System Logs** → **VPN** → **PPPoE Service** page. These are mostly low-level diagnostic or debugging details. It may be used for troubleshooting login issues, such as by searching for "AUTH: User." For details on using the advanced log filter or to override the general logging options for these PPPoE Service logs, see Section 11.1 and Section 11.3, respectively.

Note if your pfSense system is acting as a PPP client, those logs will be available at the **Status** → **System Logs** → **PPP** page as covered in Section 24.2.2.

32 L2TP Service

The Layer 2 Tunneling Protocol, or L2TP, is an extended point-to-point protocol that uses UDP. It does not provide any encryption or confidentiality. To configure pfSense as an L2TP client, see Section 24.2. This chapter covers setting up an L2TP server.

To setup pfSense as an L2TP server, follow the **VPN** → **L2TP** menu link.

32.1 L2TP Configuration

Click the **Enable L2TP** checkbox on the **VPN** → **L2TP** page to access its configuration. The L2TP **Server address** and **Remote address range** fields are required.

The **Interface** drop-down is used to select the local network it should be on. This will set the local IP address for this server-side L2TP connection.

In the **Server address** field enter the local IP address that will be negotiated at the pfSense end of the link. This IP address can not match the LAN interface address nor any other address currently used on the pfSense system. In addition it can not be within the remote subnet as defined in the following configuration.

The **Remote address range** field is used to define the remote IP addresses that can be negotiated for an L2TP link. Enter a starting address. Use the drop-down to the right of it if you want to define the subnet for it. (Note it may modify your entered address to match those bits.)

By default, it will setup a configuration for a single L2TP link. You may configure up to 255 by using the **Number of L2TP users** selection.

The **Secret** password field is used to authenticate tunnel connections and encrypt important control packets. Enter it twice to confirm you typed it in correctly as it is not visible. The same secret is used for all L2TP links. While this setting is optional, a pre-configured shared secret may be required by some clients. Note that some clients do not support tunnel authentication. See further on to learn about per-user authentication.

The **Authentication type** drop-down menu is used to configure how the authentication is done. It defaults to CHAP which implies the client can request Microsoft CHAP Version 2 or traditional

CHAP MD5 style authentication. The other selections are MS-CHAPv2 for just the Microsoft CHAP Version 2 authentication and PAP where the password crosses the link in plaintext.

Some clients request the DNS server details. Leave it blank to use the DNS server(s) as already offered by pfSense's LAN. For your own settings, define the valid IP address for a DNS server usable by the VPN client in the **Primary L2TP DNS server** field. You can use 0.0.0.0 as the address to erase this configuration from the L2TP server. The **Secondary L2TP DNS server** is for an optional second DNS server.

The L2TP service can support per-user authentication using an integrated user database as covered in the following Section 32.2. To use RADIUS instead of a local user database, click the checkbox to **Use a RADIUS server for authentication**. This will open up a few more options for the RADIUS client setup. When using RADIUS, the server address and shared secret are required.

If you want to use per-link session accounting, click the **Enable RADIUS accounting** checkbox.

Enter the IP address of the RADIUS server for the clients to authenticate against in the **Server** field. (Note that it will use the standard ports for authentication and, if used, accounting.)

Enter the shared secret for using the RADIUS server in the **Secret** field. Enter it twice to make sure you typed it correctly. This is not the secret for using L2TP but for the L2TP service to use RADIUS.

To use RADIUS-issued IPs for the peers instead of using the configured **Remote address range** setting above, click the **Issue IP Addresses via RADIUS server** checkbox.

Click the **Save** button at the bottom to start the L2TP service or to reconfigure it.

Note
You may need to adjust your firewall rules to allow L2TP client traffic.

32.2 L2TP Users

If you want to use per-user authentication for setting up L2TP tunnels instead of (or in addition to) RADIUS, click the **Users** link near the top of the webpage. The main view is to show a table of the L2TP users. For each user, it will show the optional IP address for negotiating IP addresses for a peer. It will display "Dynamic" for users without an IP address restriction. It will also provide pencil and trash can action icons to edit and delete a user entry.

Click the **Add** button to add a new L2TP user. This will take you to a new page to enter a **Username** and **Password**. You may optionally enter an **IP Address** to restrict the IP address that pfSense will let them have. (This pfSense implementation doesn't allow using an address range.) Then click the **Save** button to add the user. You will then be taken back to the table list of L2TP users. That page for adding users is the same used for editing users.

When removing a user with the **Delete user** trash can icon, you will receive a warning that all current L2TP VPN sessions will be terminated. To proceed, press the **Apply Changes** button.

32.3 L2TP Logins Logging

The shortcut icon for **Related log entries** will take you to the **Status** → **System Logs** → **VPN** page to view the L2TP logs. Click on either the **L2TP Logins** link to view the last L2TP logins and logouts log entries or the **L2TP Service** link for the last *mpd* Multilink PPP daemon debugging entries.

The Logins list shows the time of the L2TP server logins and logouts (the *Action*), the User (authentication login name), and the remote IP address. You may search by the Action (either "login" or "logout"), User, or IP Address via the **Log filter** shortcut as seen in Section 11.1.

32.4 L2TP Service Log Entries

The **Status** → **System Logs** → **VPN** → **L2TP Service** page has the L2TP-related low-level diagnostic logs from the *mpd* Multilink PPP daemon. It may be used for debugging your L2TP service, such as what address(es) it is listening on and where it is receiving L2TP packets from,

On these log pages, the **Manage log** shortcut may be used to override the general logging options (Section 11.3).

33 OpenVPN

OpenVPN is flexible VPN technology that uses SSL/TLS. It can authenticate using various methods and can allow multiple clients to connect to a single OpenVPN server. Third-party apps or clients are available for many devices and operating systems for connecting to the pfSense system through the OpenVPN tunnel. In addition, the pfSense system can also be configured as an OpenVPN client connecting to a remote OpenVPN server and can be configured so all traffic routes through that tunnel.

33.1 OpenVPN Server

The main feature page from the menu is **VPN** → **OpenVPN** → **Servers**. Near the top there are also links for **Clients** (see Section 33.2), **Client Specific Overrides** for the server (see Section 33.1.3), and **Wizards** (see Section 33.1.2). This webpage provides a table of the configured OpenVPN servers, listing them by their protocol and port number; the tunnel network; crypto (cipher, authentication algorithm, Diffie-Hellman (DH) parameter size); and description. If a configuration is disabled, the entry will be displayed in a light opacity.

The entries also have corresponding action icons to edit and to delete the server. Clicking the pencil graphic will take you to the edit mode as covered in Section 33.1.1. Removing an OpenVPN server configuration can be done by clicking the trash can graphic.

You can add a server via the **Add** button (see Section 33.1.1). You can also use a wizard to help walk through the common setup of an OpenVPN Remote Access Server.

33.1.1 Add or Edit OpenVPN Servers

The **VPN** → **OpenVPN** → **Servers** → **Edit** page is for adding a new OpenVPN server or client setup or for editing an existing configuration. The Edit mode is accessed via the pencil icon **Edit** action in the Servers list. The following introduces all the many options on the webpage. (Some of these options are also discussed in the upcoming Section 33.2.1 for a client configuration.)

General Information (OpenVPN Server)

You can disable this OpenVPN service by checking the **Disable this server** checkbox. (The configuration will still exist.)

OpenVPN offers two types of encryption for its multiple server modes: Public Key Infrastructure (PKI) using certificates or static encryption using a shared key. Using PKI with Transport Layer Security (TLS) is the most common and complex way and a certificate authority and certificate are required for using this. Using static encryption is simple, but if the shared key is accessed, all current and past tunnel traffic using that key may be decrypted.

Select the mode of operation in the **Server mode** drop-down menu. The choices are:

Peer to Peer (SSL/TLS)

> This is a simple one-server/one-client VPN that uses TLS. For a similar setup but supporting more clients, use the *Remote Access (SSL/TLS)* server mode.

Peer to Peer (Shared Key)

> This one-client/one-server non-TLS configuration is the simplest setup and uses a static key. No PKI is used, so the key must be exist on both VPN peers.

Remote Access (SSL/TLS)

> This is simple TLS mode that supports multiple clients.

Remote Access (User Auth)

> This OpenVPN TLS server requires the clients to provide a username and password instead of certificate for authentication. (Choosing a backend for authentication will be offered.)

Remote Access (SSL/TLS + User Auth)

> This TLS-based OpenVPN server requires a username and password in addition to a client certificate for each authenticating client. (Choosing a backend for authentication will be offered.)

Note that based on the mode selected, the following configurations may not appear as they are not needed for some modes; for example the peer-to-peer modes do not provide the inter-client communication feature nor multiple Advanced Client Settings.

When using a Remote Access with *User Auth* server mode, you will have a **Backend for authentication** drop-down menu. This will list previously-defined authentication servers, such as RADIUS, LDAP, or Local Database as setup at the **System → User Manager → Authentication Servers** page. as described in Section 6.6. If not selected, the first choice will be used.

The **Diagnostics → Authentication** page (see Section 6.8) may be used to test this authentication using a username and password.

UDP is the preferred protocol. But if that is not reliable, you may select TCP in the **Protocol** menu. Also use this drop-down if you are using IPv6 for UDP or TCP.

OpenVPN uses pseudo devices of `tun` which is an OSI Layer 3 software-based IPv4/IPv6 network tunneling interface or `tap` which is an OSI Layer 2 virtual Ethernet NIC. In other words, `tun` passes only IP traffic and is low-overhead; and `tap` transports Ethernet frames instead, including broadcast traffic. This device type must be the same for the clients. The default is `tun`. Use the **Device mode** menu to select `tun` or `tap`. (Note that when using the tap device mode with a server mode, you will have options for server bridge as covered in the following Tunnel Settings section.)

Select the **Interface** name in the drop-down list for where you want pfSense to listen for connections. Normally this is the WAN. This also had selections of Localhost to be limited to local system and *any* to listen on all your networks. A Gateway Group (identified with "GW Group") may also be selected if previously defined via the **System** → **Routing** → **Gateway Groups** subpage (as discussed in Chapter 15).

The OpenVPN service listens on UDP port 1194 by default. An alternative port can be entered in the **Local Port** field. Use a number between 1 to 65535. If you have multiple different OpenVPN server configurations listening on the same interface, you will need to use different port numbers.

Enter any identification string to use internally in pfSense to describe this service in the **Description** text field, such as "Marysville Tunnel" or "Remote Sales Staff".

Cryptographic Settings (OpenVPN Server)

The Cryptographic Settings is the next section to complete. A public key infrastructure (PKI) is needed for the OpenVPN configuration for using the TLS server modes. This consists of a Certificate Authority (CA) certificate and key which is used to sign certificates for the server and clients; and certificates and private keys for the server and clients.

Note that the following TLS and certificate options are not available for the Peer-to-Peer Shared Key mode.

By default, OpenVPN will provide authentication of TLS packets. (And if using an external TLS Authentication Key, it will check if it is valid.) To turn this off, uncheck the **Use a TLS Key** checkbox. (Older versions had this as the **Enable authentication of TLS packets** checkbox.) (Note this option is not available for the Peer-to-Peer Shared Key mode.)

OpenVPN helps prevent DoS attacks by signing TLS control channel packets. The key used for this will be generated by pfSense. If you want to use your own OpenVPN static key, unselect the **Automatically generate a shared TLS authentication key** checkbox. Then when it is unchecked, a **Key** textbox appears that you may insert your TLS shared key in. Even if you don't have this auto-generate method, you can still just paste in your TLS key. The data will begin and end with "OpenVPN Static key V1" text.

The **TLS Key Usage Mode** drop-down menu defaults to *TLS Authentication* to use TLS for the HMAC authentication. The other choice is *TLS Encryption and Authentication* where the TLS authentication is also encrypted using the key from the static key file.

Select the CA from the **Peer Certificate Authority** drop-down. The CA certificate can be imported or generated using the **System** → **Certificate Manager** → **CAs** → **Edit** page as covered in Section 12.1.1. (The OpenVPN wizard can also be used to create the CA.)

OpenVPN (and pfSense) will also honor a Certificate Revocation List (CRL). This can be managed via the **System** → **Certificate Manager** → **Certificate Revocation** page as explained in Section 12.3. To use a CRL, select it in the **Peer Certificate Revocation list** drop-down menu. This is not required, and commonly no CRLs are defined.

The certificate to be used for the local OpenVPN server is selected in the **Server certificate** drop-down menu. Use a certificate as identified within "Server Certificates" in the available options (as other certificates may not work). The options will indicate if they are *in use*. Be sure to use one that has been signed by the previously defined CA. These certificates can be generated using the **System** → **Certificate Manager** → **Certificates** page as covered in Section 12.2. (The OpenVPN wizard can also be used to create the certificate.)

Diffie-Hellman (DH) key exchange is used to share a secret between two parties. DH Parameters are used during the connection setup. pfSense ships with some pre-generated DH parameters files (note these are not keys). The default 2048 is commonly recommended. Use the **DH Parameter length (bits)** form to select a different bit size from the 1024 through 15360 bit options. (This will use a pregenerated DH PARAMETERS file. Older versions of pfSense won't have all these choices.)

By default, the Elliptic Curve algorithm for the Diffie Hellman key exchange will use the same curve algorithm used for the server certificate. If this is not autodetected, then it will use the crypto libraries default or fall back to the *secp384r1* curve (NIST/SECG curve over a 384-bit prime field). To choose a specific curve, select it from the long **ECDH Curve** drop-down menu. The choices range from *brainpoolP160r1* through *wap-wsg-idm-ecid-wtls9*.

The Peer to Peer Shared Key mode uses a pre-shared secret file. pfSense will generate this for you. But if you want to use an existing OpenVPN Static key (V1), uncheck the **Automatically generate a shared key** checkbox; then a **Shared key** textbox will be available to insert the key.

The **Encryption Algorithm** drop-down menu has around 64 ciphers listed from *AES-128-CBC (128 bit key, 128 bit block)* to *RC5-OFB (128 bit key by default, 64 bit block)*. This includes AES, Camellia, SEED, BF (Blowfish). CAST5, DES, IDEA, RC2, and RC5 ciphers of various sizes and modes. This algorithm is used for encrypting traffic in the tunnel and the setting must match on both endpoints. The recommended default is *AES-256-CBC (256 bit key, 128 bit block)*. (Note that the Blowfish *BF-CBC (128 bit key by default, 64 bit block)* is no longer recommended due to its small blocksize.)

An OpenVPN client can advertise support for Negotiable Crypto Parameters (NCP). This allows a server to still support clients using an old cipher. But can also tell the client to use a defined cipher. For this support, the **Enable NCP** is checked by default. Under the checkbox is a list of available encryption algorithms which may be used to select or deselect (by clicking an entry again) algorithms. The selections are listed in the form on the right. The default only selection is AES-128-GCM. If your client requests a different cipher, you may choose to add it to this **NCP Algorithms** list.

The **Auth digest algorithm** is used to authenticate traffic and this setting also must be the same on both ends. It defaults to *SHA256 (256-bit)*. This drop-down menu has around 27 digest choices ranging from *MD5 (128-bit)* to *whirlpool (512-bit)*. A common recommendation is *SHA512 (512-bit)*.

The **Hardware Crypto** drop-down menu is used to select the desired cryptographic accelerator to use. It will default to *No Hardware Crypto Acceleration* and the other choices depend on the hardware your pfSense system is running on, for example: *RSAX engine support - RSA, BSD cryptodev engine - RSA, DSA, DH, AES-128-CBC, AES-192-CBC, AES-256-CBC*, and *Intel RDRAND engine - RAND*. (For enabling kernel driver support, see Section 5.4.3.)

By default, only connections using a self-sign certificate will be accepted (i.e., it will deny certificates that were made with intermediate CAs that were generated from the same CA as the OpenVPN server). To turn off this check, choose *Do Not Check* from the **Certificate Depth** menu. The verification can be increased to a maximum number of intermediate certificate issuers with the choices of: Two (Client+Intermediate+Server) which means the certificate has to be signed by a CA directly known to the server or self-signed, Three (Client+2xIntermediate+Server), Four (Client+3xIntermediate+Server), and Five (Client+4xIntermediate+Server). The default is One (Client+ Server).

When using *Remote Access (SSL/TLS + User Auth)* server mode, you may require that the client certificate's Common Name (CN) matches the username. To enforce this, select the **Strict User-CN Matching** checkbox. (It is off by default.)

Tunnel Settings (OpenVPN Server)

The required **IPv4 Tunnel Network** field is used to enter the IPv4 addresses using CIDR notation for the OpenVPN virtual network. This is the network space provided to the client. The first usable address in the range will be used for the pfSense server-side of the VPN and the other addresses for the clients. Normally you would use reserved IP address space used for internal use. This should not be an existing network on this server nor on the client (or peer) systems. Note you may have conflicts with local networks that also use internal networks address space, so you may want to use some subnet like in the middle of the large 10.0.0.0/8 netblock, such as 10.66.77.0/24. Also note that when using **Device mode** with default `tun`, the subnet must be /29 (255.255.255.248) or lower (so at least 6 hosts in the network). If using the following Server Bridge setting, you cannot set this IPv4 Tunnel Network.

If using IPv6 instead, the **IPv6 Tunnel Network** field is used to enter the IPv6 addresses using CIDR notation for the OpenVPN virtual network. The ::1 address in the range will be used for the pfSense server-side of the VPN and the other addresses for the clients.

When using **Device mode** with the `tap` option, you will have a few server bridge settings. (These options, even if visible, will be disabled if you are using a peer-to-peer mode.) This is used for bridging the TAP interface with the network interface — note, you must set this up. (See Section 13.5 about creating a bridged interface.) You cannot define the IPv4 Tunnel Network if using these server bridge settings. To enable this feature, select the **Bridge DHCP** checkbox. (It is off by default.) Then set your pre-created **Bridge Interface** in the drop-down menu. You may set it to the *none* option to ignore the following two Server Bridge options.

To allocate IPs to your connecting clients, set aside a pool start and end on the bridged network. Both of the start and end ranges must be set if used (or leave both blank). If left blank, the interface setting above will be ignored and DHCP will be passed through. If using it, enter a valid IPv4 address in both the **Server Bridge DHCP Start** and **Server Bridge DHCP End** fields. (Of course the start must be lower than the end.)

Check the **Redirect Gateway** checkbox to tell the client that all its traffic is to be redirected over the VPN. This option is not available for Peer to Peer Shared Key.

To advertise an IPv4 network that is accessible to remote VPN clients, enter its IPv4 CIDR range in the **IPv4 Local network(s)** field. (This range is then provided to the client for its configuration.) This is normally set to the LAN network. Leave blank if remote machine won't be routing here. You may list multiple values by separating them with commas. Use **IPv6 Local network(s)** to define IPv6 networks accessible from remote clients. These options are not available for the Peer to Peer Shared Key method.

For Peer-to-Peer modes, **IPv4 Remote network(s)** and **IPv6 Remote network(s)** fields may be used to enter network CIDR ranges for real networks that will be routed through the tunnel. This is not the virtual network created by OpenVPN, but an existing network. (This information is provided to the client for its configuration.)

If you want to restrict the maximum number of concurrent clients to this OpenVPN server, set it in the **Concurrent connections** menu.

By default, OpenVPN attempts to optimize sending packets and will periodically check its compression. It will temporarily disable compression if it is not efficient. The **Compression** drop-down menu is used to configure this with the following choices: disable compression, but retain compression packet framing so it could be enabled later; use LZ4, LZ4 V2 format, comp LZO, stub compression, stub compression in V2 format,; disable adaptive compression algorithm; use legacy adaptive LZO, legacy LZO, and don't use legacy LZO. Note that the LZO options are becoming deprecated by OpenVPN. The default is to have compression turned off, but packet framing for compression still enabled so a different compression setting may be used later.

To have the clients know about the same **Compression** setting, select the **Push Compression** checkbox.

To preserve the originating packets ToS (Type-of-Service, like DSCP) bits to the packets sent through the tunnel, check the **Type-of-Service** checkbox. This is not done by default.

When using the Remote Access modes (not Peer-to-Peer), the OpenVPN could handle multiple clients at a single interface. It can internally route traffic from client to client without using the interface for routing when the **Inter-client communication** checkbox is enabled. Do not check this if you need to do packet filtering per specific clients in the tunnel.

Clients using TLS must have a unique Common Name (CN) in their certificates, by default. (If a new client connects with same CN, it will be disconnected.) While it is not recommended, if you need to have multiple client connections using the same CN, set the **Duplicate Connection** checkbox.

By default, the `tun` device mode is capable of forwarding IPv6 traffic. If you don't want to forward IPv6 traffic, check the **Disable IPv6** checkbox. (This option is not available using the `tap` device mode.)

Client Settings (OpenVPN Server)

The server or remote clients on the VPN can change their IP addresses (or ports) and the VPN session will stay open if it passes the authentication. Uncheck the **Dynamic IP** checkbox if you don't want connected clients or the server to keep connected if an IP address changes.

By default, the TLS server (using `tun` mode) will allocate a single IP address in a common subnet per connecting client. Some OpenVPN clients may require a different behavior. For clients using old OpenVPN software, you may change the default *Subnet* in the **Topology** menu to *net30* to allocate a /30 subnet per client.

Advanced Client Settings (OpenVPN Server)

The OpenVPN server can provide various options to clients, including DHCP options for DNS, NTP, WINS, and NetBIOS. These options are not displayed when using the Peer to Peer Shared Key mode.

To have the client append a domain name suffix to short hostnames for DNS lookups, select the **DNS Default Domain** checkbox and enter the domain suffix in the corresponding text field. Note the use of this may vary for different OpenVPN client implementations.

To tell the VPN clients to use your defined DNS server(s), check the **DNS Server enable** checkbox. Then set the IP address for the DNS server in the **DNS Server 1** field. This could be set to the IP address of your pfSense DNS service. Additional DNS server addresses can be assigned in the other three optional **DNS Server** fields.

Some OpenVPN clients will support the **Block Outside DNS** option to restrict access to DNS to the one inside the tunnel. This is used for example for Windows 10 to prevent it from using the wrong DNS server which may disclose network activity outside of the tunnel. Most clients don't have this problem. To enable this, select the checkbox, and the client will be told about this option.

Some Windows clients may not start using the configured DNS servers as assigned via OpenVPN. To tell them to flush their DNS cache and reconfigure their DNS, check the **Force DNS cache update** checkbox.

To tell the VPN client to use your selected Network Time Protocol server, click the **NTP Server enable** checkbox and enter the primary NTP server address into the **NTP Server 1** field, For a secondary NTP server, set it in the **NTP Server 2** field.

To tell the client how to handle NetBIOS over TCP/IP (NetBT), click the **Enable NetBIOS over TCP/IP** checkbox. When this is checked, two options are displayed. The **Node Type** menu is used to select *b-node* to use local network broadcasting, *p-node* for point-to-point mode relying on WINS server, *m-node* for mixed mode to first use broadcast then query name server, and *h-node* for reversed mixed mode to query name server first, then broadcast. Commonly the *p-node* is used with SMB/CIFS. Select *none* to not set the WINS/NBT node type. The **Scope ID** field is used to specify a text string that is the NetBIOS scope ID for the client. This is appended to the NetBIOS name to make a valid DNS name.

To specify IP addresses for Windows Internet Name Service (WINS) (aka NetBIOS name servers or NBNS), check the **WINS server enable** checkbox. When this is checked, new fields are displayed to enter WINS Servers. Enter the IP addresses for the WINS servers in the **WINS Server 1** and **WINS Server 2** text fields. Note that this is not recommended, as it is often easier to use DNS.

(Old versions of pfSense also could use a custom management port for clients; this feature is no longer offered.)

Additional per-client configurations can also be defined to override these server settings or to disable a specific client. For more information, see Section 33.1.3 about the **VPN → OpenVPN → Client Specific Overrides** feature.

Advanced Configuration (OpenVPN Server)

You can enter further OpenVPN configurations in the **Custom options** textbox. Use a semicolon (;) to separate each entry. This could be used to push configuration options to the client also.

An experimental performance feature to optimize TUN or TAP tunnel or UDP for write operations, click the **UDP Fast I/O** checkbox. Note this is not compatible with the client **Limit outgoing bandwidth** (shaper) feature.

To override the operating system's default TCP and UDP send and receive buffer size for OpenVPN, select a choice in the **Send/Receive Buffer** drop-down menu. The choices depend on the system, but commonly range from 64 KB to 2 MB.

When creating gateways for OpenVPN virtual interfaces, the default is for both IPv4 and IPv6 interfaces, but you can also select just IPv4 or IPv6 only with the **Gateway creation** radio buttons.

For debugging and log file verbosity, use the **Verbosity Level** menu. Note that each level includes the details from the lower level too. Set it to 0 to only log about fatal errors. The normal usage range is 1 (the default) to 4. The recommended setting is level 3. Level 5 is for reporting about packet read and write for TCP/UDP and TUN/TAP. Levels 6 through 11 are for extra debugging information. Level 9 will provide tcpdump-style traces. To see the logging, go to the **Status** → **System Logs** → **OpenVPN** page.

Click the **Save** button to make your changes or to add this new OpenVPN configuration. It will take you back to the **VPN** → **OpenVPN** → **Servers** table view.

Note that if there is a misconfiguration, the server may not start. See its status at **Status** → **OpenVPN** (or via the **Related status** shortcut). That page shows the client connections, and offers actions to Restart, Start, or Stop the service(s) as applicable. If the server is not running, it may show *[error]* in the client list and show "Unable to contact daemon" and "Service not running?". Then you can research further in the log entries at the **Status** → **System Logs** → **OpenVPN** page (or via the **Related log** entries shortcut).

33.1.2   OpenVPN Remote Access Server Setup Wizard

The **VPN** → **OpenVPN** → **Wizards** page provides up to twelve steps to help with setting up an OpenVPN Remote Access Server. Note that this wizard lacks several of the options available in the regular server addition mode. To make those further changes after completing with the wizard or further explanations about the following wizard settings, see the previous Section 33.1.1.

First, select your desired authentication backend in the **Type of Server** drop-down. It defaults to the recommended *Local User Access*. The other choices are *LDAP*, the Lightweight Directory Access Protocol, and *RADIUS*. Often offices use features like these that better match their needs for user management. Selecting LDAP or RADIUS will set the type of server to Remote Access (User Auth) server mode where no certificate is used for authentication. Selecting *Local User Access* (which is the same as *Local Database* authentication mode) will set the Remote Access (SSL/TLS + User Auth) server mode. If that default is selected, you can skip the following LDAP and RADIUS details.

Then click the **Next** button to go to the next page of the wizard.

LDAP Server (Wizard)

If you selected LDAP as the server type, the next wizard page will be for selecting or adding an LDAP server to use from the menu. The **System** → **User Manager** → **Authentication Servers** page may be used to view your existing configurations for connecting to LDAP (or RADIUS) servers. This is covered in Section 6.6.

Or you may click the **Add new LDAP server** button to use this wizard to configure a new LDAP client for user authentication.

Add LDAP Server (Wizard)

If you selected LDAP as the server type and chose to add a new LDAP server or if you don't have any existing LDAP server configuration, the wizard will have several options for configuring the LDAP Authentication Server Parameters. (Note that older versions of pfSense don't have all the configurations available via this wizard.) More information about these settings may be read in Section 6.6.1.

Note

This wizard page does not configure the startup of an LDAP server, but is for using an external LDAP service. pfSense does not have a pre-packaged solution for an LDAP server daemon.

Enter a descriptive name in the **Name** text field for easy identification use in your system administration. Note that this name must match the hostname for the server certificate when using SSL or STARTTLS.

The address of the existing LDAP server you want to use is set in the **Hostname or IP address** field.

If it uses an alternative LDAP server port, enter the number in the **Port** field. (Port 636 is used for LDAP over TLS/SSL and TCP port 389 is for standard LDAP or STARTTLS. This type is set in the following field.)

If it provides TLS, change the **Transport** drop-down menu to *TCP - STARTTLS* which is the preferred transport for encrypting LDAP connections. The default is *TCP - Standard*. The *SSL - Encrypted* type is also available, but its official usage is deprecated.

The **Peer Certificate Authority** menu is used with SSL or STARTTLS to select the CA for the LDAP's server certificate. This defaults to *global*.

Choose the LDAP protocol version for the server in the **Protocol Version** menu. It defaults to *3* for standard LDAPv3 and the other option *2* is for the deprecated LDAPv2.

The timeout for LDAP operations defaults to 25 seconds. This can be changed in the **Server Timeout** field.

Select scope in the **Search Scope Level** menu. The options are *One Level* (the default) and *Entire Subtree*.

The **Search Scope Base DN** text field may be used to enter the Base Distinguished Name attributes.

The **Authentication Containers** text string will be prepended to the previous **Search Scope Base DN** setting. Or this may specific a full container path, The attributes are separated by semicolons. Examples include:

```
CN=Users;DC=example
```

and

```
CN=Users,DC=example,DC=com;OU=OtherUsers,DC=example,DC=com
```

To have additional attributes for the LDAP query, check the **Enable Extended Query** checkbox and enter the LDAP attributes in the **Extended Query** text field.

If you do not want to it to use an anonymous bind, set the **LDAP Bind User DN** string to the User Distinguished Name and its corresponding password in the **LDAP Bind Password** field.

The required **User Naming Attribute** field is used to refer to the logon username, The Microsoft AD attribute is *samAccountName*, used with old Windows NT 4.0 and Windows 98, and for OpenLDAP and Novell eDirectory, the default is *cn* (Common Name).

Set the required **Group Naming Attribute** field to the standard "cn" for Microsoft AD, Novell eDirectory, and OperLDAP.

The **Member Naming Attribute** field is also required. The default group member attribute name for Microsoft AD is *memberOf*, Novell eDirectory is *uniqueMember*, and OpenLDAP is *member*.

Use the **RFC 2307 Groups** checkbox if the LDAP server uses RFC 2307-style group memberships instead of the default Active Directory style.

The **Group Object Class** field is for entering the RFC 2307 object class like "group" or "posixGroup."

If you need international characters and if your LDAP server supports UTF-8 character encoding, check the **UTF8 Encode** checkbox to use UTF-8 LDAP parameters.

By default the at-sign (@) and hostname are removed from user names. To not strip these details, check the **Username Alterations** checkbox.

Then press the **Add new Server** button to complete the LDAP client addition. This will take you to the Certificate Authority Selection section of the wizard.

Your LDAP configuration may be edited or extended via the **System** → **User Manager** → **Authentication Servers** page as covered in Section 6.6.

RADIUS Server (Wizard)

If you selected RADIUS as the type of server, the next wizard page is for selecting the RADIUS server to use. The **RADIUS servers** drop-down menu will list previously-configured entries for utilizing local or remote RADIUS servers. The list is managed via the **System** → **User Manager** →

Authentication Servers page. (For information, see Section 6.6.) If you made a selection here, click **Next** to continue to the Certificate Authority Selection page in the wizard.

The wizard may also be used to setup the client to authenticate using RADIUS by clicking the **Add new RADIUS server** button.

Add RADIUS Server (Wizard)

This wizard page has four fields to quickly configure a RADIUS client for connecting to a RADIUS server. First enter a descriptive identifier for this server configuration in the **Name** field.

Note

This wizard page does not configure the startup of a RADIUS server. To run your own RADIUS service, you could use the **System → Package Manager** to install `freeradius`. See Chapter 35 for an introduction to installing packages.

Enter the address for the existing RADIUS server in the **Hostname or IP address** text field.

Enter that server's port number in the **Port** field. The RADIUS standard is port 1812.

The **Shared Secret** password field is for verifying the messages with this defined RADIUS server. (This secret would be shared to you by the RADIUS administrator — which could be you.)

For more advanced settings or to edit this setup later, use the **System → User Manager → Authentication Servers** page (see Section 6.6).

Then click the **Add new Server** button to continue on in the wizard.

Certificate Authority Selection (Wizard)

Select an existing **Certificate Authority** (CA) from the drop-down list. (See the **System → Certificate Manager → CAs** pages as discussed in Section 12.1.) You may click the **Add new CA** button to create a CA using this wizard, or use the **Next** button to use an already defined selection.

Create a New Certificate Authority (CA) Certificate

If you chose to create a new CA certificate, this wizard page will ask for a few attributes for generating it. For more details about these, see Section 12.1.

Enter an identifying name in the **Descriptive name** field. (This would be the Common Name field in a regular certificate.)

The **Key length** menu is for setting the bit size of the new key. It defaults to 2048 which is a common minimum.

The default expiration is approximately 10 years. To set a different amount of time, enter the number of days in the **Lifetime** field. Some recommend using a maximum of 825 days.

The certificate will contain the organization's operating location. Enter the two-character ISO country code, such as PR (Puerto Rico), in the **Country Code** field. The **State or Province** and **City** (aka Locality) fields should not be abbreviated. (Some use a region name for the state or province field.)

Enter the legal registered organization or company name in the **Organization** field. (Older versions of pfSense may also have an **E-mail** field for the organization.)

Click **Add new CA** button to continue in the wizard.

Choose a Server Certificate (Wizard)

Choose a server certificate by selecting one from the **Certificate** drop-down menu and then continue in the wizard to the OpenVPN server setup by pressing **Next**.

To create a certificate, click the **Add new Certificate** button.

Your pfSense system's certificates can also be managed or added via the **System** $\rightarrow$ **Certificate Manager** $\rightarrow$ **Certificates** page as covered in Section 12.2.

Create a New Server Certificate (Wizard)

This page in the wizard is only displayed if you chose to create a new server certificate.

Enter the identifying name in the **Descriptive name** field.

The **Key length** drop-down menu has selections from 512 bit to 16384 bit. The common recommendations are 2048 bit (the default) to 4096 bit. Larger key lengths offer strong security, but may be slower in new sessions setup.

The **Lifetime** field is for entering the expiration in days. It is preset to 3650 which is approximately 10 years.

Enter the **Country Code** as ISO Alpha-2 two-letter code, such as JP (Japan), IN (India), DE (Germany), or CN (China).

Enter the location in the **State or Province** and **City** (Locality) fields. (Don't abbreviate the names.)

Enter the organization or company name in the **Organization** field. (Older versions of pfSense also have an **E-mail** field for entering the email contact address for the pfSense admin generating this certificate.)

Click the **Create new Certificate** button to complete this step and to continue to the next page in the wizard.

General OpenVPN Server Information (Wizard)

Next you will enter several characteristics for the OpenVPN server starting with General Information. While this page is very long only the **Tunnel Network** field is required and the other settings will use their defaults. More information about these fields may be read in Section 33.1.1.

Select the **Interface** name in the drop-down list for where you want pfSense to listen for connections. Normally this is the WAN.

The OpenVPN service listens on UDP port 1194 by default. If you need to use TCP, select that in the **Protocol** menu. An alternative port can be entered in the **Local Port** field. (Use a number between 0 to 65535.)

Enter an identification string to use internally in pfSense in the **Description** text field. An example is "Remote Office Staff".

Cryptographic Settings (Wizard)

The Cryptographic Settings is the next section to complete. By default, it performs authentication of TLS packets. To turn this off, uncheck the **TLS Authentication** checkbox.

It also generates a shared TLS authentication key by default. Uncheck the **Generate TLS Key** checkbox if you don't want it to automatically do this. Then you may use your own by copy-and-pasting it into the **TLS Shared Key** textbox.

For Diffie-Hellman (DH) key exchange, a DH parameter is used. The recommended length is 2048 bit. You may use the **DH Parameters Length** to select a different bit size from the few options.

The default algorithm for encrypting traffic in the tunnel is *AES-256-CBC (256 bit key, 128 bit block)*. The **Encryption Algorithm** drop-down menu has many ciphers you may choose from. (It should be available for the client too.)

The **Auth Digest Algorithm** menu is used to select a digest choice for authenticating traffic. It defaults to *SHA1 (160-bit)* and a common recommendation is *SHA512 (512-bit)*. This setting also must be the same on both ends.

The **Hardware Crypto** drop-down menu is used to select the desired cryptographic accelerator to use. It will default to *No Hardware Crypto Acceleration* and the other choices depend on your pfSense hardware. (See Section 5.4.3 about accelerator hardware support.)

Tunnel Settings (Wizard)

The next section of wizard configurations are for Tunnel Settings.

The required **Tunnel Network** field is used to enter the addresses using CIDR notation for the Open-VPN network. The first address in the range will be used for the pfSense server side of the VPN and the other addresses for the clients.

To have the client send all traffic through the tunnel, check the **Redirect Gateway** checkbox.

Enter in CIDR format the network to access from the remote client in the **Local Network** field. Normally this is the LAN network, but may also be blank if not routing through this tunnel.

Enter a number in **Concurrent Connections** field for the maximum number of VPN clients allowed.

The desired compression style is selected in the **Compression** menu. *No Preference* is the default. The other choices are: *No Preference and Adaptive Compression Disabled, Disabled - No Compression, Enabled with Adaptive Compression*, and *Enabled without Adaptive Compression*.

To pass through the ToS IP header field in the tunnel, check the **Type-of-Service** checkbox.

To internally route traffic between VPN clients (using this same OpenVPN server), check the **Inter-Client Communication** checkbox. (Note this may bypass any possible packet filter rules.)

If you need to accept multiple connections using the same TLS certificate Common Name, enable the **Duplicate Connections** checkbox.

Client Settings (Wizard)

The next section (and still on the same wizard page) are the Client Settings.

Uncheck the **Dynamic IP** checkbox if you don't want connected clients to keep their connections if their IP address changes.

The **Topology** menu is used to select between the default *Subnet -- One IP address per client in a common subnet* and *net30 -- Isolated /30 network per client* which may be need for outdated OpenVPN clients.

Use the **DNS Default Domain** field for completing a short hostname to make a fully-qualified domain name for DNS lookups.

Set the **DNS Server 1** through **DNS Server 4** fields with IP addresses if you want to assign DNS servers (such as your DNS service on your pfSense system) for your VPN clients to use.

If you want your VPN clients to synchronize their clocks using your defined Network Time Protocol servers, put the addresses in the **NTP Server 1** and **NTP Server 2** fields.

If your clients will be doing WINS or SMB/CIFS, enable the **Enable NetBIOS over TCP/IP** checkbox. Then you can set the desired behavior in the **NetBIOS Node Type** drop-down menu from the options of *none, b-node, p-node, m-node*, and *h-node*. The name to be appended to a NetBIOS name to make a valid DNS name (if needed) is entered in the **NetBIOS Scope ID** field.

If you are using a Windows Internet Name Service (WINS) server, enter it IP addresses in the **WINS Server 1** and **WINS Server 2** fields. (Note that is not desirable since it can use DNS instead.)

After all that click the **Next** button to continue in the wizard.

Firewall Rule Configuration (Wizard)

Your pfSense firewall rules need to allow the OpenVPN tunnel to work. You can manually create rules to allow traffic from OpenVPN clients to and through this OpenVPN server. Or you can let the wizard automatically add them. These options are not on by default. To permit connections from any client anywhere on the Internet to connect to your OpenVPN server, select the **Firewall Rule** checkbox. Check the **OpenVPN Rule** checkbox to allow the traffic from your connected clients to pass via the OpenVPN tunnel. Then click the **Next** button to continue in the wizard.

Wizard Completion

Your OpenVPN Remote Access Server configuration should be complete at this point in the wizard. Click the **Finish** button to proceed. If it detects any other configuration needs, it will prompt you about them and may take you to corresponding wizard page to resolve it. When this wizard is successful, the OpenVPN service will be started up and you will be taken back to the **VPN** → **OpenVPN** → **Servers** page listing the servers (as discussed in Section 33.1).

Note that you don't use the wizard later to edit a completed OpenVPN server configuration, but use the pencil icon for the Edit action in the **VPN** → **OpenVPN** → **Servers** table (as covered in the following section). (With some old versions of pfSense, if you use the **Wizards** feature again it will be mostly preset with the previous wizard run which may or may not be useful, such as a possibly already-used port number.) To add another OpenVPN server from scratch use the **Add** button from that front page.

33.1.3   OpenVPN Client Specific Overrides

The OpenVPN Server configurations may also contain custom client settings which may be setup on the **VPN** → **OpenVPN** → **Client Specific Overrides** page. After the OpenVPN client has been authenticated, configurations for the client's X.509 Common Name or username (when using password authentication) are provided to the client, such as per-client static interface assignments or fixed routes, custom DNS servers, or restricting global client configurations. This feature may also be used to disable a specific OpenVPN client.

The default view shows a table of your client-specific configurations (CSC). The entries show the Common Name (or username) used for matching and your custom description. They also indicate if they are disabled or not and provides action icons to edit or delete the client-specific configurations.

Click the **Add** button to configure a new Client Specific Override. The following sections introduce the options for adding or editing a CSC on the **VPN** → **OpenVPN** → **Client Specific Overrides** → **Edit** page. The **Common Name** field is required.

General Information (Client Specific Override)

Configurations will be created for all your local OpenVPN servers. To be specific instead, select one or more of your local servers that can use the following configured override options in the **Server List** menu. It contains the list of your already-configured TLS-based OpenVPN servers identified with their internal ID number and custom description. If a server is added later and a server is not defined here, the new server will also get a CSC setup.

To keep this configuration but not use it, check the **Disable this override** checkbox.

Enter the OpenVPN client's X.509 Common Name in the required **Common name** field. If the server is using password authentication instead of a certificate, enter the username here. (Again this is used to select which client to override the settings for.)

> **Warning**
> pfSense allows creating new configurations for existing configurations by using the same Common Name and local OpenVPN server name, The most recent CSC entry edited or added takes precedence.

Enter a brief explanation or identifier in the **Description** text field. This is used in the table display of your available CSC Overrides.

You may disable this specific client from connecting to your VPN, by checking the **Block this client connection based on its common name** checkbox. Note if there is a compromised password or key, use a Certificate Revocation List (CRL) as covered Section 12.3.

Tunnel Settings (Client Specific Override)

For custom virtual IP endpoints for the client tunnel, enter a CIDR address range for the VPN in the **Tunnel Network** or **IPv6 Tunnel Network** fields. For IPv6, use the same IPv6 prefix as in your local server's **IPv6 Tunnel Network** setting. For IPv4, if your server is using the subnet topology, enter the client's IP address and use the same subnet mask configured for the server's **IPv4 Tunnel Network**. When using the net30 topology for your server, the second usable network address in the range will be for the client and the first will be this local server's address.

For custom routing table entries for the client to access the server-side networks, enter one or more networks separated by commas (,) in the **IPv4 Local Network/s** and/or **IPv6 Local Network/s** fields.

Custom internal routes to another client may be defined in the **IPv4 Remote Network/s** and/or **IPv6 Remote Network/s** fields. These are also defined using CIDR ranges and multiple entries may be added when separated with commas. When using this, it is required that the server's routing table also contain the same routes; this is done by filling in the OpenVPN server's **IPv4 Local network(s)** and/or **IPv6 Local network(s)** fields (as described in Section 33.1.1).

To have the all the client's outgoing IP traffic redirected over this VPN, check the **Force all client generated traffic through the tunnel** checkbox. (This will override the client's default gateway route.)

Client Settings (Client Specific Override)

In addition to these custom overrides, the client may also receive other settings from the OpenVPN server. To not use those global server definitions, select the **Prevent this client from receiving any server-defined client settings** checkbox.

To have specific DHCP options provided to the client, enable the corresponding checkboxes and provide the values. The DHCP options include the default DNS domain, up to four DNS server IP addresses, one or two IP addresses for the NTP servers, the NetBIOS over TCP/IP Node Type and Scope ID, and one or two IP addresses for WINS servers. For details about these DHCP options, see Section 33.1.1.

You may enter additional client-specific options in the **Advanced** text box. Separate them using a semicolon (;).

After clicking the **Save** button you will be taken back to the page showing all your CSC overrides.

33.2 OpenVPN Clients

The **VPN** → **OpenVPN** → **Clients** page is for running your pfSense system as a peer connecting and tunneling with a remote OpenVPN server. It contains a table listing the existing clients identified by the protocol (like UDP), server hostname or IP address followed by port number, and your defined description. Entries displayed lightly (50% opacity) have disabled configurations. Each client has corresponding actions to edit or delete the corresponding client. (Editing the client will provide the same view as when adding a new client as described in the following section.)

To create a new client, click the **Add** button at the bottom of the table.

The **Related Status** and **Related log** entries shortcuts will lead to **Status** → **OpenVPN** and **Status** → **System Logs** → **OpenVPN**, respectively. On the status page, see the table for Client Instance Statistics as introduced in Section 33.5.

33.2.1 Add or Edit OpenVPN Clients

The **VPN** → **OpenVPN** → **Clients** → **Edit** page is accessed by editing an existing client or adding a new client. This page has over thirty options to configure the client side of the OpenVPN tunnel. (While some of these options overlap with the server-side configuration, Section 33.1.1, many are unique to the client side.) The only required field is for the **Server host or address**, but if you use the default Peer to Peer SSL/TLS server mode, a client certificate or a username/password pair must also be provided.

If editing an existing OpenVPN client, you will also have shortcuts for restarting and stopping the service.

General Information (OpenVPN Client)

If you want to keep this configuration but not use it — that is no tunnel enabled, click the **Disable this client** checkbox.

In the **Server mode** drop-down select the style for connecting to the remote server: *Peer to Peer (SSL/TLS)* for using a certificate or *Peer to Peer (Shared Key)* to not use TLS.

Define if the remote OpenVPN server is using IPv4 or IPv6 and UDP or TCP in the **Protocol** drop-down menu. Select *UDP* for UDP over IPv4 (this is the default), *UDP6* for UDP over IPv6, *TCP* for TCP over IPv4, or *TCP6* for TCP over IPv6. Note that the address selected for the **Interface** must match the protocol.

It uses the `tun` tunneling network interface by default. If you want to use the virtual Ethernet device instead select `tap` in the **Device mode** menu.

The OpenVPN client daemon will bind to the address for your WAN device by default. If you want it to connect from a different network, select it from the **Interface** menu. Any options identified with "GW Group" were previously defined via the **System** → **Routing** → **Gateway Groups** subpage as covered in Section 15.2. If the *any* choice is selected, it will not bind to a specific local address. Note again that the protocol just defined must match the protocol for your selected interface address.

By default, the client daemon will use a random dynamic port for its source port. If you need a specific source port, configure the number in the **Local port** field. To have it use the random dynamic port, enter 0 (zero) for the value.

Enter the address of the remote OpenVPN server (or peer) in the **Server host or address** field. This is required.

Commonly the OpenVPN service listens on port 1194. If you need it to connect to a different remote port, enter the number in the **Server port** field.

If you need to connect to the remote OpenVPN server via an HTTP proxy, enter the HTTP proxy server's address and port number in the **Proxy host or address** and **Proxy port** fields.

If the HTTP proxy needs authentication, change the **Proxy Auth. - Extra options** menu from *none* to *basic* for standard HTTP authentication or *ntlm* for the Microsoft NT Lan Manager authentication scheme. Then additional fields will be available to enter the proxy authentication **Username** and **Password** (and a confirmation field for the password again).

Use the **Description** field to enter a name or text string that will help the pfSense admin recognize the corresponding configuration.

User Authentication Settings (OpenVPN Client)

The user authentication fields are only available for the default Peer to Peer SSL/TLS server mode. (It doesn't use a username and password for the Shared Key mode.)

If the client certificate is not selected, enter the username and password for authentication in the **Username** and **Password** fields. (Also enter the password again in the confirmation field.)

By default, the client will requery for the username and password when there is a verification error. If you want it to be a fatal error, select the **Do not retry connection when authentication fails** checkbox.

Cryptographic Settings (OpenVPN Client)

When you are using the TLS mode you will have multiple options for TLS and certificates. These aren't used for the shared key mode,

You will have a checkbox selected by default for using the recommended HMAC authentication for the TLS control channel. This feature is not used to encrypt nor authenticate the tunnel. If you want pfSense to provide a new key for this TLS control channel protection, keep the **Automatically generate a shared TLS authentication key** checkbox checked. After saving this page's configurations and re-entering these client settings (by clicking the Edit action icon in the table of clients), you can then see the TLS key which could be copied for use on its OpenVPN peer. If the key already exists, then the checkbox to auto-generate it will not be displayed.

If you deselect that checkbox or if it doesn't exist you will have the **Key** textbox. Commonly you would paste in the key there. The format must begin and end with the "OpenVPN Static key V1" markers.

If you don't want to use the TLS control channel protection, uncheck the **Enable authentication of TLS packets** checkbox.

When using TLS, select the CA in the **Peer Certificate Authority** menu. If you need to import (or create) a CA, Section 12.1 about the **System → Certificate Manager → CAs** page. This is not needed if the upcoming **Client Certificate** field is set to *None*.

If you want pfSense to honor a CRL (certificate revocation list), select one from the **Peer Certificate Revocation list** menu. This may be used when a key has been compromised. To setup a CRL for a certificate, see Section 12.3 for the **System → Certificate Manager → Certificate Revocation** feature.

This configuration interface defaults to use a username/password authentication. To change this, select the certificate in the **Client Certificate** menu. The entries will indicate the type of certificate and if it is already in use. The certificate must be signed by the earlier defined CA. To import (or create) a certificate to be known by pfSense, go to the **System → Certificate Manager → Certificates** page as covered in Section 12.2. If the client certificate is not selected, the username/password must be provided.

When using the shared key server mode (and not TLS), you will be able to introduce a shared key. By default, the **Automatically generate a shared key** checkbox is selected. When you save this pages's configuration and then view it by editing it, you will see the new OpenVPN static key in the following textbox. This may be copied and shared with the remote peer's configuration.

Or uncheck that checkbox to enter a key already shared to you for use with the remote peer in the **Shared Key** textbox. It will be identified with the "OpenVPN Static key V1" markers at the beginning and end of the data.

The cipher algorithm for encrypting the packets in the tunnel must match on both the client and server. It is set in the **Encryption Algorithm** drop-down menu. The entries indicate their default key size. OpenVPN recommends using a Cipher Block Chaining mode (CBC) which is also required when using static key mode. While OpenVPN defaults to Blowfish *BF-CBC (128 bit key by default, 64 bit block)*, it is not longer recommended due to collision attacks because of its small block size. *AES-256-CBC* is another commonly recommended setting. It defaults to its first choice which is commonly *AES-128-CBC (128 bit key, 128 bit block)*. If encryption is disabled, select the bottom *None (No Encryption)* choice.

The OpenVPN client and server will negotiate crypto support using the Negotiable Crypto Parameters (NCP) feature. If you don't want this client configuration to use this, uncheck the **Enable NCP** checkbox. When using it, the allowed algorithms are defined in the right-side **NCP Algorithms** list. On the left side, select or deselect algorithms to be supported. (Click on an already-highlighted entry in the left column to remove it from being selected.) By default, the only selection is AES-128-GCM.

The message digest used to authenticate received packets using HMAC is set in the **Auth digest algorithm** menu. It defaults to *SHA1 (160-bit)* To disable packet authentication set it to *None (No Authentication)*.

The **Hardware Crypto** menu is used to enable hardware-based crypto engine functionality. It defaults to not use hardware crypto acceleration. The choices depend on the pfSense hardware, such as: *RSAX engine support - RSA, BSD cryptodev engine - RSA, DSA, DH, AES-128-CBC, AES-192-CBC, AES-256-CBC*, and *Intel RDRAND engine - RAND*. (See Section 5.4.3 about this hardware support.)

Tunnel Settings (OpenVPN Client)

The IPv4 addresses used for the private virtual network may be defined using the **IPv4 Tunnel Network** text field. You don't need to set this if the OpenVPN server provides addresses. This uses CIDR notation (like 10.0.8.0/24). The second usable IP address (after the network address) is used for this client's virtual interface. When using the `tun` device mode, the first usable IP address is the remote peer's address. Or for `tap` it uses the subnet mask for the virtual Ethernet segment.

If you are using IPv6 and the OpenVPN server isn't providing addresses, set the virtual network addresses in the **IPv6 Tunnel Network** field also using CIDR notation (like fe80::/64). The ::2 address will be used for the client. For `tap` device mode, it uses the prefix for the virtual Ethernet segment.

For setting up the routing table after the established connection, define the networks in the **IPv4 Remote network(s)** field using CIDR notation. It can support multiple routes, so delimit them with commas. When using the `tun` device mode, the gateway is the remote peer's IP address as defined in the earlier **IPv4 Tunnel Network** option.

For setting up the routing for IPv6, use the **IPv6 Remote network(s)** field. This also supports multiple routes in CIDR notation separated by commas.

The bandwidth of the outgoing tunnel data can be limited down to 100 bytes per second using the **Limit outgoing bandwidth** option. Enter a number in bytes per second with a minimum of 100 and a maximum of 100000000 (which is 100 MBytes). Leave it blank (the default) to not use this shaper. Note that values below 1000 may cause timeouts. (This feature cannot be used with the following **UDP Fast I/O** option.)

OpenVPN can selectively compress packets sent over the tunnel and will periodically disable this compression when it is not efficient. This may be adjusted using the **Compression** drop-down menu. The default is to have compression turned off, but with packet framing for compression still enabled so a different compression setting may be used later. The other options include: use LZ4, LZ4 V2 format, comp LZO, stub compression, stub compression in V2 format,; disable adaptive compression algorithm; use legacy adaptive LZO, legacy LZO, and don't use legacy LZO. (The LZO options will be deprecated by OpenVPN.) Note that the server may be able to tell the client to change this setting.

When using the TLS server mode and `tun` device mode, the client will have an IP address in a common subnet. To change this to OpenVPN's default where the client has its own /30 point-to-point subnet (which may waste IPs), set the **Topology** menu to *net30 -- Isolated /30 network per client.* (This may be required on old Windows clients.) Note that `tap` device mode always uses one IP address in a common subnet for the client. This topology setting has no effect with IPv6.

DSCP and ECN fields in packet headers are not retained in the packets sent in the tunnel by default. To include type of service (ToS) fields in the sent packets, enable the **Type-of-Service** checkbox.

When using the `tun` device mode, it will be capable of forwarding IPv6 traffic. To turn off this default, select the **Don't forward IPv6 traffic** checkbox.

If you don't want this client to update its routing table based on the settings pushed from the OpenVPN server, select the **Don't pull routes** checkbox.

To not execute any local commands to install routes, click the **Don't add or remove routes automatically** checkbox.

Advanced Configuration (OpenVPN Client)

If your OpenVPN client needs addition configurations, set them in the **Custom options** textbox. These are for official openvpn.conf settings. At the time of this book's printing, pfSense uses OpenVPN version 2.4.6. Use a semicolon (;) to separate multiple options.

To enable the experimental optimizations for TUN or TAP tunnels or UDP for write operations, check the **UDP Fast I/O** checkbox. Note this is not compatible with the previous client **Limit outgoing bandwidth** option.

To override your system's default send and receive buffer sizes for TCP and UDP, choose a size in the **Send/Receive Buffer** drop-down menu. The choices depend on the system, but commonly range from 64 KB to 2 MB.

When creating an OpenVPN virtual interface, a gateway is setup for both IPv4 and IPv6. You can choose to only do this for just IPv4 or IPv6 via the **Gateway creation** radio buttons.

To adjust the logging or debugging output from the OpenVPN client daemon, use the **Verbosity level** menu. Use 0 to only show log fatal errors. Levels 1 through 4 are the normal usage range. The default value is 1. Level 5 will log packet reads and writes. Levels 6 through 11 are for more detailed debugging. The client logging can be seen on the **Status** → **System Logs** → **OpenVPN** page.

After defining your selections for the OpenVPN client setup, click the **Save** button. After the configuration is loaded, the **VPN** → **OpenVPN** → **Clients** page will be displayed showing the table of clients.

33.3   OpenVPN Virtual Interface

When OpenVPN tunnels are setup, the base FreeBSD system will have virtual network devices created such as `ovpns1` and `ovpnc1` for the first OpenVPN server and client virtual devices. If you want to use pfSense configurations with this interface for gateways and policy routing, address translation, and more, you can assign a pfSense-style network interface to the virtual device. See the **Interfaces** → **Interface Assignments** page as covered in Section 13.1 about assigning interfaces.

You don't need to assign the interface to do firewall rules with it. If you do create an pfSense interface, you may end up with redundant firewall rule tables.

33.4   OpenVPN Firewall Rules

Firewall rules will need to be enabled to allow the traffic to and from and through the OpenVPN tunnels. On the server side's **Firewall** → **Rules** page you will have a new tab (link) for **OpenVPN** to configure rules for the virtual interface. This may be used to allow traffic through the tunnel. See Section 16.2 about the various rule settings.

The firewall logs may show traffic on the virtual network device names like `ovpns1` for the first OpenVPN server virtual interface and `ovpnc1` for the first OpenVPN client virtual interface. You may be able to use the firewall logs interface to add rules using the plus (+) icon. (See Section 16.18 for details.)

33.5   OpenVPN Status

When OpenVPN is configured as a server or as a client, the **Status** → **OpenVPN** page lists your OpenVPN clients, peer-to-peer connections, and its OpenVPN internal routing table, depending on how your OpenVPN is setup and used. Much of these details are retrieved via the running OpenVPN management interfaces. If you are using custom options that modify the management features, the status may not work for this page.

The main tables are sortable; you may click on the column headers to re-order the rows. Icons indicate the status for service instances and you can stop or restart (or start) the specific services. Shortcuts are also available to access the OpenVPN configurations and its logging.

For an OpenVPN server, the client connections view shows the common name (of the client certificate), its real IP address and port, virtual IP address, connected since time, and bytes received and sent. An icon is also available to kill the corresponding client connection.

If you have routing, a **Show Routing Table** button will be available. Click it to see the server's internal routing which will show the virtual IP address, the client common name, the client's real IP address and port, and the last reference time.

Peer to Peer Server Instance Statistics						
Name	Status	Connected Since	Virtual Address	Remote Host	Bytes Sent / Received	Service
Server UDP4:1194	up	Sat May 25 23:42:16 2019	10.200.0.1	172.16.1.4	5.83 MiB / 944 KiB	⊘ C ⓒ

Figure 33.1: **Status → OpenVPN — Peer to Peer Server Instance**

The Peer to Peer Server Instance Statistics (as seen in Figure 33.1) shows the status for an OpenVPN connected peer, whether the connection is up or not, connected since time, virtual IP address (like assigned in the **IPv4 Tunnel Network** field), the real IP address of the remote peer, and bytes sent and received. The table also provides actions to restart and stop this peer-to-peer OpenVPN service. If the status is down, but there is a client daemon process, then the circle check icon will indicate it is running.

Client Instance Statistics							
Name	Status	Connected Since	Local Address	Virtual Address	Remote Host	Bytes Sent/Received	Service
Client UDP4	up	Sat May 25 23:55:48 2019	10.0.2.15:26810	10.200.0.2	10.185.49.132:1194	938 KiB / 5.33 MiB	⊘ C ⊙

Figure 33.2: **Status → OpenVPN — Client Instance**

The Client Instance Statistics table (like seen in Figure 33.2) is on the client-side of a peer. This will show its type and protocol (like UDP), if it is up or not, connected since, its local IP address (and local port), virtual address, remote host address (and its OpenVPN port), bytes sent, and bytes received. If the virtual address field is empty, this implies that the tunnel network has not been provided or it is not configured. Note that when the client daemon process is running, the circle check icon will still indicate it is running even if the status is down. It will also provide actions to restart and stop the OpenVPN client service.

33.6 OpenVPN Log Entries

The logs at the **Status → System Logs → OpenVPN** page are for the OpenVPN server and for the OpenVPN clients. Note that this view doesn't identify the server versus client processes, so it may be difficult to recognize what log entries are for the client. You may be able to identify the OpenVPN client process by seeing the IP address for the remote server in the "link remote:" logged messages.

The logging verbosity level for the server and clients may be adjusted. See the **Verbosity Level** setting in the server and client configurations in the bottom Advanced Configuration section as described in Section 33.1.1 and Section 33.2.1.

To search these logs, use the **Log filter** shortcut. To modify the logging settings, follow the **Manage log** shortcut. For details, see Section 11.1 and Section 11.3.

If you see a log entry of "Authenticate/Decrypt packet error: packet HMAC authentication failed" this may be due to copying a wrong key.

34 Load Balancing and Failover

The pfSense system can be used for managed IP forwarding by providing Layer 3 network redirection to other systems, with manual or automated failover. This is available via the **Services → Load Balancer** and **Status → Load Balancer** menu pages. This technology is powered by the OpenBSD `relayd` daemon which manages the packet-level redirection rules with PF packet filter rules to forward traffic between it and target servers. For high availability and automated failover, it can monitor (aka health-checks) the target hosts before forwarding to them.

Note that this feature may be deprecated in later versions of pfSense. An alternate solution is *HAProxy*, a TCP, HTTP, and HTTPS load balancer, which is available to be installed from the pfSense packages (Section 35.3).

pfSense also provides network redundancy by sharing the same IP addresses over multiple pfSense systems and a multi-WAN setup for Internet gateway failover. These are covered in Section 16.10 and Section 15.2.2 respectively.

Unmanaged connection redirections to other hosts can also be done via the packet filter using stateful address translation. For details, see Chapter 17.

An alternate method and definition of load balancing by prioritizing traffic can be done via the ALTQ technology. This is discussed in Chapter 25.

The **Services → Load Balancer** pages have links to take you to the page views for the **Pools** for listing or defining destination server(s) for a specific service, the mode of operation (load balancer or failover), and what monitor to use; **Virtual Servers** which lists or defines the listening connection and what destination(s) it uses; **Monitors** which lists or defines the techniques for checking if the target server is up; and **Settings** for a few additional daemon tunables.

On the top right of the pages are shortcuts for **Related status** and **Related log entries** which are also covered in this chapter.

34.1 Load Balancer Pools

A *pool* defines a single destination or a cluster of systems providing a network service. A *virtual server* (configured in an upcoming section) enables the pfSense load balancer to monitor that these target systems are up and to redirect traffic to and from them.

The pools list and additions are available via the main **Services** → **Load Balancer** page. No pools are configured by default, but when defined, this page has a table briefly describing them. Use the **Add** button to add a load balancer pool.

Adding a pool does not start the load balancing or failover service yet, but just adds a definition (known as a table) for the destinations and what monitor is used to check it. The daemon is enabled (after adding this pool) via the **Services** → **Load Balancer** → **Virtual Servers** page as covered in Section 34.2.

For each entry, the Pools table shows the mode as Load Balance or Manual Failover; the single active failover server or the cluster of load balancing servers; the port the remote server listens on; the check-health monitor (with a link to review or edit the monitor configurations as covered in Section 34.3.1); and an optional description that briefly explains or identifies the purpose of this target pool. These are explained in the upcoming sections.

A different view of this same pool information is available at **Status** → **Load Balancer** as seen in Section 34.5.

The entries have corresponding action icons to edit, copy, or remove the entry. Click the **Edit pool** pencil icon to make changes as described in the following section. Click the **Copy pool** clone icon to duplicate the entry so you can create another pool entry based on similar settings. To remove a pool, click its **Delete pool** trash can icon. It will first check that no virtual servers use the corresponding pool.

34.1.1   Add or Edit Load Balancer Pool

Adding or editing a pool is accessed via the **Services** → **Load Balancer** → **Pools** page by clicking the **Add** button, **Edit pool** pencil icon (to modify an existing entry), or **Copy pool** clone icon (to start a new entry based on a previously added pool). The form has several fields and the name, port, and an enabled target server address is required.

Enter a unique single word in the required **Name** field. It cannot contain a space or a slash (/). It cannot be longer than 16 characters. It cannot match an existing alias name and cannot be one of pfSense's reserved table names (bogons, bogonsv6, negate_networks, snort2c, sshguard, sshlockout, tonatsubnets, virusprot, vpn_networks, or webConfiguratorlockout.) This name is selected in the upcoming Virtual Servers configuration.

The **Mode** drop-down field is used to select if you want this pool to define a **Load Balance** cluster of servers or an individual enabled **Manual Failover** destination server (and optionally a disabled choice too).

The connections are somewhat balanced using the round-robin looping of the PF packet filter translation.

Choosing **Manual Failover** from the drop-down puts it into a simple failover mode. The **Status** → **Load Balancer** page can be used to see if the daemon detected that the destination server is down and to manually select an alternate destination (with its corresponding radio button).

While this option is called *Manual*, automated failover can be activated using the Virtual Server's **Fall-back Pool** selection.

Note that the **Load Balance** selection also provides a type of failover support, as the daemon will remove servers from the pool of destination servers if they are not available.

You may want to add an explanation about this pool entry in the **Description** field, especially if you have many pools with vague names.

Enter a valid port number or port alias name in the required **Port** field. This is the listening port on the remote server. Port aliases can be setup via the **Firewall → Aliases → Ports** page as covered in Section 16.5. Note that if using an alias list, it will only use the first port number if the corresponding Virtual Server configuration only listens on a single port.

On host checks, the daemon will temporarily mark a destination host as down if the check fails. To make it more tolerant by trying it more times, set a count number in the **Retry** field. To keep the default of zero, leave the field blank. The maximum is 65535.

The health check is defined in the **Monitor** drop-down field. By default, the choices are ICMP (the default), TCP, HTTP, HTTPS, and SMTP. You may have different selections as seen and setup via the **Services → Load Balancer → Monitors** page.

Note

If you need a specific type of monitoring, you may want to set it up first. See Section 34.3 for details.

The IP addresses in the load balance pool or the failover pools are entered, one at a time, in the **Server IP Address** field. This is address of the target server listening on the port defined above. You may enter an IPv4 or IPv6 address or subnet. If using a subnet, use a small range with slash (/) notation like /26 through /32, as it cannot be larger than 64 addresses. Note that host aliases do not work. Click the **Add to pool** button after each entry.

Below the address entry field and button, there are two lists for the pool members. When using the default Load Balance mode, each addition will be added to the right *Enabled (Default)* list. You may add multiple entries in the Load Balance mode.

The Manual Failover mode only has a single address or subnet. The first addition is placed on the right *Enabled (Default)* side. The second or later entries (when clicking **Add to pool** an additional time) will go into the left *Disabled* column.

The *Disabled* list is not known by the `relayd` daemon and will not be used for redirection. It is only used manually by the pfSense administrator. The **Move to disabled list** button under the right list may be used to move the selected entry (or multiple entries) to the left column.

In Load Balance mode, the **Move to enabled list** button on the left side may be used to move disabled members to the default (right) list.

If you make a mistake or need to remove an entry or entries, select them and click the corresponding **Remove** button. (It may prompt you to verify this action.)

Note that at least one enabled IP address is required. For either mode, the value of using this feature is to have a list of generally available servers in the Enabled list. The **Status → Load Balancer → Pools** page may be used to manually select hosts including from the *disabled* to switch what pool to monitor and redirect to. This is covered in Section 34.5.

Click the **Save** button to introduce these pool settings. This will take you back to the table view of all pools. You will need to also click the **Apply Changes** button to use the new pool's configuration. (But if you don't have a virtual server setup, applying the changes doesn't matter yet — and can be done after adding that.)

Note

You may have firewall rules that restrict the monitoring or access to the pool hosts (at the defined port). See the **Firewall** → **Rules** page to review your settings or to allow access for your load balancer.

34.2   Virtual Servers

The **Services** → **Load Balancer** → **Virtual Servers** subpage lists the existing listening server addresses and ports. These are *virtual* as the real service is provided at the destinations defined in the enabled pool. No virtual servers are configured by default. Click the **Add** button to add one.

The table (when virtual servers are defined) lists the protocol "tcp" which in pfSense implies that it will do PF packet filter redirection or "dns" which means it will be a limited Layer 7 DNS relay; the local IP address and port that the pfSense server is redirecting (or relaying) for; the pool (defined earlier) of destination servers; and an automatic fall-back pool (if used for failover). The upcoming section explains these in more detail.

Each entry will have action icons to modify, duplicate, or remove the corresponding virtual server configuration. Click the **Edit virtual server** pencil icon to adjust its settings (as covered in the following section). Use the **Copy virtual server** clone icon to make a copy of the configuration — it will take you to the entry form with values preset using the original copy. To remove a virtual server, click the **Delete virtual server** icon which will then prompt you to confirm the removal. After making changes, you may need to use the **Apply Changes** button for them to be activated.

For status details about these same enabled virtual servers, see the **Status** → **Load Balancer** → **Virtual Servers** subpage (see Section 34.6).

34.2.1   Add or Edit Load Balancer Virtual Server

The form for adding or editing a virtual server configuration is accessed by clicking the **Add** button from the **Services** → **Load Balancer** → **Virtual Servers** button or by using the **Edit virtual server** pencil icon or **Copy virtual server** clone icon actions. The *virtual server* needs a name and a local IP address to listen on.

Enter a keyword to identify it in the **Name** field. Each virtual server must have a different name with a maximum of 32 characters. It cannot contain slashes (/) nor any spaces. If you need a more detailed name or longer explanation, enter it in the optional **Description** field.

In the **IP Address** field enter the IP address or host alias name to listen on. If the load balancer is redirecting internal services for outside use, then the address could be the WAN IP address, for example. You may also use a host alias as previously setup via **Firewall** → **Aliases** (see Section 16.5).

The **Port** field is used to define the port for the incoming connections. If your virtual server's listening port is the same as the port used for the destination server(s) in the pool, you can keep this field empty.

Note

Just like the destination addresses and port used by a pool need to be allowed in the packet filter, the traffic into this virtual server also needs to be allowed by the PF packet filter firewall. See and adjust your settings in **Firewall** → **Rules** as needed.

Note it does not make sense to have the virtual server handling on the same port as something else already on the same IP address. It may not work as you expect, so keep track of your different listening services and network translations.

The next selection is the **Virtual Server Pool** drop-down menu. Select the load balancer pool that was previously defined (and seen at **Services** → **Load Balancer**) for your destination(s). By default, it has the first load balancer pool defined.

The Layer 3 redirection load balancer can auto failover to use a different pool if the main pool is all down. To enable this, select the previously-defined pool in the **Fall-back Pool** drop-down menu. (Note this option cannot be used with following **Relay Protocol** set to "DNS".)

This Load Balancer implementation managed by pfSense is mainly for Layer 3 redirection. This is the default mode "TCP" as set in the **Relay Protocol** drop-down menu. It has very limited use as a Layer 7 application relay for the historic DNS protocol via the "DNS" selection. This DNS feature tells the `relayd` daemon to listen only on UDP and relay via UDP. This enables tracking of the stateless UDP by using DNS headers.

Warning

This DNS feature is broken for most modern uses of DNS. Recent implementations of DNS use EDNS0 (Extension Mechanisms) support and accept DNSSEC records which breaks this DNS-based state checking.

In addition, changing the **Relay Protocol** for an existing virtual server to "DNS" may have unexpected results. You may need to click the **Restart Service** shortcut button to restart `relayd`.

Click the **Save** button to introduce these changes. This will take you back to the table view of your virtual servers. To activate these new configuration changes, click the **Apply Changes** button. Note it may take several seconds for the service to be active.

34.3   Load Balancer Monitors

A monitor is a health-check to confirm that the destination server or specific service is up. The `rel ayd` daemon periodically checks the members of the pool and the redirection is only enabled for those that are up. By default, pfSense has some predefined monitors seen at **Services → Load Balancer → Monitors**. These may be selected when setting up the load balancer pool (see Section 34.1.1).

The default monitor definitions are: ICMP to do an ICMP or ICMPv6 ECHO_REQUEST ping to the host; TCP to do a simple TCP connect to see if the host is up; HTTP to do a simple HTTP HEAD request of the default path (/) and check that it returns a "200 OK" status; HTTPS does the same HTTP check but wrapped in SSL; and SMTP which checks if the returned data from the connection is a "220" mail service ready greeting. (No load balancer using a monitor is configured by default, but when a pool is added, the default monitor choice is ICMP.)

More specific HTTP and HTTPS monitors may be setup as shown in the following section. In addition, a generic method for optionally sending some data and checking what it returns is available.

You may choose to copy an existing monitor configuration to speed up creating a monitor. (Creating a new monitor may be a better idea than modifying one of the predefined defaults as that would make your system different than other pfSense standard setups.) Then the basic step would be to give it a new name and whatever change as needed such as entering an HTTP hostname to check for.

34.3.1   Add or Edit Load Balancer Monitor

Introducing a new health-check or modifying an existing one is done via the **Services → Load Balancer → Monitors** subpage by clicking the **Add button**, the **Copy monitor** clone icon action, or the **Edit monitor** pencil icon action.

If cloning an existing monitor, be sure to set a new name.

The **Description** field is not optional (like in most pfSense forms). Enter a brief summary or explanation of the purpose of this monitor there.

Then enter the type of health-check if not using the default ICMP in the **Type** drop-down field. Note that the type may introduce an additional form for type-specific settings. For example, for HTTPS, select the result that should be in the returned header's status line in the **HTTPS Code** drop-down field. The choices contain many status codes from "100 Continue" to "505 HTTP Version Not Supported." The default is the successful "200 OK."

When finished, click the **Save** button.

34.4   Load Balancer Settings

A few tunables for the `relayd` daemon may be configured via the **Services → Load Balancer → Settings** subpage. These global settings are for all the load balancer configurations and not specific to a specific load balancer pool or virtual server.

It will attempt to check a host's state for up to 1000 milliseconds. This may be changed by entering the number in milliseconds in the **Timeout** field.

It checks each host every 10 seconds. To change this, enter how often in seconds in the **Interval** field.

It will start up three daemon processes, each able to handle all relayed connections. To change the number of processes at startup, set the **Prefork** field. The allowed range is 1 to 32.

Click the **Save** button to save the configurations. Then it will indicate the changes need to be applied, so click the **Apply Changes** button to reload the load balancer.

34.5 Load Balancer Pools Status

To see what pools and virtual servers are currently up see the **Status** → **Load Balancer** page and **Status** → **Load Balancer** → **Virtual Servers** subpage. (Status for the virtual servers is covered in the next section.)

The main page shows the pools. For each, it shows the configured mode (like Load balancing or Manual failover) and the name of the monitor (like TCP). The most important use is to quickly see if the destination servers in the cluster (or individual failover) are up, down, or disabled and to manually select what servers should be in use.

Servers that the health-check monitor determined are up are marked in light green and those that are currently unavailable due to monitoring are in light red. Pool entries that have been in use will have a percentage number indicating its availability. This may be used as an indicator (when compared to others in the same pool) on how often it was available for use. Those at 0.00% have probably never been in use, so you may want to check your IP address or monitor or that remote system to verify it is correct and up.

The Servers column lists all of the load balancing or manual failover server addresses (with port numbers). For load balancing it has checkboxes and for manual failover it uses radio selection buttons.

Unchecking a load balancing server selection implies that it will be disabled; pfSense will know about the configuration but the `relayd` daemon will not.

For manual failover, just select the other single server to failover to. (Note that the load balancer will not automatically change the *manual* failover based on monitoring.)

While the interface allows you to uncheck all the load balancing servers to disable them, it will always require at least one enabled even if its monitoring indicates it is unavailable (with red). (When the page is reloaded, one will be checked.)

Click the **Save** button to change the server selections (or single manual selection). Then press **Apply Changes** to activate it.

Clicking the **Reset** button simply reloads the page (after prompting if okay) with the previously-enabled settings displayed.

34.6   Load Balancer Virtual Servers Status

A sortable table view of the virtual server style load balancers is available at the **Status** → **Load Balancer** → **Virtual Servers** subpage. This shows its name, IP address and port number (colon delimited), each of its servers in the pool, status, and description.

The status is shown in light green for a working or active entry. It is light red if the virtual service is down. Or if the `relayd` daemon is not running or the status is unknown it is in light blue. This may also indicate the total sessions count and statistics about the last and average sessions. (These details may be a minute old.)

34.7   Load Balancer Logs

For the logging messages for the `relayd` load balancer, see the **Status** → **System Logs** → **Load Balancer** page. After completed remote host monitoring checks, it logs about changed states such as going from up to down. A state of *unknown* may indicate that the host hadn't been checked yet or is disabled. The new state notification may also report round trip times and their availability percentage. The logs may also contain messages about corresponding PF tables updates.

To search these logs, use the **Log filter** shortcut. By default, it will display the latest 50 entries. To modify this or its other log view settings, see the **Manage log** shortcut. For details, see Section 11.1 and Section 11.3.

35 Add-on Software Packages

pfSense has many software suites installed (and enabled by default) in the core system. This software includes a modified FreeBSD kernel and base operating system which provides a standard Unix environment and a good collection of system and network administration tools and services; the pfSense startup and management software and interactive webpages; and third-party packages.

These packages, also known as FreeBSD *ports*, further enhance the system. A new install of pfSense will have over a hundred of these packages already installed, such as bind-tools command-line DNS lookup tools, dpinger IP device monitoring tool, perl5 language, php72 PHP Scripting Language, and python27 language. These represent thousands of files — configurations, binaries, databases, and more.

Note

Many of the FreeBSD package installs are not complete and pfSense is not a complete FreeBSD operating system. To reduce the disk usage most documentation, locale, and example files were removed by pfSense. Notably, the command-line `man` tool and most manuals are also not available.

The pfSense project also provides its own pfSense-specific packages. This is for add-on software that has been adapted for pfSense. These may provide server management interfaces, networking diagnostic tools, system maintenance commands, and various features to extend your pfSense system's capabilities. A pfSense package may also introduce a new menu item and a new pfSense management page to administer or view details related to the package. All these optional packages configurations aren't covered in this book, but the settings and use of these webpages are similar in use as the standard pfSense configuration pages.

Around 71 pfSense packages are available, such as *acme* Automated Certificate Management Environment through *zabbix* IT infrastructure monitoring. A list of packages is provided in Section 35.1. None of these pfSense add-on packages are installed by default with pfSense. Your currently-installed packages are listed via the main **System → Package Manager** page. The pfSense packages collection can be viewed and installed via the **System → Package Manager → Available Packages** page as described in this chapter.

The pfSense packages mostly provide the hooks into pfSense or administration interfaces available via the pfSense management pages. Most of these pfSense packages also depend on FreeBSD packages which provides the base technology. The installer will also install them. Also note that some of these add-ons may not be adequately verified with different releases of pfSense which may result in not working as expected or generating errors.

This chapter and feature is about pfSense packages and not about viewing, selecting, or managing FreeBSD packages. A few pfSense internal packages are also installed but their details are hidden from these features as they are core components (not add-ons) which are maintained using the standard system update method available via the **System → Update** page as covered in Chapter 9.

35.1 Available pfSense Packages

The following lists add-on packages available for pfSense. (This list may vary depending on the pfSense version.)

acme
> Automated LetsEncrypt Certificate Management Environment

apcupsd
> APC Uninterruptible Power Supply (UPS) monitoring and control.

arping
> Broadcasts a who-has ARP packet on the network and prints answers.

arpwatch
> Monitors Ethernet activity and reports changes.

Avahi
> Service discovery on a local network using mDNS/DNS-SD.

Backup
> Tool to backup and restore files and directories.

bandwidthd
> Track and display TCP/IP network utilization.

bind
> Authoritative and recursive DNS server suite.

blinkled
> Monitoring network activity using LEDs on ALIX, WRAP, Soekris, etc.

cellular
> Cellular Cards (like Huawei) interface.

Cron
> Manage scheduled commands.

darkstat
> Packet sniffer for network statistics reporting.

Filer
> Interface to edit files and set permission modes.

freeradius2 and freeradius3

RADIUS protocol services. Supports MySQL, PostgreSQL, LDAP, Kerberos.

frr

BGP, OSPF, and OSPF6 routing daemon as an alternative to Quagga OSPF and OpenBGPD.

FTP_Client_Proxy

Basic FTP Client Proxy using OpenBSD's ftp-proxy.

gwled

Use LEDs for monitoring gateway status on ALIX, WRAP, Soekris, etc.

haproxy and haproxy-devel

TCP/HTTP(S) Load Balancer.

iftop

Realtime interface monitor for the shell console.

iperf

Network throughput, loss, and jitter testing tool.

LADVD

LLDP (Link Layer Discovery Protocol), CDP (Cisco Discovery Protocol), EDP (Extreme Discovery Protocol), and NDP (Nortel Discovery Protocol) link layer advertisements sending and decoding tool.

LCDproc

LCD display driver.

Lightsquid

Web proxy reporting tool for Squid.

lldpd

Link-Layer protocols to know on which port is a server.

mailreport

Periodic e-mail reporting tool.

mtr-nox11

Enhanced traceroute and ping network diagnostic tool.

Netgate_Coreboot_Upgrade

Coreboot of Netgate hardware update tool.

net-snmp

Net-SNMP implementation of the SNMP protocol suite with interface.

nmap

Network exploration and port scanner with operating system detection and security auditing tool.

Notes

Keep track of notes for your pfSense system.

nrpe
> NRPE interface for setting up Nagios monitoring.

ntopng
> An interactive network probe with NetFlow/sFlow emitter/collector and statistics.

nut
> Network Uninterruptible Power Supply (UPS) tools using the SNMP, APCUPSD, or NUT protocols.

Open-VM-Tools
> VMware management utilities.

OpenBGPD
> Border Gateway Protocol (BGPv4) daemon (as an alternative to Quagga OSPF and FRR).

openvpn-client-export
> Export OpenVPN Windows Client or Mac OS X Viscosity configurations.

pfBlockerNG
> Manage various PF blocking lists from various feeds including MaxMind GeoIP database.

Quagga_OSPF
> OSPF routing protocol (as an alternative to OpenBGPD and FRR).

routed
> Routing Information Protocol (RIP) v1 and v2 daemon.

RRD_Summary
> Summarize traffic passed In/Out totals for the previous and current months.

Service_Watchdog
> Monitors and restarts stopped services.

Shellcmd
> Manage commands for system startup.

siproxd
> NAT proxy for multiple SIP devices.

snmptt
> An SNMP trap handler which can log or pass SNMP traps.

snort
> Network intrusion prevention and detection system (IDS/IPS) using protocol, signature, and anomaly-based inspection.

softflowd
> Flow-based network traffic analyzer with Cisco NetFlow data export.

squid
> Web proxy cache daemon with HTTP/HTTPS reverse proxying, SSL filtering, C-ICAP antivirus integration, and Exchange-Web-Access (OWA) Assistant.

squidGuard

Squid URL redirector using blacklists.

Status_Traffic_Totals

Report traffic passed In/Out for months, days, and hours.

stunnel

A TLS encryption wrapper between remote client and a server to add TLS support.

sudo

User privilege delegation and escalation.

suricata

Network IDS, IPS and Security Monitoring engine by OISF.

syslog-ng

Provide an independent syslogging service.

System_Patches

Apply and maintain custom system patches.

Telegraf

A server agent for collecting, aggregating, and reporting metrics.

tftpd

Trivial File Transfer Protocol (TFTP) network service.

tinc

An alternate IP-level Virtual Private Network (VPN) tunneling and encryption daemon.

zabbix-agent, zabbix-agent22, and zabbix-agent32

Client for Zabbix network, hardware, and application monitoring system.

zabbix-proxy, zabbix-proxy22, and zabbix-proxy32

A Zabbix proxy for collecting data and distributed monitoring.

35.2 Installing Packages

Click the **System** → **Package Manager** → **Available Packages** subpage link to view the list of pfSense packages available to install for your pfSense version. (There may be short delay as it downloads the list of available packages.)

It will show the package name, its version, and a brief description for each package. It will also list what packages it depends on (if any). The package name may be a clickable link to go to the webpage for that corresponding pfSense package for more information. The version string link takes you to the external pfSense development history webpage (currently at GitHub) specifically for that pfSense package.

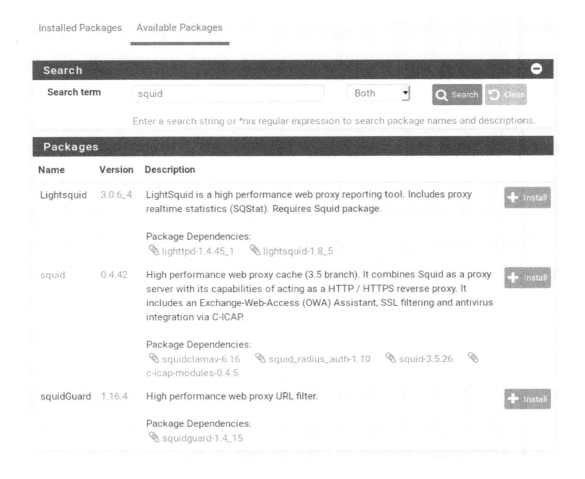

Figure 35.1: Available Packages Search

To reduce the list of many package choices, enter a keyword or regular expression in the **Search term** text field and press its **Search** button. This will do a case-insensitive match against both the name and description fields. To just search the name or description, select it from the drop-down menu. For example, searching for "dns" will reduce the list of packages to just a few choices. (An example is seen in Figure 35.1.) Click the **Clear** button to reset the search and view all the available package selections again.

Note that this list won't show your already-installed pfSense packages. To see those, use the **Installed Packages** link as described in the following section.

Each entry will have a corresponding **Install** button. Click your choice to begin its installation. It will bring up a prompt on the **System → Package Manager → Package Installer** page to verify this step. Click the **Confirm** button to continue.

Note that the packages will be downloaded from a pfSense mirror using HTTPS, so be sure that your firewall rules allows an HTTPS connection initiated from your pfSense system. Also, if you need to use an HTTP Proxy to download packages, set it up on the **System** → **Advanced** → **Miscellaneous** subpage (Section 5.4.1).

Commonly any dependencies are from official FreeBSD packages, but some may depend on pfSense packages. The dependency management is handled automatically.

Don't exit the **Package Installer** page until it completes. This may take a few seconds to a few minutes, depending on the size and number of dependencies to download, extract, and configure. A progress bar will be displayed and will change color to green when finished.

A dynamic package installer view will show this progress. It may indicate it is updating its package repo catalog; list the packages it is downloading, extracting, and installing; and show that it is doing various configuration steps. Some packages may also provide messages to be displayed at install time to explain about other needs or how to use this software. Generally, pfSense-installed packages don't need you to read or act on these messages.

When completed, the top of the page will say the installation successfully completed.

Depending on the package, you may have a new menu link in one of the menus to access the package's configuration or to otherwise view its details. The location and naming within the menus is not consistent, so look around. For example, the pfSense *bind* package settings are available via the **Service** → **BIND DNS Server** menu link and the **Diagnostics** → **Backup/Files/Dir** menu entry leads you to the *Backup* package settings.

35.3 Package Manager

Upgrading, removing, or listing your currently-installed packages may be done via the **System** → **Package Manager** page. When loading, it may have a short delay as the list of packages is retrieved and formatted. By default (or in a new installation of pfSense), no packages are installed and none will be listed. To install a package, use the **Available Packages** link as covered in the previous section.

When you have packages installed, it will show the name of the package, its categories to help identify it (like *net* for networking related packages), its version number, its short description, and its list of FreeBSD package dependencies (if any).

The version string may be a clickable link to an external webpage (currently GitHub) with the development history. If it has package dependencies, it will link to external webpages with more details about it.

An icon will indicate the package status on the left column for each entry. A check mark simply means it is up-to-date and appears okay. The packages are checked to see if there is a newer package available from pfSense and it will suggest upgrading it with a link to do so. It will indicate with an exclamation mark if there is a configuration for the package, but the package itself is no longer installed.

Each entry also has actions to deinstall and re-install. If an external webpage about the software is known, it will also have an information icon to link to it.

Click the **Remove package** trash can icon to delete the package. This will remove its package files, but may keep its configurations or databases on your disk.

Or to download and install the package again, press the **Update package** or **Reinstall package** icon.

These actions will need to be verified by pressing a **Confirm** button A progress bar will be displayed and a dynamic view will show the output for the removal or reinstallation steps. At the bottom, there should be some indication of success and the top of the page should indicate the action was successfully completed. Click the **Installed Packages** link at the top to get back to the list of installed packages.

35.4 Package Logging

Some add-on packages may do logging. To view these debugging or diagnostic outputs, see the **Status** → **Package Logs** page. By default, no packages are installed that do logging, so this page will be empty.

For package logs it may show up to the latest 50 entries. This count is configured via the **GUI Log Entries** field on the **Status** → **System Logs** → **Settings** page (Section 11.2).

Note that some package logging goes to existing system logs, so you will need to find and view them via one of the pages accessed via the **Status** → **System Logs** pages. For example, the *bind* package logging is in the **Status** → **System Logs** → **System** → **DNS Resolver** page view.

36 High Availability Synchronization

pfSense provides synchronization methods for sharing firewall state information and for sharing some pfSense configuration settings with one or more pfSense systems. Multiple systems knowing the same configurations can help prevent a single point of failure. The options for these are available via the **System → High Avail. Sync** page.

36.1 State Synchronization (pfsync)

The state or progress of network connections may be tracked by the PF firewall in a state table. This may be used to match traffic to already-established connections. The state entries may be shared with other pfSense peers using the *pfsync* protocol so they may be consistent in the case of failover.

To enable transferring or accepting the state changes to or from another firewall, check the **Synchronize states** checkbox.

Use the **Synchronize Interface** drop-down form to select the interface to be used. The state changes are sent using multicast by default.

If you don't want to use multicast, enter a specific IPv4 address for the other pfSense system to synchronize with in the **pfsync Synchronize Peer IP** input field.

 Warning
The *pfsync* traffic is not encrypted. It is recommended that this connection is secured using IPsec or with a dedicated cable connection between the pfSense systems.

36.2 Configuration Synchronization (XMLRPC Sync)

Several different categories of configurations may be transferred from the pfSense system to another pfSense system. This configuration synchronization will only happen when enabled and the pfSense peer's version is the same pfSense version.

Enter the remote pfSense system's IP address in the **Synchronize Config to IP** field. This is the IP address for the backup system.

 Warning
Do not configure your backup pfSense systems to synchronize their copied configurations back to the main systems. You don't want to mistakenly overwrite the production configurations with the backups.

Enter the other pfSense system's username and password (as used for its web login) in the **Remote System Username** and **Remote System Password** fields. (Repeat the password in the corresponding field to confirm it was typed in correctly.) Note that the backup server's password will be replaced with the current system's password after the configuration synchronization.

The page also lists several checkboxes for enabling or disabling types of configurations to synchronize to the peer. These include:

Synchronize Users and Groups
Users (and their passwords) and groups. This includes the *admin* user and the next UID and GID counter fields.

Synchronize Auth Servers
LDAP and/or RADIUS authentication servers configurations.

Synchronize Certificates
Certificate Authorities, Certificate Revocation Lists, and/or certificates.

Synchronize Rules
PF packet filter firewall rules. When this is checked, if you have time-based or calendar schedules configured, they are also transferred as if the **Synchronize Firewall schedules** was checked. Note that firewall rules that are marked with the **No XMLRPC Sync** checkbox are not synchronized to the backup firewall.

Synchronize Firewall schedules
Calendar and time-based schedules for the firewall.

Synchronize Firewall aliases
Network, port, and URL Aliases.

Synchronize NAT
Network Address Translation rules. Note that NAT rules that are marked with the **No XMLRPC Sync** checkbox are not synchronized to the backup firewall.

Synchronize IPsec
IPsec configurations.

Synchronize OpenVPN
OpenVPN configurations. Note when this is checked, it also will synchronize the CAs, CRLs, and/or certificates as if the **Synchronize Certificates** was checked.

Synchronize DHCPD

DHCP Server settings. Note when the **Failover peer IP** DHCP server option (Section 19.4) is configured, the backup server's DHCP failover IP address is replaced with the master pfSense system's DHCP interface's address. (That way they are a peer for each other.)

Synchronize Wake-on-LAN

Wake-on-LAN (WoL) Server settings.

Synchronize Static Routes

Static routes and gateway configurations.

Synchronize Load Balancer

Load balancer pools and virtual servers configurations.

Synchronize Virtual IPs

Virtual IPs for CARP-based high availability configurations. Note that CARP **Skew** settings will be increased by 100 for the backup system (and clamped to a maximum of 254) so the backup will have a lower preference. (See Section 16.10.1 for details.)

Synchronize traffic shaper (queues)

ALTQ traffic shaper configurations.

Synchronize traffic shaper (limiter)

Dummynet traffic shaper limiters configurations.

Synchronize DNS (Forwarder/Resolver)

DNS Forwarder (dnsmasq) and/or DNS Resolver (Unbound) configurations.

Synchronize Captive Portal)

Captive portals configurations including vouchers.

Note that there are many other pfSense settings that are not synchronized.

Click the **Save** button to enable these settings.

36.3 Syncing the Configuration

When enabled, on normal configuration changes there are over 250 settings when changed that can trigger the configuration synchronization from this system to the other pfSense system.

It can also be triggered manually to test it. If you have high availability enabled and the **Synchronize Config to IP** setting defined, the **Status** → **Filter Reload** page will have a **Force Config Sync** button which may be used to perform the configuration synchronization. Note this will push the selected configurations to the remote system overwriting those configurations there.

37 The Text Console Menu

This chapter introduces the capabilities provided at the text-based console menu.

As mentioned in the installation chapter, pfSense provides a simple menu at the local terminal display — or via a remote SSH (secure shell) login. By default, you can use a SSH client (like PuTTY or OpenSSH's `ssh`) to login remotely to the pfSense system.

The text console menu (as seen in Figure 37.1) provides various basic system management tasks and troubleshooting or diagnostic capabilities. But it does not provide menus or text-based wizards for full pfSense configurations as found in the normally-used webConfigurator (covered in Chapter 4 and throughout this book). It does provide access to the Unix shell which does provide a very low-level and high-powered access for expert use of the core FreeBSD system and the many software components that run pfSense.

The text console will display the assigned network identifiers, interface names, and their configured network types and addresses. A menu of 17 numbered choices is displayed. (Note that some older systems may have additional options.) The console may show log messages periodically, such as successful webConfigurator logins or upgrade messages. When logged in via SSH, if you press Enter at a blank option prompt, it will log you out. If you enter some invalid option, it will just redisplay the menu again.

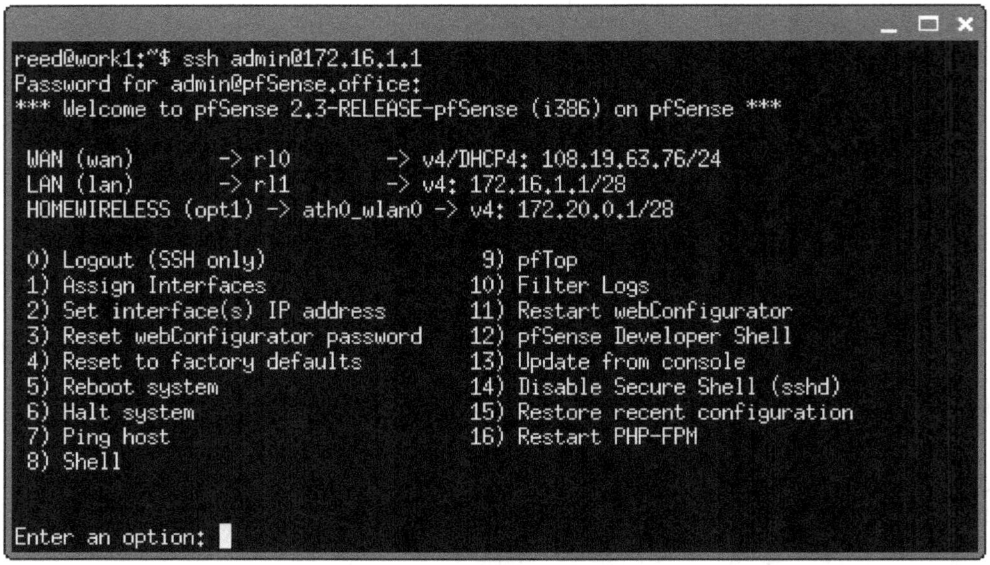

Figure 37.1: Menu at Text Console

37.1   0) Logout (SSH only)

When remotely logging in via SSH, you can enter "**0**" at the option prompt and your SSH connection
will be closed. Note that this doesn't stop the SSH service — that can be done via text console menu
option "14" (see following Section 37.15) or via the web interface under **System** → **Advanced** →
Secure Shell (see Section 5.3.2).

37.2   1) Assign Interfaces

This option is the same as the installation step described in Section 2.11. This may be used to do a basic setup of a VLAN, and to assign the WAN, LAN, and any additional network interfaces. Normally
these assignments are done after installation using the webConfigurator as covered in Chapter 13, but
this may be useful for emergencies when it cannot be accessed.

It will list the detected network interfaces by their FreeBSD device names, MAC addresses, and their
vendor and model description. It will also indicate if the network device is live with "(up)."

It will first ask if you want to do VLAN assignments, then select the interfaces for the WAN, LAN,
and an *Optional* interfaces.

Note that if you change the assignments, it will not change their networking configurations. The network device will be configured with the existing configuration as known for the pfSense interface.

For more details on the interface assignments via the text console, see Section 2.11.

37.3   2) Set interface(s) IP address

This may be used to enable using DHCP to configure the WAN interface or to may manually enter addresses for the WAN or LAN (or additional) interfaces. As with option #1, these are normally configured at the web interface (Chapter 13) after pfSense is already running, but this text-based method may be needed when the web interface isn't available.

It will display a numbered list of the pfSense network interfaces and their associated FreeBSD device names (such as assigned using the previous text console menu option). These will also indicate if the WAN is using DHCP or is static (manually) configured.

To set the IP address for the WAN, select it (usually the number "1" option). (If you only have one network interface, it will automatically start asking to configure it as the WAN.) It will ask if you want to use DHCP to configure the IPv4 address. If you enter "n" then it will prompt for you to enter the address and then its CIDR subnet. (The subnet will accept numbers 1 through 31, such as "24" for 255.255.255.0.) The IPv4 address may be skipped by leaving it blank to continue to the IPv6 instead). If you enter an invalid address, it will prompt again.

Then it will ask if you want to use DHCPv6 to configure an IPv6 address or you may manually enter it. (The IPv6 subnet masks range from 1 to 127.) Note that /64 (ffff:ffff:ffff:ffff:0:0:0:0) IPv6 allocations (with over 18 quintillion addresses) are usually given to end users, /48 (ffff:ffff:ffff:0:0:0:0:0) for business customers who may have multiple virtual LANs, and /32 (ffff:ffff:0:0:0:0:0:0) for ISPs.

The next entry defines if it has a gateway. Note that the gateway address must be within the same subnet previously configured.

If your WAN is statically configured and you don't have a LAN interface, then it will ask if you want to enable DHCP service on the WAN, And if you have a static IPv6 address, then it will prompt to enable DHCPv6. If you select "y" for yes, then you will be prompted to enter the starting address for assignment to DHCP clients and then the end address of the range. Note the address must be in the subnet for this interface being configured. (Of course, the end address ust be equal or greater than the start address.) If you are providing DHCP or DHCPv6 service, you may use the webConfigurator to further configure it; see Chapter 19 or Chapter 20 for details.

For the LAN, you may enter the IPv4 or IPv6 address details. (It it won't ask to use DHCP.) For the gateway, if it is on the LAN, just press Enter to leave it blank. Then it will ask if you want to run a DHCP service for the LAN network. If you were already running the DHCP and you choose "n", then it will be stopped.

This may also ask if you want to use HTTP instead of the default HTTPS for the webConfigurator access. This could be for temporary use to modify its certificate. Note if you previously disabled the default anti-lockout firewall rule for the web interface and SSH access, it will be re-enabled.

To change these settings, see the **System** → **Advanced** → **Admin Access** page as covered in Section 5.3.1.

When completed, the filter and routing rules are reloaded and the DHCP server is started if desired. In addition, the new address(es) may be used for accessing the pfSense webConfigurator in a web browser.

37.4   3) Reset webConfigurator password

Option "3" is used to reset the admin password back to the default *pfsense*. This may be useful at the local console terminal if the password is unknown, such as taking over management of a pfSense system. This will prompt to proceed by choosing "**y**" to make the change.

Warning
Resetting the password may be dangerous. By default, your LAN network will be able to login using the commonly-known password. Or if you only have a WAN and it is on the Internet, the world may be able to login.

The webConfigurator may be used to change the password via the **System** → **User Manager** → **Users** page. Click the **Edit user** pencil icon action for the *admin* user and on the new page under User Properties, set your new desired password (and confirm it by entering it again), and click the **Save** button. (This is explained in Section 6.2.)

37.5   4) Reset to factory defaults

This option will remove add-on packages, remove the custom configurations (including the `config.xml` file) and various log files, and the default configuration file is copied into place. It will also enable the initial wizard at boot to detect if any default WAN or LAN interfaces are found.

This option will remove all your settings. It will prompt before proceeding and then reboot immediately after.

(The corresponding feature in the webConfigurator is **Diagnostics** → **Factory Defaults** covered in Section 7.10.)

37.6   5) Reboot system

This option "5" may be used to reboot the hardware and operating system. It will prompt first, so press "**y**" for a normal reboot. It will attempt to cleanly stop all add-on packages programs and other services and then reboots the system. Depending on the system, it may take a few minutes for pfSense to be live again.

You may also have options to *reroot* (if you aren't using ZFS) to stop the running software without resetting the hardware, remount the disks, and do the system startup using the same running operating system kernel; boot into *single user mode* which will restart the hardware but only boot up to a console prompt (where you need local access) without the pfSense services running; and reboot with forced consistency check of the file system.

(The web interface's **Diagnostics** → **Reboot** option, as described in Section 7.4, may also be used to reboot the system.)

37.7   6) Halt system

Option "6" powers off the system. It will prompt first for a "**y**" to proceed with this system power-down. Like with the reboot, it will also attempt to cleanly stop all the programs and services. (The webConfigurator **Diagnostics** → **Halt System** feature, as covered in Section 7.3, can also be used to shutdown the system.)

37.8   7) Ping host

Option "7" will prompt for a host name or IP address to ping for network testing and measurement. It is useful for basic network troubleshooting and will ping the host three times, one second a part, and then prompt to continue back to the main menu as shown in the following example. The round-trip times are reported and the summary also reports round-trip statistics and packet loss percentage. The tool is also useful to confirm that local DNS works by using a hostname.

```
Enter an option: 7


Enter a host name or IP address: 8.8.4.4

PING 8.8.4.4 (8.8.4.4): 56 data bytes
64 bytes from 8.8.4.4: icmp_seq=0 ttl=49 time=10.837 ms
64 bytes from 8.8.4.4: icmp_seq=1 ttl=49 time=12.002 ms
64 bytes from 8.8.4.4: icmp_seq=2 ttl=49 time=12.548 ms
```

```
--- 8.8.4.4 ping statistics ---
3 packets transmitted, 3 packets received, 0.0% packet loss
round-trip min/avg/max/stddev = 10.837/11.796/12.548/0.714 ms

Press ENTER to continue.
```

For fault isolation, you can first ping the local network interfaces, and then hosts and gateways further (and further) away can be pinged (one at a time). Note that the packet filter rules may restrict the ICMP ECHO_REQUEST (or ICMP6_ECHO_REQUEST) or ECHO_RESPONSE (or ICMP6_ECHO_REPLY) packets.

pfSense also has this feature via the web interface by using the **Diagnostics** → **Ping** option as seen in Section 27.2. Or the **Diagnostics** → **Test Port** feature, covered in Section 27.4, can be used to test TCP connections.

37.9   8) Shell

The Unix command line shell is accessed via option "8." The shell feature is expected to only be used by experienced Unix system administrators and is not the normal way to administer a pfSense system. To exit the shell (and return back to the menu), enter "**exit**" and press Enter.

It provides full root (uid 0) privileges and runs *tcsh*, an extended C-shell with many useful features like history editing and filename completion. To use a POSIX-like, Bourne-style standard command interpreter instead, run "**sh**" at the current prompt (and use *exit* twice to get back to the pfSense console menu).

A complete Unix system is available with the standard tools, like *chmod*, *cp*, *df*, *dig*, *grep*, *ifconfig*, *ls*, *mv*, *netstat*, *ps*, *rm*, *route*, *sed*, *top*, *traceroute*, *vmstat*, and hundreds of other tools. Note that pfSense runs on FreeBSD and some of its command-line options and command output may be different than used and seen on other Unix-type systems. But overall, it is very similar to GNU/Linux systems. The system has a normal Unix layout. Many log files are available under /var/log/ and the /conf/ directories, and many configurations and system control scripts are in the /etc/ and /usr/local/etc/ directories. It is advised that you don't modify these files, as the pfSense system may regenerate them or overwrite them based on its settings.

Firewall and network tools like *ntpq*, *pfctl*, *relayctl*, *unbound-control*, and others are also available. It offers additional scripting languages like Python, Perl, Lua, PHP, and AWK.

pfSense also allows running Unix tools and shell commands via the web interface by using the **Diagnostics** → **Command Prompt** option (as covered in Section 7.1).

37.10   9) pfTop

A real-time display of the active states and rule statistics for the packet filter is available using option "9." Within pfTop, press "**q**" to quit and return to the pfSense console menu.

pfTop is a useful diagnostics tool for troubleshooting and analyzing the systems packet filtering behavior. For example, you can quickly see what connections are transferring the most data or running at the highest speeds or what firewall rules are getting matched most frequently.

The interactive display's header line indicates if the packet filter is "Up" (enabled), what states are shown on the current display and the total count of state entries, the current pfTop view, the sort order, size of the cache (used for figuring out throughput rate and peak speed), and the current system clock time. The display is updated every five seconds; press the Spacebar to update the stats immediately or use "**s**" to set a different number of seconds to delay.

The default interactive display view shows the active states, rules, and queues (as many as will display on a single terminal screen). The information includes the protocol type (like tcp or icmp), direction (in or out), source address and port, destination address and port, its state (source:destination), age of the state entry, expiration timeout for the state entry (based on the last time a packet matched the state), number of packets that matched that state entry, and the total bytes for those packets. A wide terminal will show more details or more verbose output formats. For example, with a default 80 column or narrow display, the state may be listed using numbers, such as the following for TCP: 0 for closed, 1 for listening for connection, 2 for active and SYN sent, 4 for established, 9 for closed and FIN acknowledged, and 10 for wait after close. For UDP, 2:1 (MULTIPLE:SINGLE) indicates the UDP state was established.

To view more entries use the page down and page up or down and up arrow keys. The State number listed in the header will change to show what state range is displayed. The views include: 0) default, 1) long for all details, 2) state, 3) time, 4) size, 5) rules, 6) label, 7) speed, and 8) queue. You can use the right or left arrows, press "**v**" or numbers "**0**" through "**8**" to switch views. The rules view lists each packet filter actions and how many packets that have matched.

It is not sorted by default. The sort keys include (the shortcut listed in parentheses): total bytes (B), latest expiry time (E), most packets (P), connection age (A), source address (F), destination address (T), source port (S), destination port (D), recent rate (R), and peak speed (K). Use the "**o**" key to rotate through these different sort orders or use the shortcut key. To reverse the order (for example to sort by most bytes versus fewest bytes), use "**r**" or toggle using the shortcut key. Use "**N**" to not sort.

pfSense also provides limited pfTop information via the web interface by using the **Diagnostics** → **pfTop** option, but that is not interactive nor as useful. For details, see Section 16.14.

37.11   10) Filter Logs

This option "10" will output all the firewall logged details such as the following. On an active system with the default log sizes, this may be around 512 KB of messages of approximately 3310 lines. (If nothing displays, this simply may mean that nothing has used your firewall or no rules have logging configured.) Then it continues to wait to display additional lines. Press Control-C to exit this (but note that a connection over SSH may also exit).

```
May  5 17:23:44 pfSense filterlog: 7,16777216,,1000000105, ↩
    ath0_wlan0,match,block,in,6,0x00,0x00000,1,Options,0,36,fe80 ↩
    ::40a:936f:f513:719,ff02::16,HBH,PADN,RTALERT,0x0000,
...
May  5 17:31:16 pfSense filterlog: 5,16777216,,1000000103,rl0, ↩
    match,block,in,4,0xc0,,1,56137,0,none,2,igmp ↩
    ,36,71.97.37.1,224.0.0.1,datalength=12
...
May  5 17:40:46 pfSense filterlog: 5,16777216,,1000000103,rl0, ↩
    match,block,in,4,0x0,,50,0,0,DF,17,udp ↩
    ,128,147.75.208.212,108.19.63.76,4500,4562,108
```

The firewall rules for logging are explained in Section 16.2.1. The webConfigurator may also be used to view the firewall logs via the **Status** → **System Logs** → **Firewall** pages, as covered in Section 16.18 and its following sections.

(Behind the scenes, the pfSense *filterlog* tool listens on the pflog0 interface for packets marked to be logged by PF and then logs them to a customized system log daemon that supports circular log files which writes them to /var/log/filter.log in plain text. See Chapter 11 for more details about logging.)

37.12   11) Restart webConfigurator

The web-based user interface backend is restarted using option "11." This will kill the HTTP server(s) and startup new HTTP server(s). If using Captive Portal (which is covered in Chapter 29) it will also restart the Captive Portal's HTTP server. This is a recovery mechanism just in case the pfSense interface doesn't work. (It will also make sure the RRD-based graphing is enabled.)

37.13   12) PHP shell + pfSense tools

Option "12" invokes the pfSense developer shell which provides a scriptable interface to the system using the PHP language with access to the pfSense configurations, common Unix shell commands, and built-in commands. This is an advanced feature that most pfSense administrators do not use. Note that this is not a Unix shell prompt.

Warning
The Developer Shell scripts may be dangerous and may remove or reset important configurations.

It displays "pfSense shell:" prompts to enter a single or series of commands. If the lines are not built-in commands, then they are appended to a playback buffer. You may use the up arrow to access previously typed commands history. The built-in commands are:

exit, quit

Leave this shell and return to the console menu.

?, help

Outputs some examples of using the pfSense Developer Shell. (The playback buffer will be cleared.)

exec

This will run the current playback buffer in PHP. (Then the playback buffer will be cleared.) Note that the standard pfSense PHP functions are included, for access to many capabilities and configurations of pfSense. Lines that are prefixed with an "!" exclamation mark are ran via the Unix shell. If the playback buffer fails to execute, such as due to a syntax error, the PHP interpreter should output a warning or parse error indicating the line near where the bug is at and a Call Stack dump. In addition, the web interface may indicate that it detected a crash report or programming bug; see Section 4.6 for more details.

reset

Clears the playback buffer.

record *playbackname*

This will copy the existing buffer and start appending the command lines to the filename defined in the required argument. The file is stored in the /etc/phpshellsessions/ directory (which already contains other scripts).

stop, stoprecording

Stop saving (stop recording) the command lines to the playback file as previously started with the "record" command.

run *playbackname*, **playback** *playbackname*

This will execute the previously saved or recorded script as defined by the required argument (and located in the /etc/phpshellsessions/ directory). Some of the scripts may support arguments that may be passed along on the command-line.

showrecordings

This will list the available scripts (in the /etc/phpshellsessions/ directory) which includes the default scripts and the recorded playback scripts. These can be ran individually by using the "`run`" command.

The standard scripts (also known as playback commands) which can be ran with "`run playbackname`" follow:

changepassword

This script prompts for username and then for the password to change that user's password. Note that the main pfSense user is named "admin."

disablecarp

This will tell the system to stop accepting incoming CARP packets and bring down its virtual interfaces used for CARP. The `enablecarp` script can be used to re-enable it. CARP is covered in Section 16.10.

disablecarpmaint

This will stop the CARP maintenance mode as described in Section 16.10.2 and will advertise it is a member of the redundancy group as defined in the Virtual IP CARP Settings' **Advertising frequency** configuration (see Section 16.10.1).

disabledhcpd

This will disable the DHCP servers on all interfaces. (The corresponding script `restartdhcpd` may be used to re-start the DHCP service.) See Chapter 19 and Chapter 20 for details on setting up DHCP and DHCPv6 services.

disablereferercheck

By default, use of the web interface forms is only allowed if the referring page (HTTP_REFERER) is the pfSense system. This script will disable this check, but note this may allow a man-in-the-middle attack. This may also be disabled using the web interface via **System → Advanced → Admin Access** page using the **Disable HTTP_REFERER enforcement check** checkbox.

enableallowallwan

This opens up the packet filter firewall to allow all IPv4 and IPv6 traffic. It will also turn off the blocking of RFC 1918 private networks and bogon networks. This can be used to temporarily gain access to a pfSense system or its network.

enablecarp

This will tell the system to enable its CARP interfaces and the virtual interfaces used for CARP. It also tells the system to start accepting incoming CARP packets. The `disablecarp` script can be used to stop it. CARP is covered in Section 16.10.

enablecarpmaint

This makes it so the CARP advertising to the redundancy group is at the lowest level such as entered on the **Status → CARP** page (see Section 16.10.2).

enablesshd

This will start the SSH server for remote access into the pfSense console. This can also be done using option "14" from the console menu.

externalconfiglocator

This looks on all attached disks for the main pfSense configuration file, `config.xml`. It attempts both MSDOS and regular (FreeBSD's UFS) file systems. If the configuration file is found and is sane, then it backs up the current file and uses the newly-found configuration.

gatewaystatus

This will return the recent status for the configured gateways. For example:

```
Name       Monitor       Source          Delay    StdDev     ←
    Loss    Status
WAN_DHCP   10.18.49.1    10.18.49.132    4.19ms   1.002ms   0.0%   ←
       none
```

See the **Status** → **Gateways** page (Section 15.1.3) for further details.

generateguicert

This will generate a self-signed 2048-bit certificate that will be used for the HTTPS web interface. It will be valid for 2000 days and will use the system's hostname for the admin@ email address and common name. The web server(s) are restarted. Note that the web browser may need to get the new certificate and confirm a security exception to use it. Certificate creation and management are handled via the **System** → **Certificate Manager** menu features as described in Chapter 12.

gitsync

This feature may be used to update parts of the system using GIT. If not already installed, it installs the `git` package.

installpkg *packagename*

This installs the package named with the required command-line argument. Note that it prefixes the package name with "pfSense-pkg-" but many pfSense packages no longer use that naming. See Chapter 35 for details about the add-on packages.

listpkg

This will list the installed add-on packages. See Chapter 35 for information.

pfanchordrill

This will display the PF packet filter and translation rules for all the PF *anchors*. The packet filter configuration can be organized into different rulesets, each identified by an anchor name, such as: ipsec, miniupnpd, natearly, natrules, openvpn, relayd, tftp-proxy, and userrules.

pftabledrill

The PF packet filter configurations uses tables of addresses and ports to simplify its rule sets. This feature will output the contents for all its tables, such as bogons, bogonsv6, snort2c, sshguard, sshlockout, virusprot, and webConfiguratorlockout, This will also output the contents for active user-defined tables. Note that the output may be very long. These may also be viewed via the **Diagnostics** → **Tables** page (see Section 16.17).

removepkgconfig

This script will clear the package configuration data and remove many startup and management scripts for default services and add-on packages.

removeshaper

This deletes the firewall's Traffic Shaper and queueing rules from the pfSense configuration. For more information, see Chapter 25.

resetwebgui

This will reset the webConfigurator interface and its dashboard to the system defaults to use the standard pfSense theme, have the menu panel be able to scroll off the display, have two columns in the dashboard, and only display the system information and interfaces dashboard widgets. See Section 5.1.4 for details.

restartdhcpd

This will stop currently running DHCP servers and restart them including the Router Advertisement Daemon (radvd) if needed. (The corresponding script `disabledhcpd` may be used to disable the DHCP services.)

restartipsec

This stops the IKE daemon and terminates all IPsec connections, then waits two seconds and starts a new IKE daemon instance. IPsec is covered in Chapter 30.

svc *action servicename*

This allows you to stop, restart, start, or retrieve status for various services. This functionality can also be accessed via the web interface at **Status → Services** as introduced in Section 7.7. This requires two additional command-line arguments for an action and for the service name; additional arguments may be needed as specific to the service.

uninstallpkg *packagename*

This removes the package named with the required command-line argument. Note that it prefixes the package name with "pfSense-pkg-" but many pfSense packages no longer use that naming.

37.14   13) Update from console

Selecting option "13" will run the pfSense upgrade script which is used to update the pfSense operating system (also known as the *firmware*). The system update can also be done via the web interface's **System → Update** option; see Chapter 9 for details.

This update may be done without interaction. If the system is already up-to-date, you may receive output like the following:

```
>>> Updating repositories metadata...
Updating pfSense-core repository catalogue...
pfSense-core repository is up-to-date.
Updating pfSense repository catalogue...
pfSense repository is up-to-date.
All repositories are up-to-date.
Your packages are up to date
```

Older versions (with menu option "13" as "Upgrade from console") may have a submenu for the firmware update. The choices are: 1) Update from a URL; 2) Update from a local file; or Q) Quit. Select "**2**" if you have a previously downloaded update tarfile that you can use. Or use "**1**" to do an update over the web. It will allow you to enter a URL to the upgrade tarfile or use "**auto**" to use its default for the latest upgrade.

Warning

The system upgrade will make your system unavailable to you and your users for up to several minutes.

It may display numerous lines of output during the upgrade. (An example of the output is in Section 9.3.) When completed, if required, it will warn that a reboot is required and prompts to proceed with the upgrade and reboot.

37.15   14) Enable or Disable Secure Shell (sshd)

If the SSH server is already running the menu option will say "Disable" and if is not running "Enable." The Secure Shell server (known as *sshd*) provides secure communications over insecure networks for untrusted hosts; in this usage it allows a remote SSH client (like mentioned at the start of this chapter) to authenticate and then provides a terminal session on the pfSense system.

By default, the SSH server is not enabled (it is not running).

When option "14" is entered, it will indicate the SSH server's current status and if you'd like to proceed (to enable or disable). Choose "**y**" to write the new configuration and to start or stop the server. The firewall rules will be reloaded after this change.

The web interface provides further SSH options to select a custom port and to disable password-based logins and require authorized keys for logins only. See Section 5.3.2 for more details.

37.16   15) Restore recent configuration

Entering "15" will bring up a submenu for listing and restoring backups of the pfSense XML configuration file. Press "**q**" to return to the main menu.

At the restore backup menu, enter "**1**" to list all the saved backups (as found under the /conf/ backups/ directory). Each will be numbered, starting with the largest number representing the oldest version, and a date stamp and a configuration format version will be listed. The most recent will be displayed last. The entries will include an identification of the user who made the change and hopefully a brief description about it or the name of the program that made the change.

To revert to a previous backup, enter "**2**" at the menu and then at the next prompt enter the number of the configuration file you'd like to restore. It will then ask you to confirm by showing the details again, as shown below:

```
Restore Backup from Configuration History

1) List Backups
2) Restore Backup
Q) Quit

Please select an option to continue: 2
Which configuration would you like to restore?
 1-33 : 2

Is this the backup you wish to restore?
02. 5/14/16 10:26:08    v15.0   admin@172.16.1.4
    Changed backup revision count to 39

Y/N? : Y

Successfully reverted to timestamp 5/14/16 10:26:08 with  ←
    description "admin@172.16.1.4: Changed backup revision count ←
    to 39".
You may need to reboot the firewall or restart services before  ←
    the restored configuration is fully active.
```

As suggested, you need to restart services or reboot the pfSense system to fully use the restored configuration. (For example, a LAN interface may not reflect a changed LAN IP address in the pfSense configuration.)

See Section 8.2 for more information on the configuration history and the web-based interface for it. The web interface will also allow removing old backups, comparing between two XML files, and updating the count of maximum backups to save.

37.17   16) Restart PHP-FPM

PHP-FPM is the FastCGI Process Manager used with the PHP programming language ran via the NGINX web server. (This is what powers the dynamic webConfigurator webpages.) This feature will kill the existing program, generate a new configuration for it, and start the program again.

37.18   98) Move configuration file to removable device

This is used to prepare a separate disk (like a USB flash drive) with your pfSense configuration. Then it can be used for a *pre-flight install* later. This menu option only exists on older pfSense versions and only if pfSense has detected some capable storage devices. It will prompt you to enter the device name with a *msdos* (aka FAT) file system. Then will mount it, move the configuration, remove other related configurations, and then remount the new file system so the configurations are accessed from it.

37.19   99) Install pfSense to a hard drive, etc.

Only old pfSense systems booted with the LiveCD have the 99 Install menu option. This is used to run the disk selection and partitioning menus and then install pfSense to a hard disk. Note that these old installation steps are quite different than the recent installers.

37.20   100) Verify webConfigurator is running

This is an unlisted menu option which may be used to show that the web server is running and the webConfigurator is available. Enter "100" to run the `links` console-based web browser to connect to the localhost's web server. It will take you to the local pfSense login prompt. Note that the browser doesn't support cookies and the login won't fully work.

In this text-based web browser, you can visit other websites by pressing "**g**" (for *go*) and then entering the URL to visit. Pressing the **Escape** key will bring up the `links` menu.

The simplest way to exit is by pressing "**q**" for quit or Control-C.

Index

www.ingramcontent.com/pod-product-compliance
Lightning Source LLC
LaVergne TN
LVHW062300060326
832902LV00013B/1976